HAL•LEONARD ESSENTIAL SONGS

FOR ORGANS, PIANOS & ELECTRONIC KEYBOARDS

E-Z PLAY TODAY

265

Love Songs

ISBN 978-1-4234-8382-3

HAL•LEONARD CORPORATION

7777 W. BLUEMOUND RD. P.O. BOX 13819 MILWAUKEE, WI 53213

CONTENTS

All for Love
from Walt Disney Pictures' THE THREE MUSKETEERS

Registration 3
Rhythm: Pop Rock or 8-Beat

Words and Music by Bryan Adams,
R.J. Lange and Michael Kamen

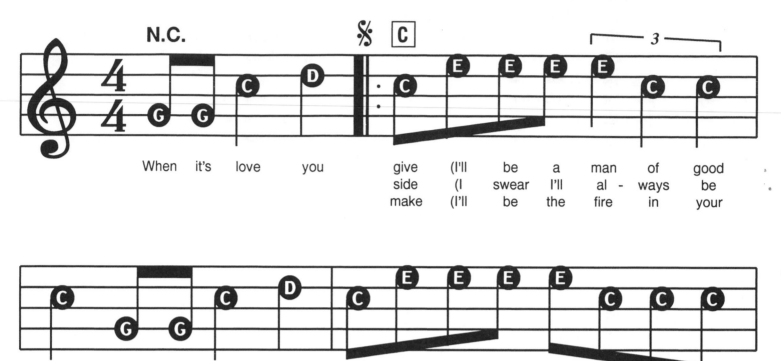

When it's love you give (I'll be a man of good
side (I swear I'll al - ways be
make (I'll be the fire in your

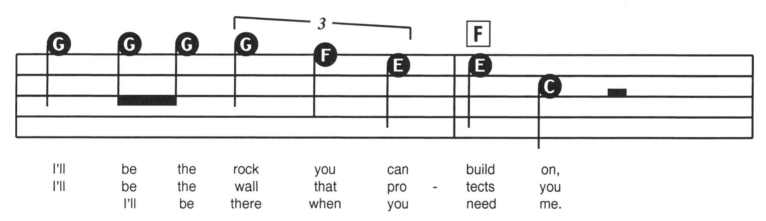

faith.) then in love you'll live. (I'll make a stand. I won't break.)
strong.) then there's a rea - son why. (I'll prove to you we be - long.)
night.) then it's love you take. (I will de - fend, I will fight.)

I'll be the rock you can build on,
I'll be the wall that pro - tects you
I'll be there when you need me.

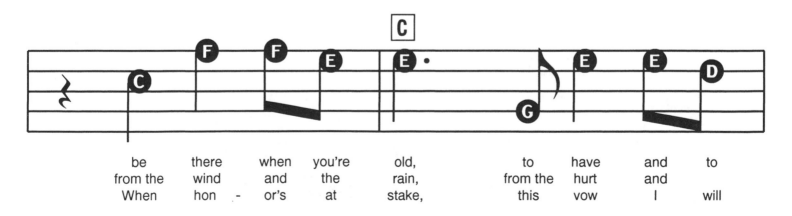

be there when you're old, to have and to
from the wind and the rain, from the hurt and
When hon - or's at stake, this vow I will

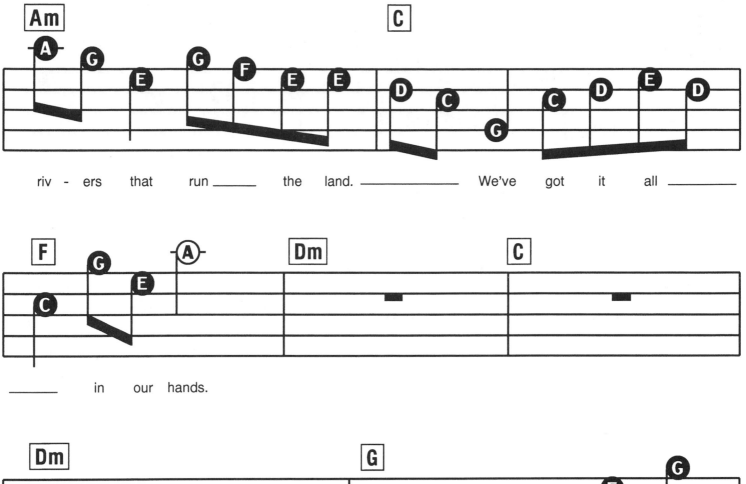

riv - ers that run _____ the land. _____ We've got it all _____

_____ in our hands.

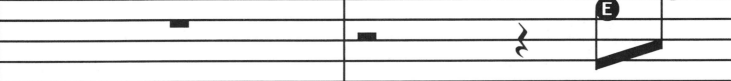

Now it's

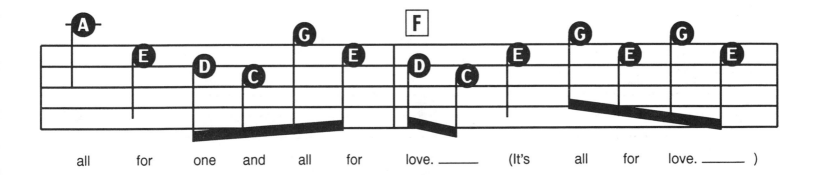

all for one and all for love. _____ (It's all for love. _____)

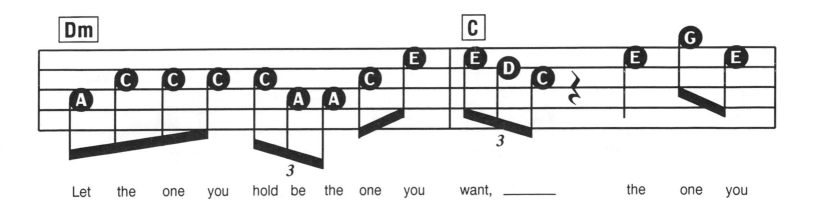

Let the one you hold be the one you want, _____ the one you

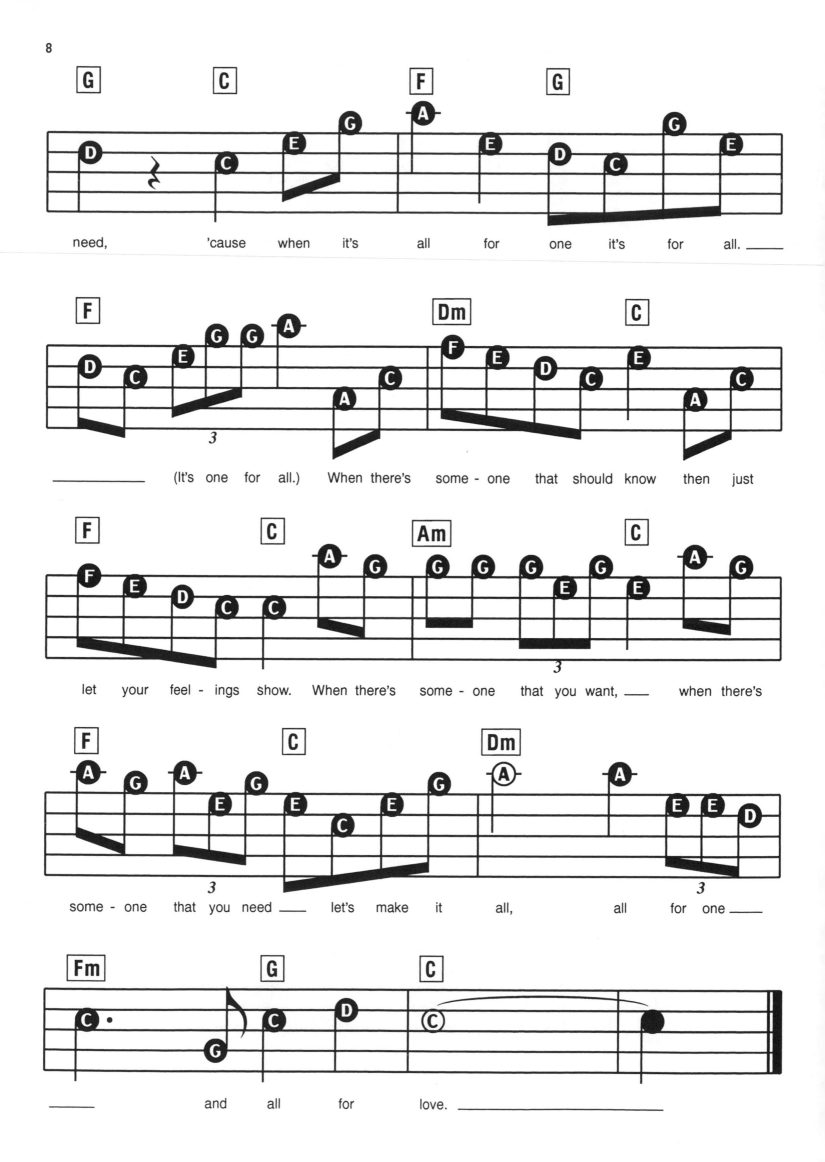

All Out of Love

Registration 2
Rhythm: Rock or 8-Beat

Words and Music by Graham Russell
and Clive Davis

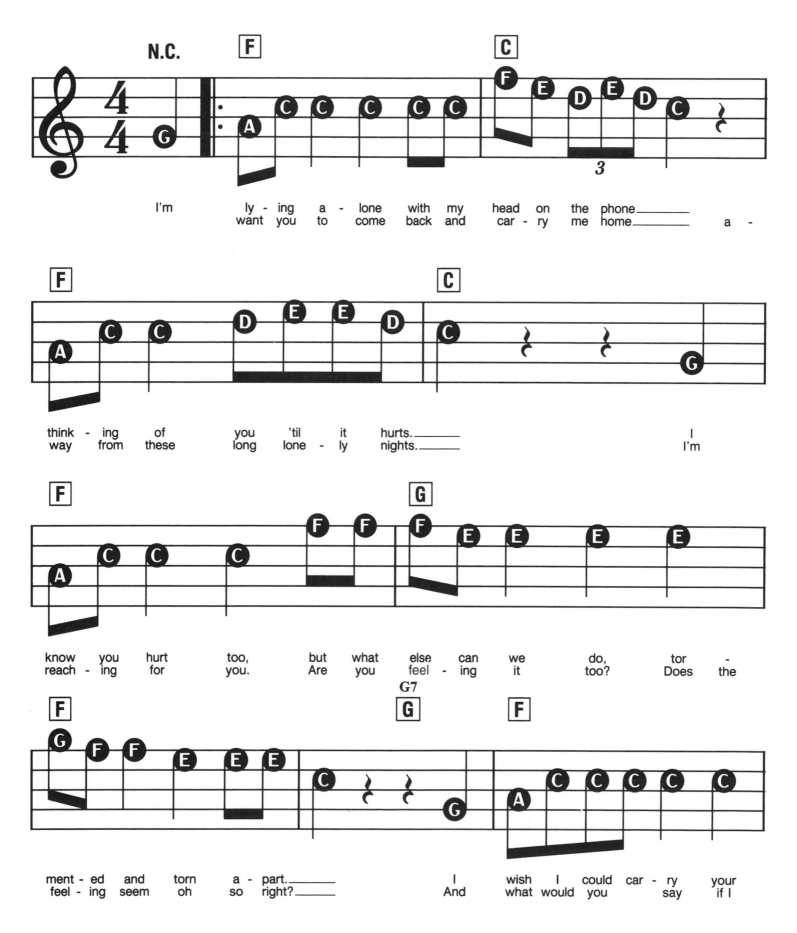

I'm   ly - ing a - lone   with my   head on   the phone_____   a -
want you   to   come   back and   car - ry   me home_____

think - ing   of   you   'til   it   hurts._____   I
way   from   these   long   lone - ly   nights._____   I'm

know   you   hurt   too,   but   what   else   can   we   do,   tor -
reach - ing   for   you.   Are   what   you   feel - ing   it   do   too?   Does   the

ment - ed   and   torn   a - part._____   I   wish   I   could   car - ry   your
feel - ing   seem   oh   so   right?_____   And   what   would   you   say   if   I

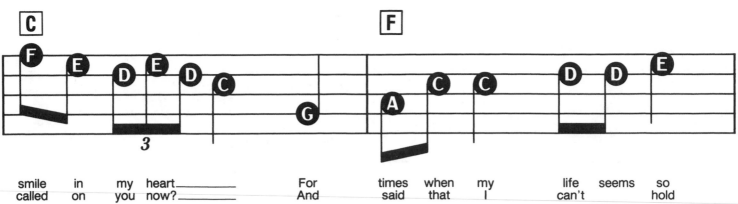

smile   in   my   heart_____   For
called   on   you   now?_____   And
times   when   my   life   seems   so
said   that   I   can't   so   hold

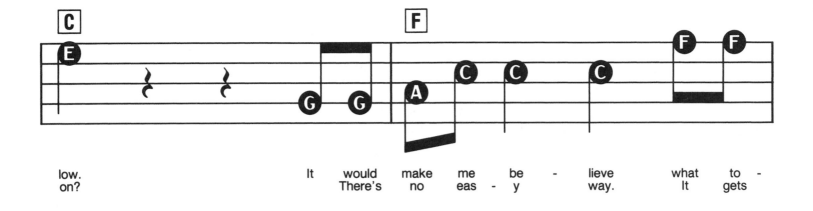

low.
on?

It   would   make   me   be - lieve   what   to -
There's   no   eas - y   way.   It   gets

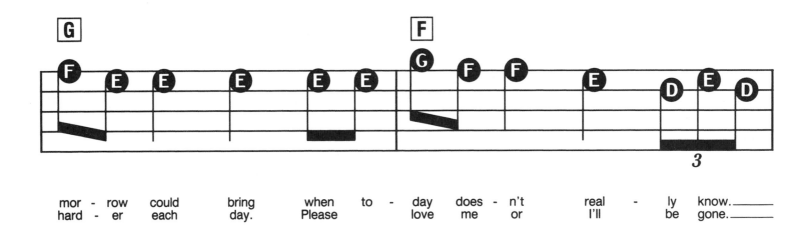

mor - row   could   bring   when   to - day   does - n't   real - ly   know._____
hard - er   each   day.   Please   love   me   or   I'll   be   gone._____

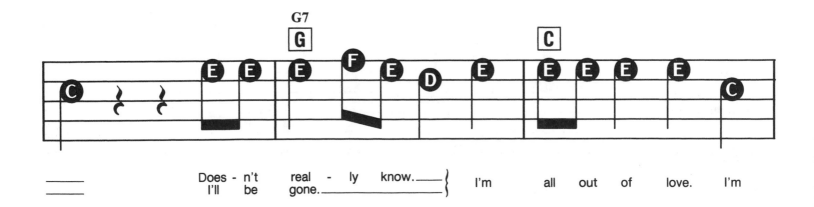

_____   Does - n't   real - ly   know._____ }   I'm   all   out   of   love.   I'm
I'll   be   gone._____

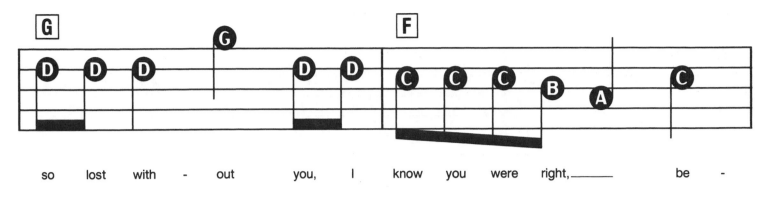

so lost with - out you, I know you were right,_____ be -

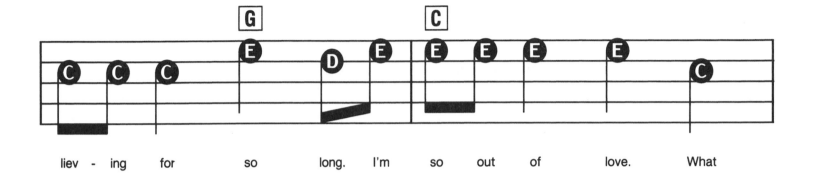

liev - ing for so long. I'm so out of love. What

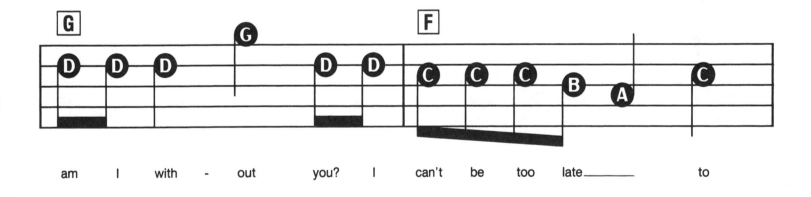

am I with - out you? I can't be too late_____ to

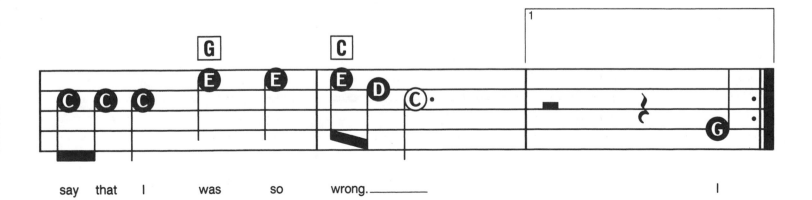

say that I was so wrong._____ I

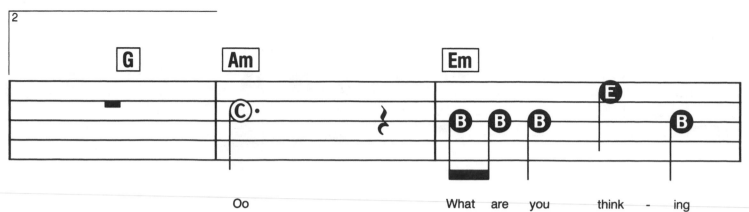

Oo   What are you think - ing

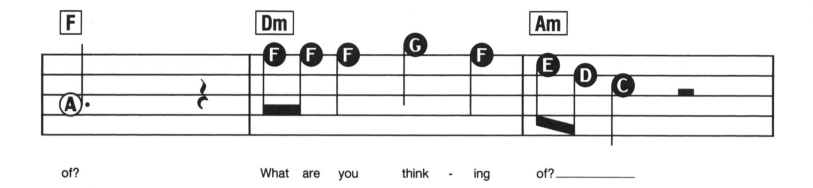

of?   What are you think - ing of?_____

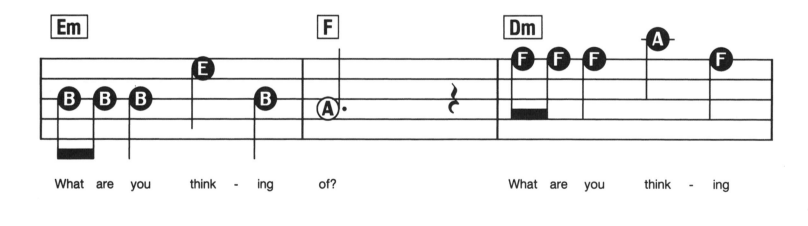

What are you think - ing of?   What are you think - ing

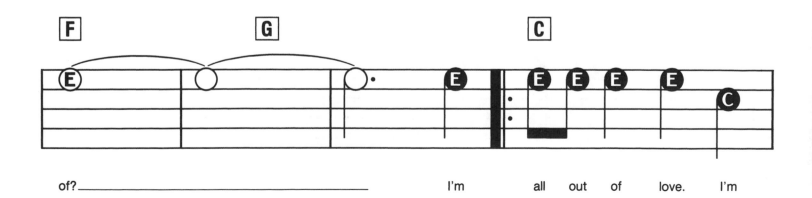

of?_____   I'm all out of love. I'm

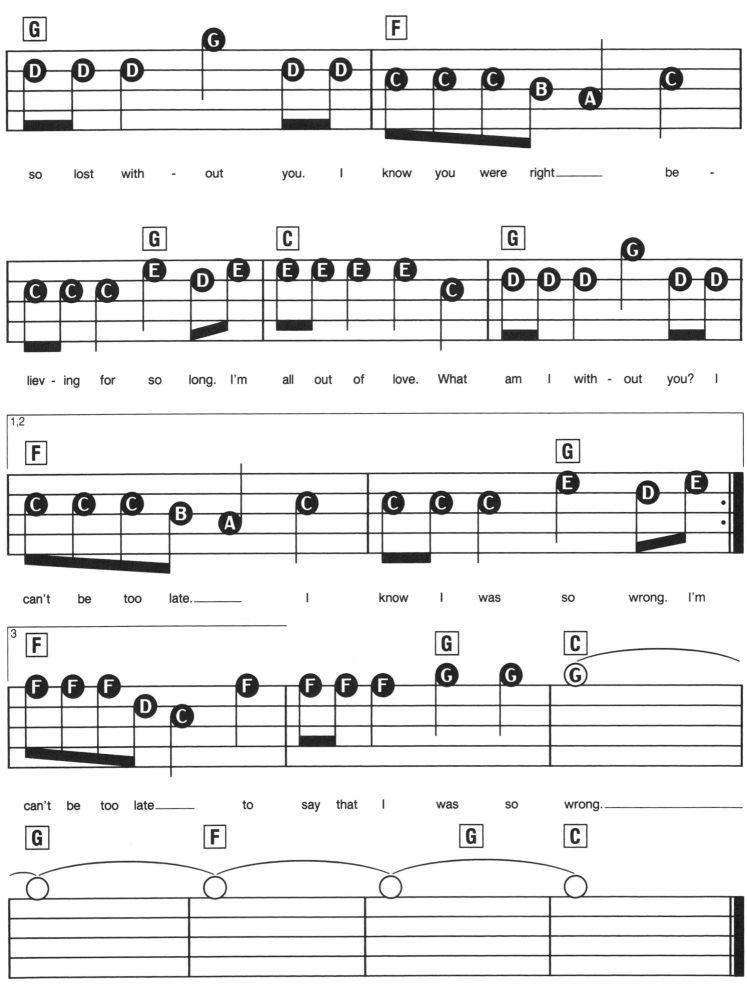

All I Ask of You
from THE PHANTOM OF THE OPERA

Registration 8
Rhythm: 8-Beat or Ballad

Music by Andrew Lloyd Webber
Lyrics by Charles Hart
Additional Lyrics by Richard Stilgoe

Raoul: No more talk of dark-ness, for - get these wide - eyed fears: I'm
let me be your light; you're

here, noth - ing can harm you, my words will warm and calm you.
safe, no one will harm find you, your fears are far be - hind you.

Let me be your free - dom, let day - light dry your tears; I'm
Christine: All I want is free - dom, a world with no more night; and

here, with you, be - side you, to guard you and to guide you.
you, al - ways be - side me, to hold me and to hide me. *Raoul:* Then

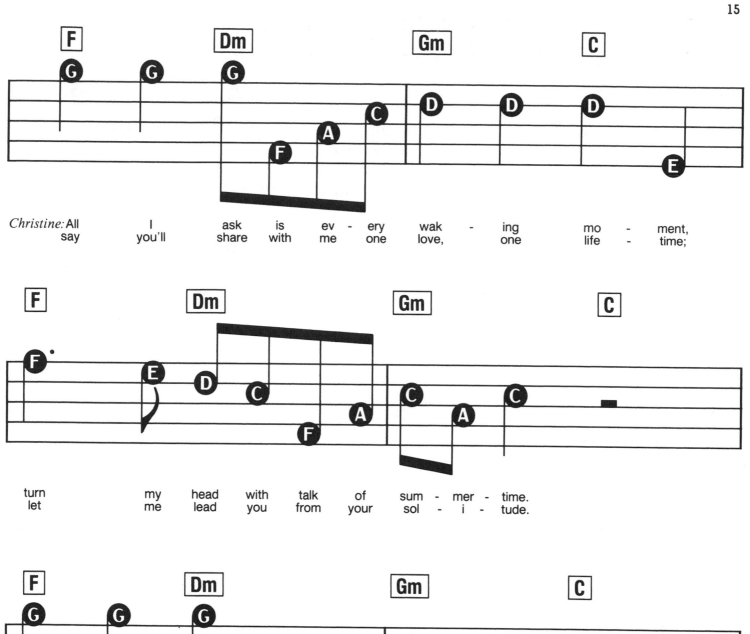

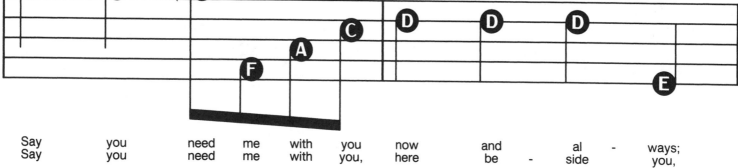

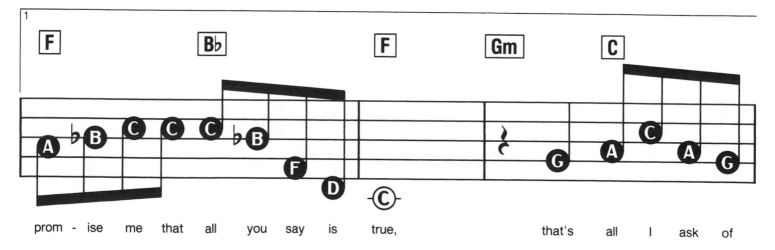

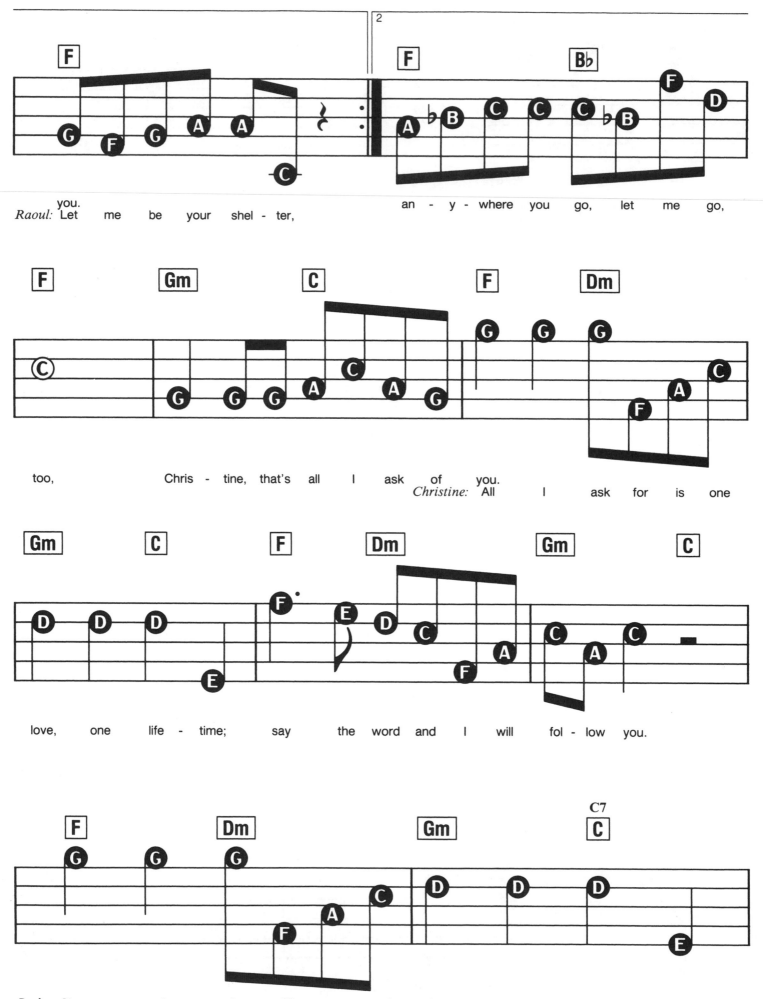

Raoul: Let me be your shel - ter, an - y - where you go, let me go,

too, Chris - tine, that's all I ask of you. *Christine:* All I ask for is one

love, one life - time; say the word and I will fol - low you.

Both: Share each day with me, each night, each morn - ing.

All My Loving

Registration 9
Rhythm: Rock

Words and Music by John Lennon
and Paul McCartney

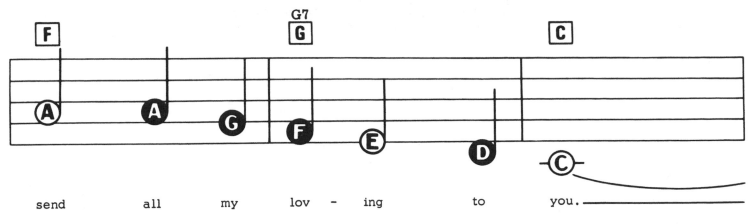

send   all   my   lov - ing   to   you.

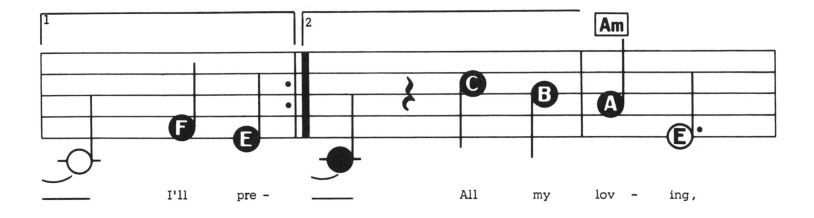

I'll   pre -   All   my   lov - ing,

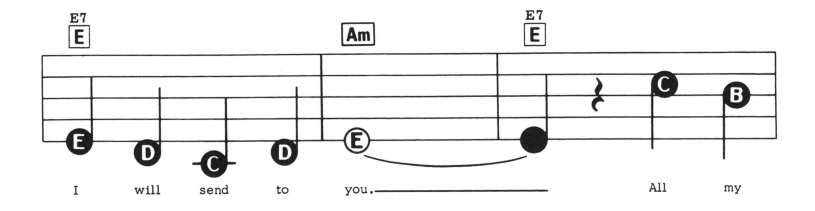

I   will   send   to   you.   All   my

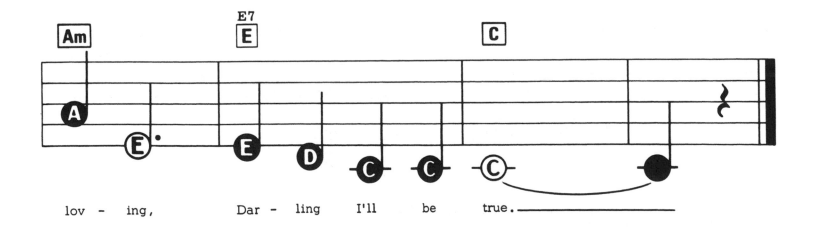

lov - ing,   Dar - ling   I'll   be   true.

Almost Paradise
Love Theme from the Paramount Motion Picture FOOTLOOSE

Registration 8
Rhythm: Rock or 8-Beat

Words by Dean Pitchford
Music by Eric Carmen

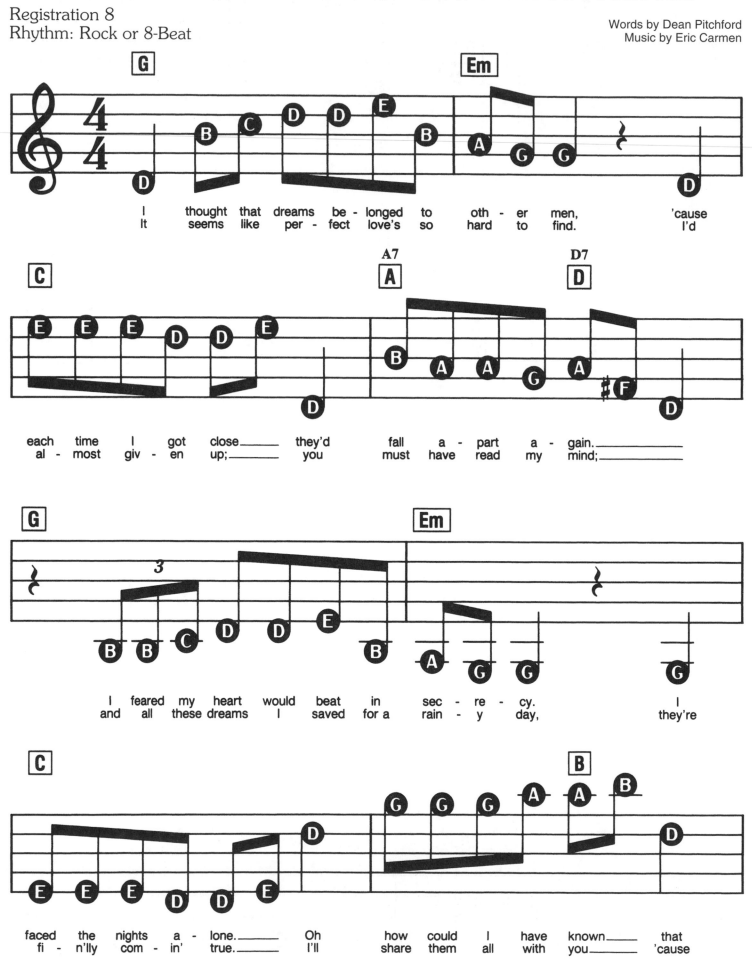

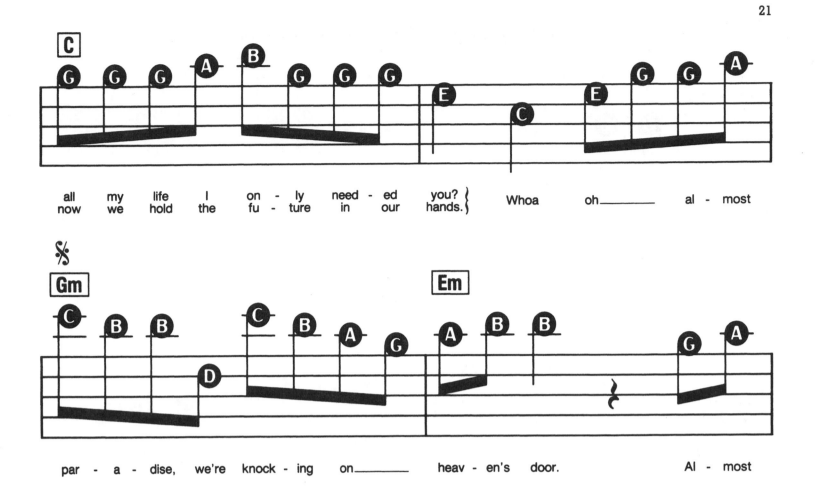

all my life I on - ly need - ed you? Whoa oh_____ al - most
now we hold the fu - ture in our hands.

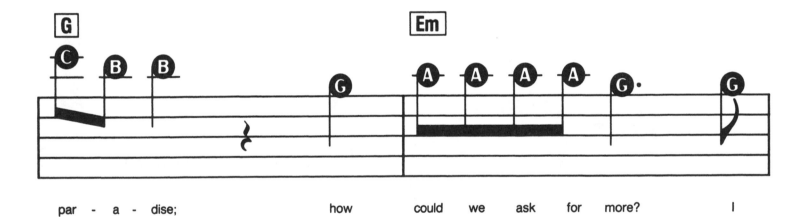

par - a - dise, we're knock - ing on_____ heav - en's door. Al - most

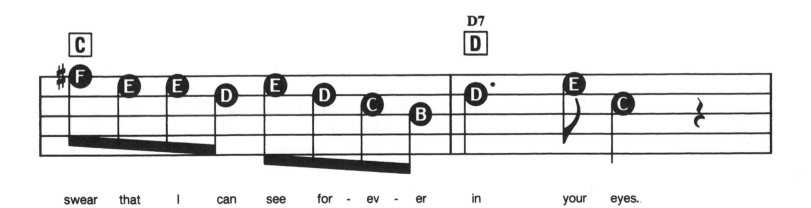

par - a - dise; how could we ask for more? I

swear that I can see for - ev - er in your eyes.

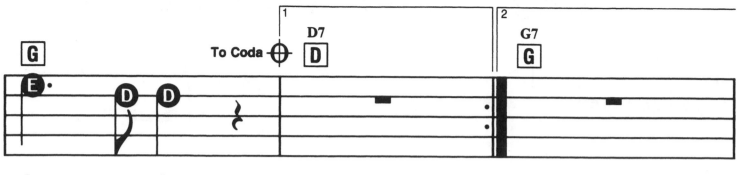

Par - a - dise.

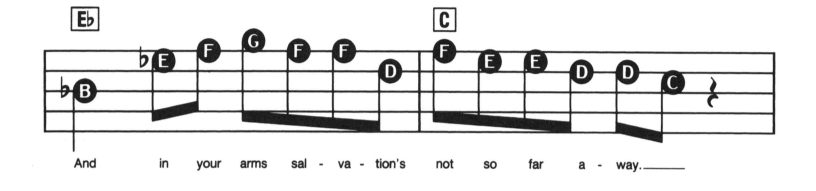

And in your arms sal - va - tion's not so far a - way.___

D.S. al Coda
(Return to %
Play to ⊕ and
skip to Coda)

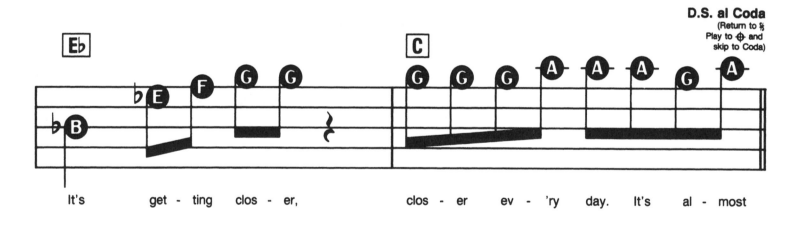

It's get - ting clos - er, clos - er ev - 'ry day. It's al - most

CODA
⊕

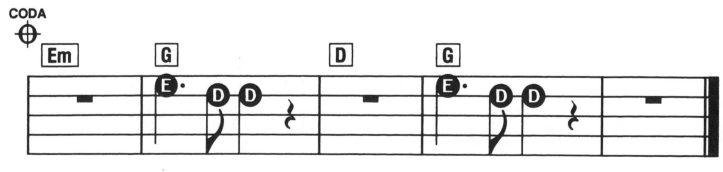

Par - a - dise, par - a - dise.

Baby, I Love Your Way

Registration 8
Rhythm: Rock or 4/4 Ballad

Words and Music by
Peter Frampton

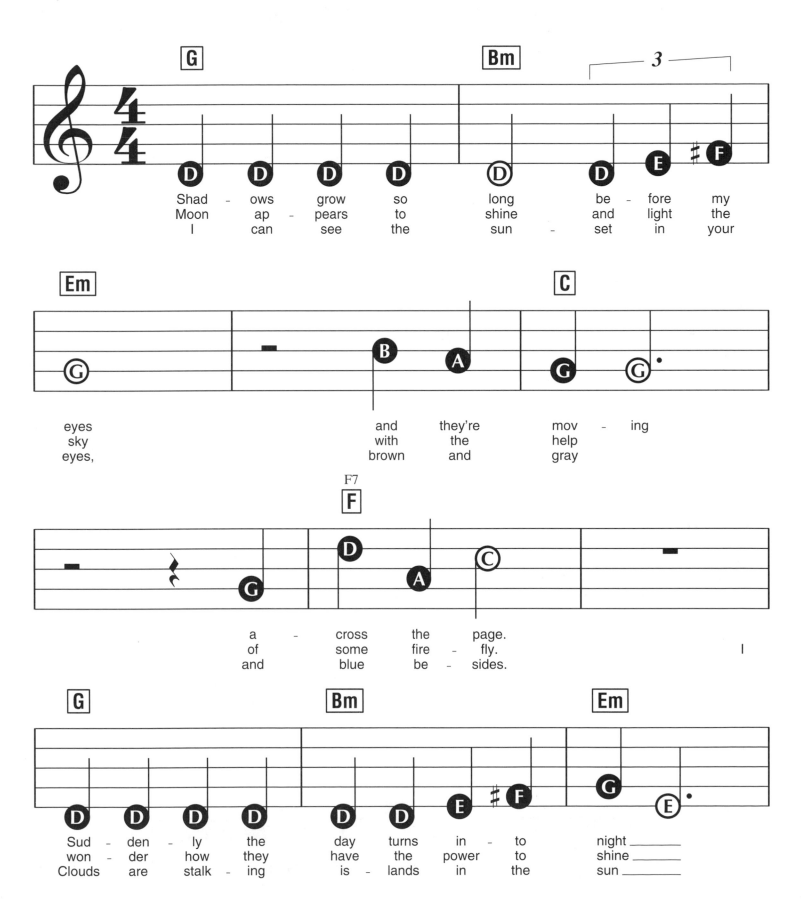

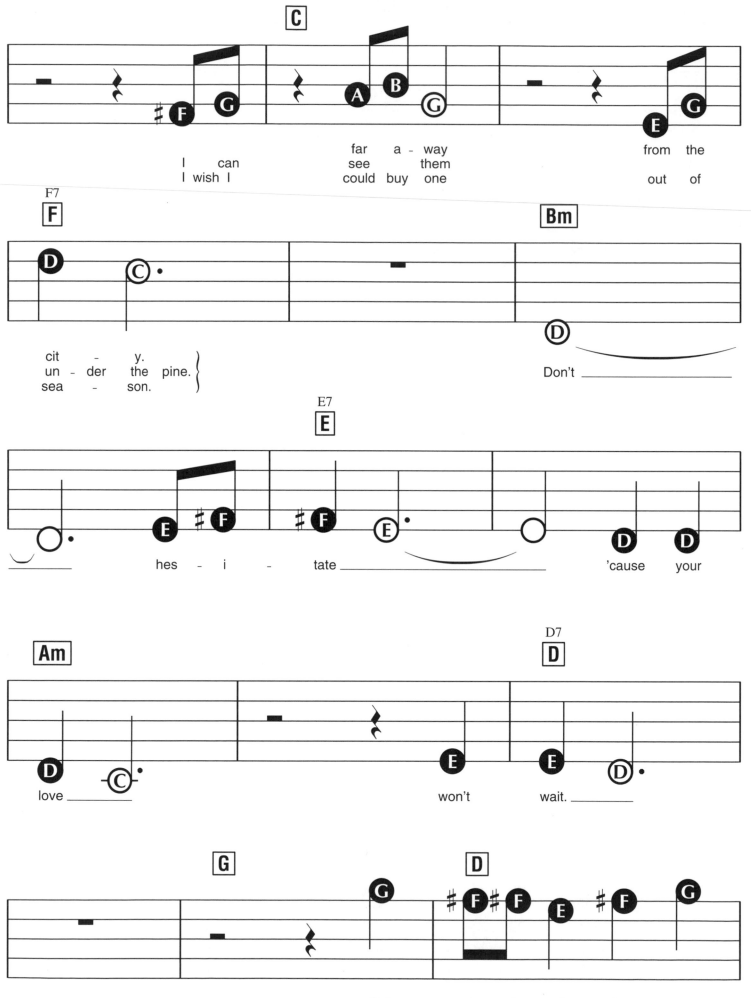

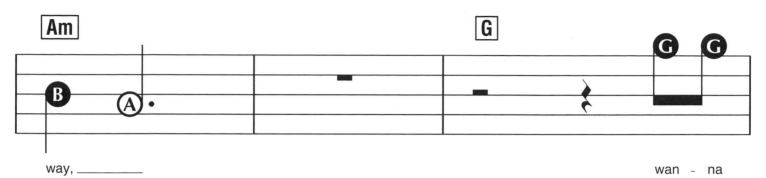

way, _____

wan - na

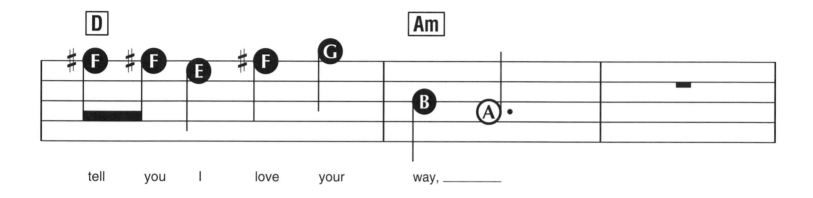

tell   you   I   love   your   way, _____

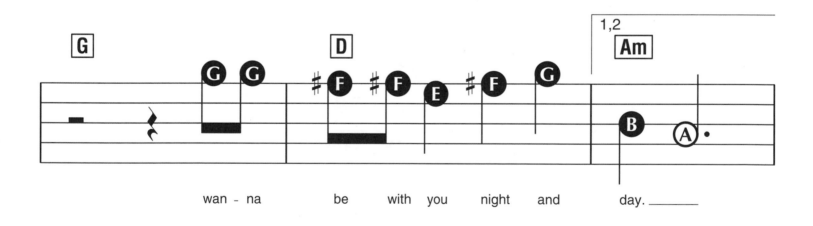

wan - na   be   with   you   night   and   day. _____

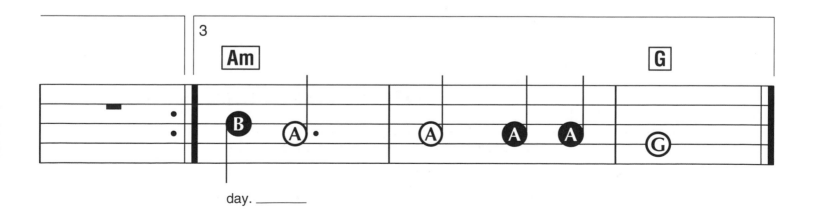

day. _____

Always on My Mind

Registration 10
Rhythm: Ballad or Slow Rock

Words and Music by Wayne Thompson,
Mark James and Johnny Christopher

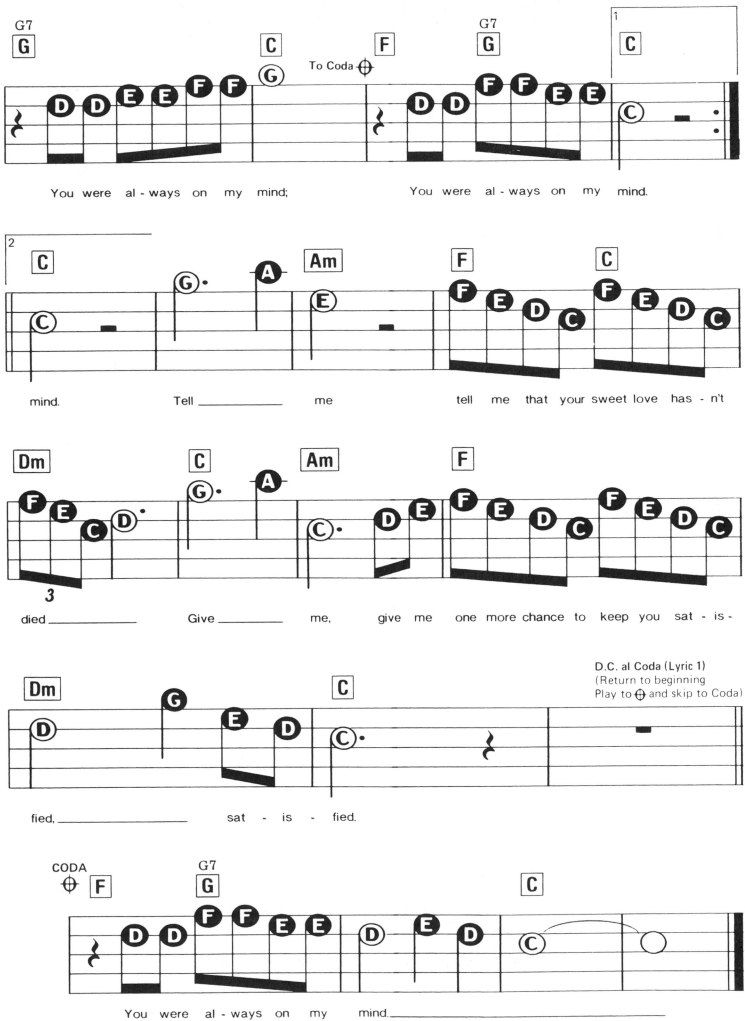

Amanda

Registration 5
Rhythm: Slow Rock or Ballad

Words and Music by
Tom Scholz

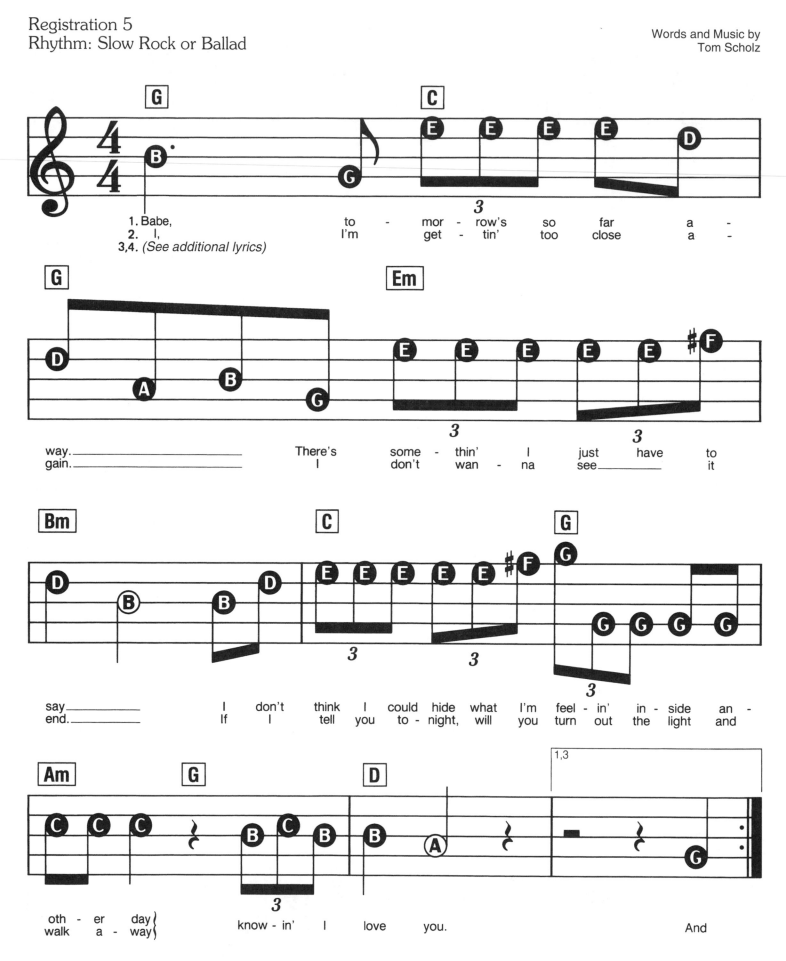

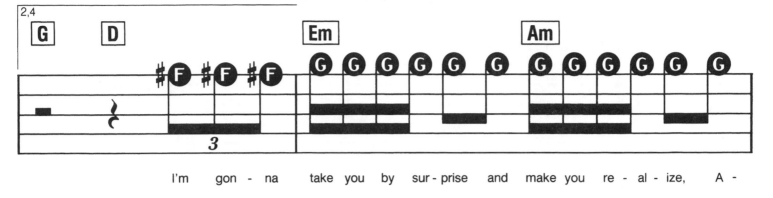

I'm gon - na take you by sur - prise and make you re - al - ize, A -

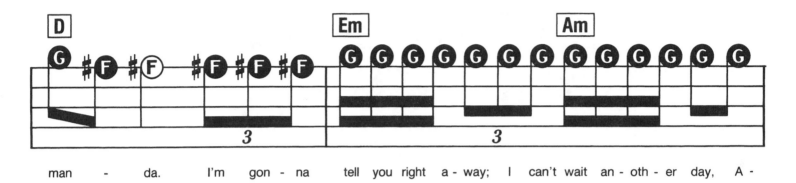

man - da. I'm gon - na tell you right a - way; I can't wait an - oth - er day, A -

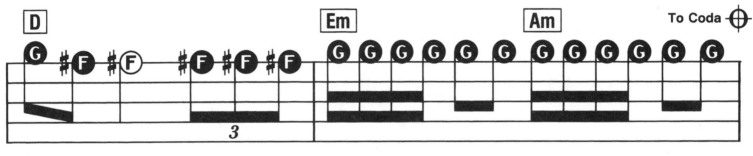

man - da. I'm gon - na say it like a man and make you un - der - stand, A -

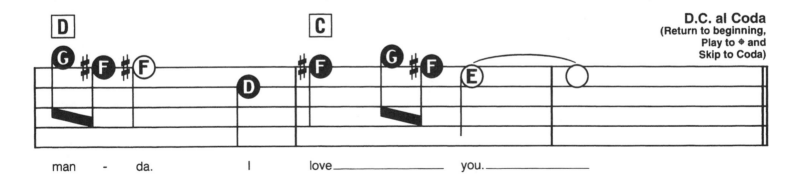

man - da. I love_____ you._____

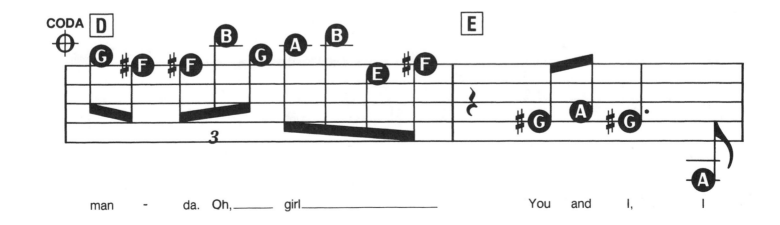

man - da. Oh,_____ girl_____ You and I, I

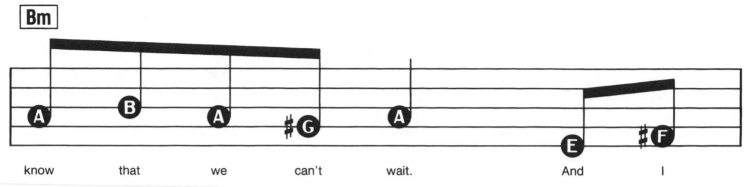

know that we can't wait. And I

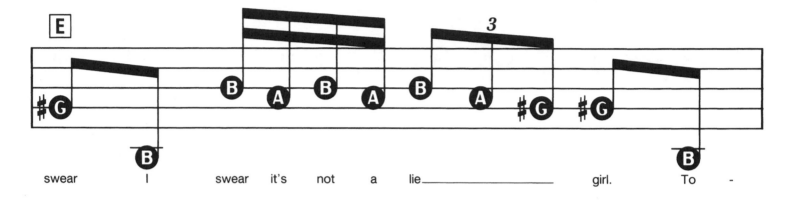

swear I swear it's not a lie_____ girl. To -

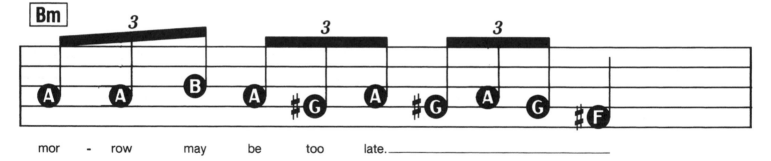

mor - row may be too late._____

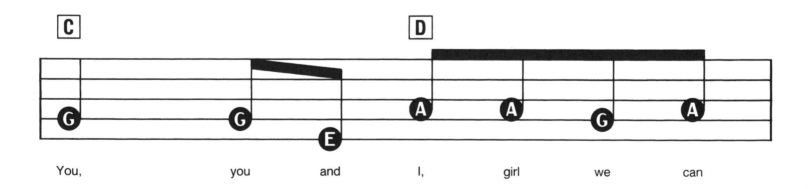

You, you and I, girl we can

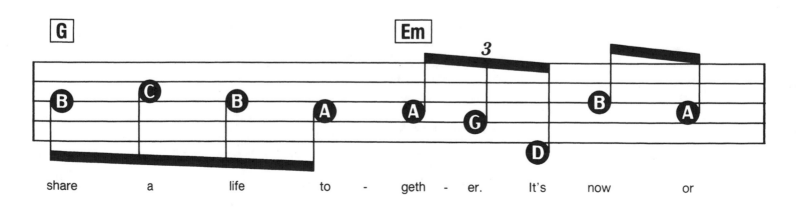

share a life to - geth - er. It's now or

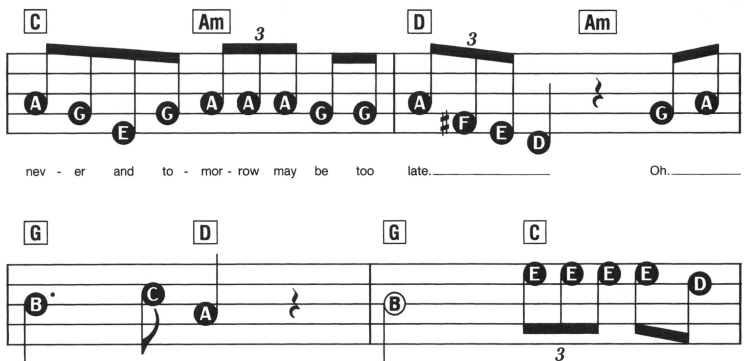

nev - er and to - mor - row may be too late._____ Oh._____

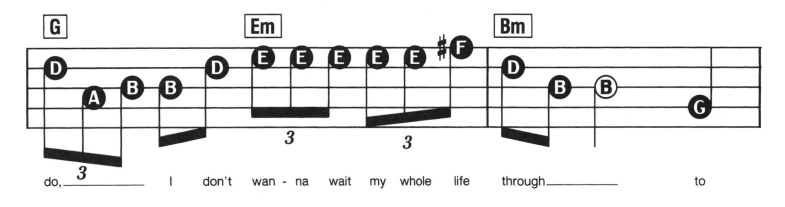

And feel - in' the way I

do,_____ I don't wan - na wait my whole life through_____ to

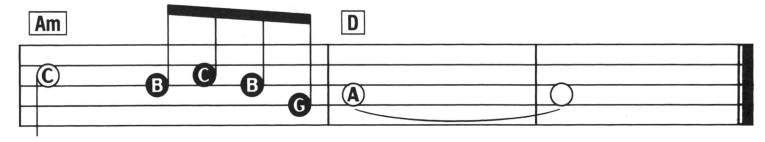

say I'm in love with you._____

Additional Lyrics

3. And, I feel like today's the day.
   I'm lookin' for the words to say.
   Do you wanna be free?
   Are you ready for me to feel this way?
   I don't wanna lose ya.

4. So, it may be too soon I know.
   The feelin' takes so long to grow.
   If I tell you today will you turn me away.
   And let me go?
   I don't wanna lose you.

And I Love Her

Registration 8
Rhythm: Rock or Jazz Rock

Words and Music by John Lennon
and Paul McCartney

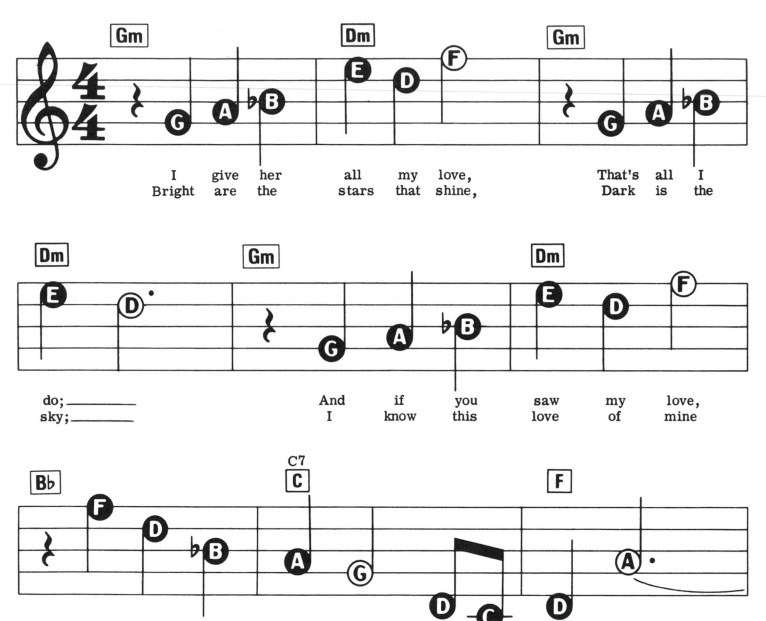

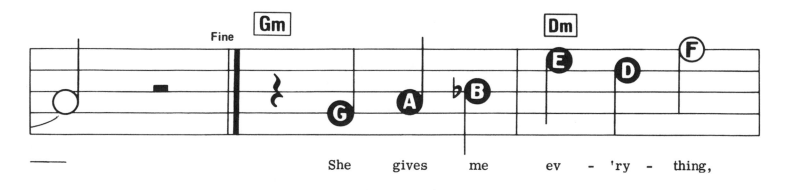

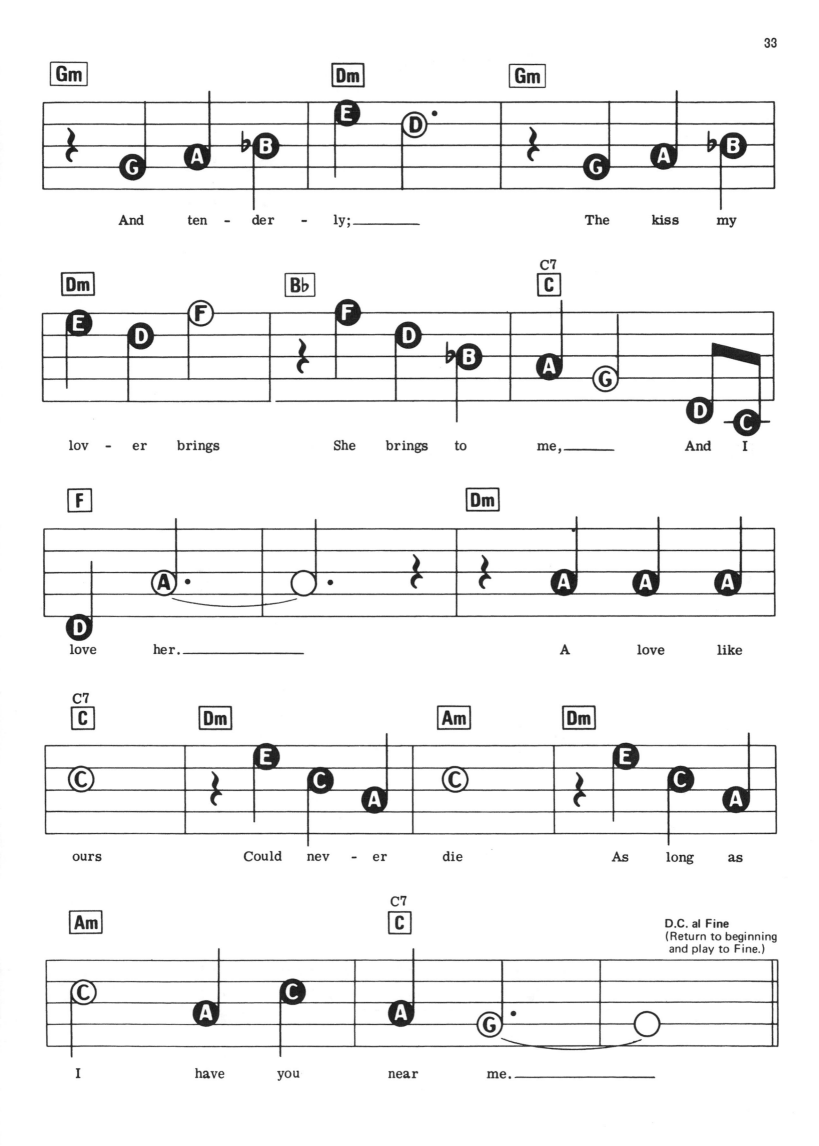

Back at One

Registration 2
Rhythm: 8-Beat or Rock

Words and Music by
Brian McKnight

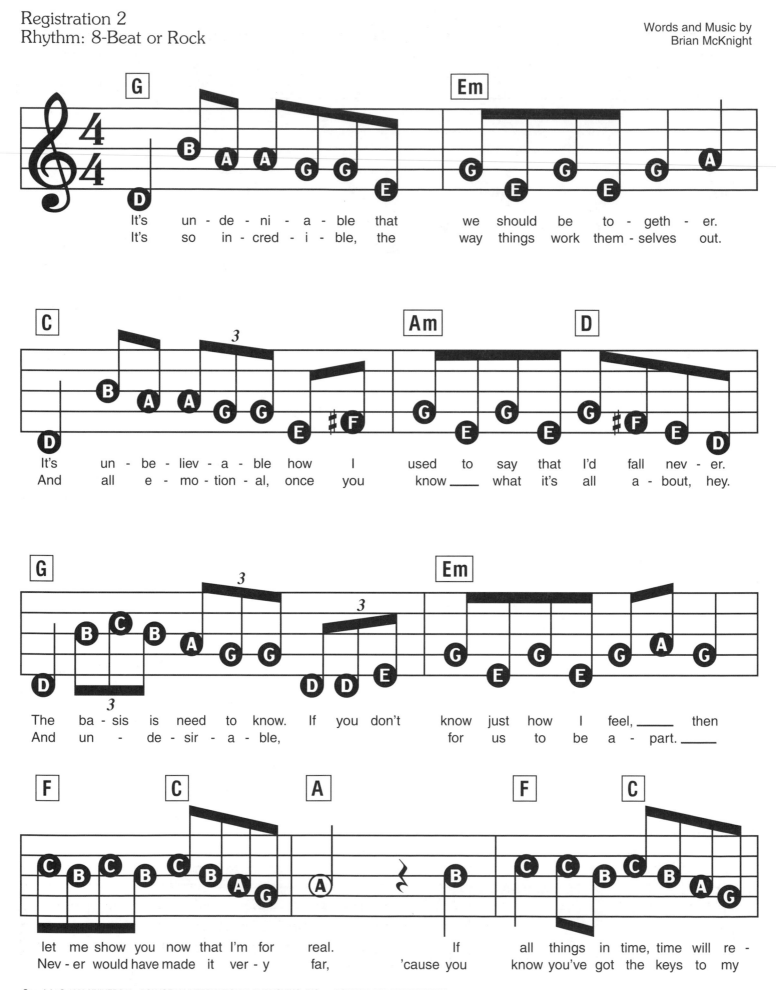

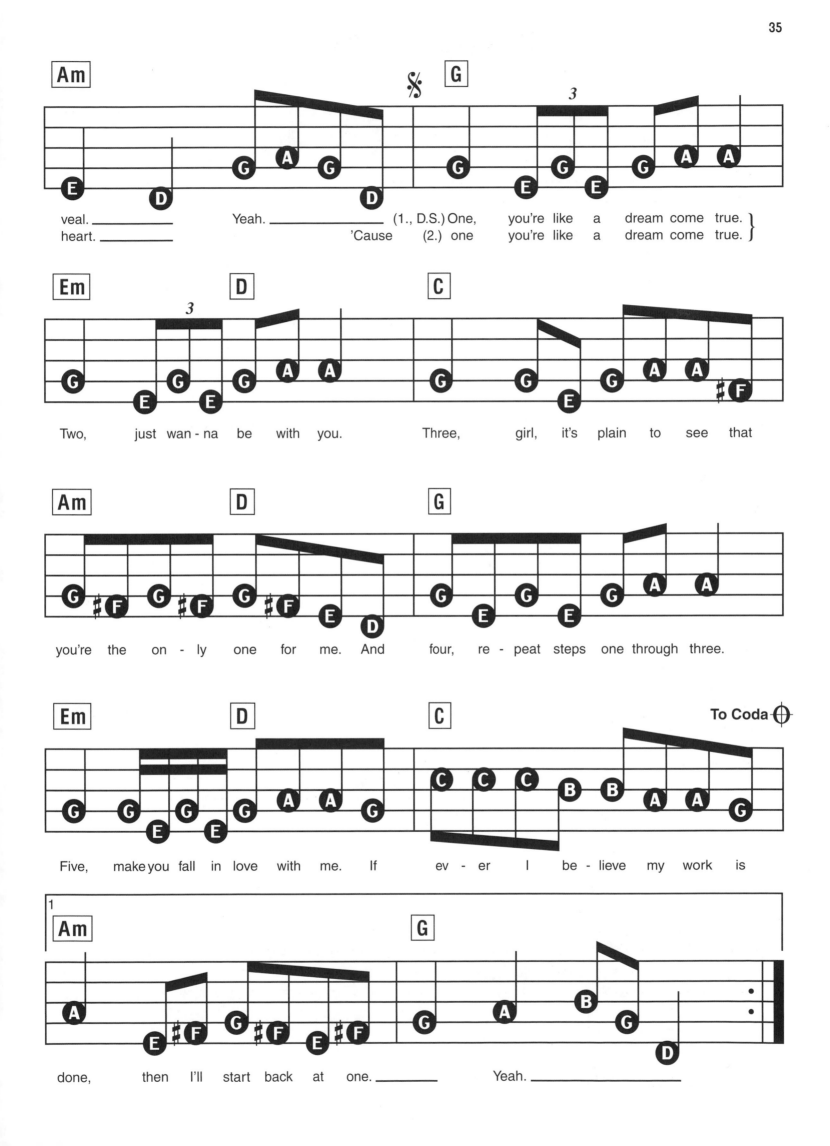

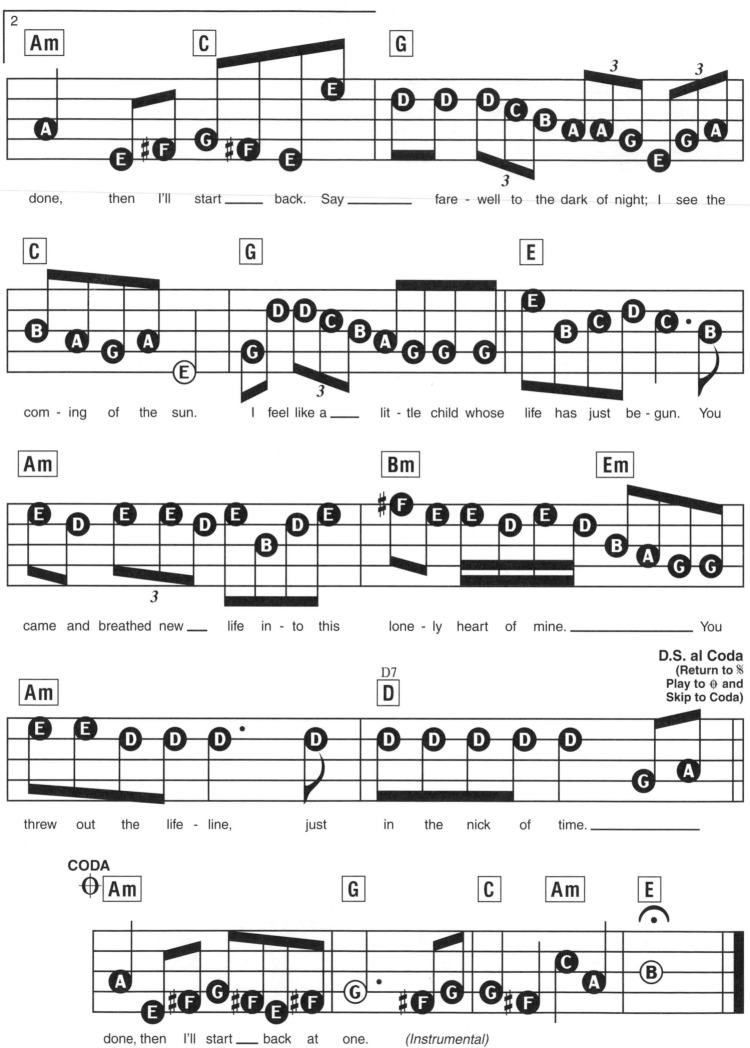

Breathe

Registration 7
Rhythm: Country Pop or Ballad

Words and Music by Holly Lamar
and Stephanie Bentley

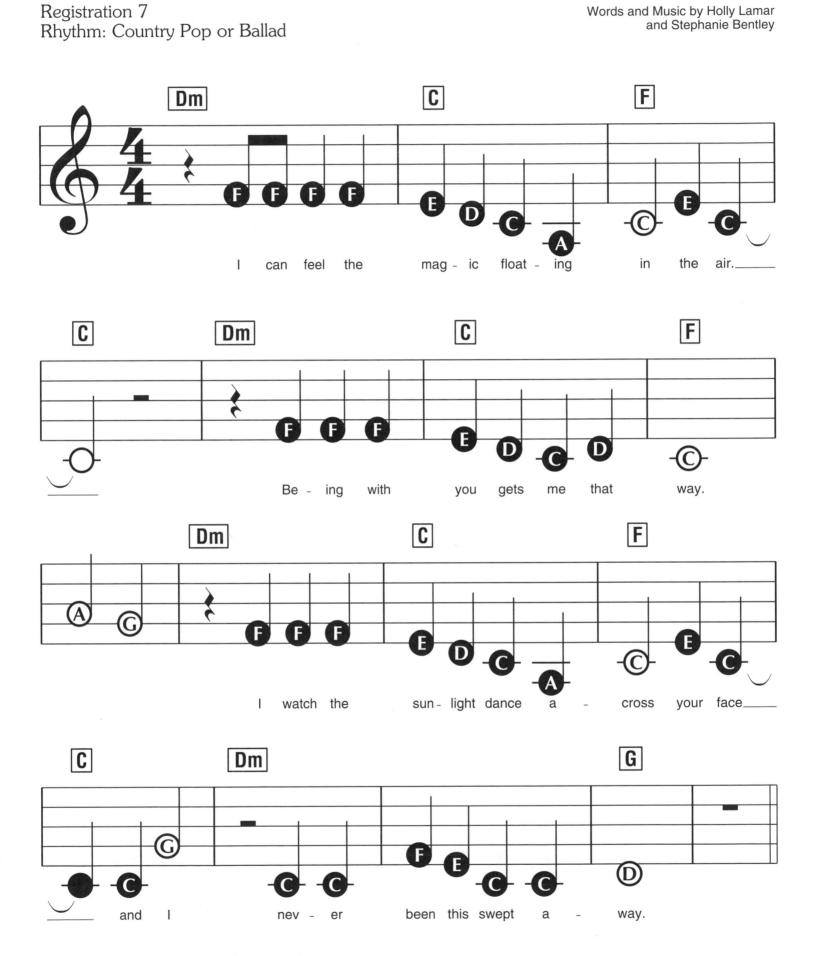

38

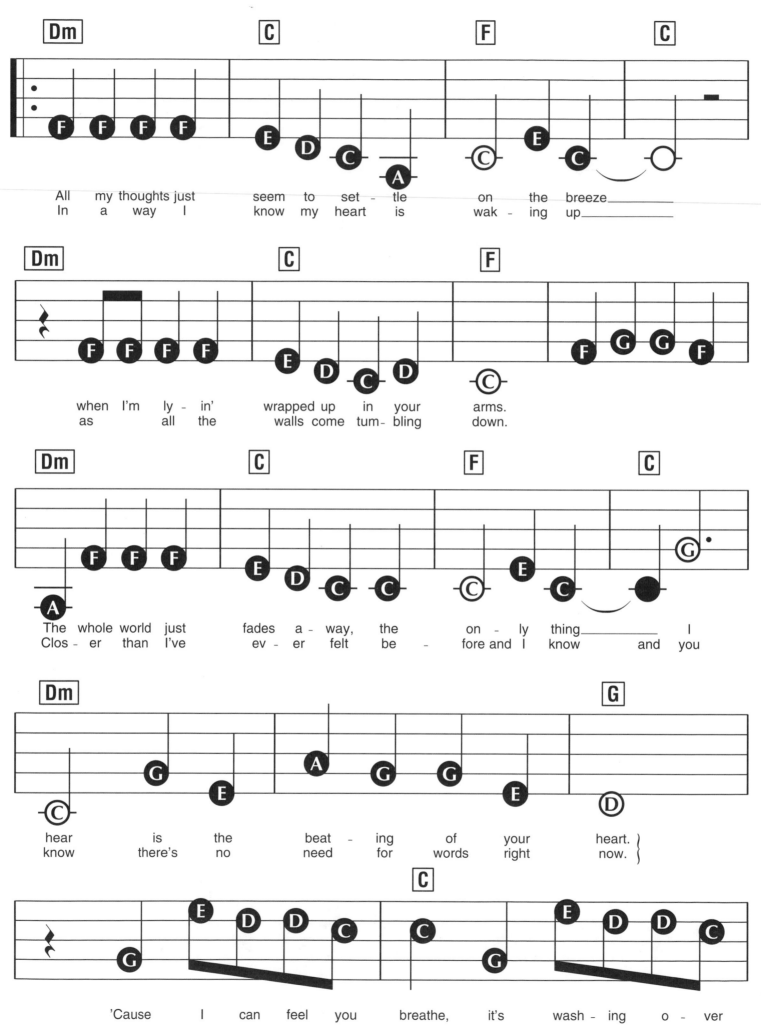

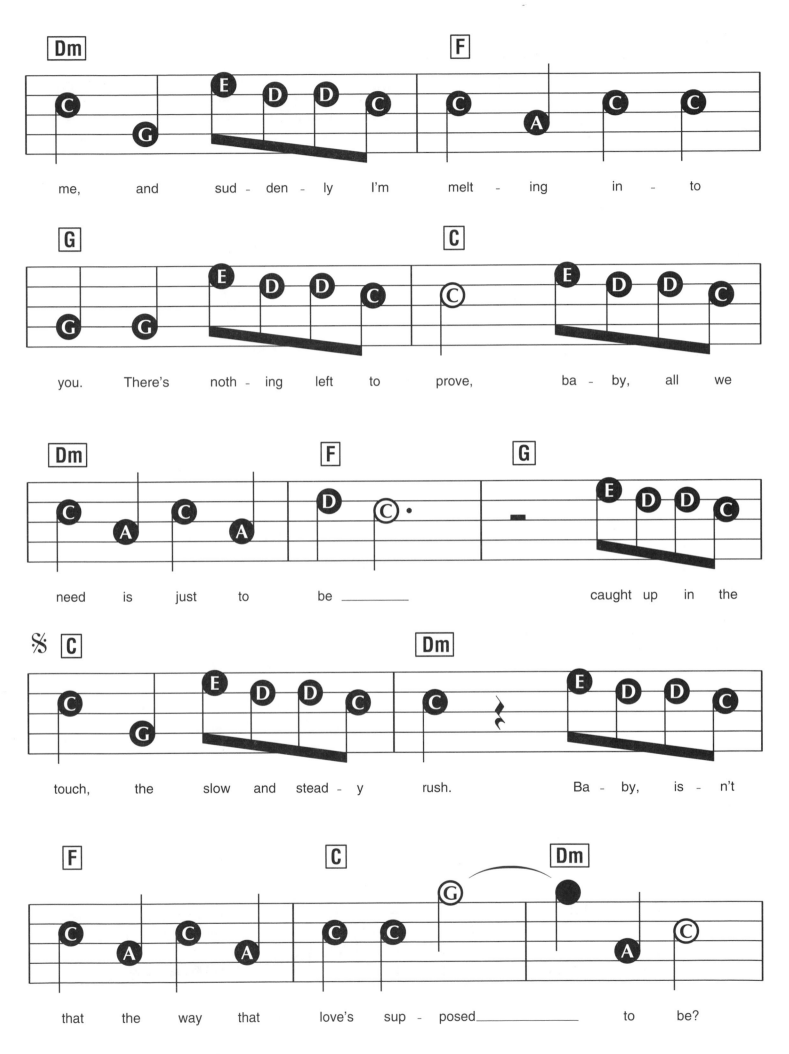

To Coda

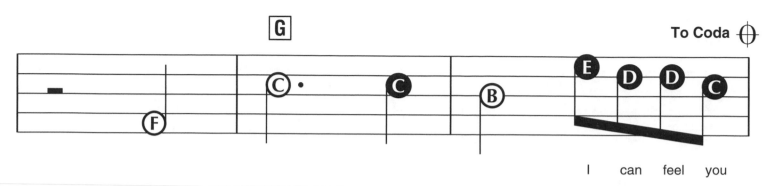

I can feel you

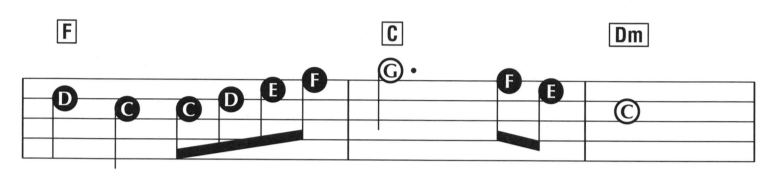

breathe. _____

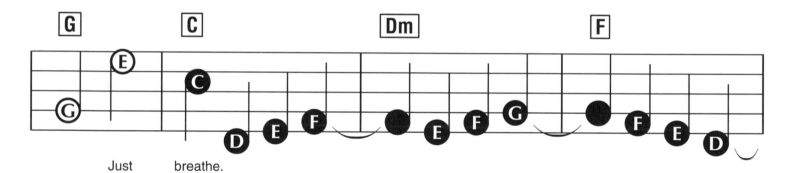

Just   breathe.

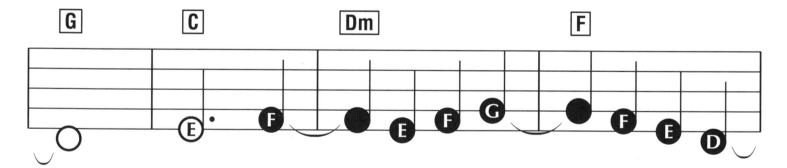

D.S. al Coda
(Return to %
Play to ⊕ and
Skip to Coda)

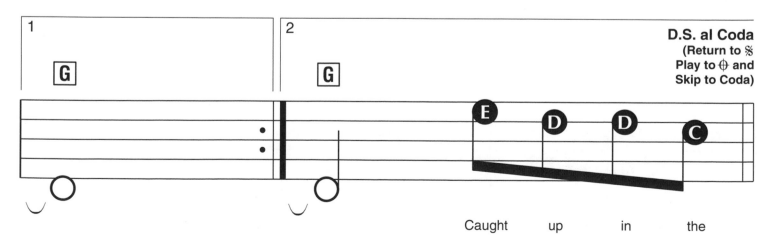

Caught   up   in   the

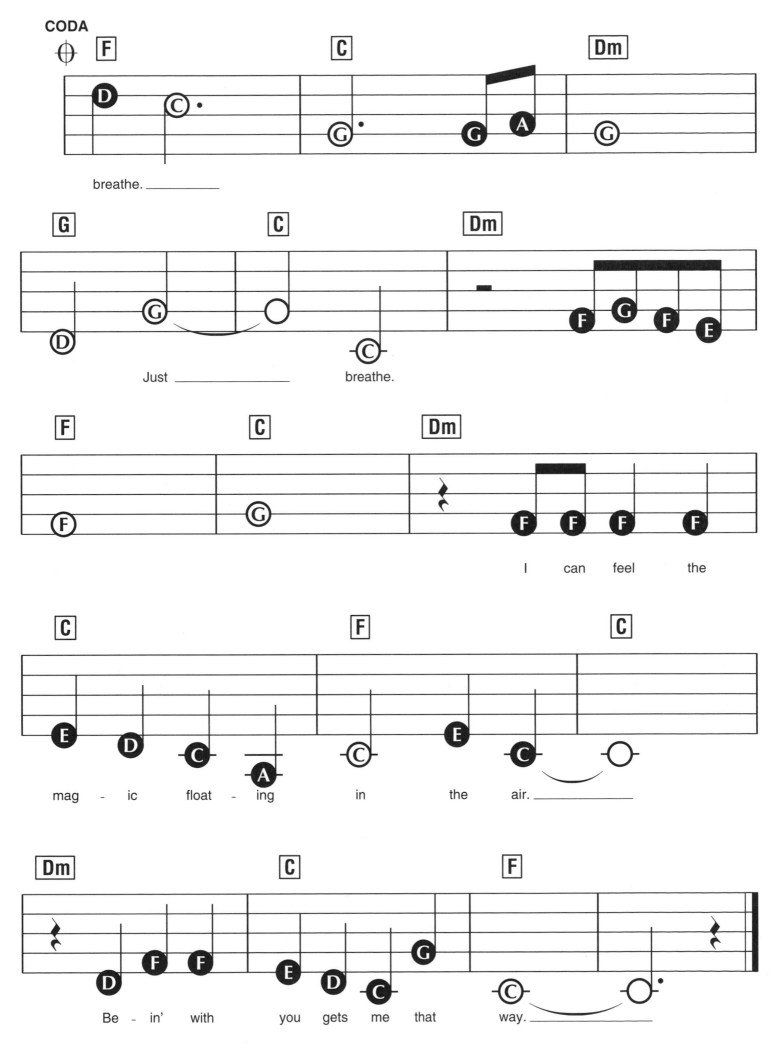

Best of My Love

Registration 4
Rhythm: 8-Beat or Rock

Words and Music by Maurice White
and Al McKay

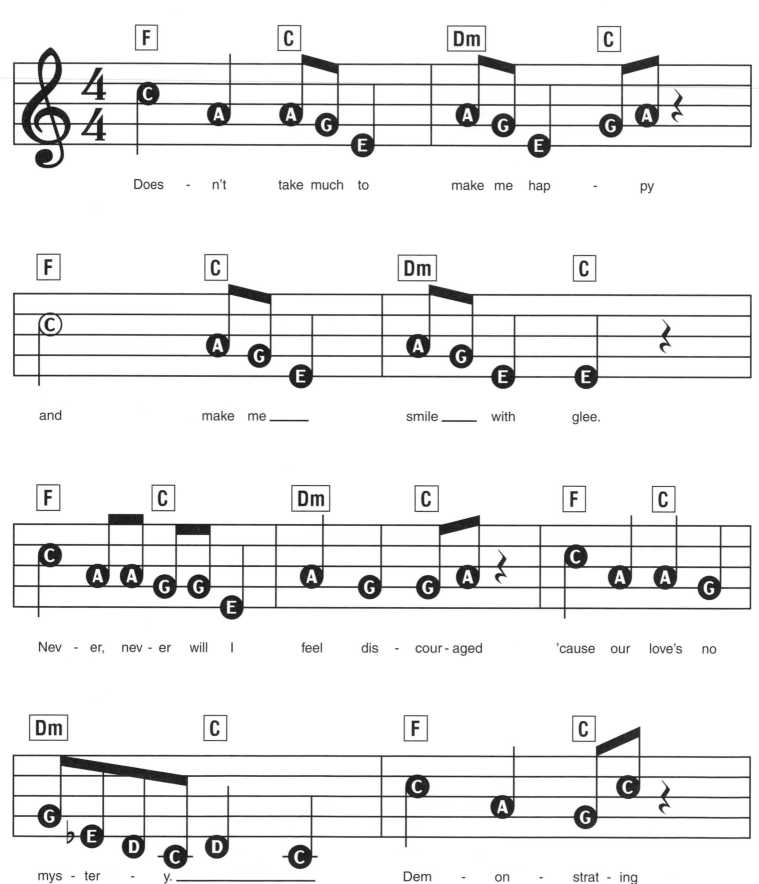

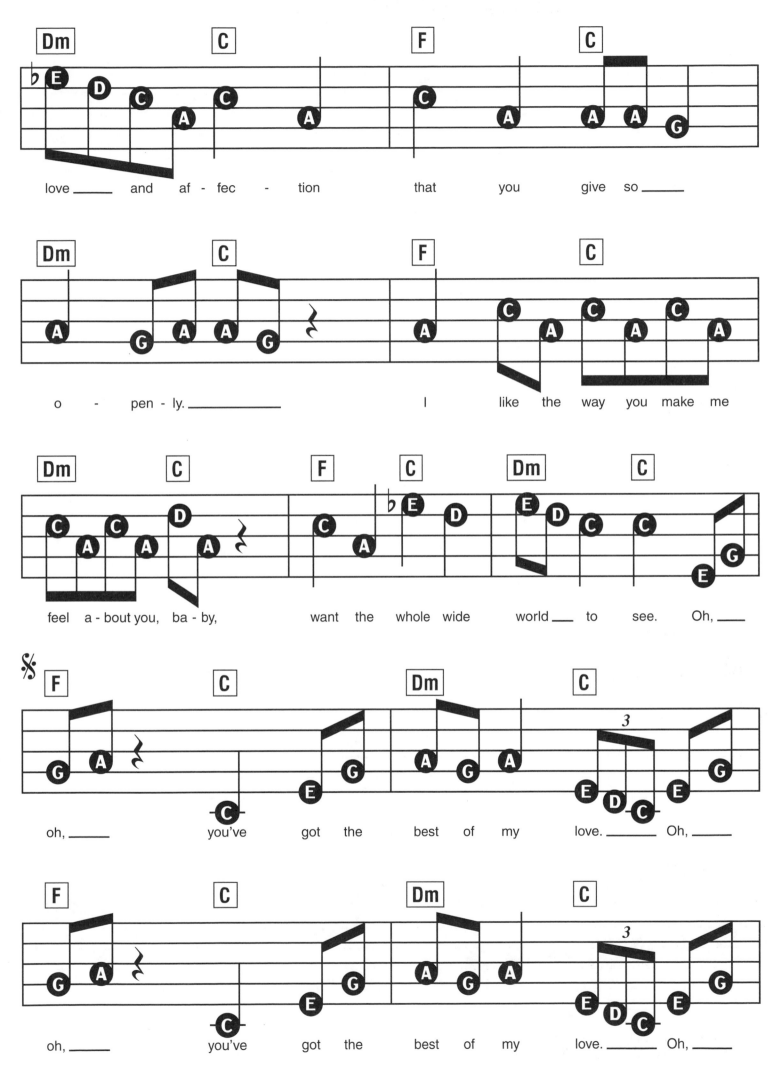

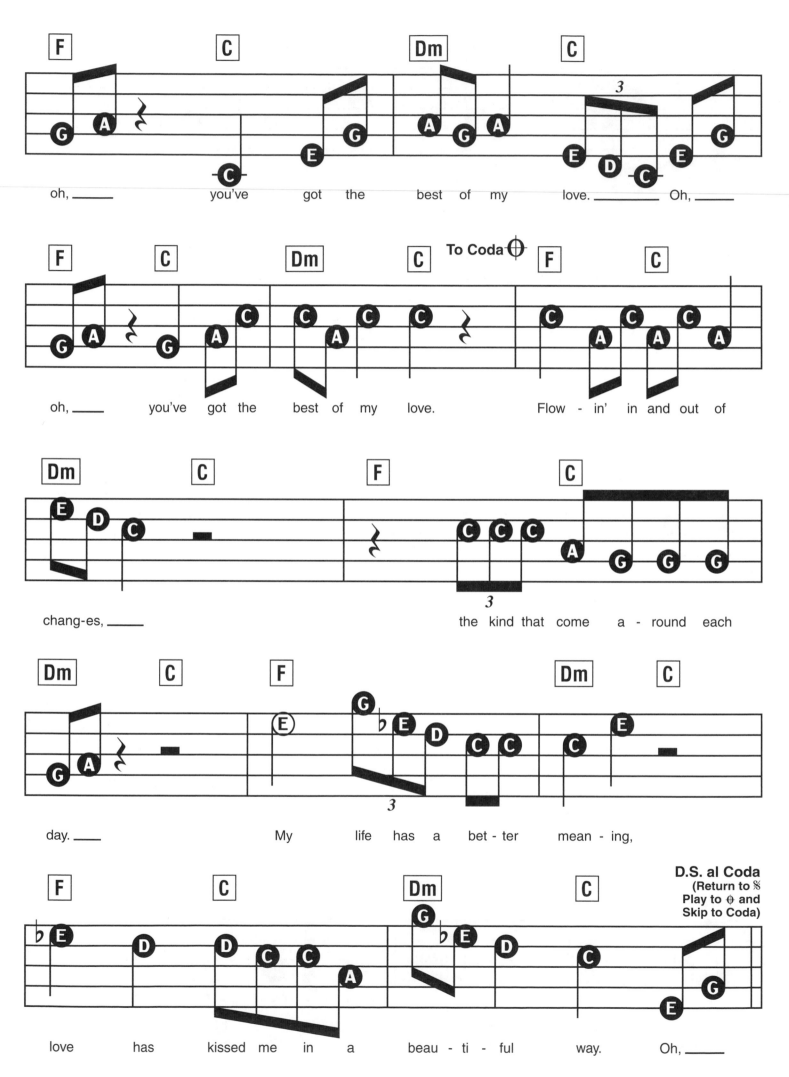

45

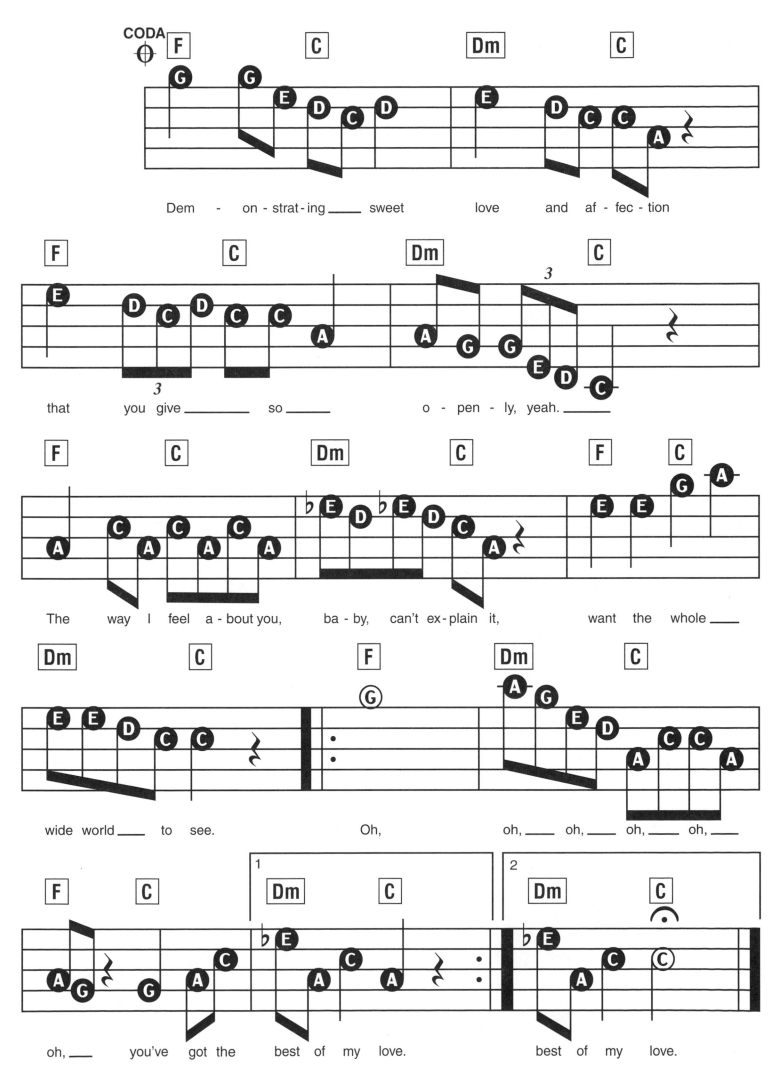

Can You Feel the Love Tonight
from Walt Disney Pictures' THE LION KING

Registration 2
Rhythm: Rock or 8-Beat

Music by Elton John
Lyrics by Tim Rice

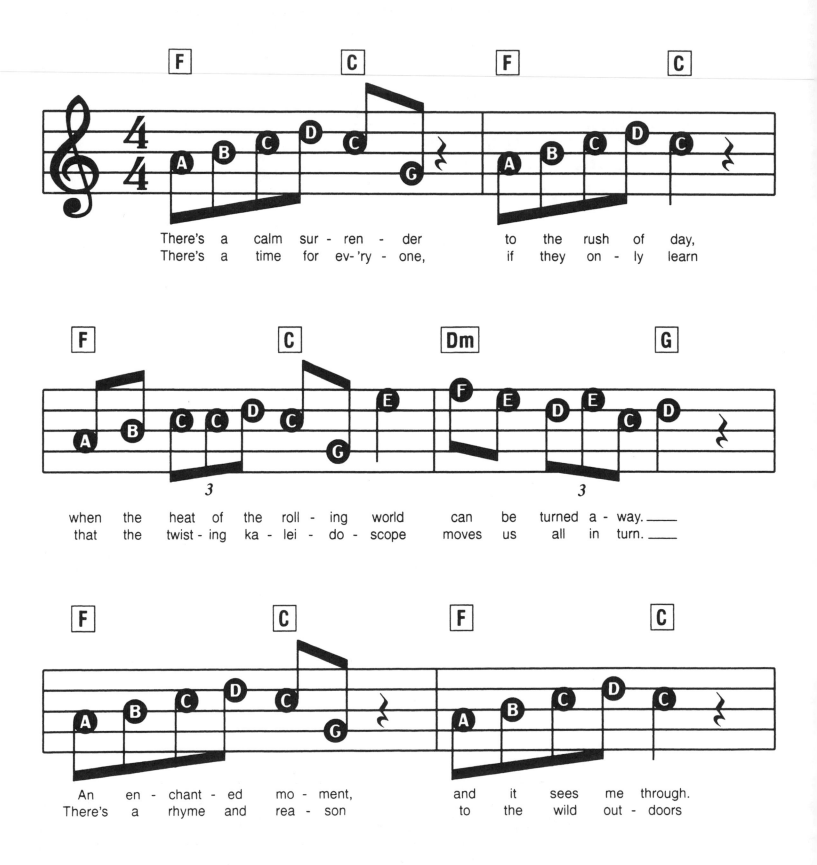

There's a calm sur - ren - der   to the rush of day,
There's a time for ev - 'ry - one,   if they on - ly learn

when the heat of the roll - ing world can be turned a - way. ____
that the twist - ing ka - lei - do - scope moves us all in turn. ____

An en - chant - ed mo - ment,   and it sees me through.
There's a rhyme and rea - son   to the wild out - doors

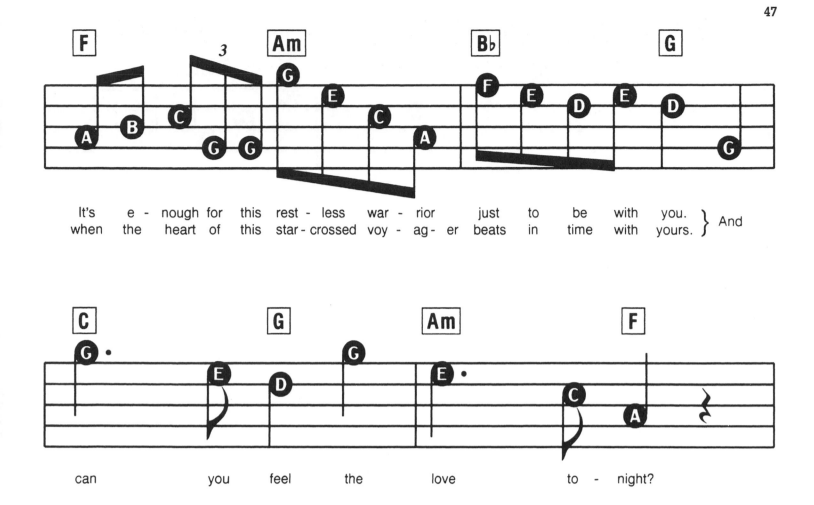

It's e - nough for this rest - less war - rior just to be with you. } And
when the heart of this star - crossed voy - ag - er beats in time with yours.

can you feel the love to - night?

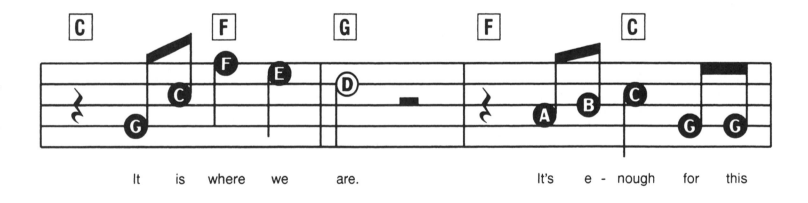

It is where we are. It's e - nough for this

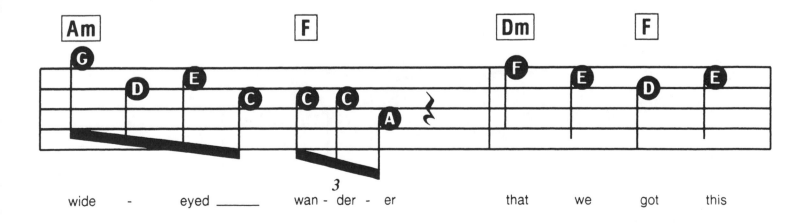

wide - eyed _____ wan - der - er that we got this

Can't We Try

Registration 4
Rhythm: Medium Rock Ballad

Words and Music by Dan Hill
Additional Lyrics by Beverly Chapin-Hill

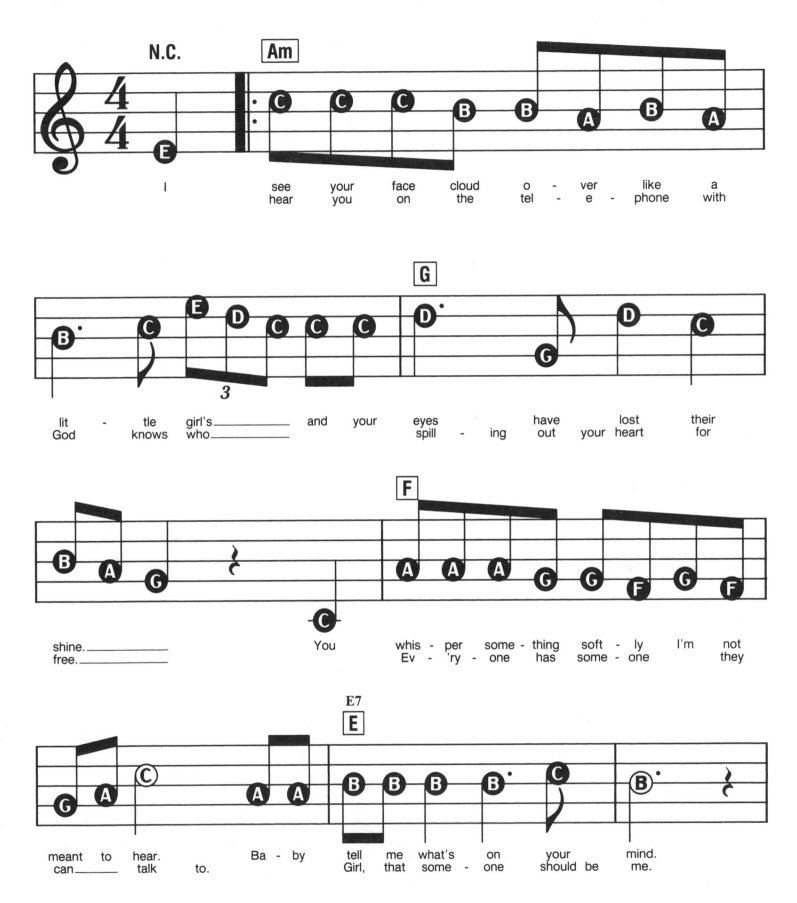

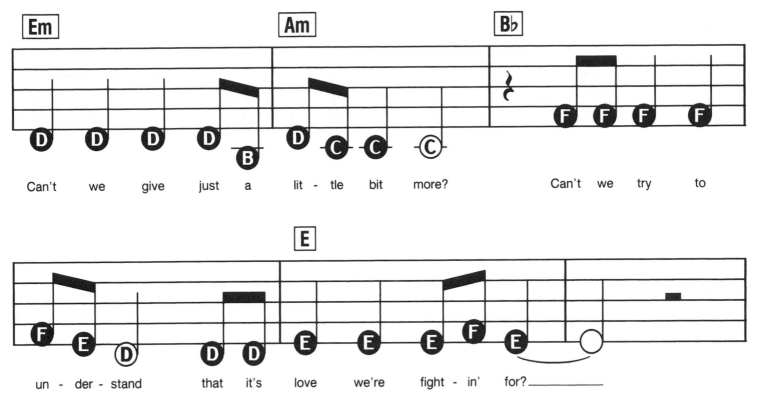

Can't we give just a lit - tle bit more? Can't we try to

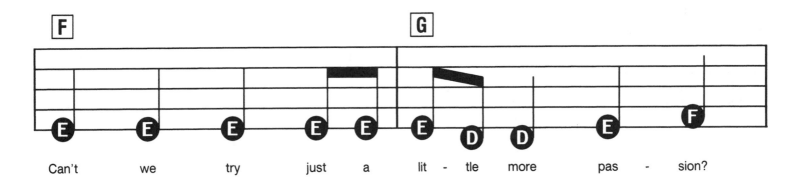

un - der - stand that it's love we're fight - in' for? _____

Can't we try just a lit - tle more pas - sion?

Can't we try just a lit - tle less pride?

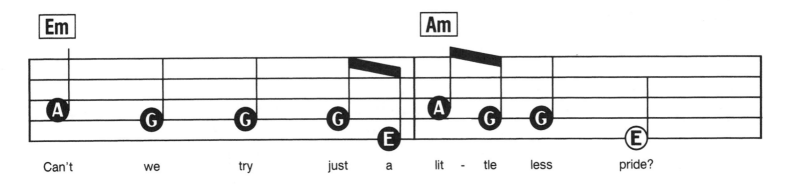

Love you so much, ba - by, that it

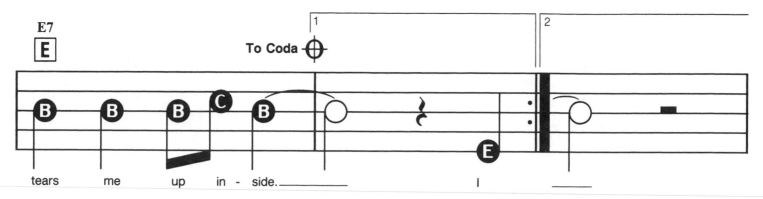

tears me up in - side._____ I _____

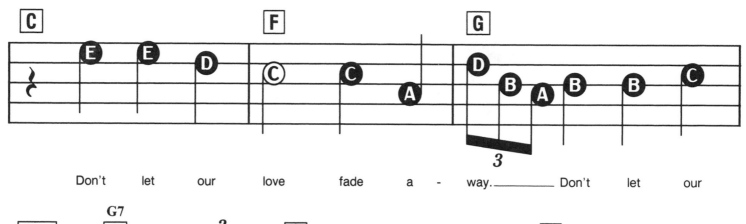

Don't let our love fade a - way._____ Don't let our

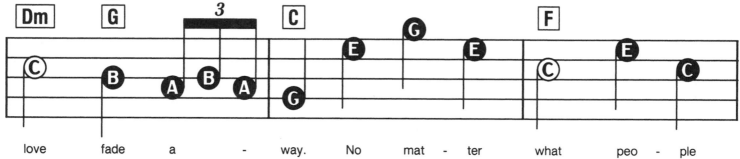

love fade a - way. No mat - ter what peo - ple

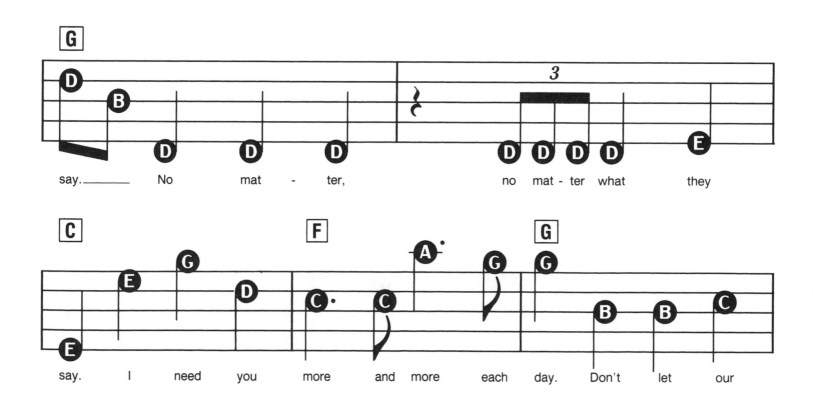

say._____ No mat - ter, no mat - ter what they

say. I need you more and more each day. Don't let our

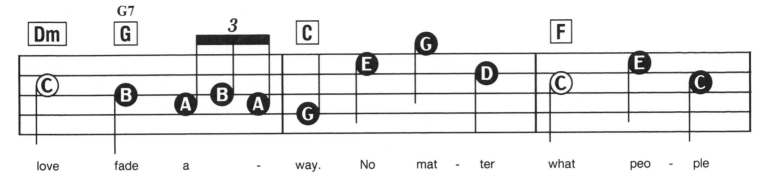

love fade a - way. No mat - ter what peo - ple

D.S. al Coda
(Return to ‰
Play to ⊕ and
skip to Coda)

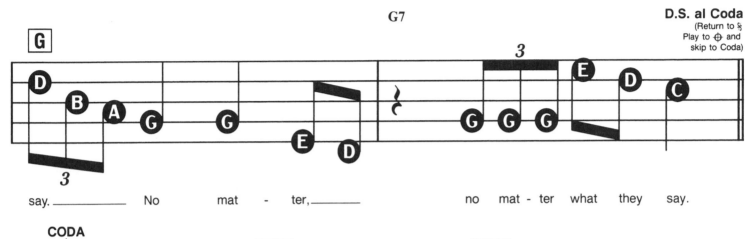

say._____ No mat - ter,_____ no mat - ter what they say.

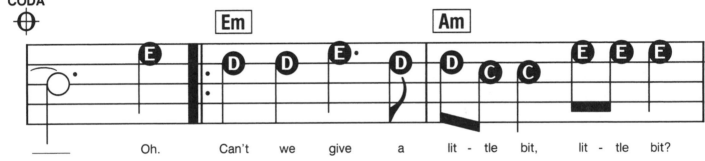

_____ Oh. Can't we give a lit - tle bit, lit - tle bit?

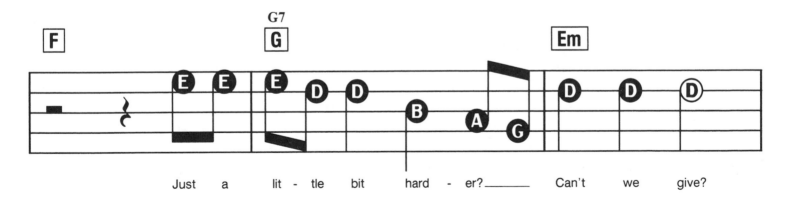

Just a lit - tle bit hard - er?_____ Can't we give?

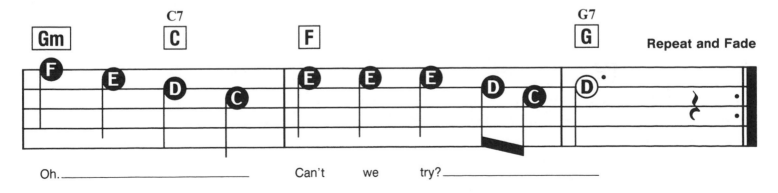

Oh._____ Can't we try?_____

Can't Help Falling in Love
from the Paramount Picture BLUE HAWAII

Registration 3
Rhythm: Ballad or Swing

Words and Music by George David Weiss,
Hugo Peretti and Luigi Creatore

Wise   men   say   on - ly
Shall   I   stay?   Would   it

fools   rush   in, _____   but   I   can't
be   a   sin _____   if   I   can't

help   fall - ing   in   love   with   you.
help   fall - ing   in   love   with   you?

Like   a   riv - er   flows   sure - ly   to   the   sea,

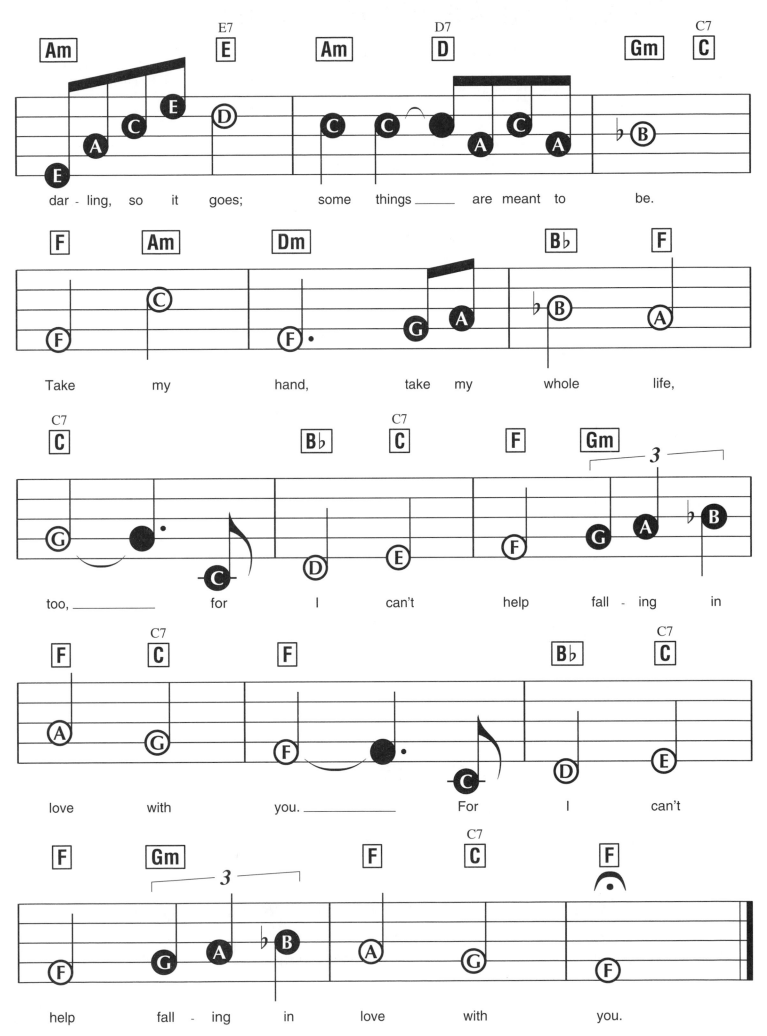

The Colour of Love

Registration 5
Rhythm: Rock

Words and Music by Jolyon Skinner,
Barry Eastmond, Wayne Brathwaite and Billy Ocean

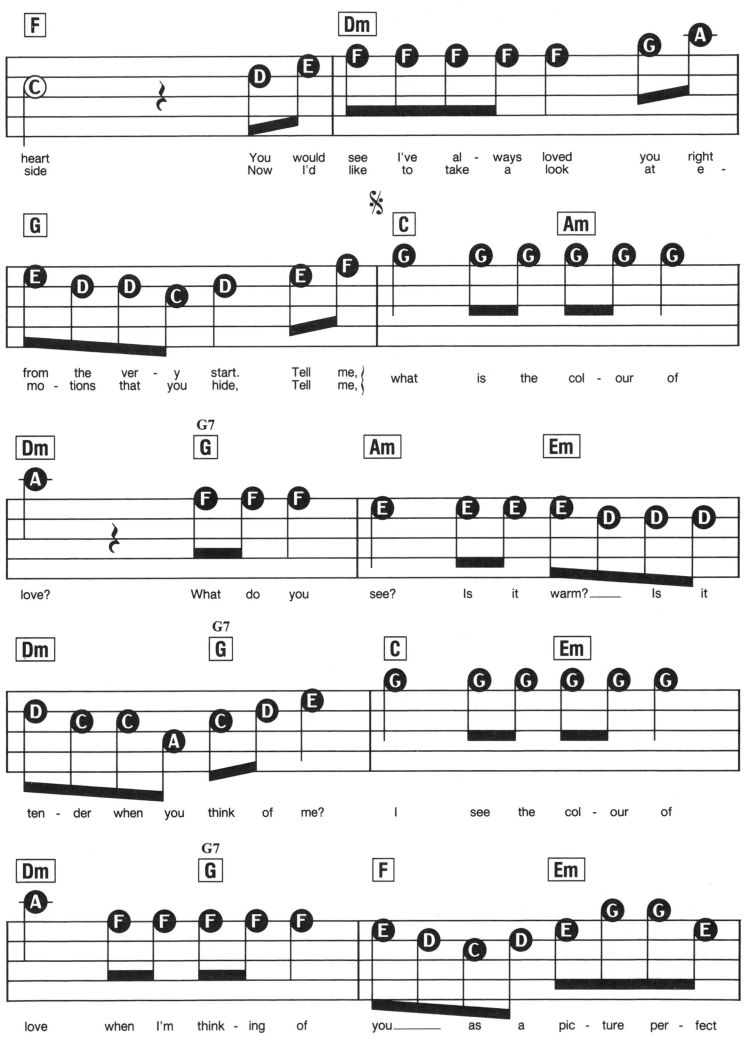

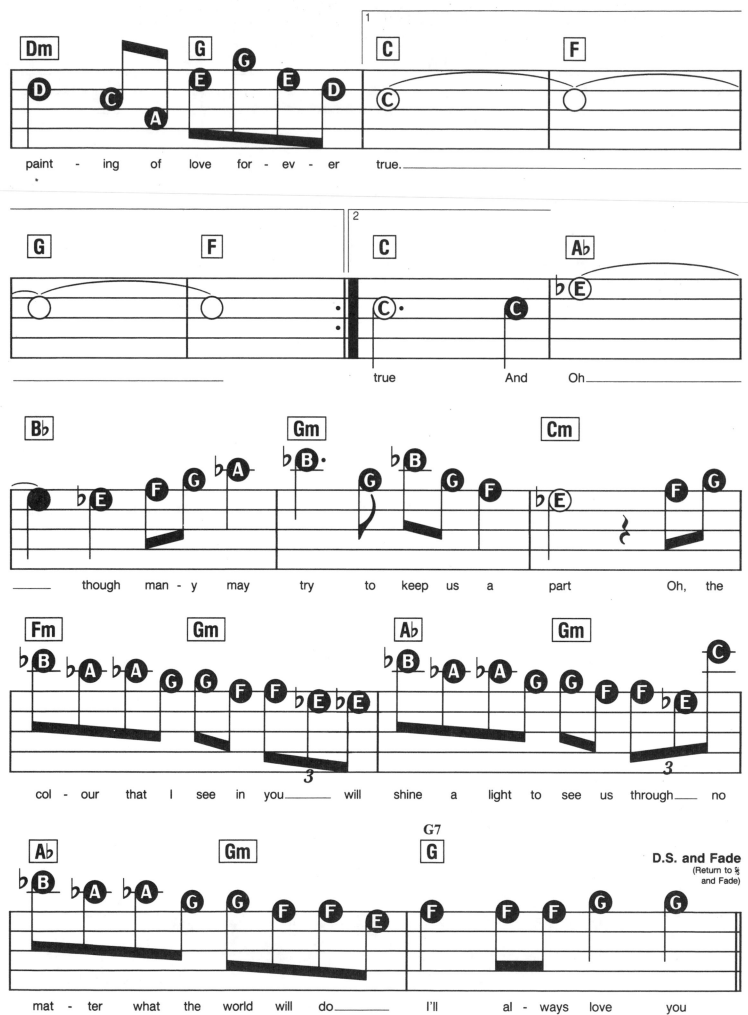

Could I Have This Dance
from URBAN COWBOY

Registration 4
Rhythm: Waltz

Words and Music by Wayland Holyfield
and Bob House

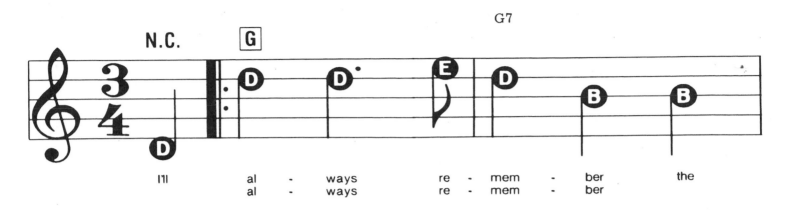

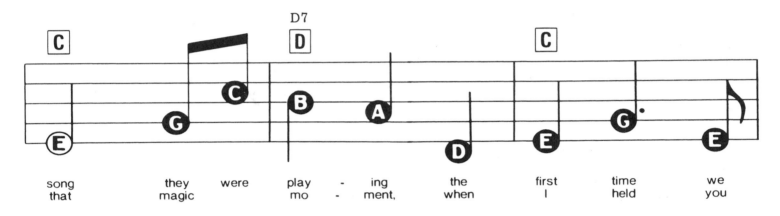

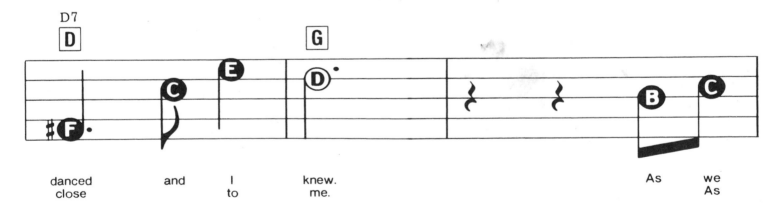

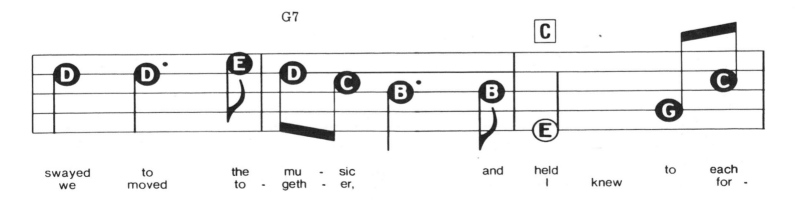

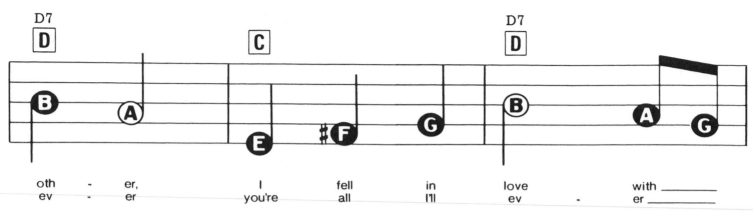

oth - er,   I   fell   in   love   with _____
ev - er   you're   all   I'll   ev - er _____

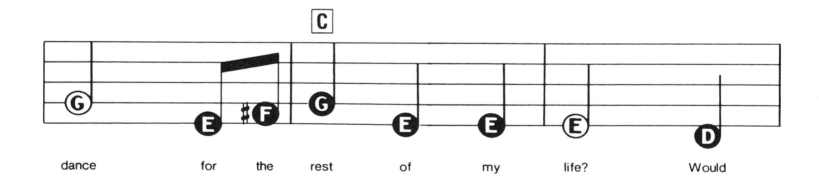

you.   Could   I   have   this
need.

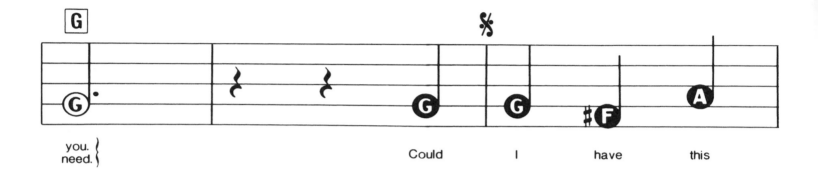

dance   for   the   rest   of   my   life?   Would

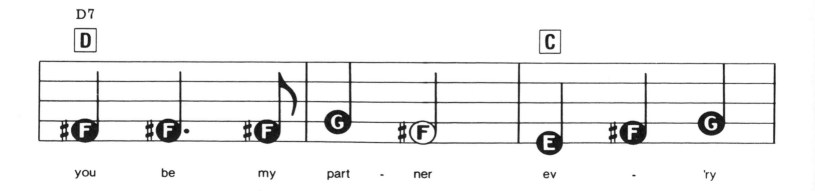

you   be   my   part - ner   ev - 'ry

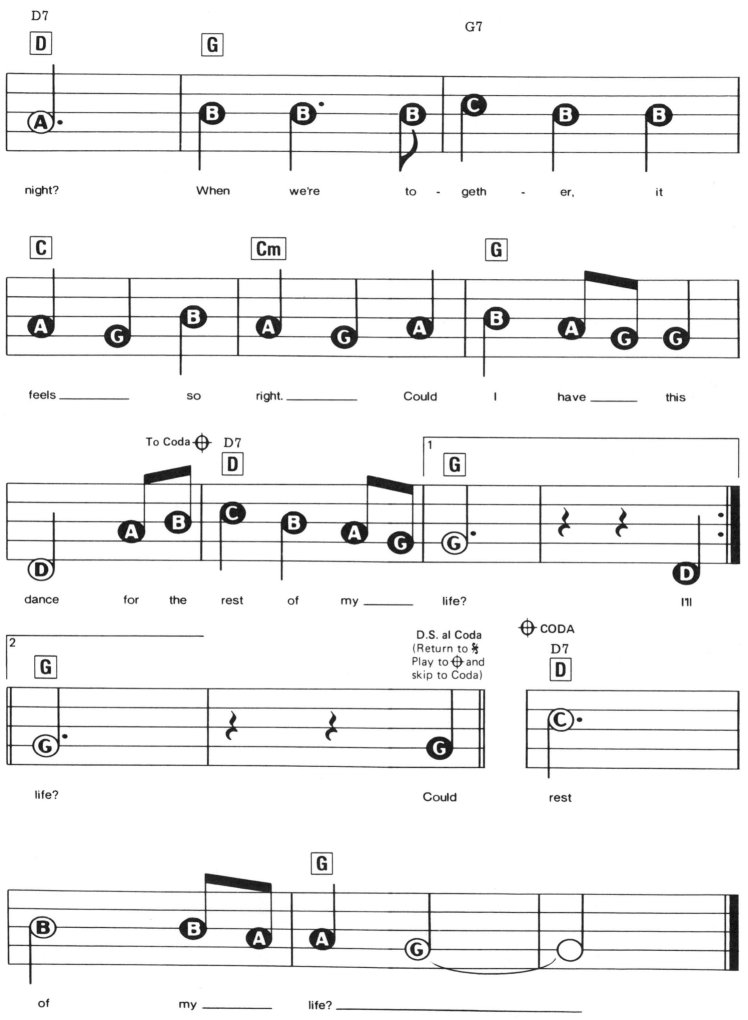

Endless Love

Registration 1
Rhythm: Rock or 8-Beat

Words and Music by
Lionel Richie

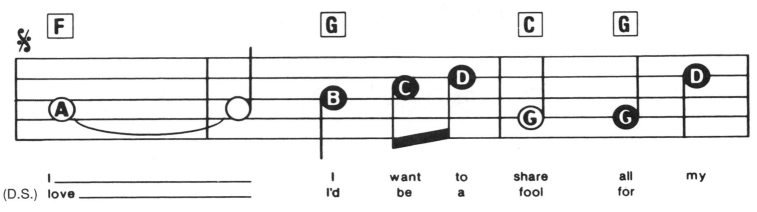

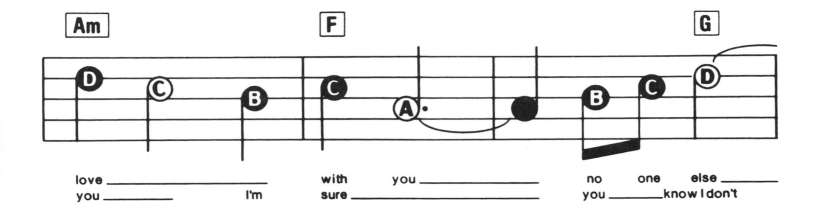

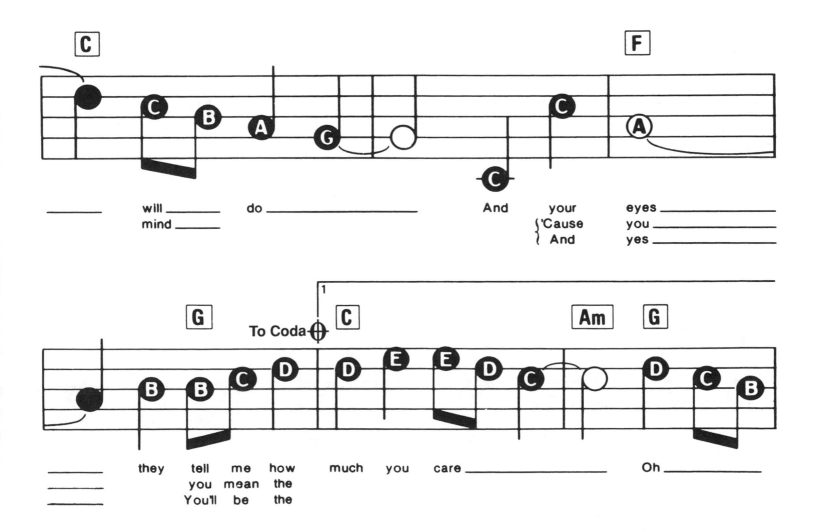

64

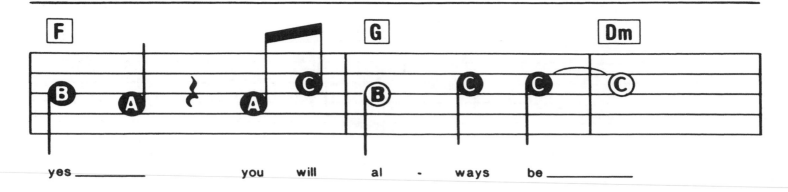

yes _____ you will al - ways be _____

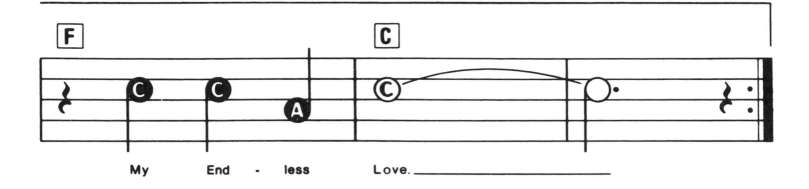

My End - less Love. _____

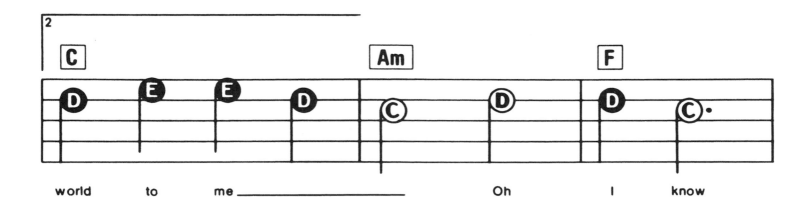

world to me _____ Oh I know

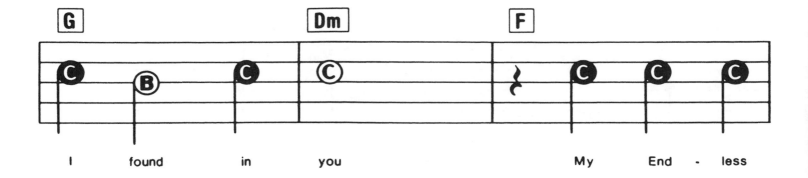

I found in you My End - less

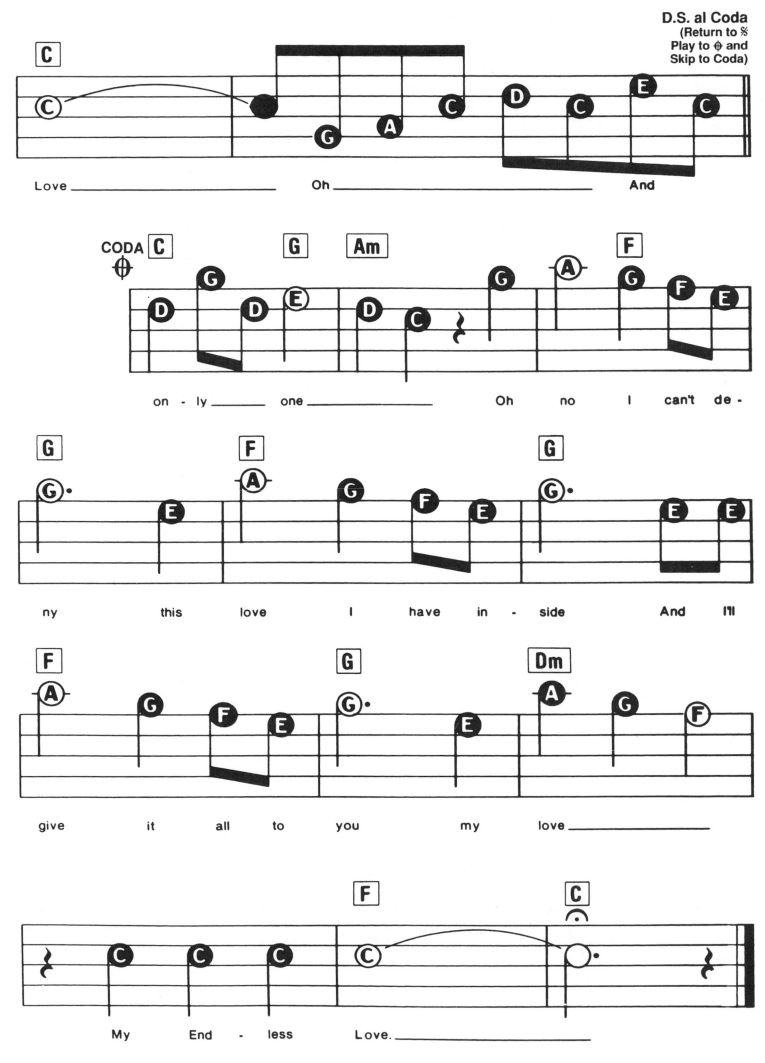

Eternal Flame

Registration 4
Rhythm: Rock or 8-Beat

Words and Music by Billy Steinberg,
Tom Kelly and Susanna Hoffs

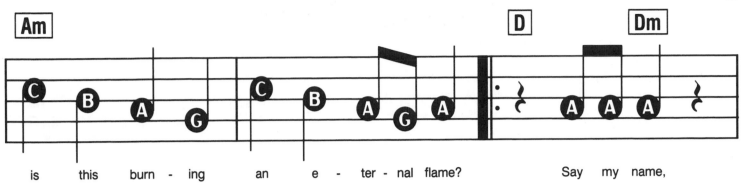

is this burn - ing an e - ter - nal flame? Say my name,

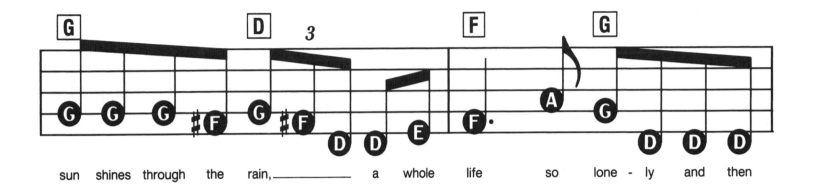

sun shines through the rain,_____ a whole life so lone - ly and then

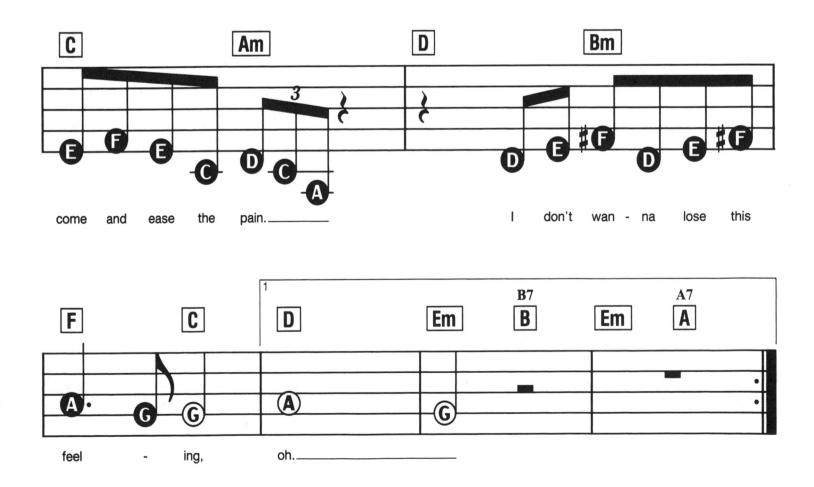

come and ease the pain._____ I don't wan - na lose this

feel - ing, oh._____

The First Time Ever I Saw Your Face

Registration 9
Rhythm: Ballad

Words and Music by
Ewan MacColl

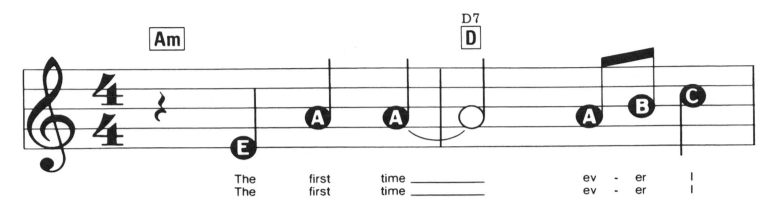

The first time _____ ev - er I
The first time _____ ev - er I

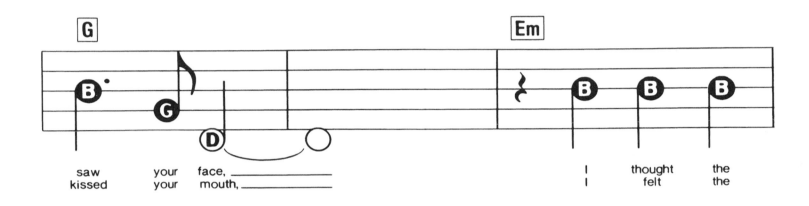

saw your face, _____   I thought the
kissed your mouth, _____   I felt the

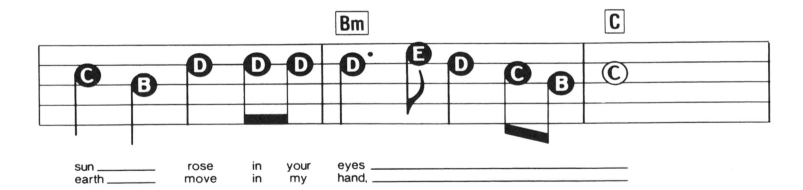

sun _____ rose in your eyes _____
earth _____ move in my hand, _____

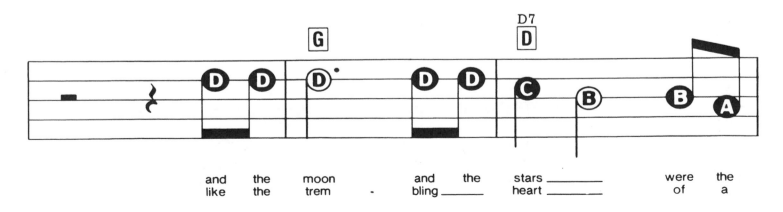

and the moon _____ and the stars _____ were the
like the moon trem - bling _____ heart _____ of a

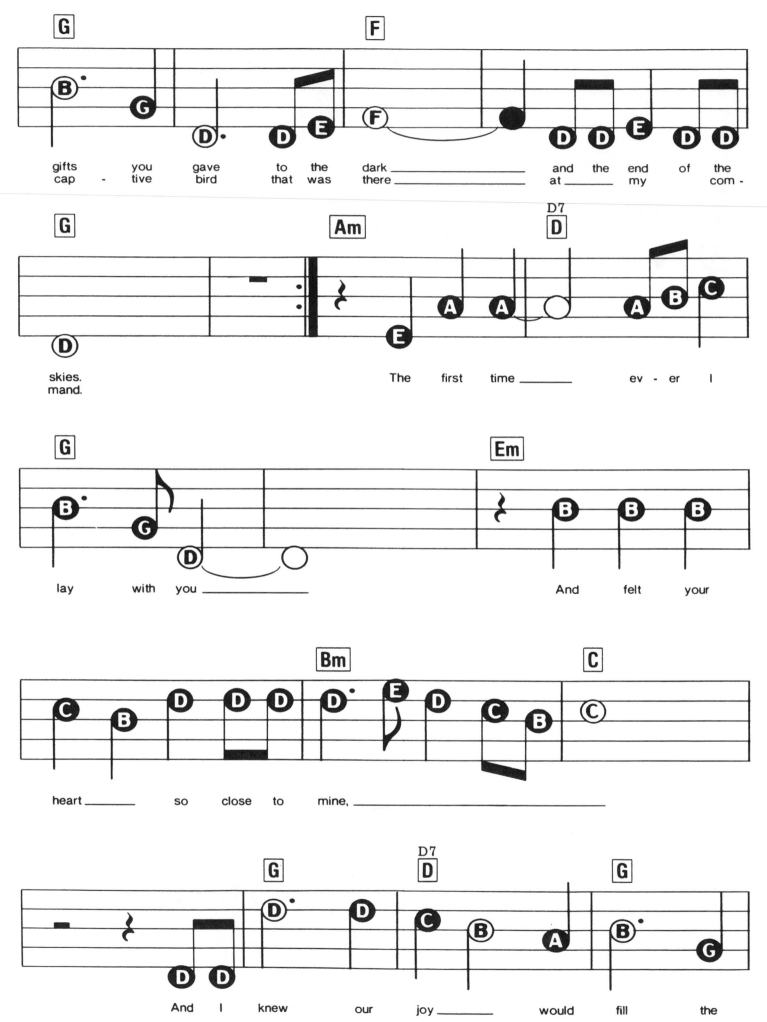

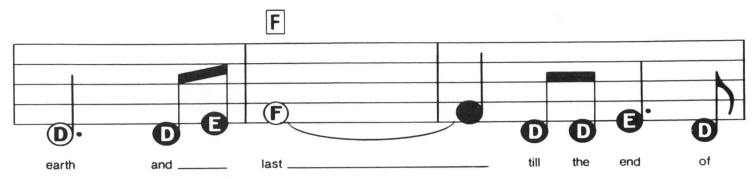

earth and _____ last _____ till the end of

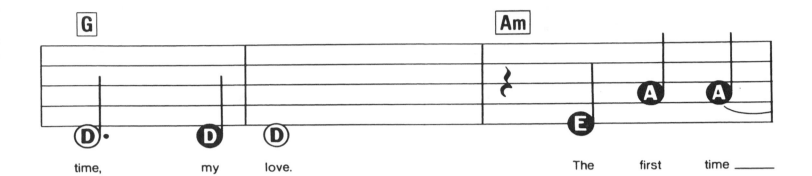

time, my love. The first time _____

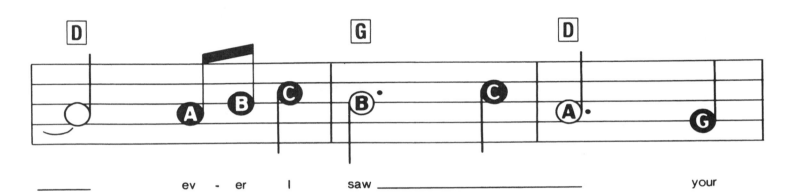

_____ ev - er I saw _____ your

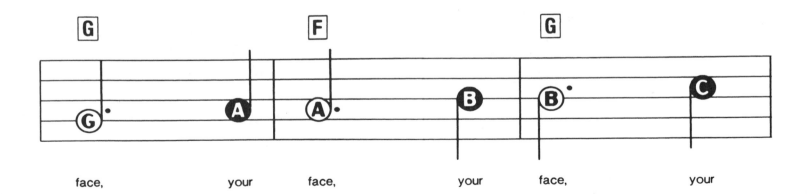

face, your face, your face, your

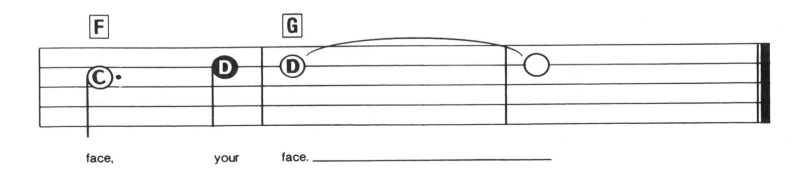

face, your face. _____

For the First Time
from ONE FINE DAY

Registration 8
Rhythm: Ballad or Pop

Words and Music by James Newton Howard,
Jud Friedman and Allan Rich

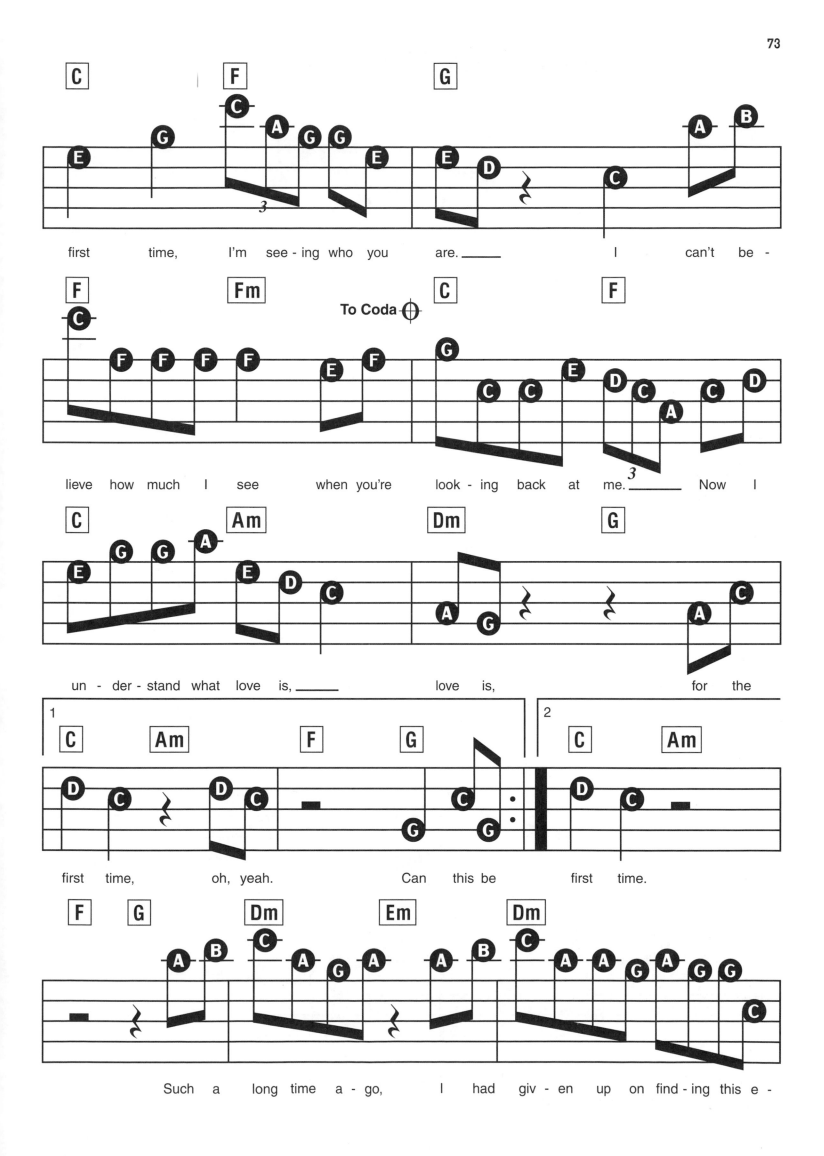

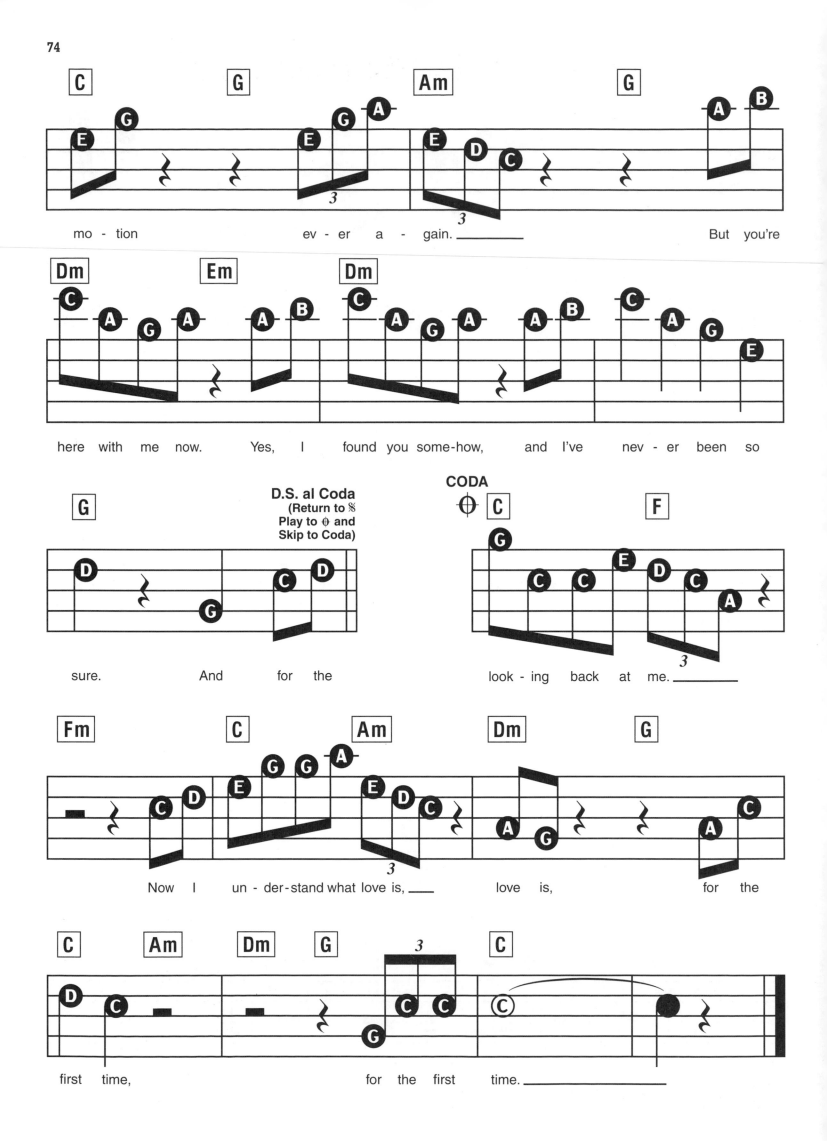

From This Moment On

Registration 4
Rhythm: 4/4 Ballad or 8-Beat

Words and Music by Shania Twain
and R.J. Lange

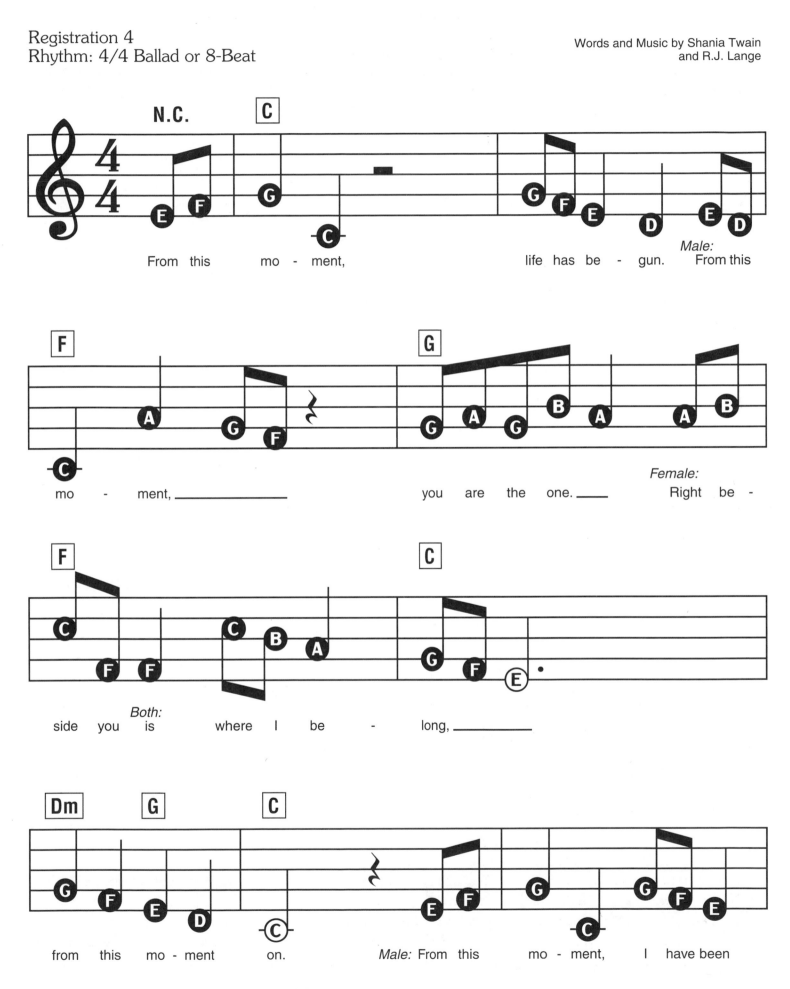

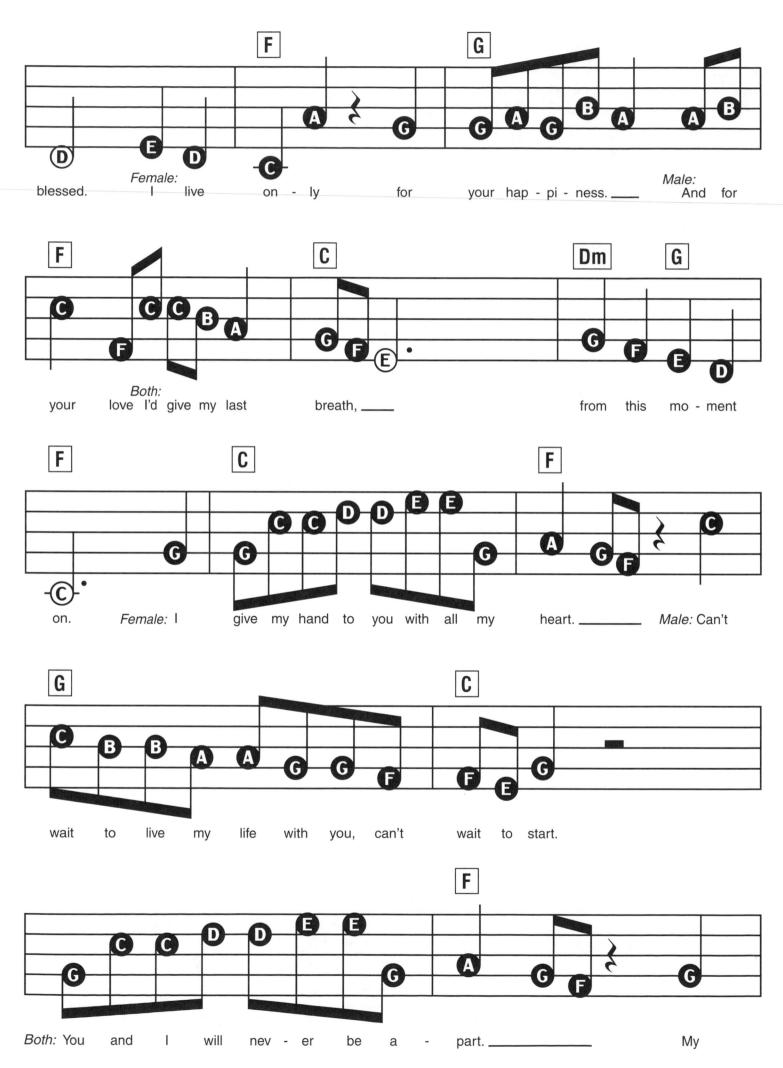

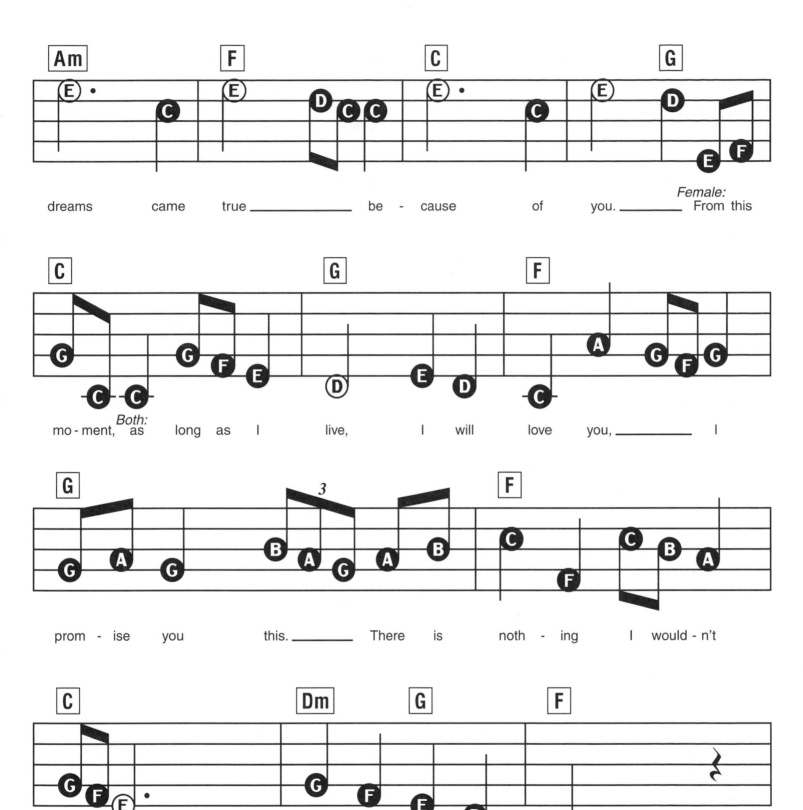

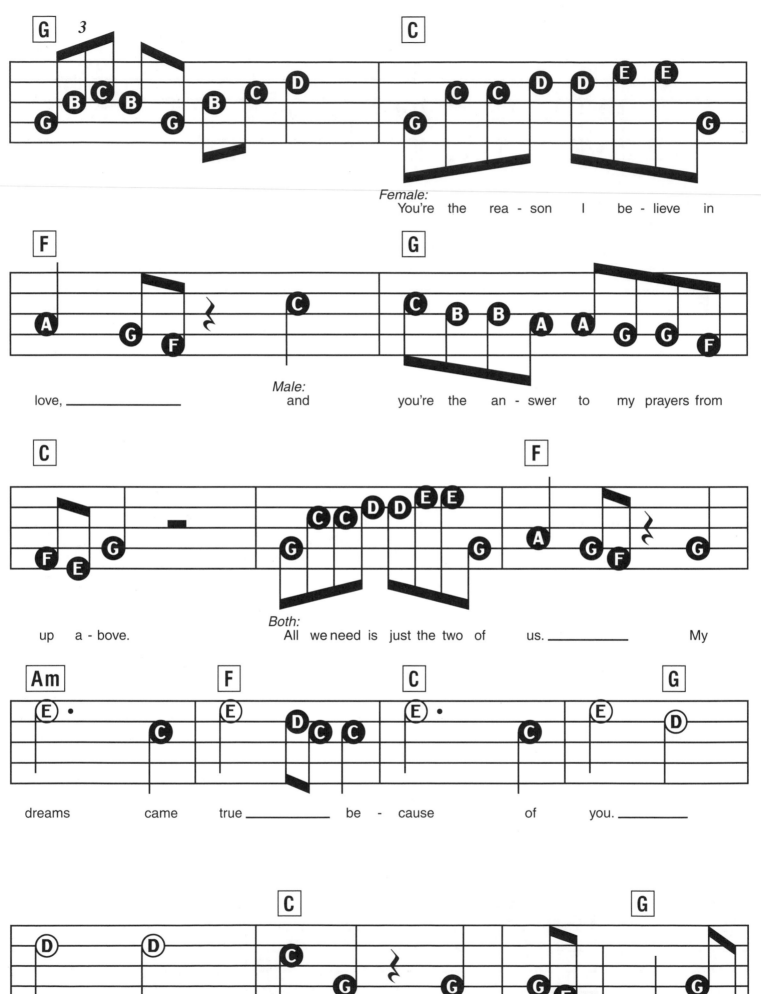

Female:
You're the rea - son I be - lieve in love, _____

Male:
and you're the an - swer to my prayers from up a - bove.

Both:
All we need is just the two of us. _____ My dreams came true _____ be - cause of you. _____

From this mo - ment, as long as I live, I will

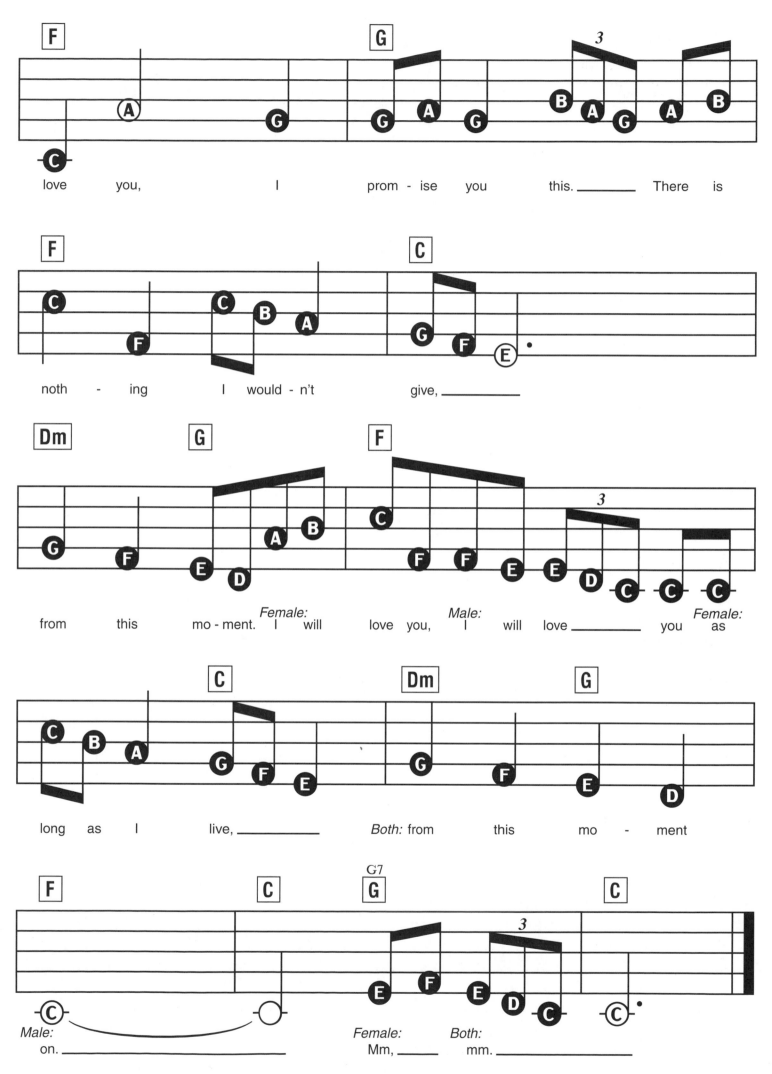

79

Glory of Love
Theme from KARATE KID PART II

Registration 1
Rhythm: Rock

Words and Music by David Foster,
Peter Cetera and Diane Nini

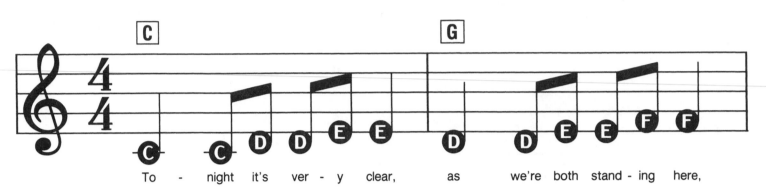

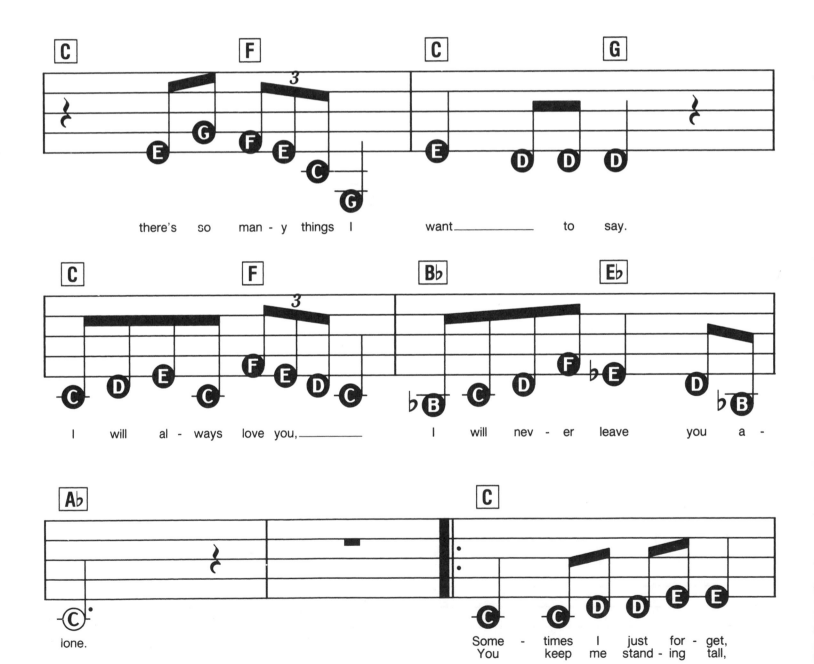

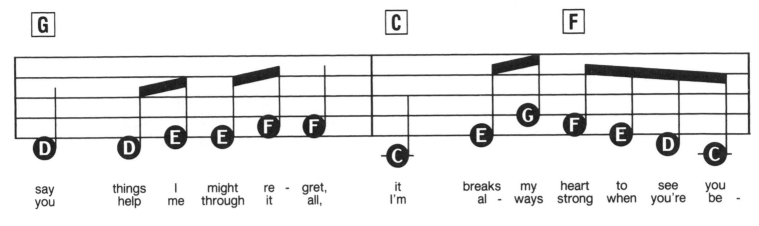

say things I might re-gret, it breaks my heart to see you
you help me through it all, I'm al-ways strong when you're be -

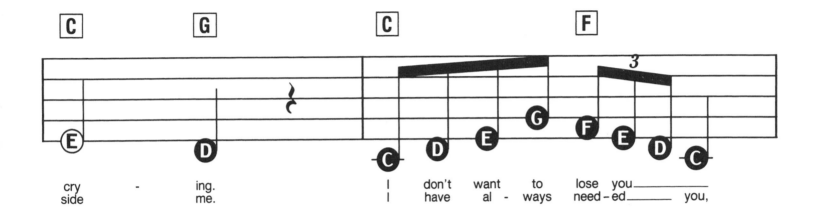

cry - ing. I don't want to lose you_____
side me. I have al-ways need-ed_____ you,

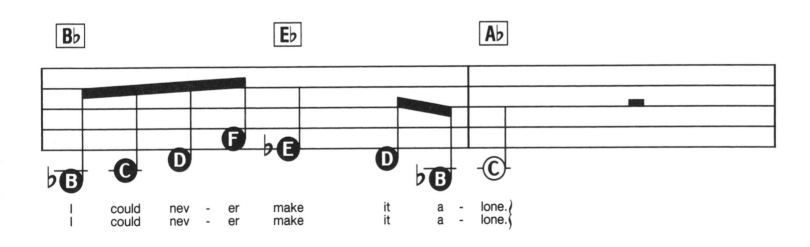

I could nev - er make it a - lone.
I could nev - er make it a - lone.

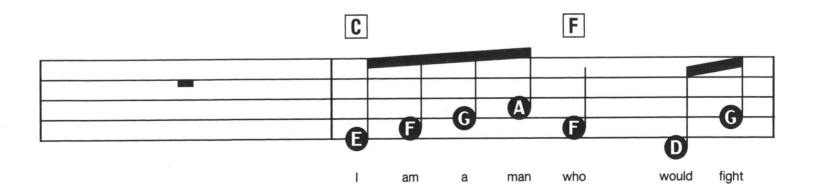

I am a man who would fight

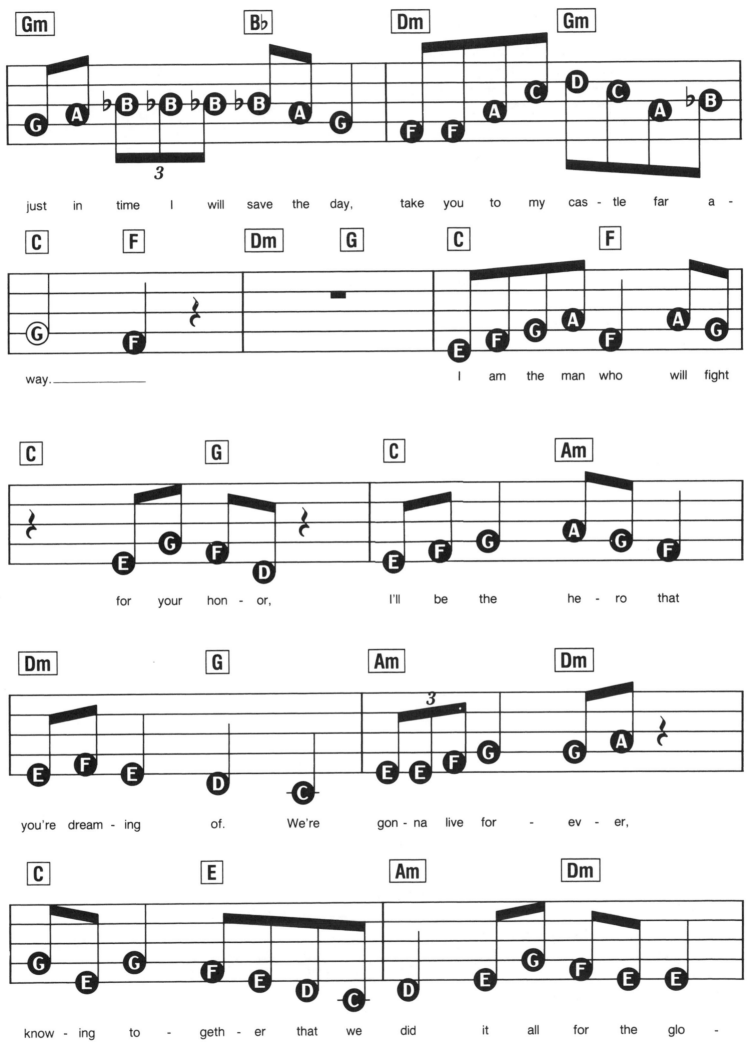

84

Have I Told You Lately

Registration 2
Rhythm: Rock or 8-Beat

Words and Music by
Van Morrison

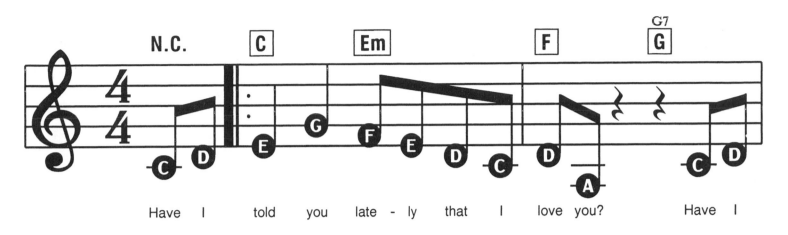

Have I told you late - ly that I love you? Have I

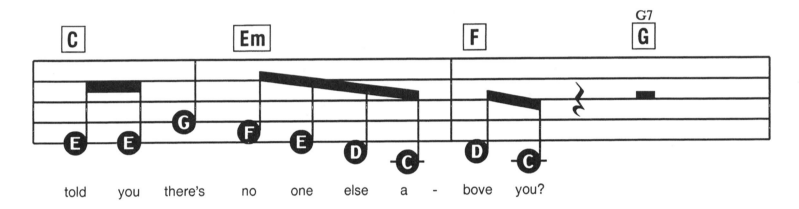

told you there's no one else a - bove you?

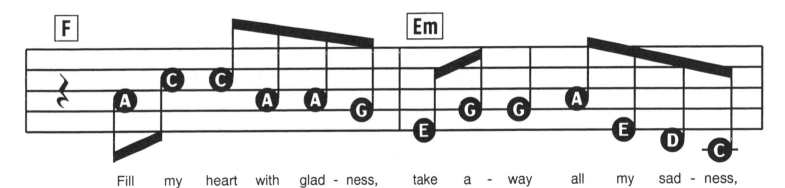

Fill my heart with glad - ness, take a - way all my sad - ness,

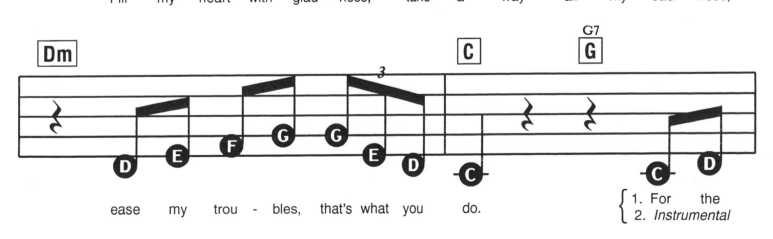

ease my trou - bles, that's what you do.

1. For the
2. *Instrumental*

86

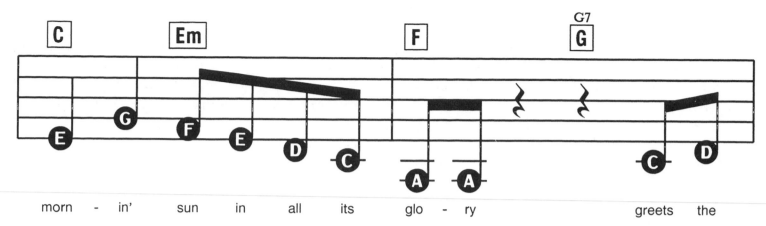

morn - in' sun in all its glo - ry greets the

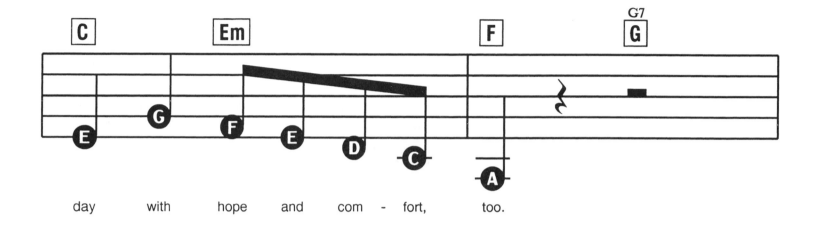

day with hope and com - fort, too.

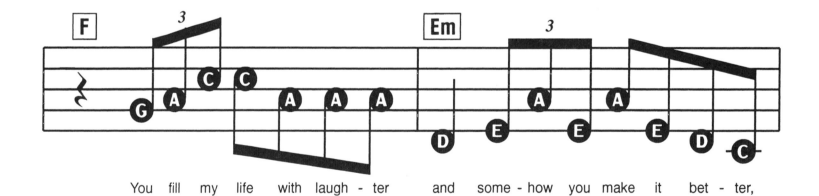

You fill my life with laugh - ter and some - how you make it bet - ter,

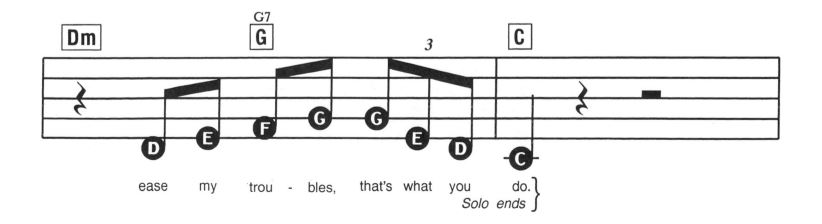

ease my trou - bles, that's what you do.
Solo ends

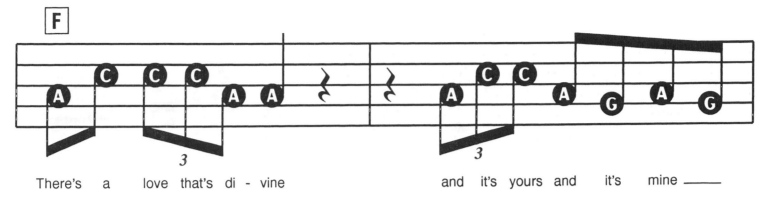

There's a love that's di-vine and it's yours and it's mine ____

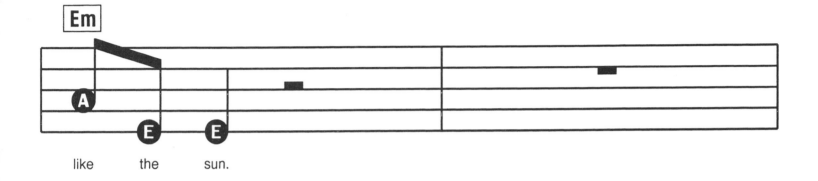

like the sun.

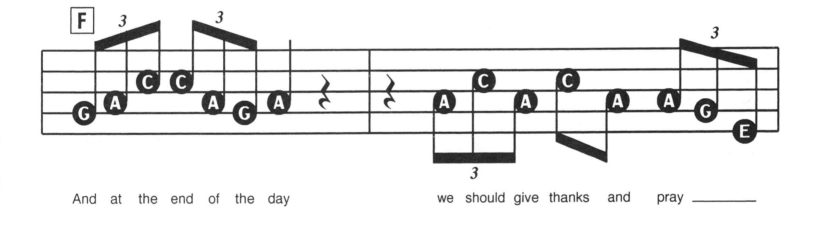

And at the end of the day we should give thanks and pray _____

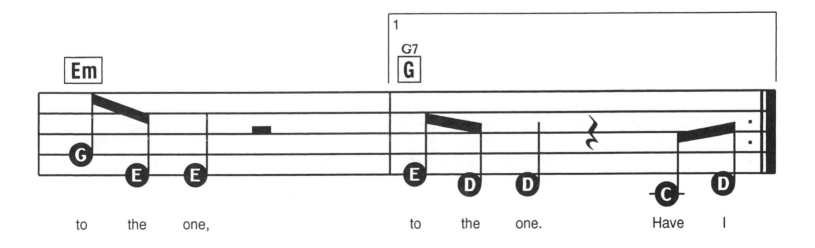

to the one, to the one. Have I

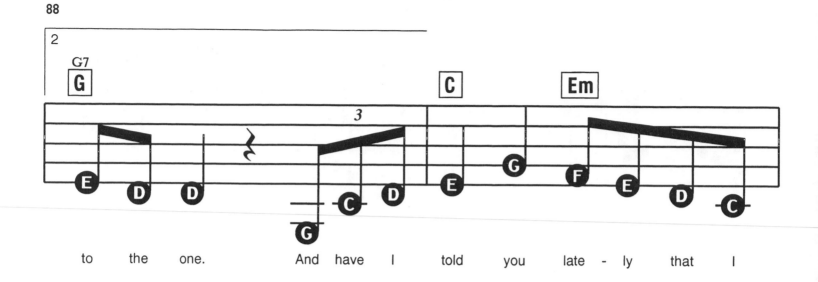

to the one. And have I told you late - ly that I

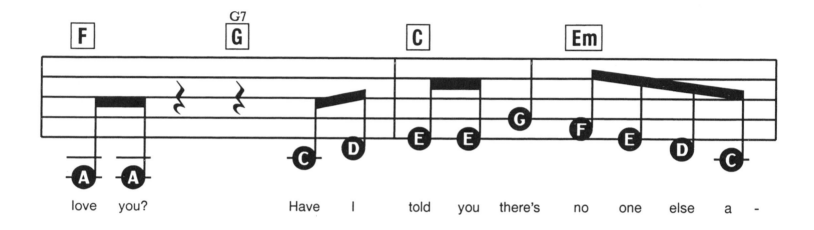

love you? Have I told you there's no one else a -

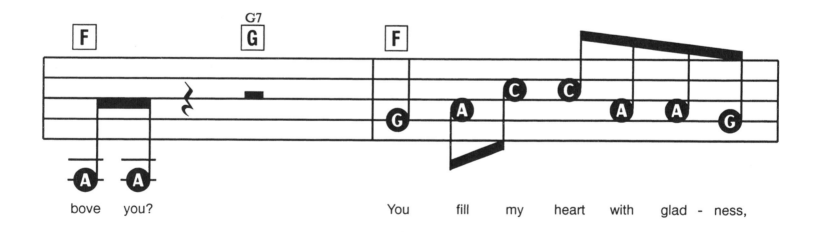

bove you? You fill my heart with glad - ness,

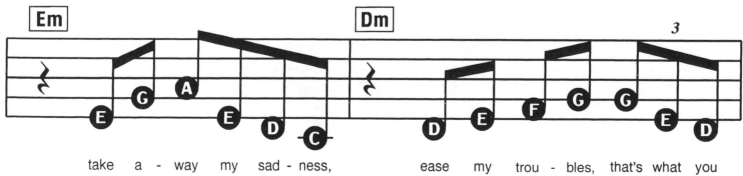

take a - way my sad - ness, ease my trou - bles, that's what you

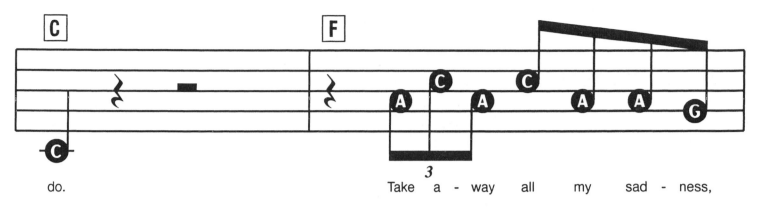

do. Take a - way all my sad - ness,

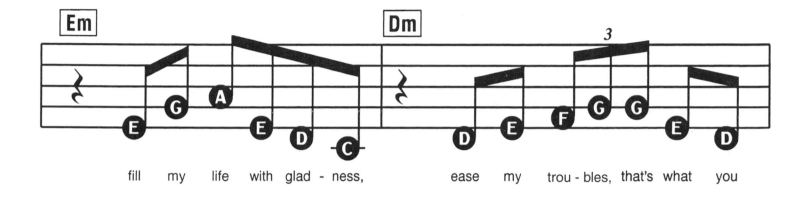

fill my life with glad - ness, ease my trou - bles, that's what you

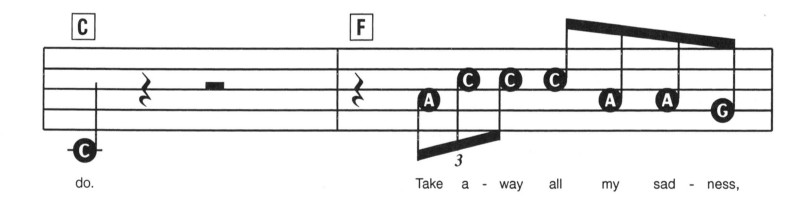

do. Take a - way all my sad - ness,

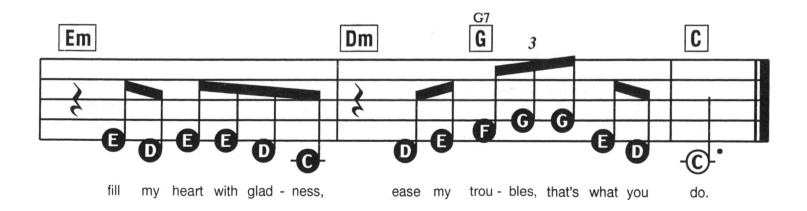

fill my heart with glad - ness, ease my trou - bles, that's what you do.

Here and Now

Registration 8
Rhythm: 8-Beat or Rock

Words and Music by Terry Steele
and David Elliot

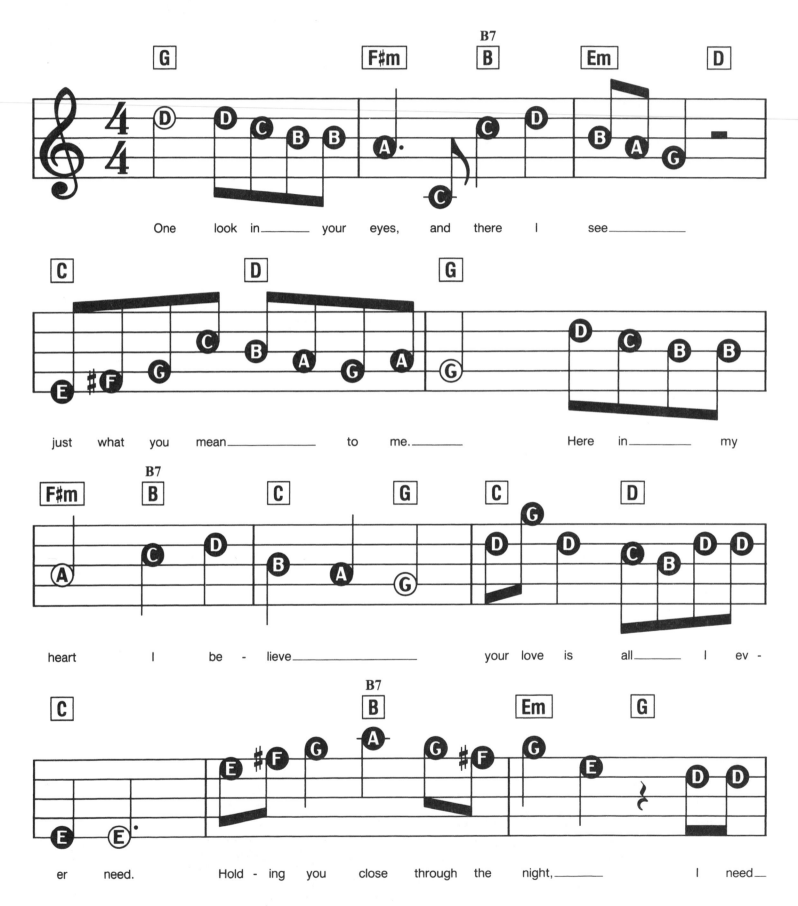

One look in your eyes, and there I see just what you mean to me. Here in my heart I be - lieve your love is all I ev - er need. Hold - ing you close through the night, I need

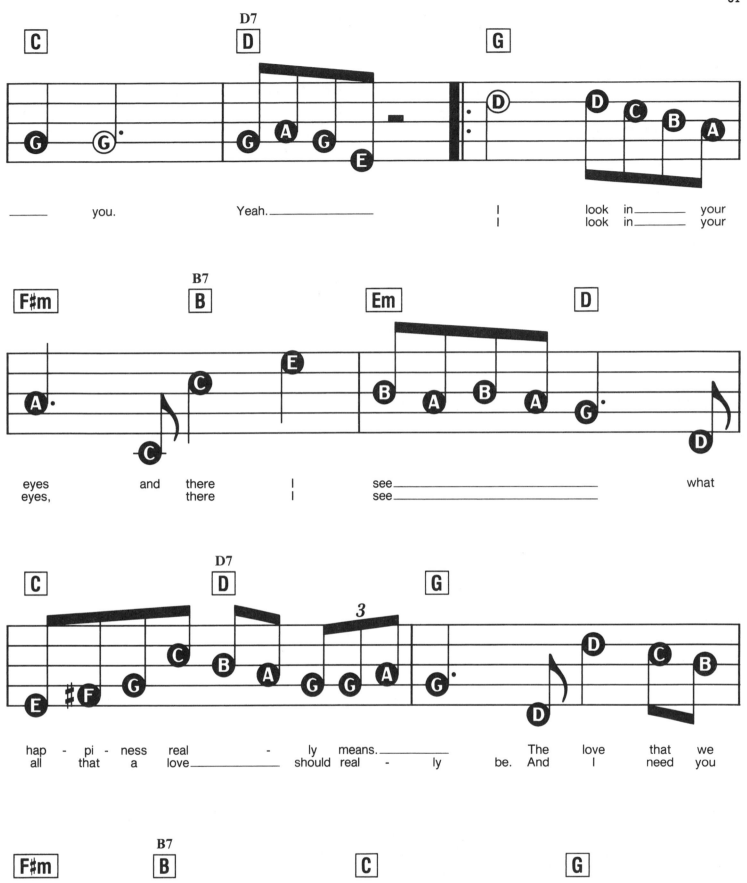

you.   Yeah.   I   look in   your
    I   look in   your

eyes   and   there   I   see   what
eyes,   there   I   see

hap - pi - ness real - ly means.   The   love   that   we
all   that   a   love   should real - ly   be. And   I   need   you

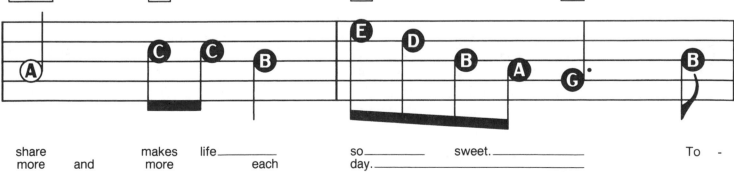

share   and   makes   life   so   sweet.   To -
more   and   more   each   day.

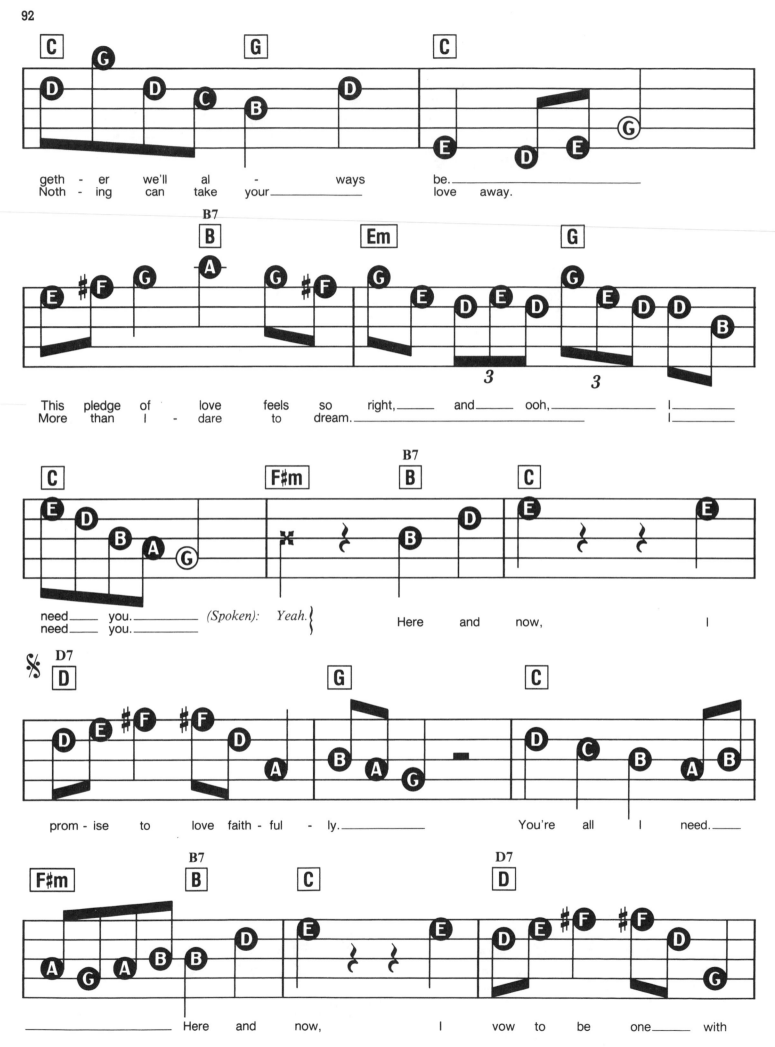

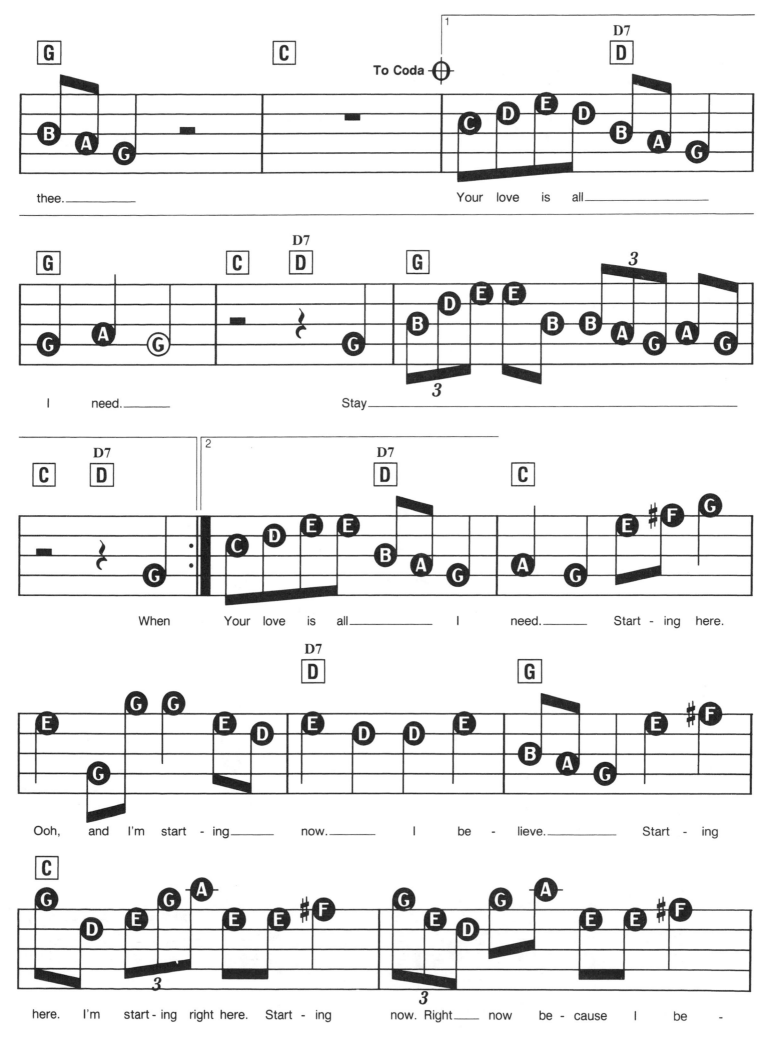

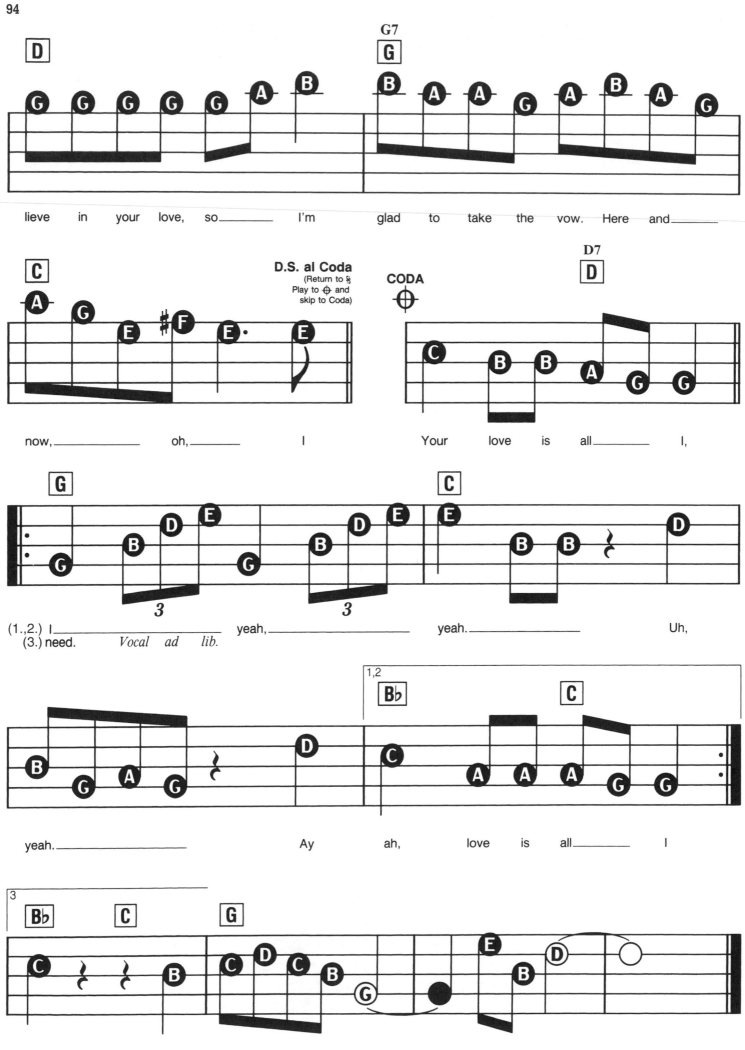

How Deep Is Your Love
from the Motion Picture SATURDAY NIGHT FEVER

Registration 4
Rhythm: Rock or Disco

Words and Music by Barry Gibb,
Robin Gibb and Maurice Gibb

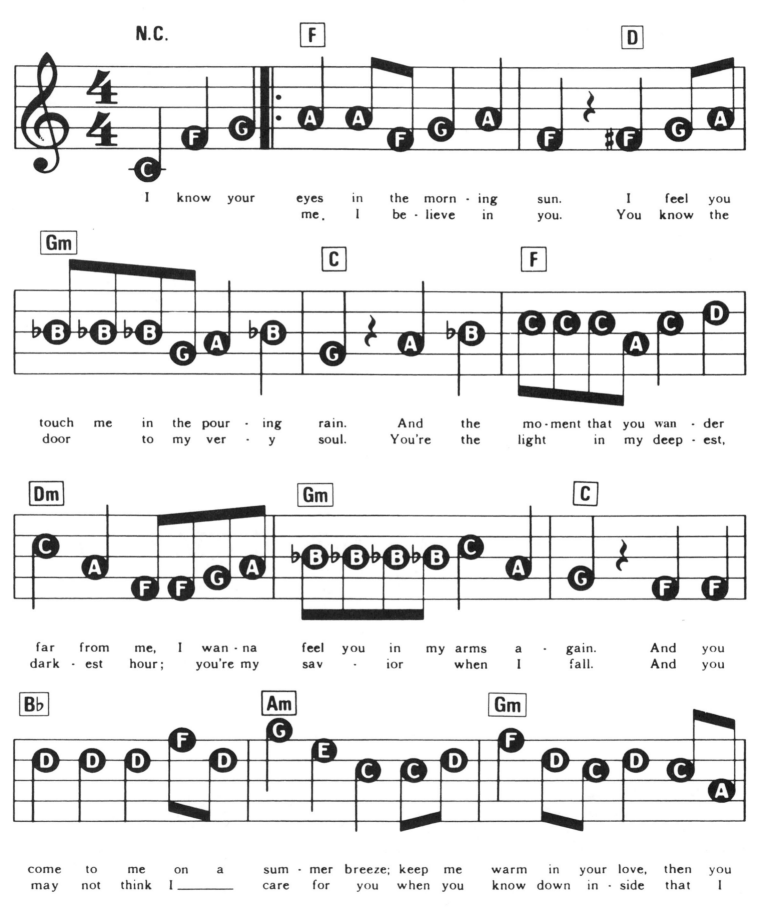

I know your eyes in the morn - ing sun. I feel you
me, I be - lieve in you. You know the

touch me in the pour - ing rain. And the mo - ment that you wan - der
door to my ver - y soul. You're the light in my deep - est,

far from me, I wan - na feel you in my arms a - gain. And you
dark - est hour; you're my sav - ior when I fall. And you

come to me on a sum - mer breeze; keep me warm in your love, then you
may not think I _____ care for you when you know down in - side that I

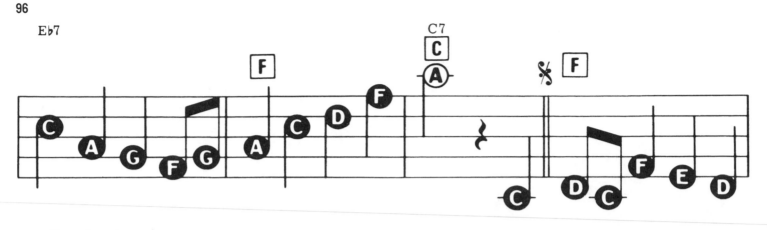

soft · ly leave.
real · ly do. } And it's me you need to show: How deep is your love? How

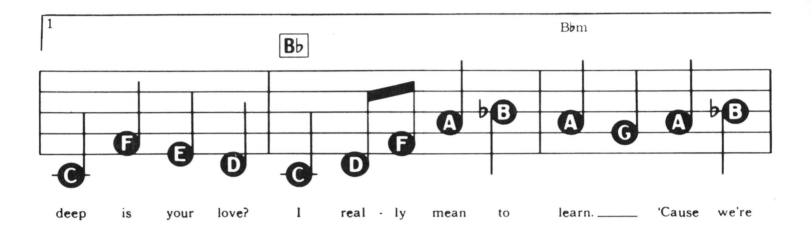

deep is your love? I real · ly mean to learn. _____ 'Cause we're

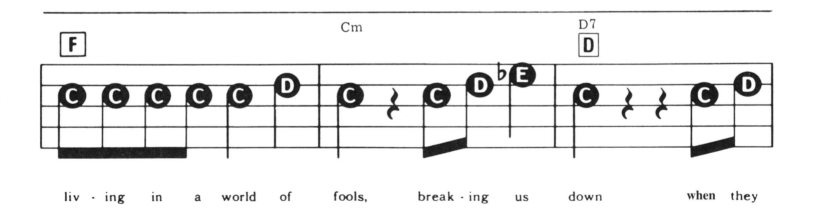

liv · ing in a world of fools, break · ing us down when they

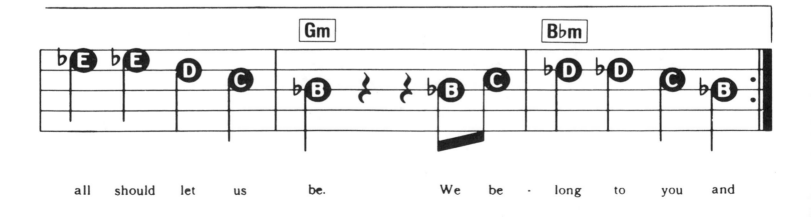

all should let us be. We be · long to you and

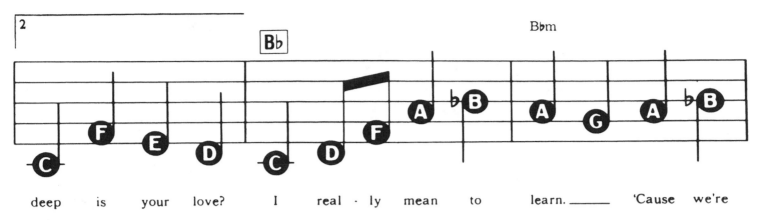

deep   is   your   love?   I   real · ly   mean   to   learn. _____ 'Cause we're

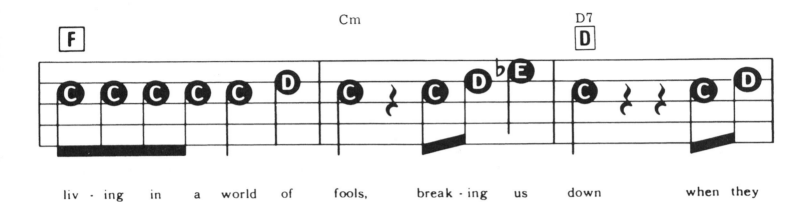

liv · ing   in   a   world   of   fools,   break · ing   us   down   when they

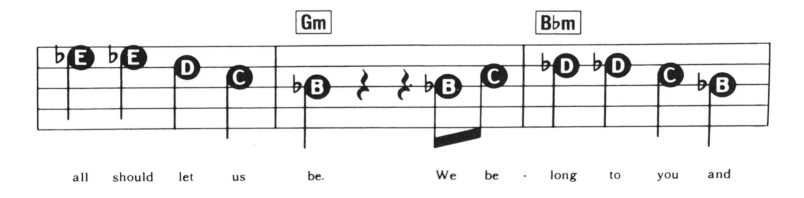

all   should   let   us   be.   We be · long   to   you   and

D.S. and Fade
(Return to 𝄋
and fade)

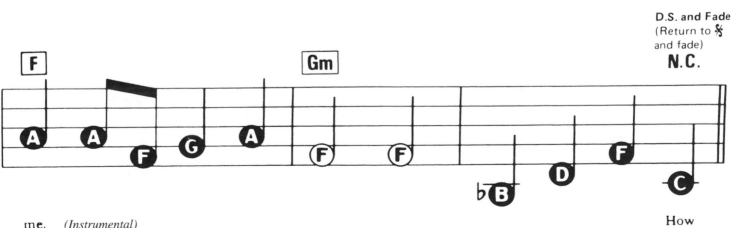

me. *(Instrumental)*   How

How Am I Supposed to Live Without You

Registration 3
Rhythm: Rock or Pops

Words and Music by Michael Bolton
and Doug James

99

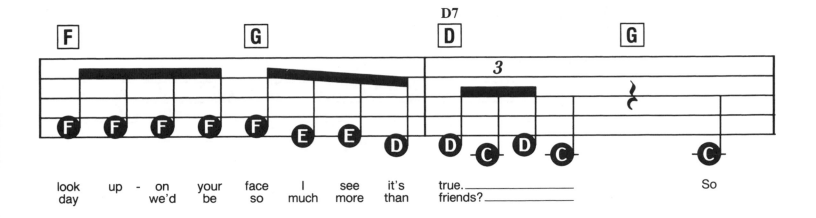

look up - on your face I see it's true._____ So
day up - we'd be so much more than friends?_____

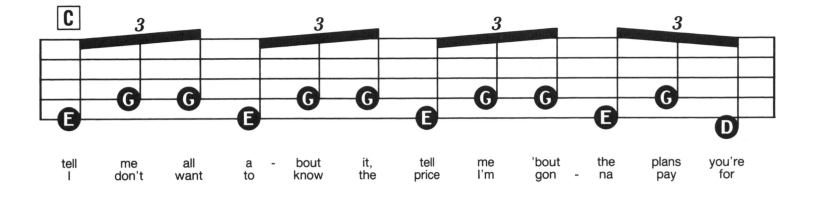

tell me all a - bout it, tell me 'bout the plans you're
I don't want to know it, the price I'm gon - na pay for

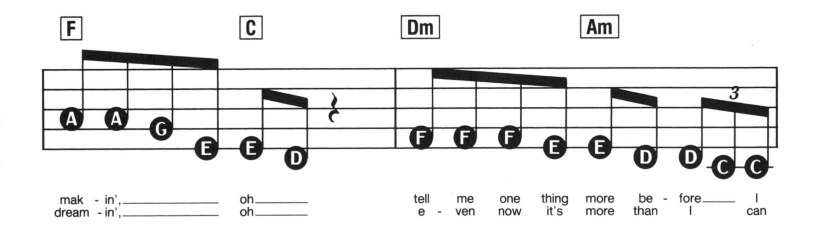

mak - in',_____ oh_____ tell me one thing more be - fore_____ I
dream - in',_____ oh_____ e - ven now it's more than I can

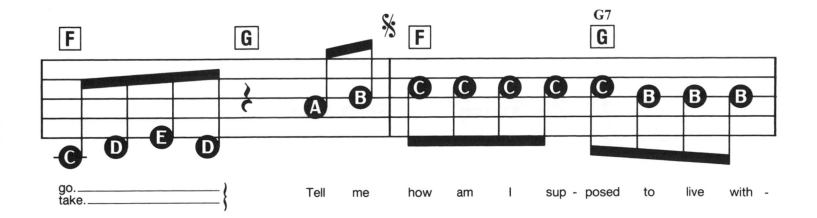

go._____ Tell me how am I sup - posed to live with-
take._____

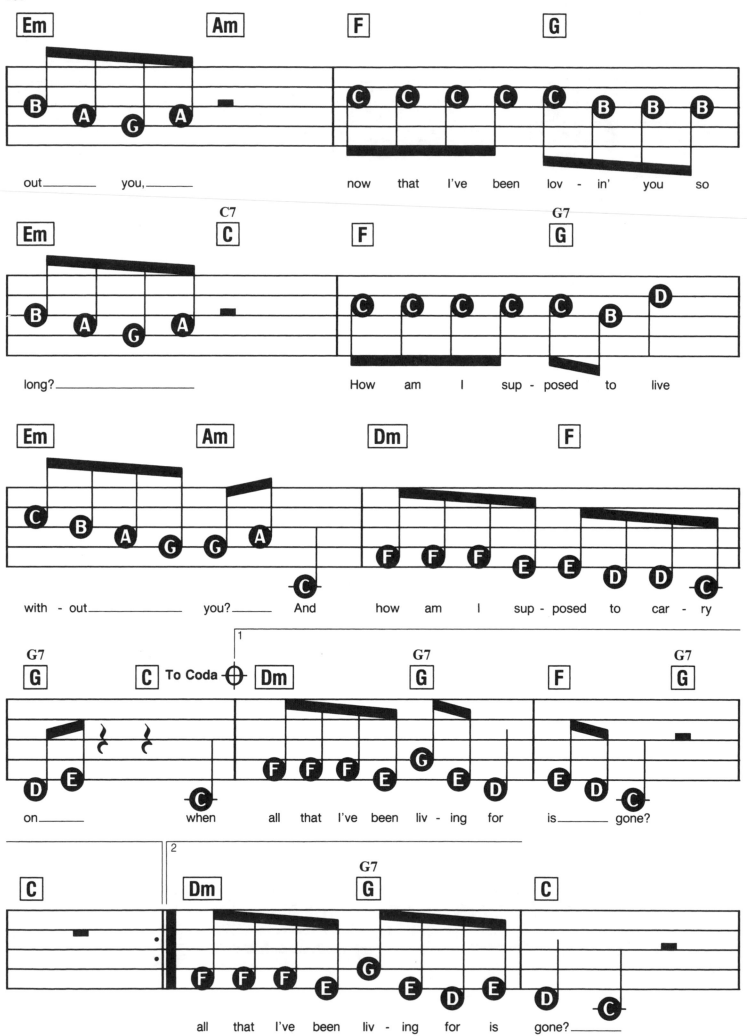

101

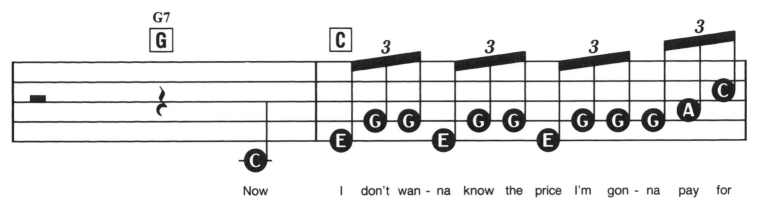

Now   I   don't wan - na know the price I'm gon - na pay for

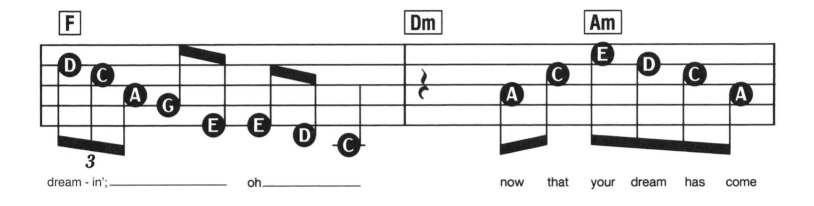

dream - in';_____ oh_____   now   that   your dream has come

D.S. al Coda
(Return to %
Play to ⊕ and
skip to Coda)

CODA

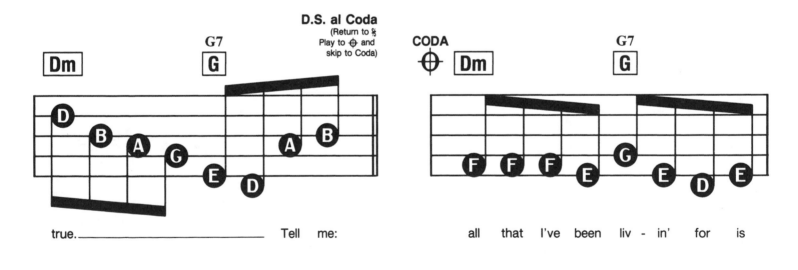

true._____ Tell me: all   that   I've   been liv - in'   for   is

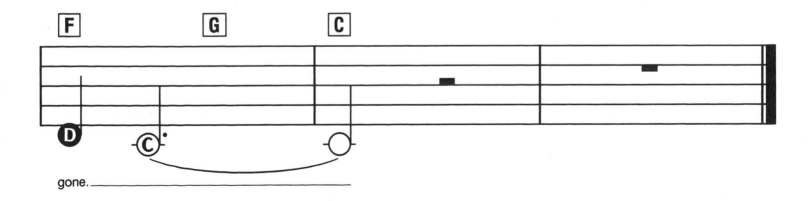

gone._____

I Can't Stop Loving You

Registration 8
Rhythm: Swing or Fox Trot

Words and Music by
Don Gibson

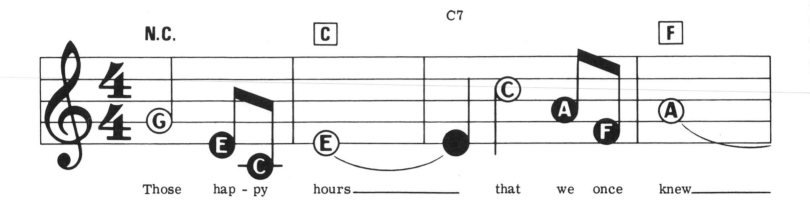

Those hap-py hours_____ that we once knew_____

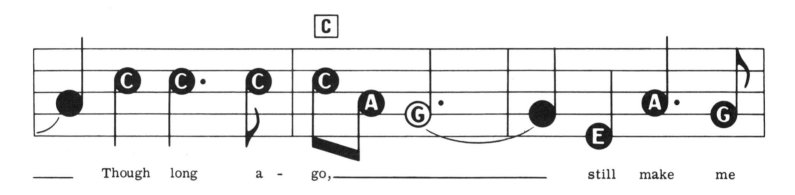

_____ Though long a - go,_____ still make me

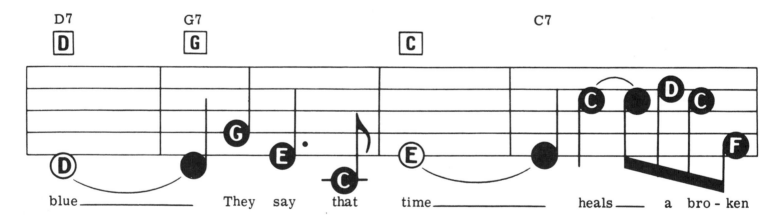

blue_____ They say that time_____ heals_____ a bro-ken

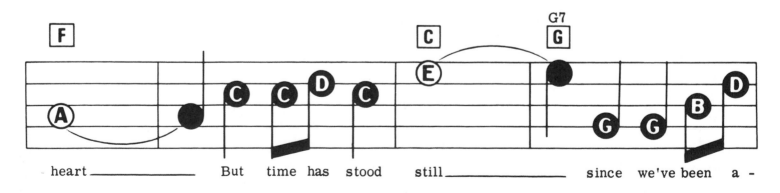

heart_____ But time has stood still_____ since we've been a-

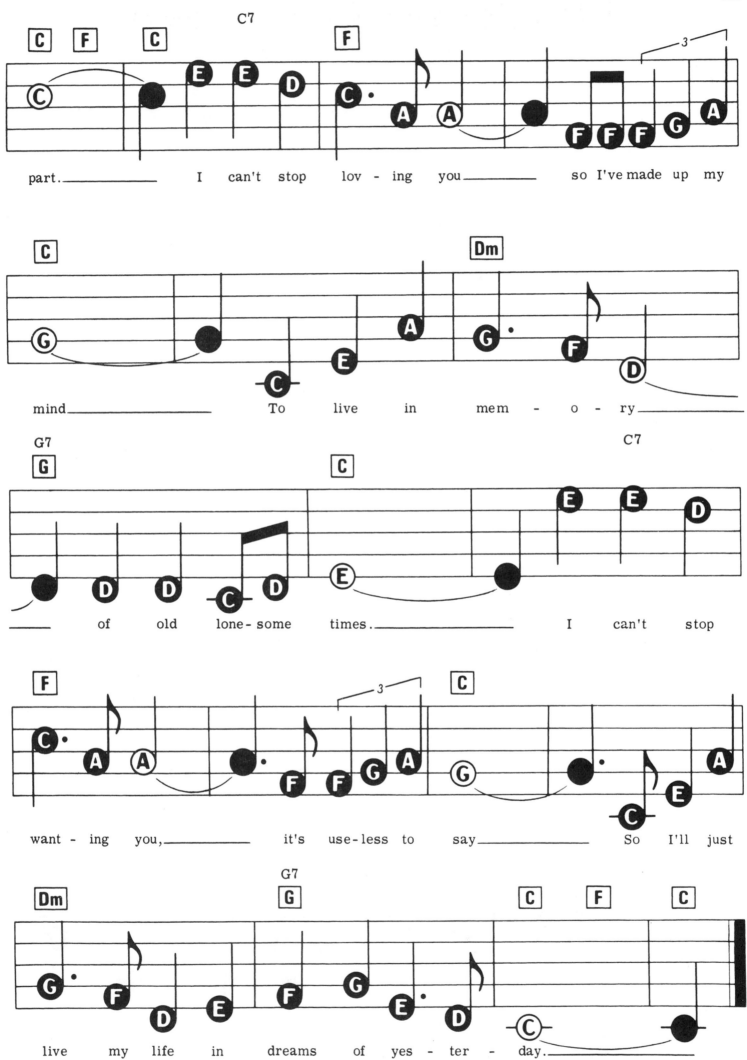

I Finally Found Someone

from THE MIRROR HAS TWO FACES

Registration 2
Rhythm: Rock or 8 Beat

Words and Music by Barbra Streisand,
Marvin Hamlisch, R.J. Lange and Bryan Adams

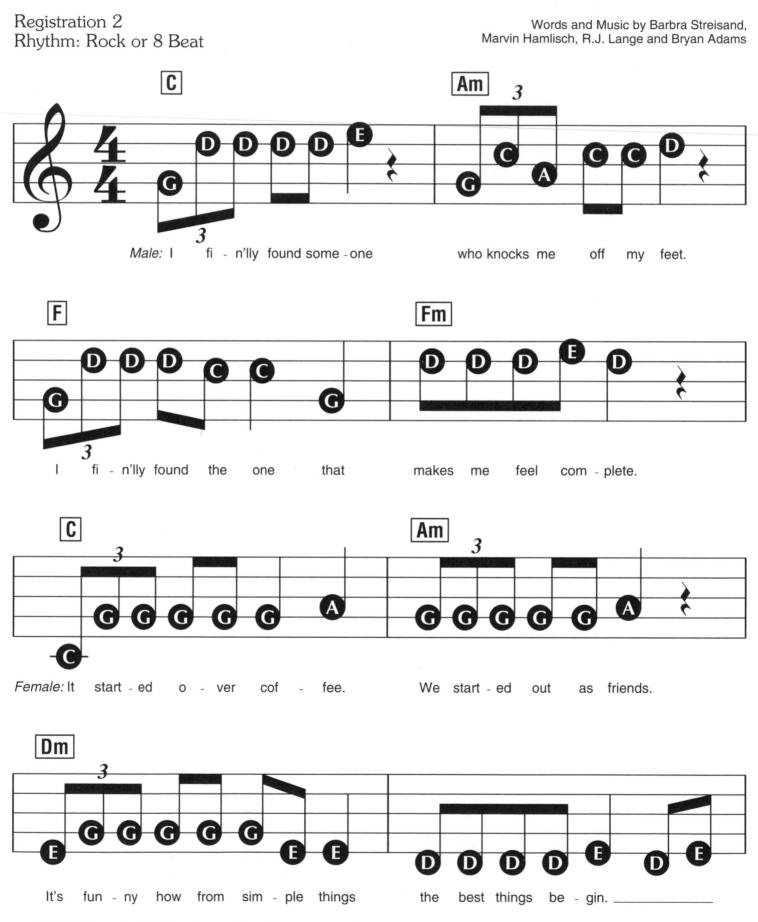

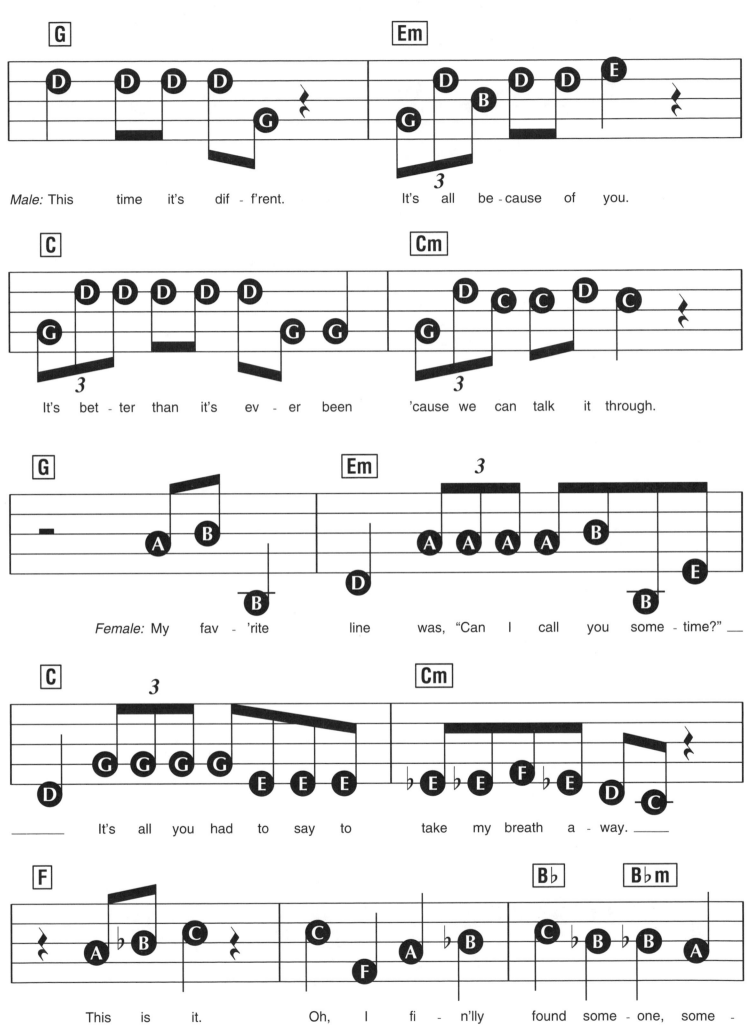

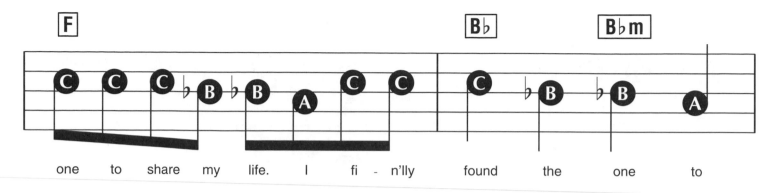

one to share my life. I fi - n'lly found the one to

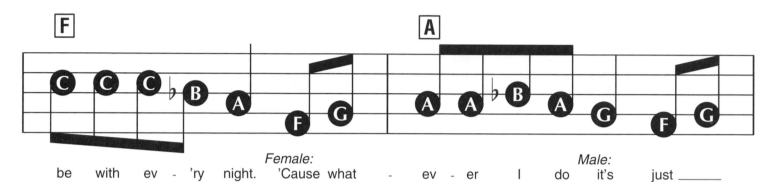

be with ev - 'ry night. 'Cause what - *Female:* ev - er I do it's *Male:* just _____

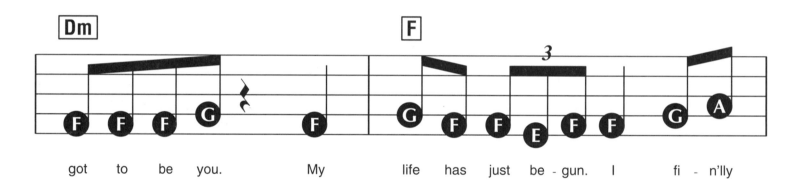

got to be you. My life has just be - gun. I fi - n'lly

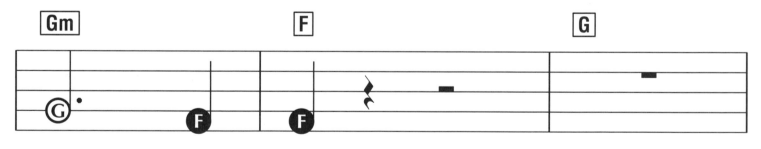

found some - one.

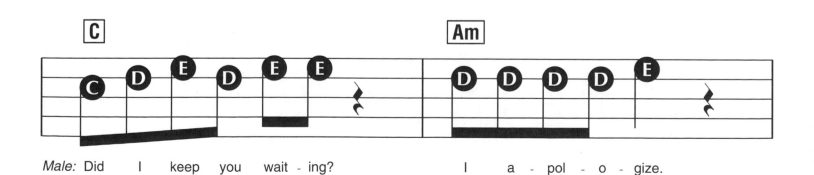

Male: Did I keep you wait - ing? I a - pol - o - gize.

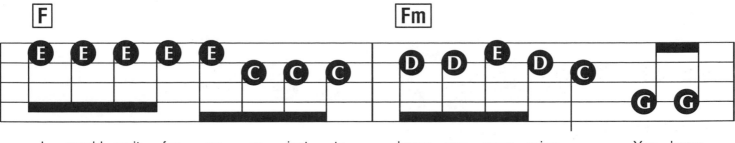

I would wait for - ev - er just to know you were mine. _____ You know,

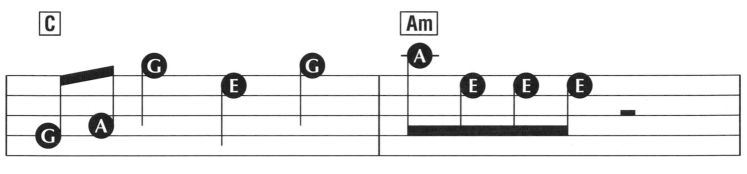

I love your hair, I love what you wear.

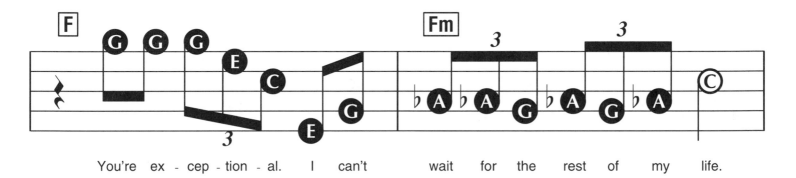

You're ex - cep - tion - al. I can't wait for the rest of my life.

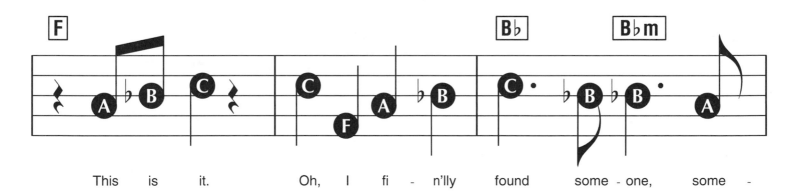

This is it. Oh, I fi - n'lly found some - one, some -

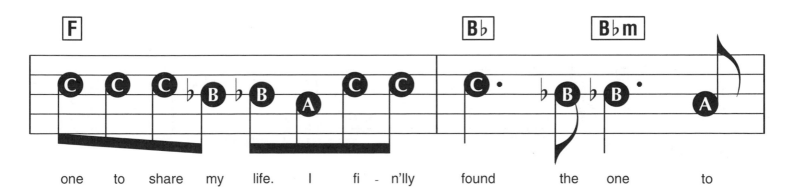

one to share my life. I fi - n'lly found the one to

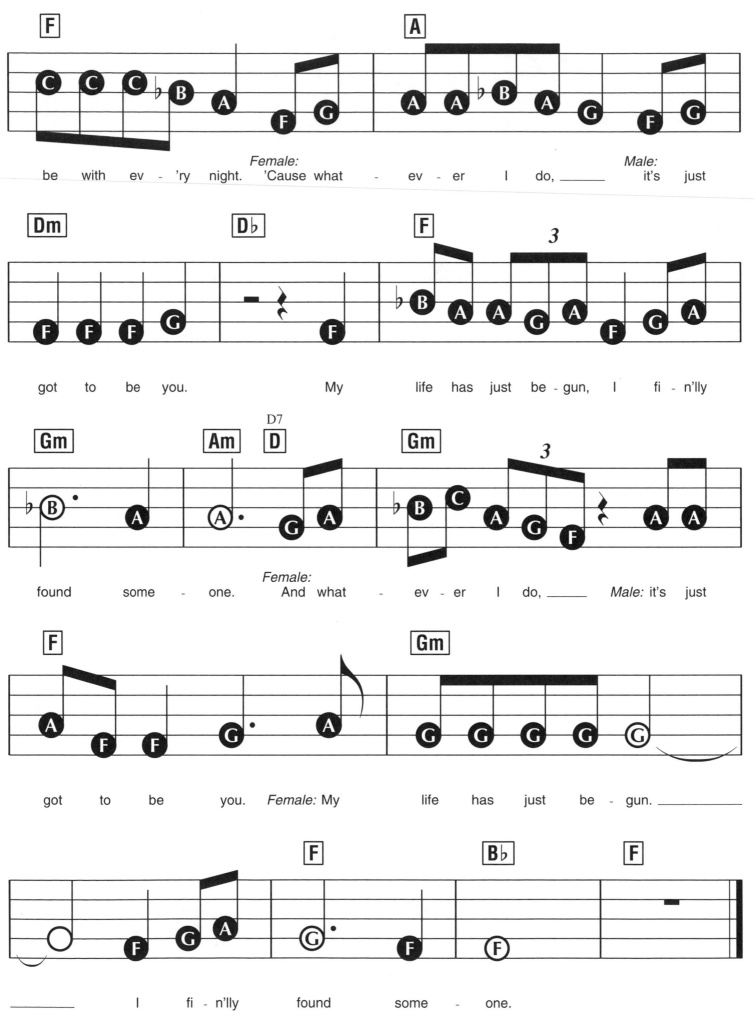

I Honestly Love You

Registration 1
Rhythm: 8-Beat or Pops

Words and Music by Jeff Barry
and Peter Allen

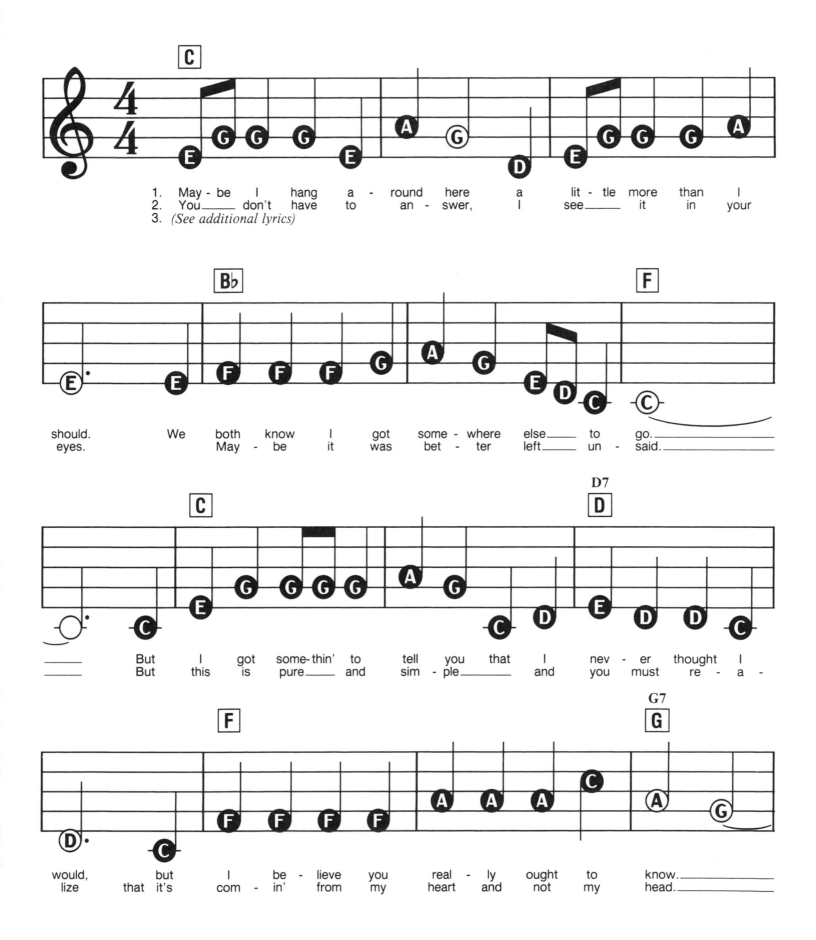

1. May - be I hang a - round here a lit - tle more than I
2. You___ don't have to an - swer, I see___ it in your
3. *(See additional lyrics)*

should. We both know I got some - where else___ to go.
eyes. May - be it was bet - ter left___ un - said.

_____ But I got some - thin' to tell you that I nev - er thought I
_____ But this is pure___ and sim - ple___ and you must re - a -

would, but I be - lieve you real - ly ought to know.___
lize that it's com - in' from my heart and ought not my head.___

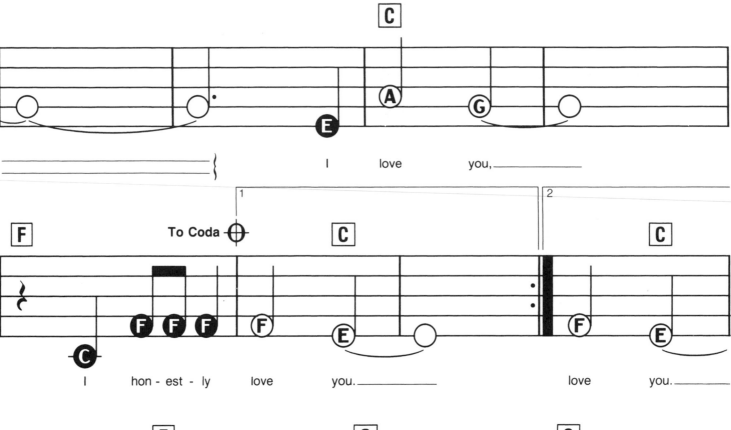

I love you,

I hon-est-ly love you. love you.

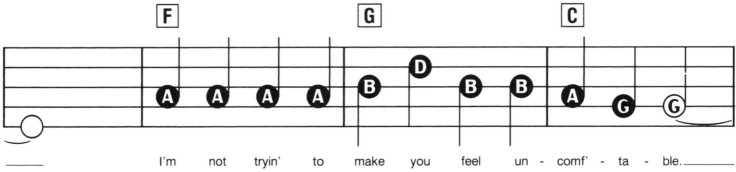

I'm not tryin' to make you feel un - comf' - ta - ble.

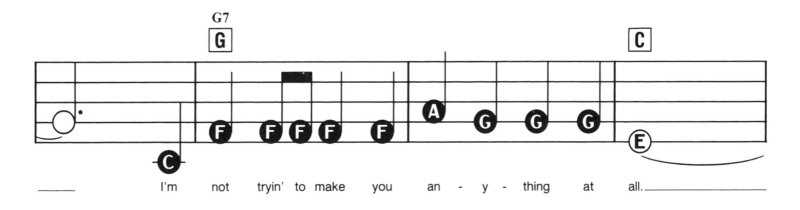

I'm not tryin' to make you an - y - thing at all.

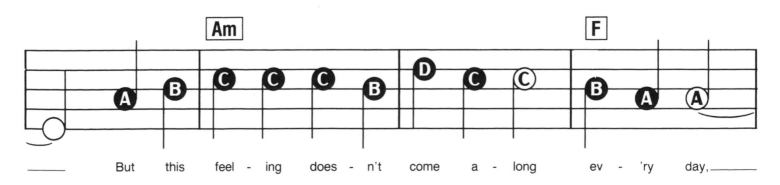

But this feel - ing does - n't come a - long ev - 'ry day,

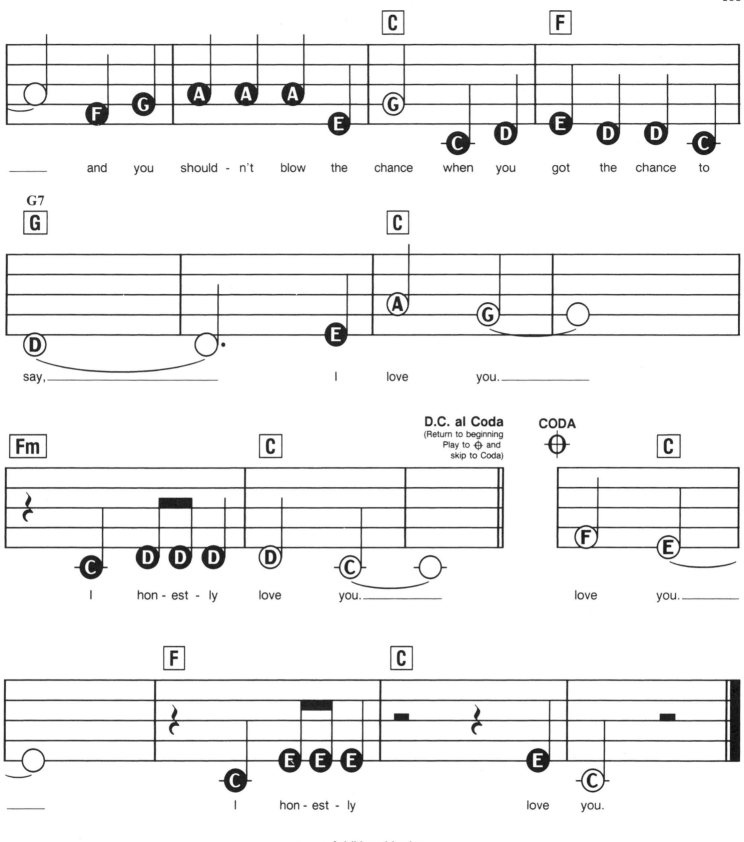

Additional Lyrics

3. If we were both born
   In another place and time,
   This moment might be ending with a kiss,
   But there you are with yours
   And here am I with mine.
   So I guess we'll just be leaving it at this,
   I love you.
   I honestly love you.
   I honestly love you.

I Just Called to Say I Love You

Registration 2
Rhythm: Rock

Words and Music by
Stevie Wonder

No New Year's Day to cel- e- brate,
rain, no flow- ers bloom,
high, no warm Ju- ly,
sun, no Hal- low- een,

no choco- late cov- ered can- dy hearts to give a- way.
no wed- ding Sat- ur- day with- in the month of June.
no har- vest moon to light one ten- der Au- gust night.
no giv- ing thanks to all the Christ- mas joy you bring.

No first of spring,_____ no song to sing,
But what it is_____ is some- thing true,
No au- tumn breeze,_____ no fall- ing leaves,
But what it is_____ though old so new,

in fact here's just an- oth- er or- di- nar- y day.
made up of these three words that fly to south- ern skies.
not e- ven your time for like no
to fill your heart birds to three

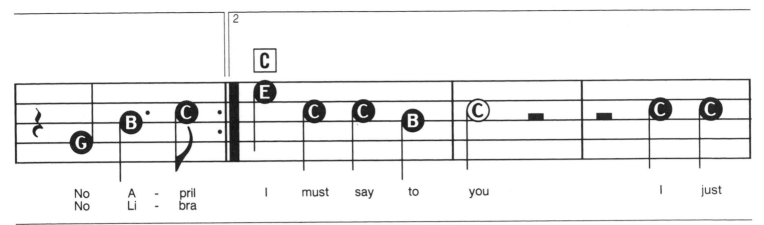

No A - pril I must say to you I just
No Li - bra

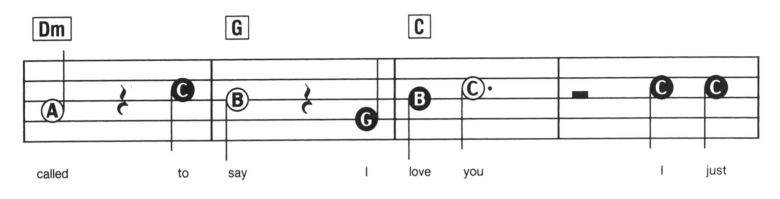

called to say I love you I just

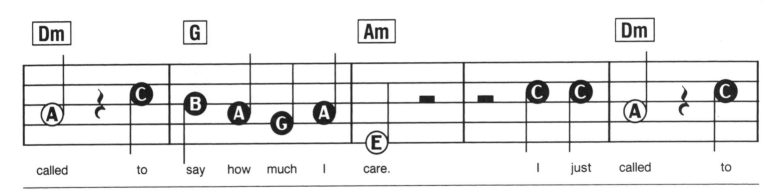

called to say how much I care. I just called to

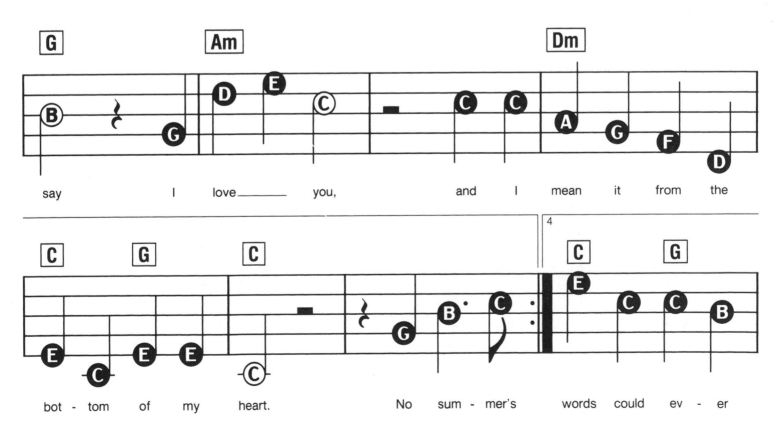

say I love_____ you, and I mean it from the

bot - tom of my heart. No sum - mer's words could ev - er

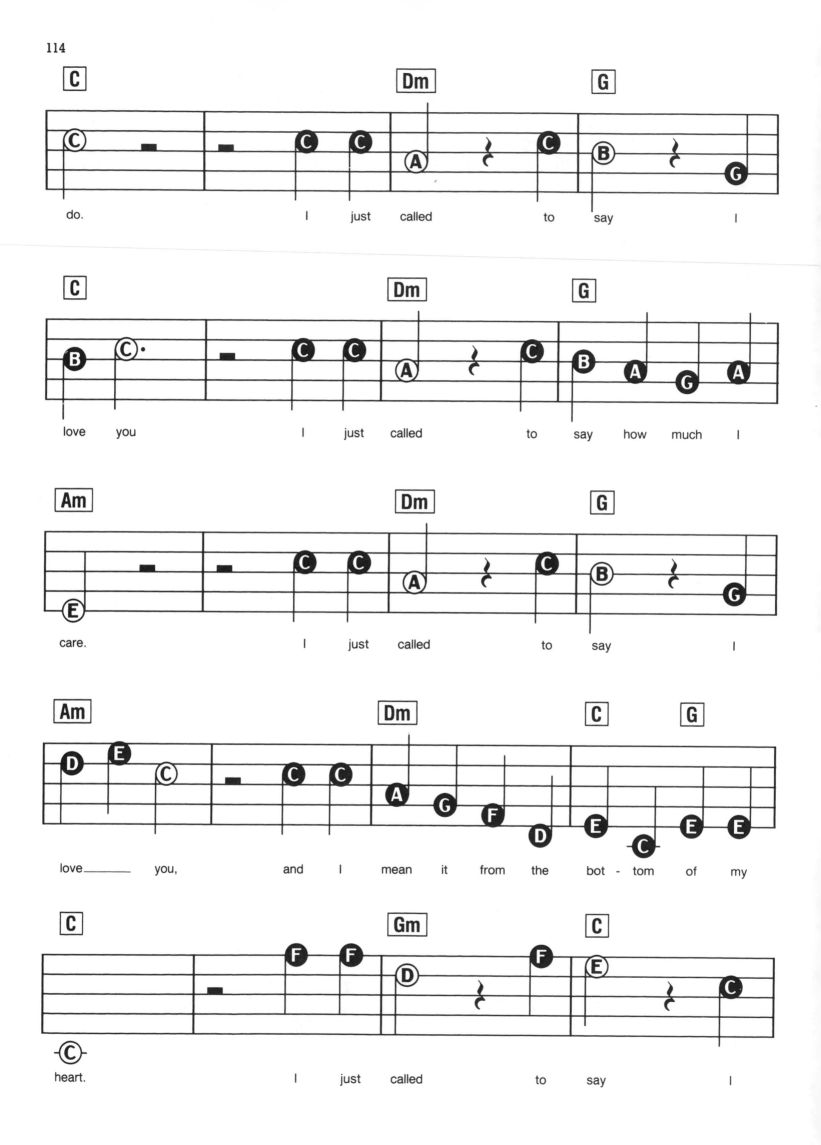

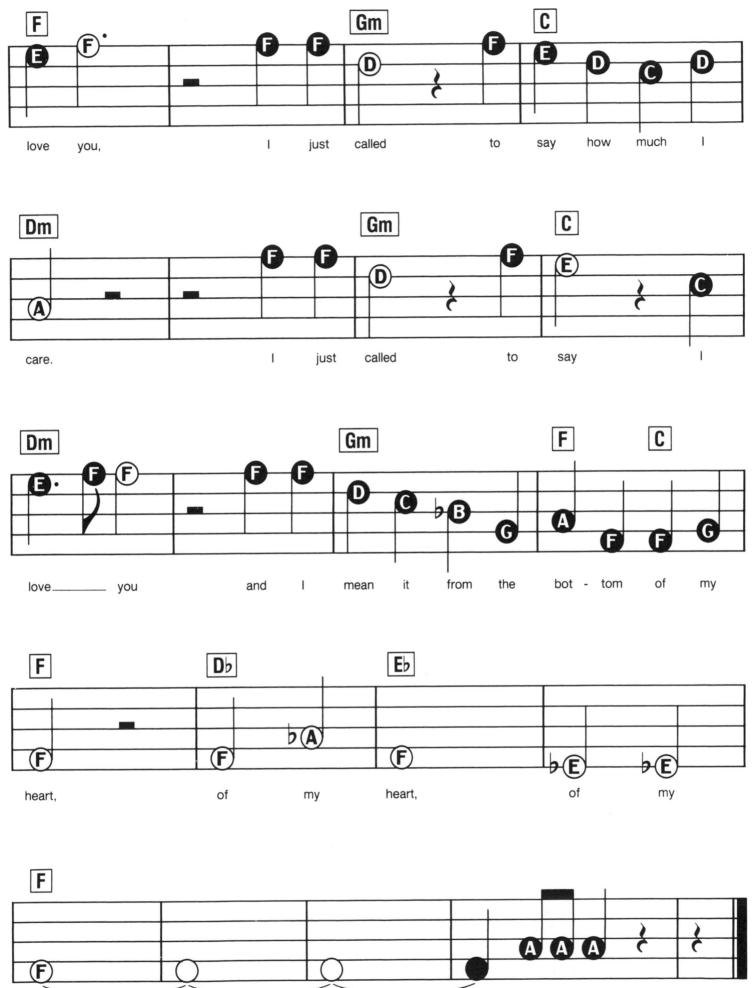

I Think I Love You

Registration 2
Rhythm: Rock or 8-Beat

Words and Music by
Tony Romeo

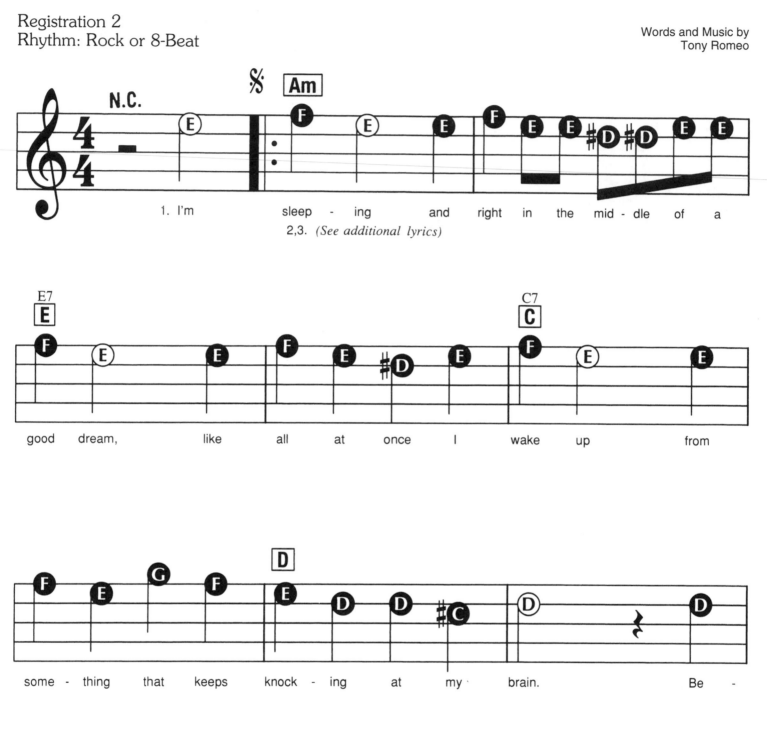

1. I'm sleep - ing and right in the mid - dle of a
2, 3. *(See additional lyrics)*

good dream, like all at once I wake up from

some - thing that keeps knock - ing at my brain. Be -

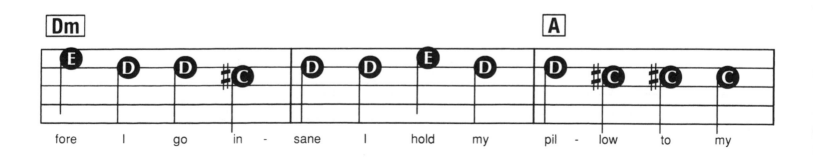

fore I go in - sane I hold my pil - low to my

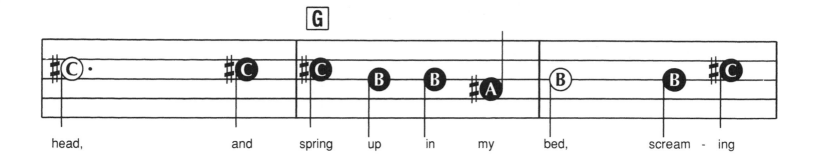

head, and spring up in my bed, scream - ing

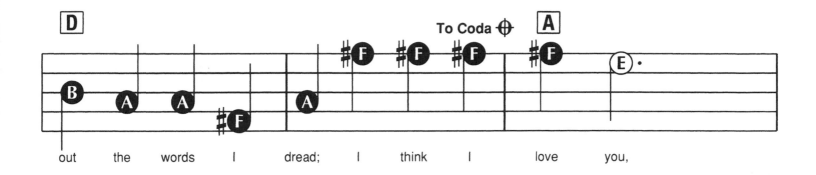

out the words I dread; I think I love you,

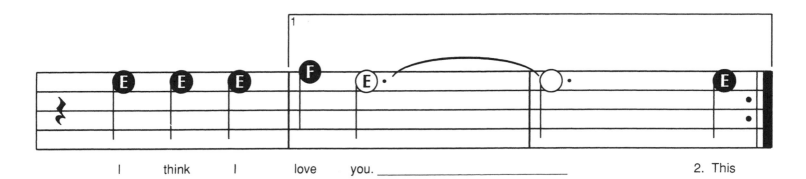

I think I love you. _____ 2. This

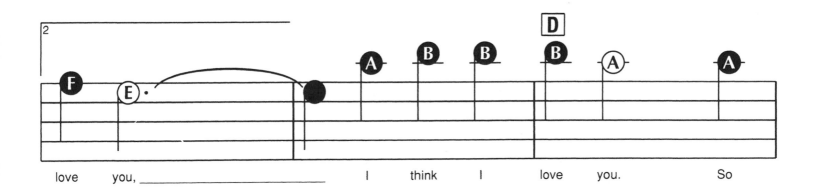

love you, _____ I think I love you. So

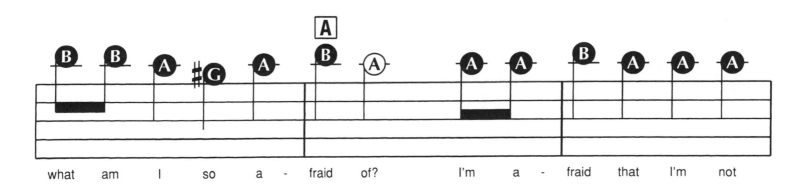

what am I so a - fraid of? I'm a - fraid that I'm not

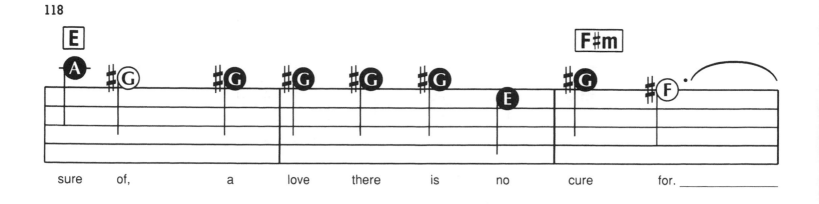

sure of,   a   love   there   is   no   cure   for. _____

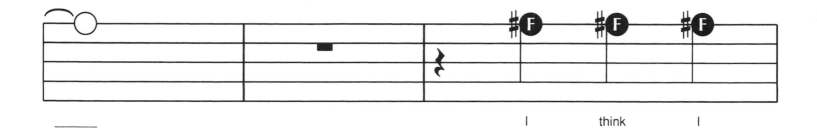

_____   I   think   I

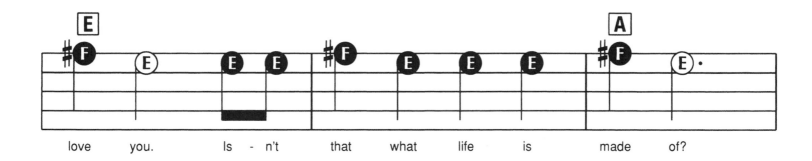

love   you.   Is - n't   that   what   life   is   made   of?

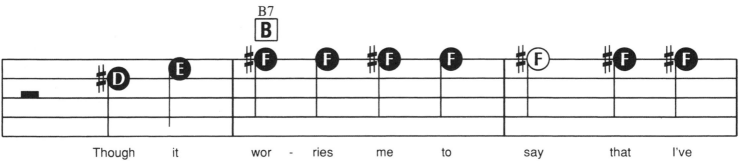

Though   it   wor - ries   me   to   say   that   I've

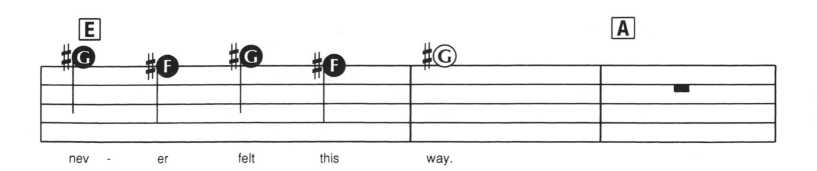

nev - er   felt   this   way.

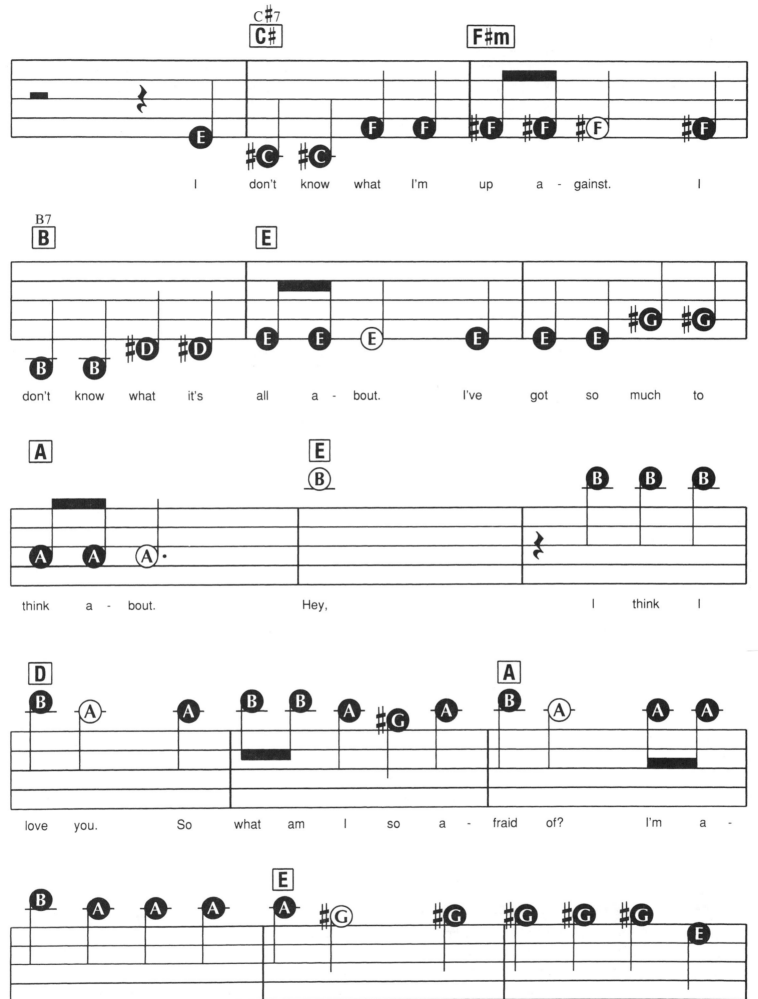

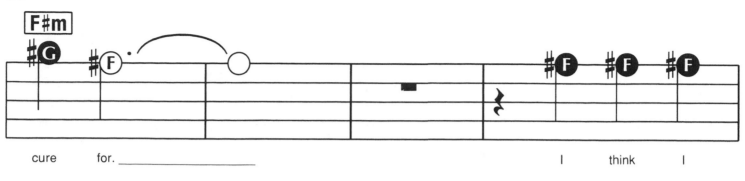

cure   for. _____   I   think   I

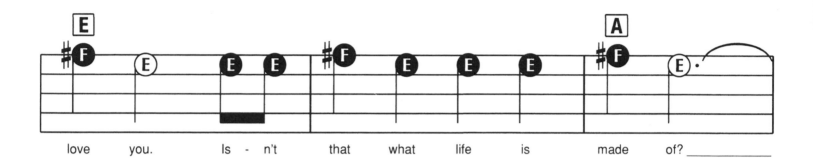

love   you.   Is - n't   that   what   life   is   made   of? _____

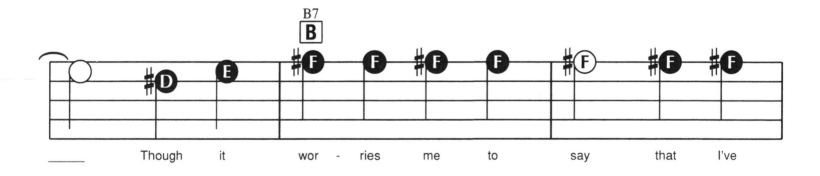

_____   Though   it   wor - ries   me   to   say   that   I've

D.S. al Coda
(Return to 𝄋
Play to ⊕
Skip to Coda)

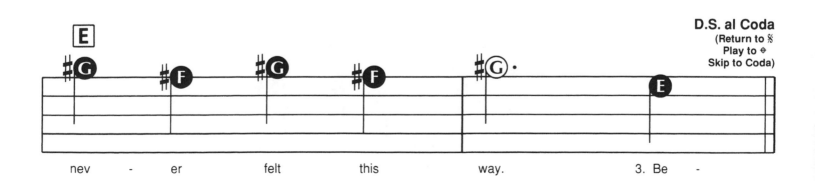

nev - er   felt   this   way.   3. Be -

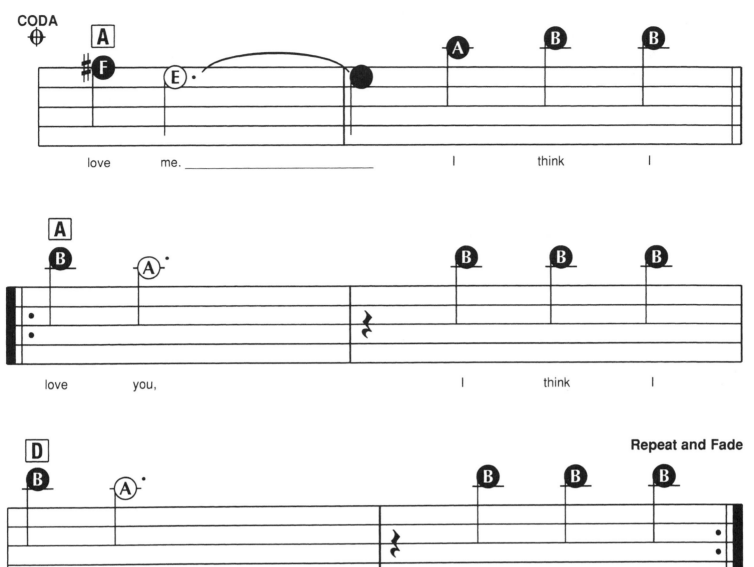

Additional Lyrics

2. This morning I woke up with this feeling,
   I didn't know how to deal with.
   And so I just decided with myself,
   I'd hide it to myself.
   And never talk about it and didn't I go and shout it
   When you walked into the room:
   I think I love you. (etc.)

3. Believe me you really don't have to worry,
   I only want to make you happy.
   And if you say "Hey go away," I will.
   But I think better still.
   I'd better stay around and love you,
   Do you think I have a case? Let me ask you to your face.
   Do you think you love me?
   I think I love you! (etc.)

I Will Remember You
Theme from THE BROTHERS McMULLEN

Registration 1
Rhythm: Ballad

Words and Music by Sarah McLachlan,
Seamus Egan and Dave Merenda

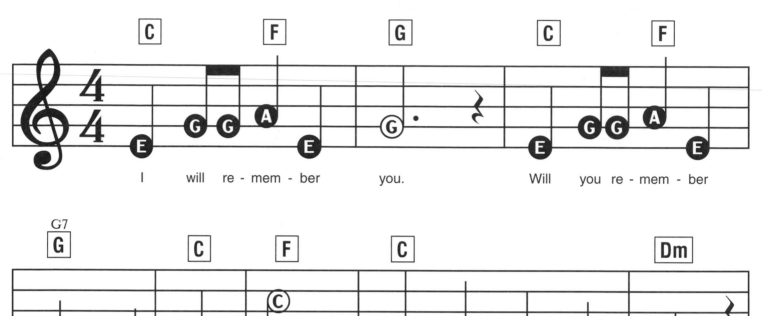

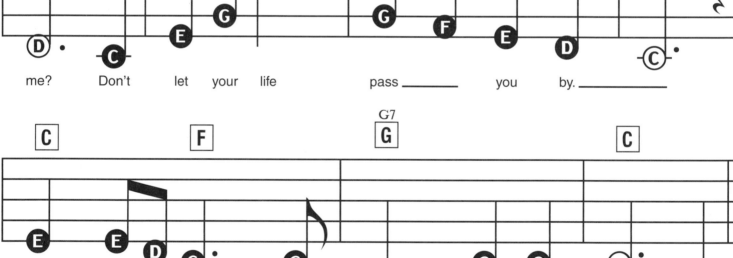

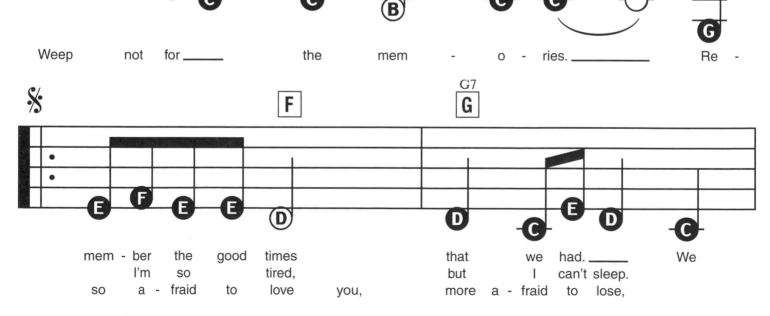

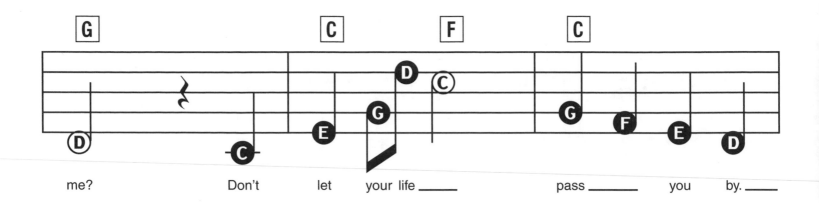

me? Don't let your life ____ pass ____ you by. ____

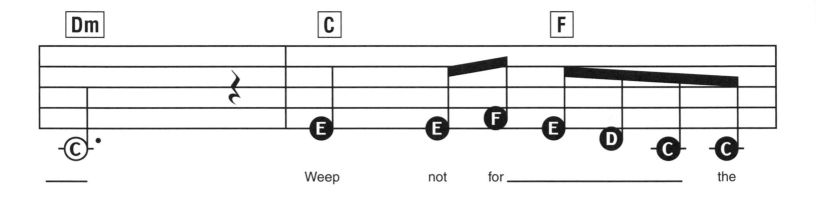

____ Weep not for ____ the

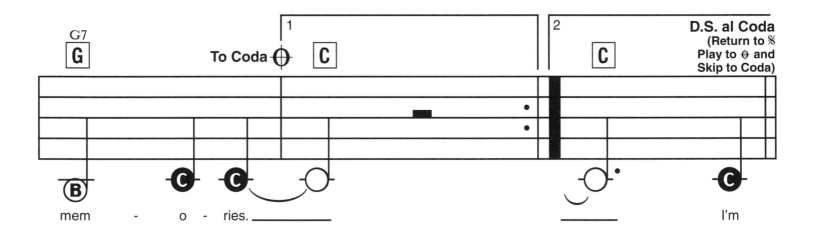

mem - o - ries. ____ ____ I'm

CODA

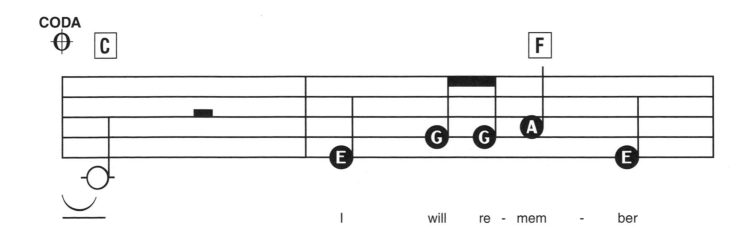

____ I will re - mem - ber

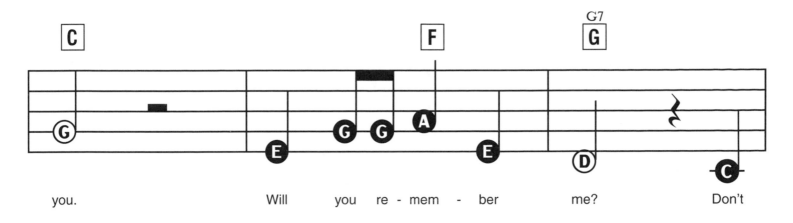

you.　　　　Will　you　re - mem - ber　me?　　Don't

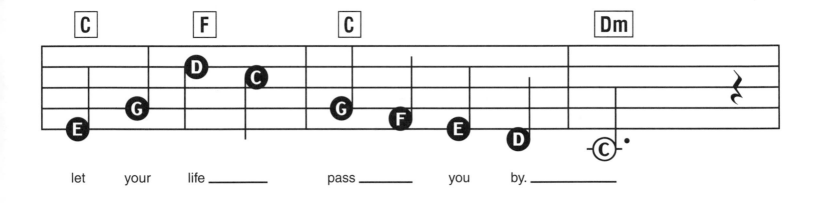

let　your　life _____ pass _____ you　by. _____

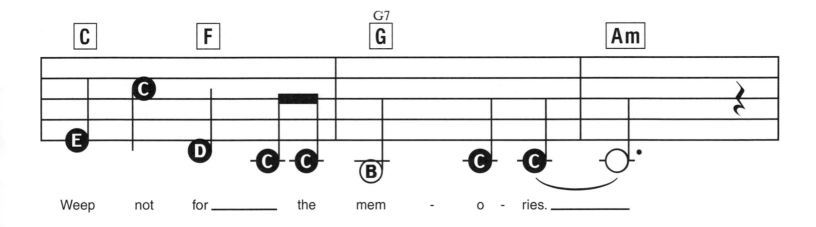

Weep　not　for _____ the　mem - o - ries. _____

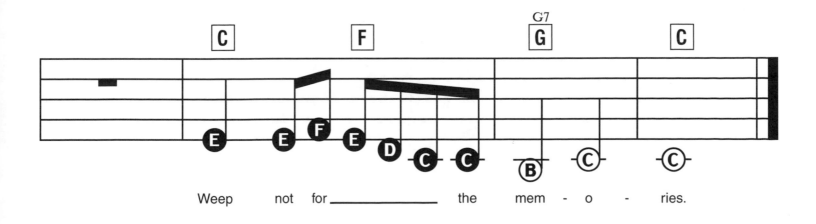

Weep　not　for _____ the　mem - o - ries.

I'll Be

Registration 4
Rhythm: Waltz

Words and Music by
Edwin McCain

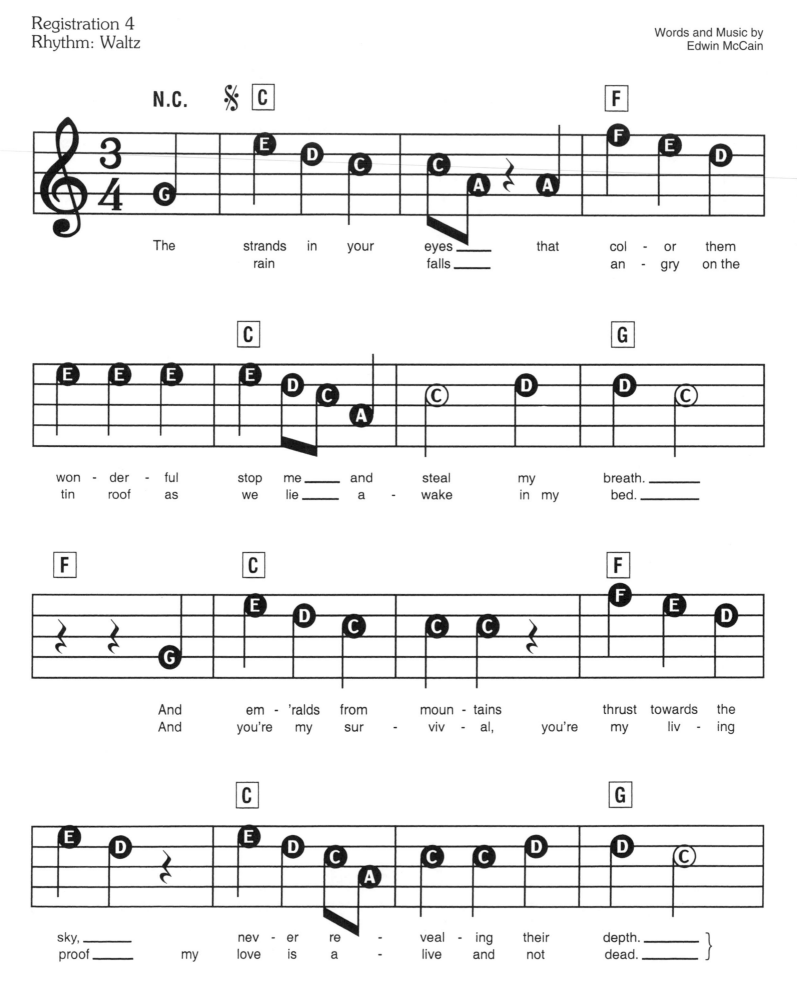

The strands in your eyes ____ that col - or them
rain falls ____ an - gry on the

won - der - ful stop me ____ and steal my breath. ____
tin roof as we lie ____ a - wake in my bed. ____

And em - 'ralds from moun - tains thrust towards the
And you're my sur - viv - al, you're my liv - ing

sky, ____ nev - er re - veal - ing their depth. ____ }
proof ____ my love is a - live and not dead. ____ }

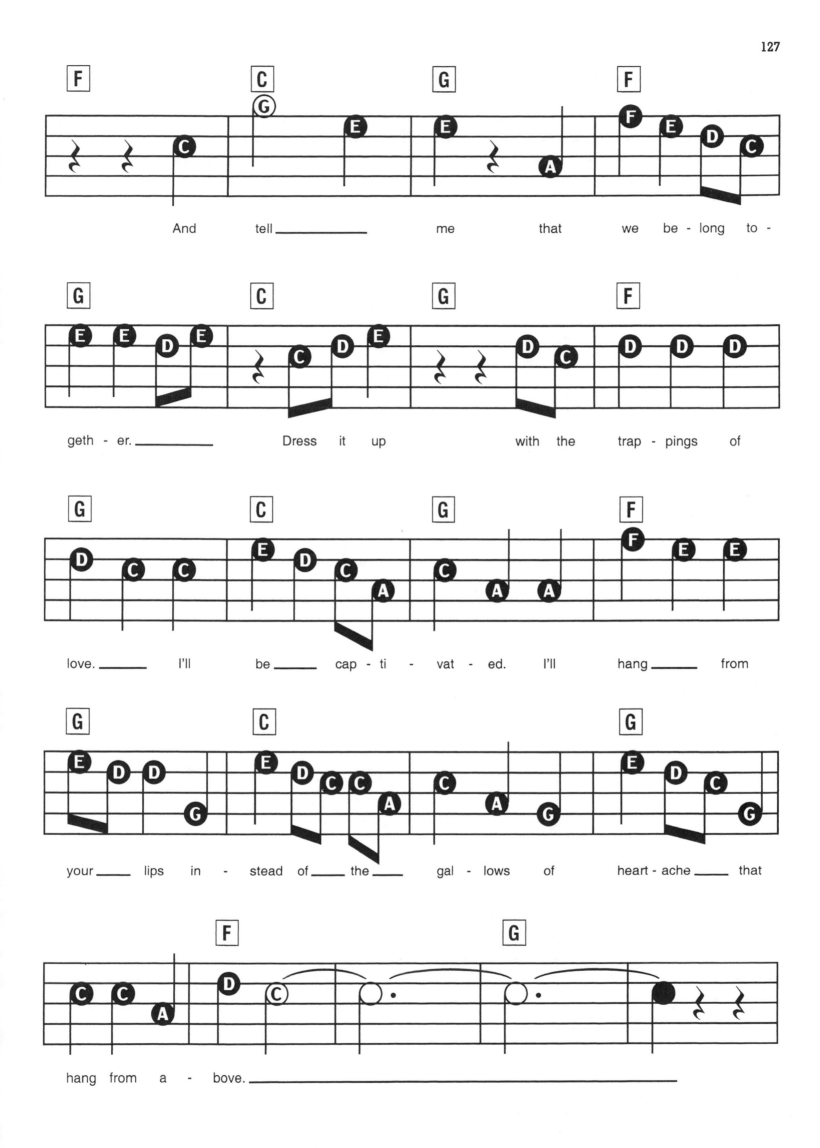

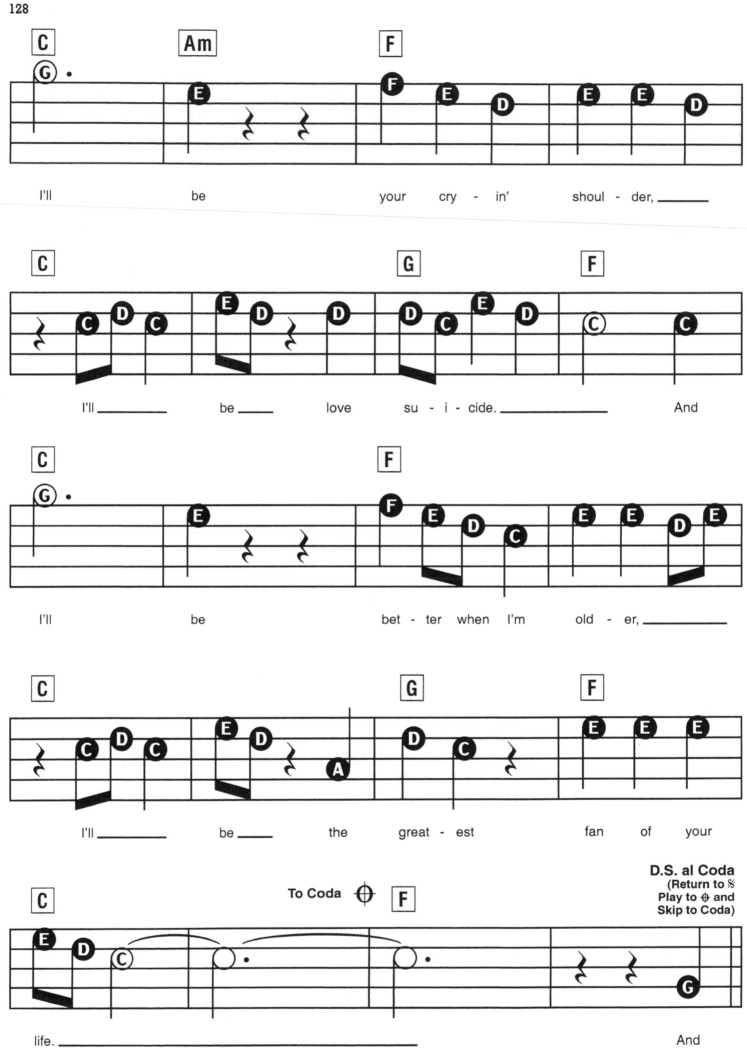

CODA

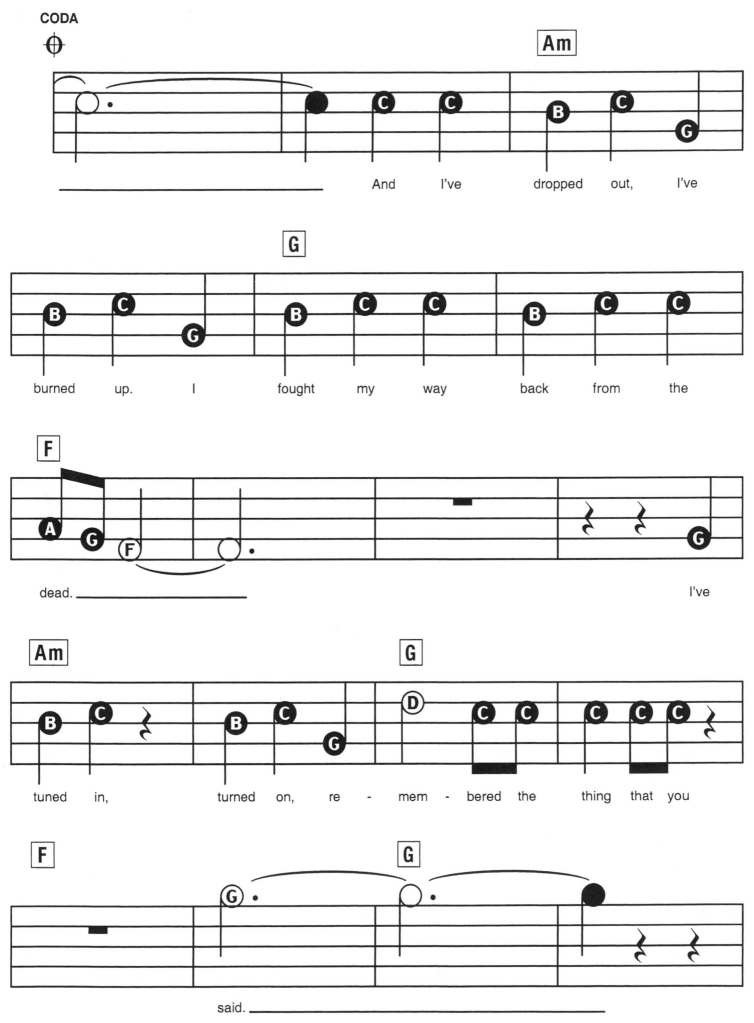

Am

And I've dropped out, I've

G

burned up. I fought my way back from the

F

dead. I've

Am   G

tuned in, turned on, re - mem - bered the thing that you

F   G

said.

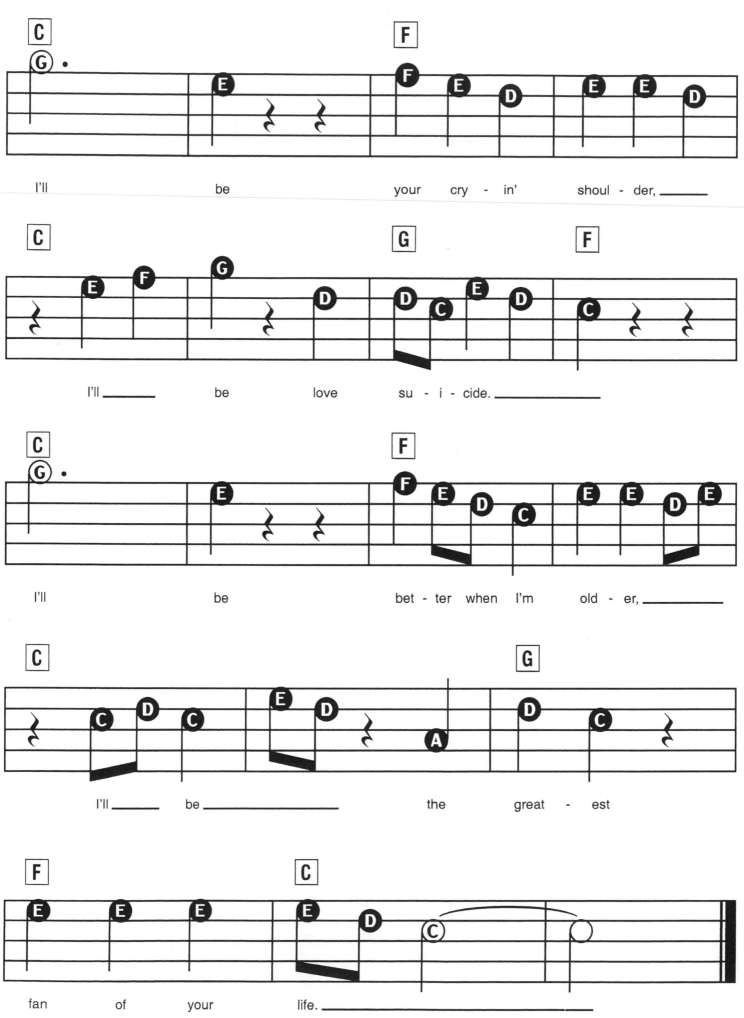

I'll Make Love to You

Registration 7
Rhythm: Slow Rock

Words and Music by
Babyface

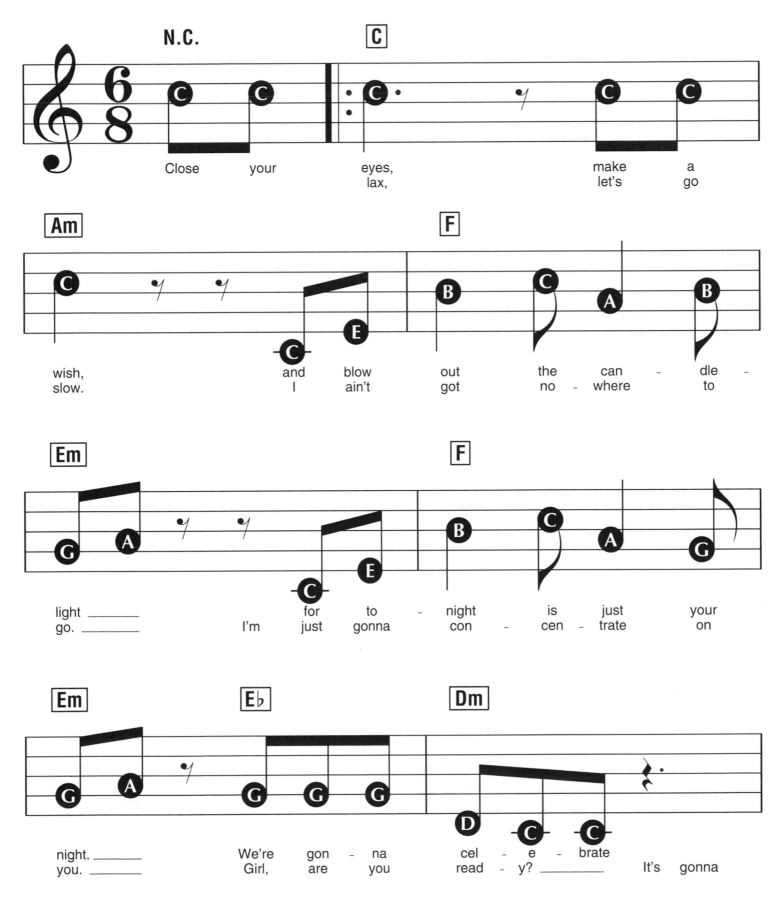

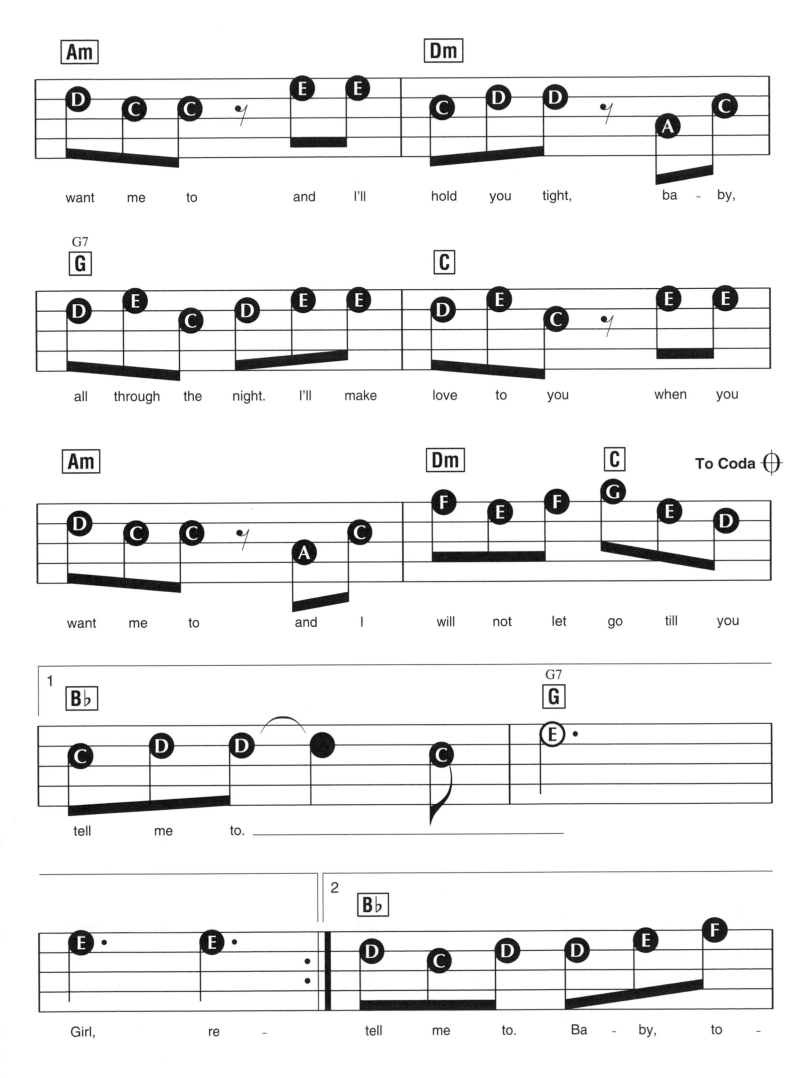

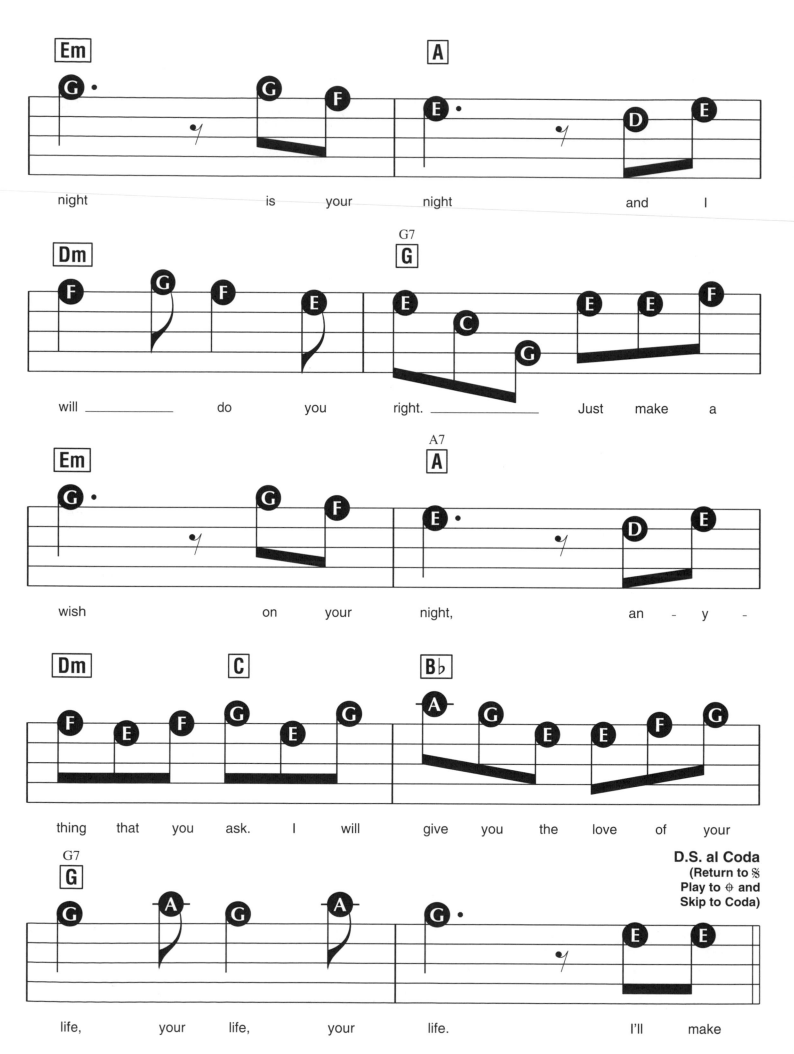

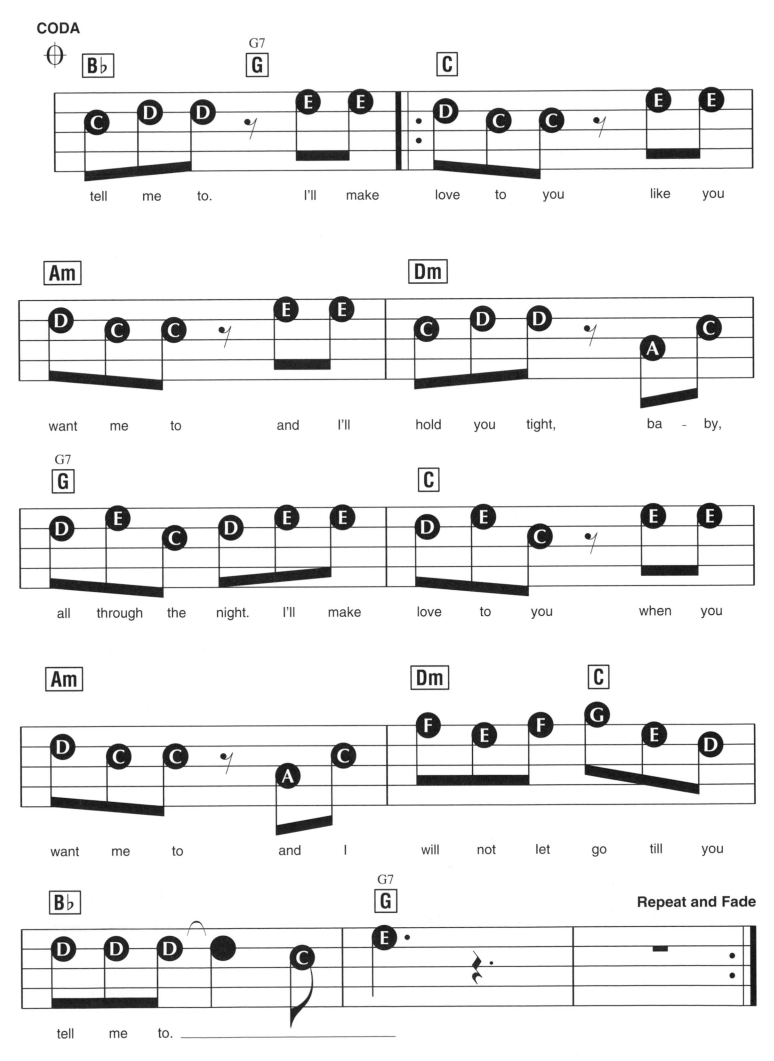

I'll Be There

Registration 9
Rhythm: Rock or 8-Beat

Words and Music by Berry Gordy, Hal Davis,
Willie Hutch and Bob West

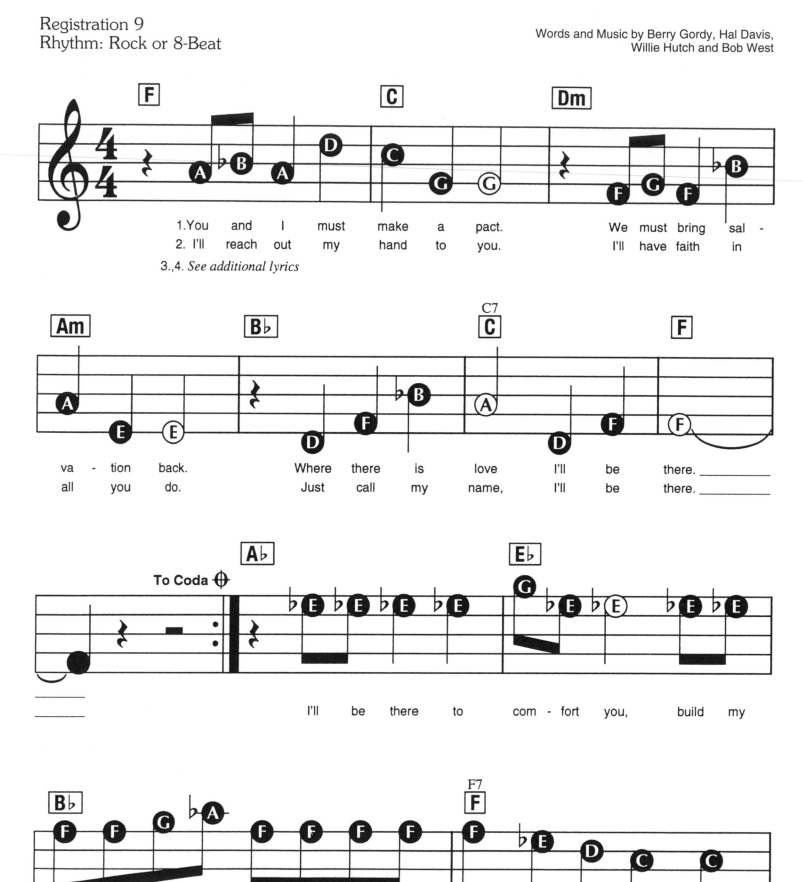

1.You and I must make a pact.
2. I'll reach out my hand to you.
3.,4. *See additional lyrics*

We must bring sal -
I'll have faith in

va - tion back.
all you do.

Where there is love I'll be there.
Just call my name, I'll be there.

To Coda

I'll be there to com - fort you, build my

world of dreams a - round you. I'm so glad that I found you.

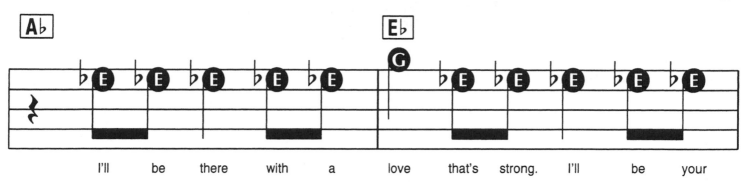

I'll be there with a love that's strong. I'll be your

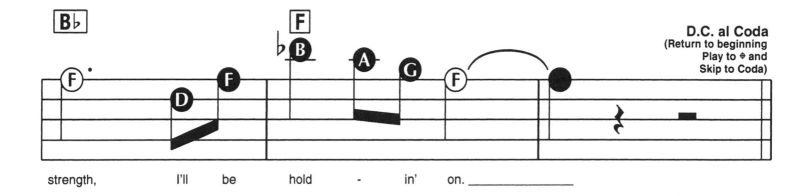

D.C. al Coda
(Return to beginning
Play to ⊕ and
Skip to Coda)

strength, I'll be hold - in' on. _____

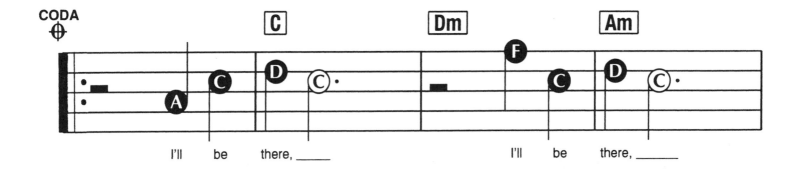

I'll be there, _____ I'll be there, _____

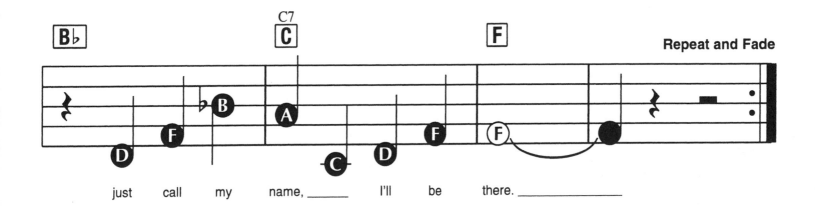

Repeat and Fade

just call my name, _____ I'll be there. _____

Additional Lyrics

3. Let me fill your heart with joy and laughter.
   Togetherness, girl, is all I'm after.
   Whenever you need me, I'll be there.

4. I'll be there to protect you
   With unselfish love that respects you.
   Just call my name, I'll be there.

I'll Be There For You

Registration 9
Rhythm: Rock or 8-Beat

Words and Music by Jon Bon Jovi
and Richie Sambora

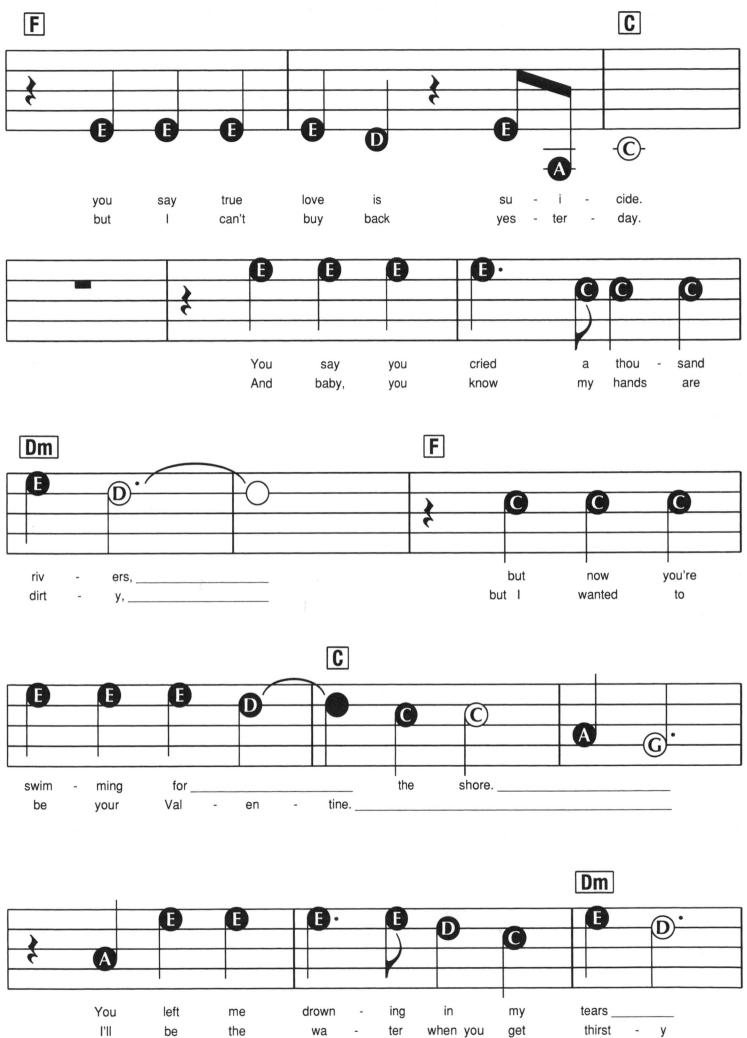

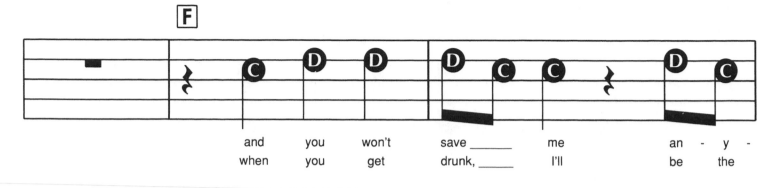

and you won't save _____ me an - y -
when you get drunk, _____ I'll be the

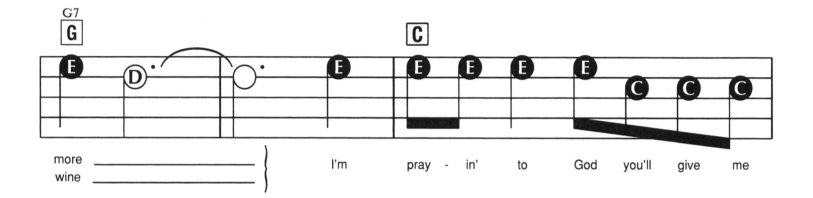

more _____ I'm pray - in' to God you'll give me
wine _____

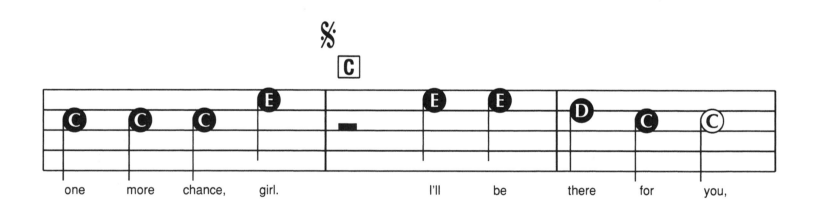

one more chance, girl. I'll be there for you,

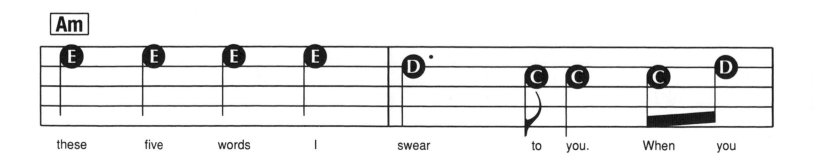

these five words I swear to you. When you

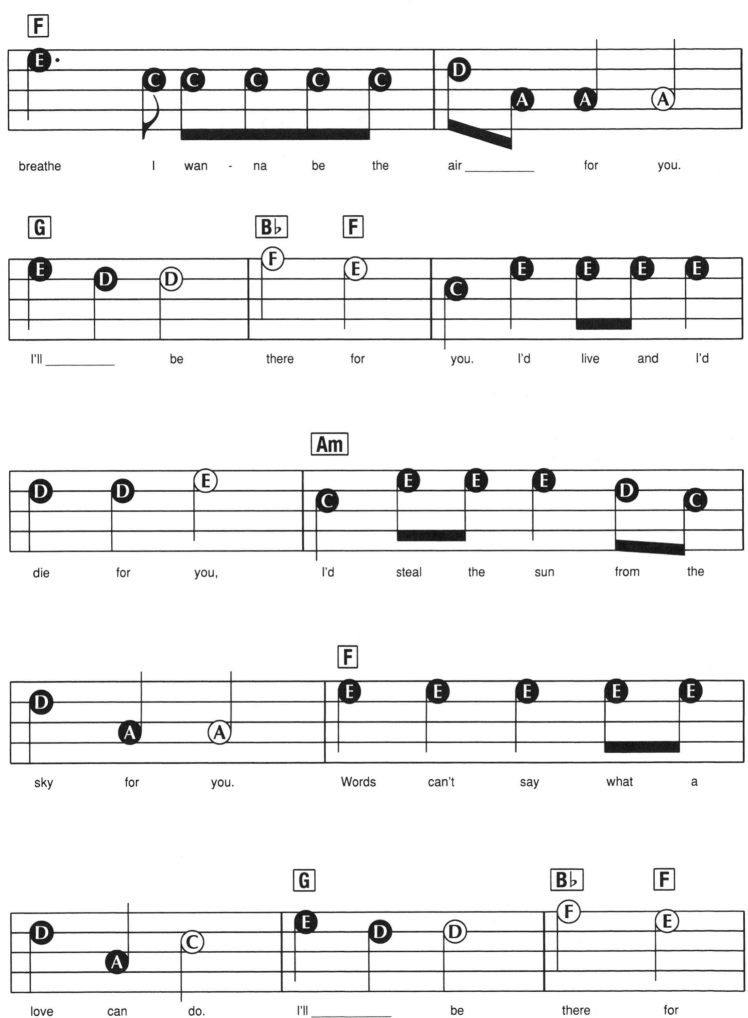

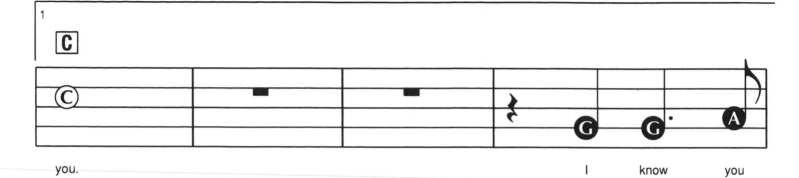

you.   I   know   you

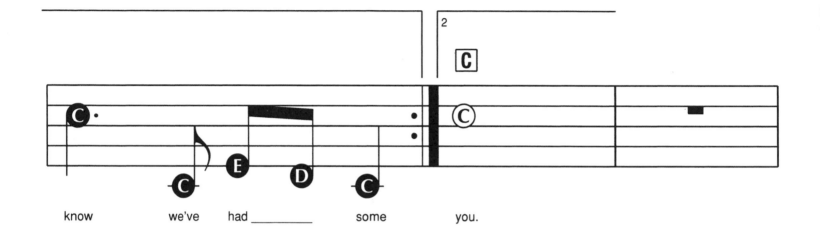

know   we've   had _____   some   you.

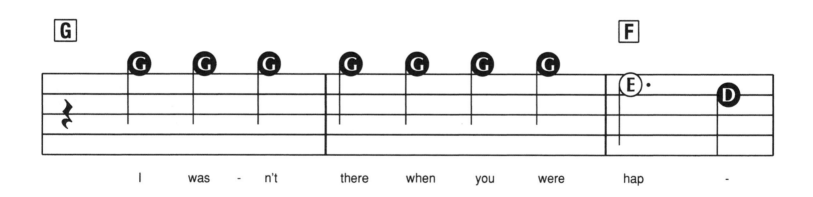

I   was - n't   there   when   you   were   hap -

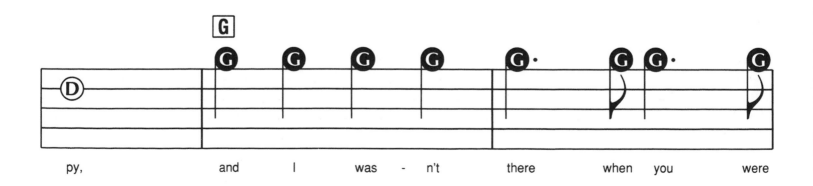

py,   and   I   was - n't   there   when   you   were

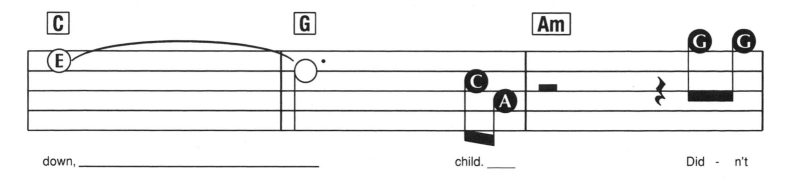

down, _____ child. ____ Did - n't

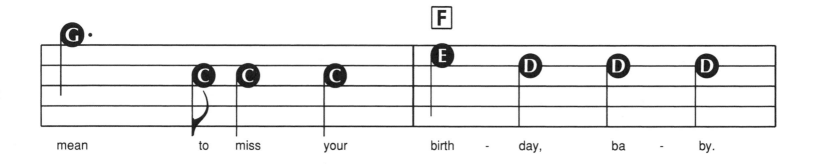

mean to miss your birth - day, ba - by.

I wish I'd seen you blow those can - dles

D.S.
Return to 𝄋, and Fade

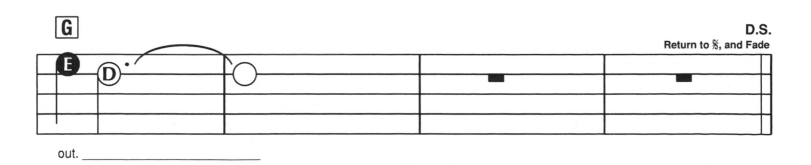

out. _____

I'll Have to Say I Love You in a Song

Registration 2
Rhythm: Slow Rock or Ballad

Words and Music by
Jim Croce

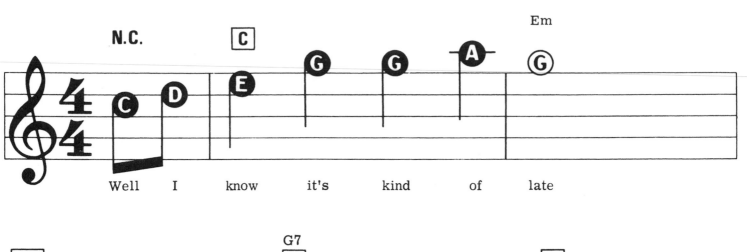

Well I know it's kind of late

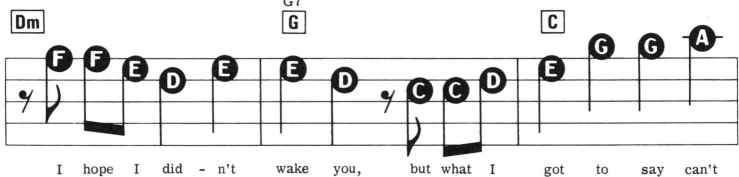

I hope I did-n't wake you, but what I got to say can't

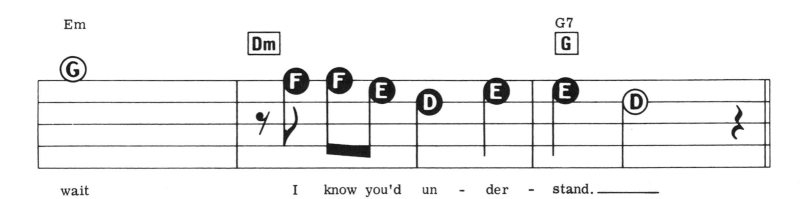

wait   I know you'd un - der - stand._____

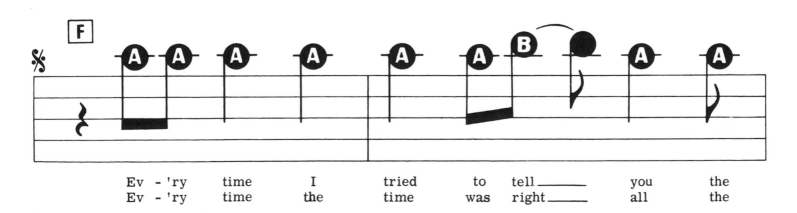

Ev - 'ry   time   I   tried   to   tell_____ you   the
Ev - 'ry   time   the   time   was   right_____ all   the

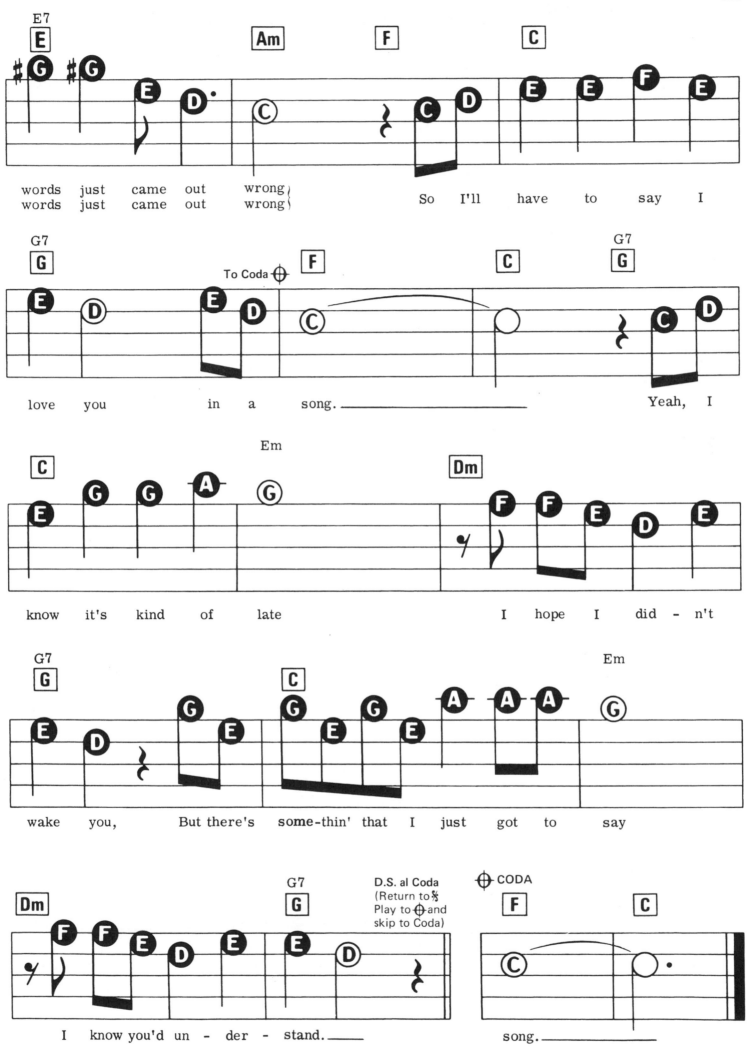

If You Leave Me Now

Registration 1
Rhythm: 8-Beat, Pops or Bossa Nova

Words and Music by
Peter Cetera

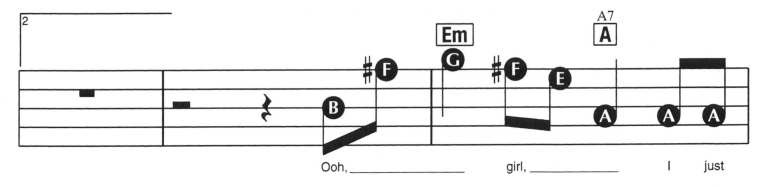

Ooh,_____ girl,_____ I just

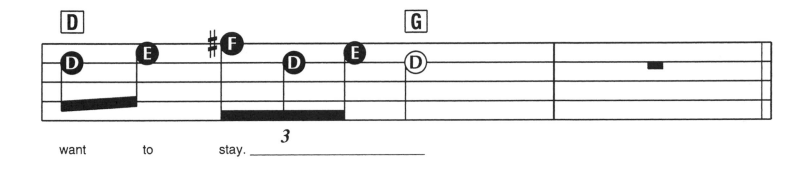

want to stay. _____

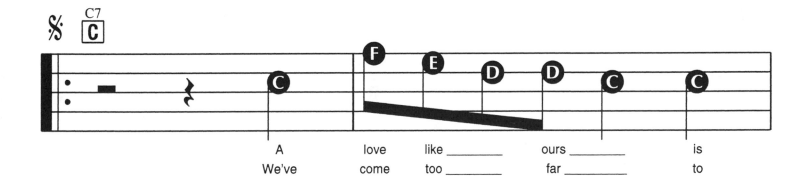

A love like _____ ours _____ is
We've come too _____ far _____ to

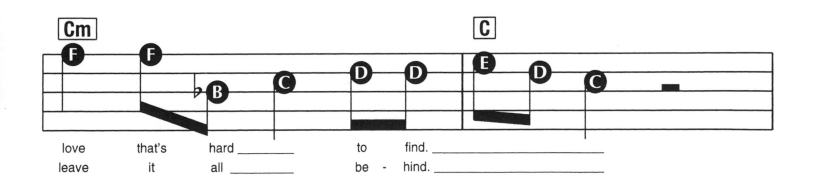

love that's hard _____ to find. _____
leave it all _____ be - hind. _____

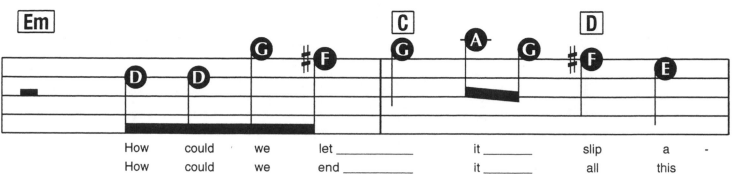

Em

How could we let _____ it _____ slip a -
How could we end _____ it _____ all this

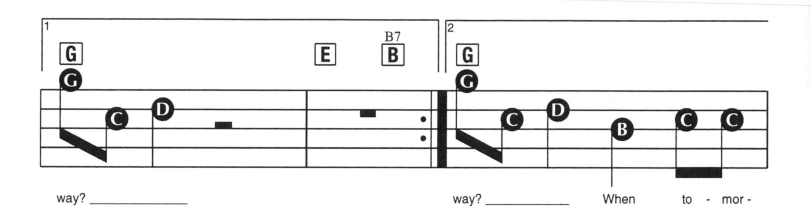

1 **G** **E** **B** (B7) **2** **G**

way? _____   way? _____ When to - mor -

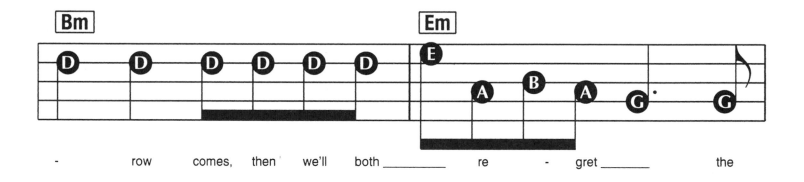

Bm   **Em**

- row comes, then we'll both _____ re - gret _____ the

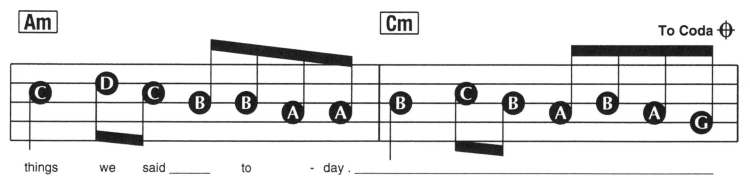

Am   **Cm**   To Coda ⊕

things we said _____ to - day. _____

D.S. al Coda
(Return to ⅍
Play to ⊕, with repeats, and
Skip to Coda)

CODA
⊕

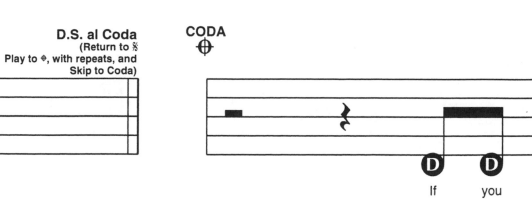

If you

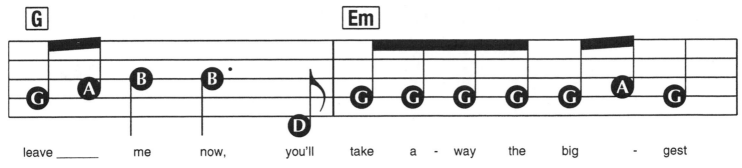

leave _____ me now, you'll take a - way the big - gest

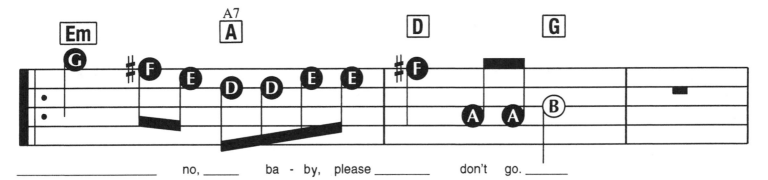

part of me. _____ Ooh, _____

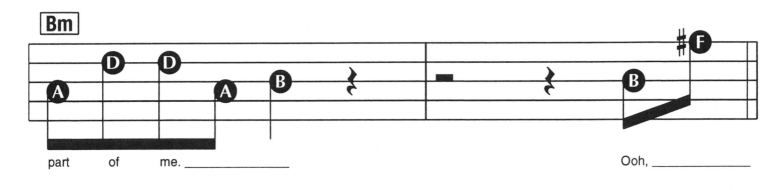

_____ no, _____ ba - by, please _____ don't go. _____

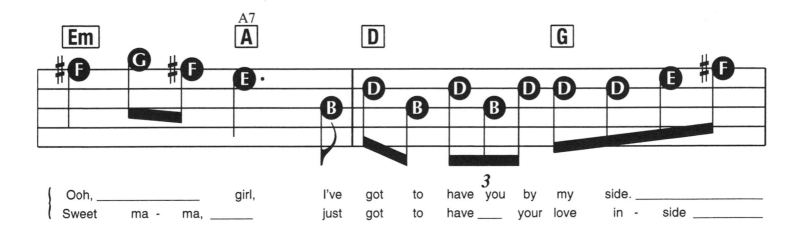

Ooh, _____ girl, I've got to have you by my side. _____

Sweet ma - ma, _____ just got to have ___ your love in - side _____

Repeat and Fade

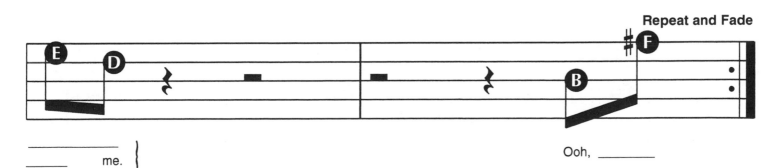

___ me. _____ Ooh, _____

It Must Have Been Love

Registration 4
Rhythm: 8-Beat or Rock

Words and Music by
Per Gessle

Lay a whis-per on my pil-low, leave the
liev-ing we're to-geth-er, that I'm

win-ter on the ground. ____ I wake up lone-ly, a stare of
shel-tered by your heart. ____ But in and out-side I turn to

si-lence in the bed-room and all a-round. Touch me
wa-ter like a tear-drop in your palm. And it's a

now, I close my eyes ____ and dream a-way.
hard win-ter's day ____ I dream a-way.

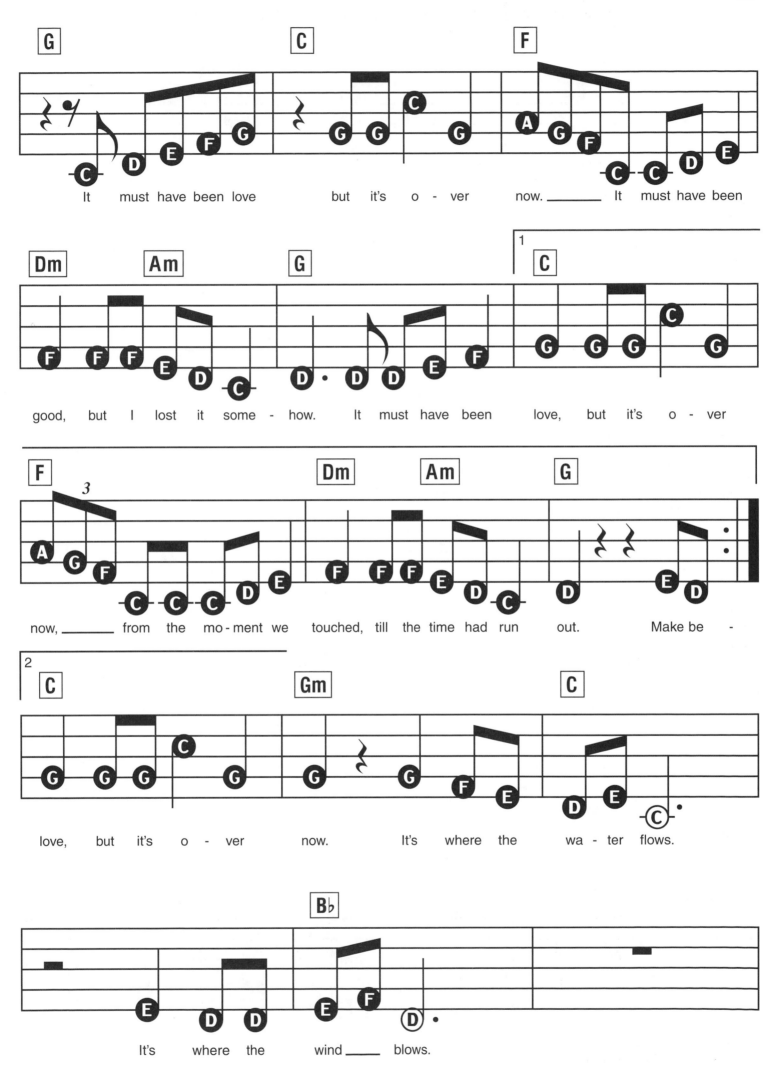

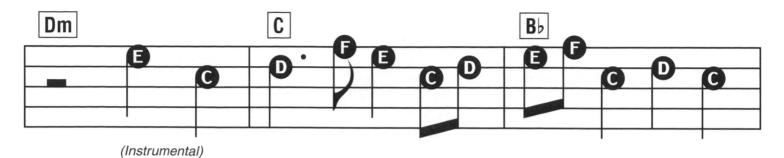

(Instrumental)

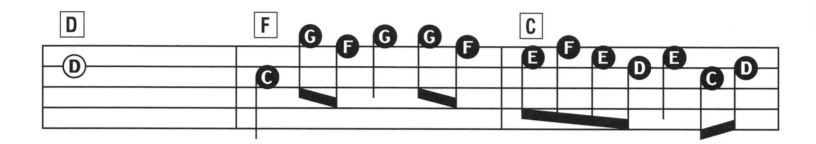

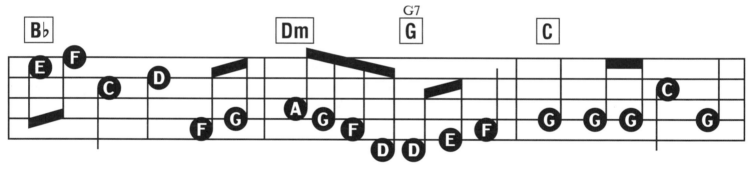

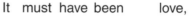

It must have been love, but it's o - ver

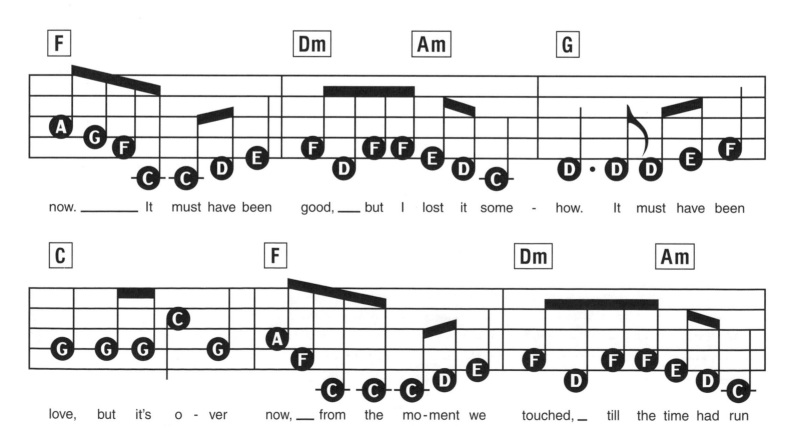

now. _____ It must have been good, _ but I lost it some - how. It must have been

love, but it's o - ver now, _ from the mo-ment we touched, _ till the time had run

153

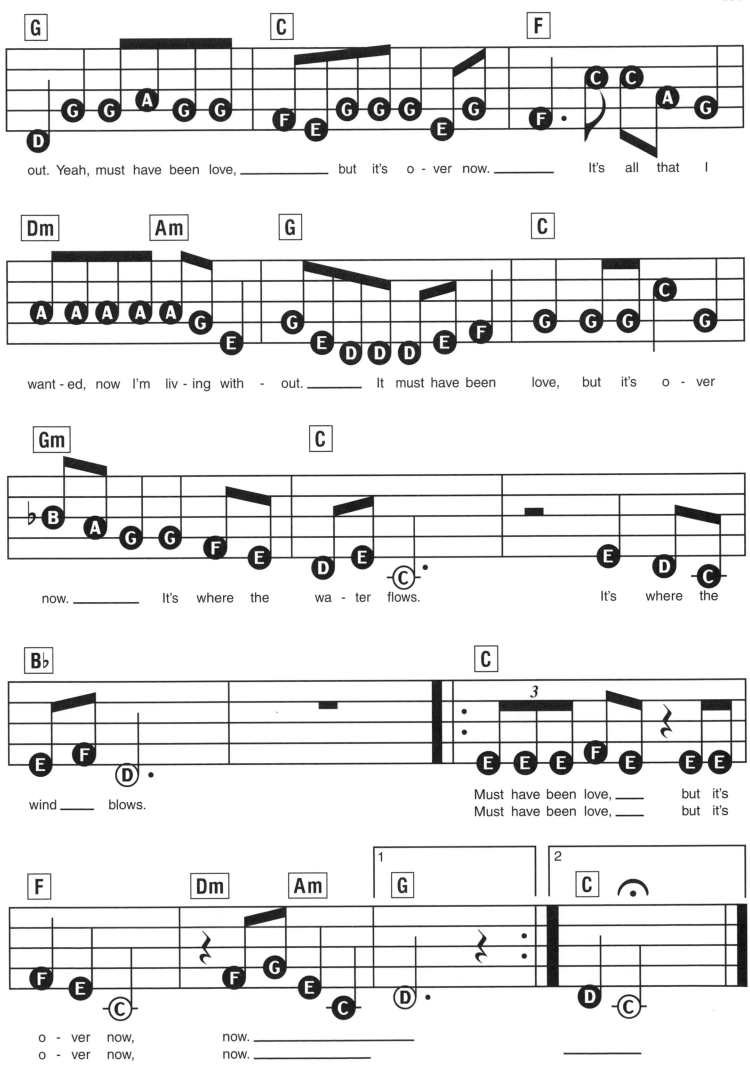

Just the Way You Are

Registration 4
Rhythm: Rock or Jazz Rock

Words and Music by
Billy Joel

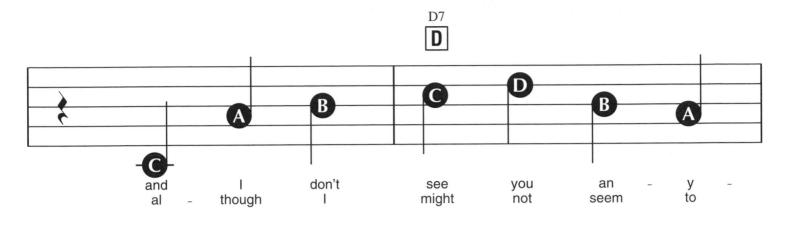

D7

and   I   don't   see   you   an – y –
al – though   I   might   not   seem   to

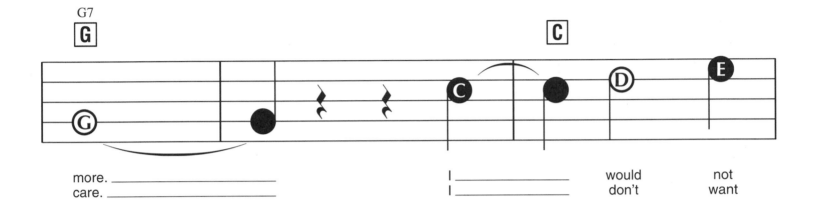

G7   C

more. _____   I _____   would   not
care. _____   I _____   don't   want

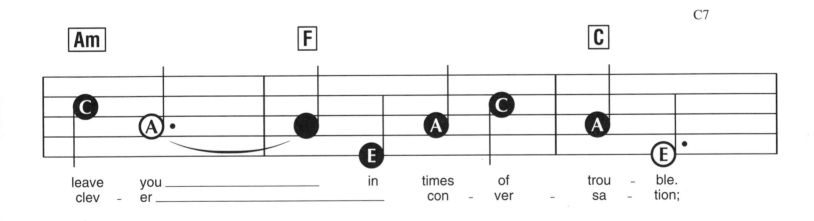

Am   F   C   C7

leave   you _____   in   times   of   trou – ble.
clev – er _____   con – ver – sa – tion;

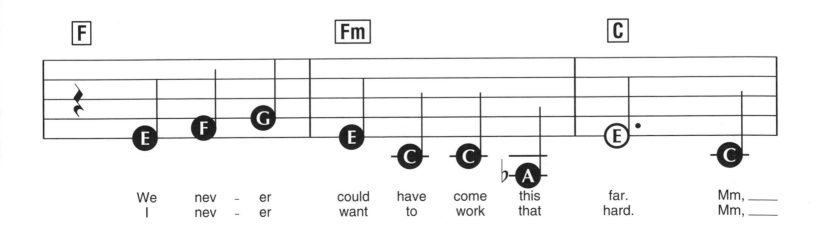

F   Fm   C

We   nev – er   could   have   come   this   far.   Mm, ____
I   nev – er   want   to   work   that   hard.   Mm, ____

C7

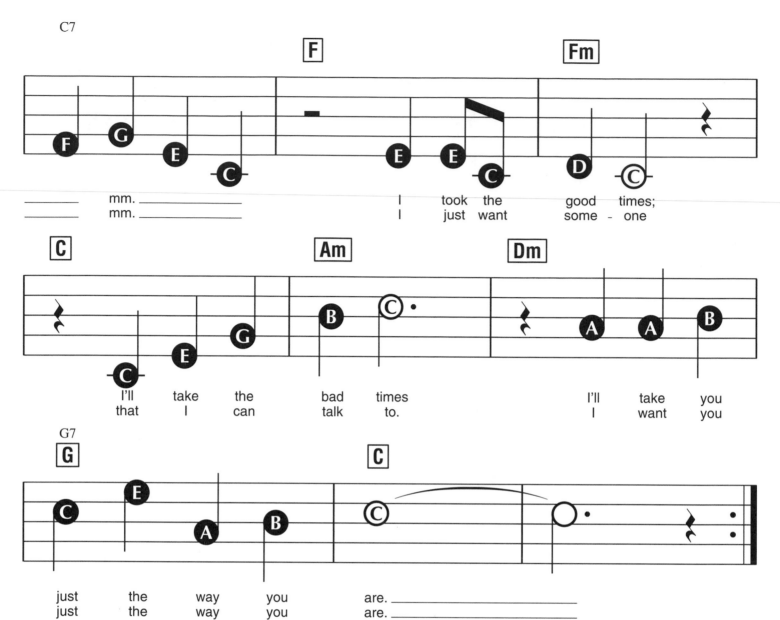

F   Fm

```
_____ mm. _____
_____ mm. _____
```

I took the good times;
I just want some - one

C   Am   Dm

I'll take the bad times I'll take you
that I can talk to. I want you

G7
G   C

just the way you are. _____
just the way you are. _____

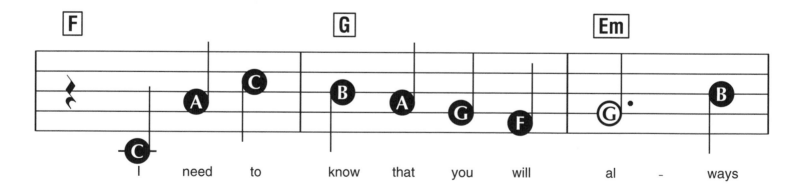

F   G   Em

I need to know that you will al - ways

A7
A   Dm   G

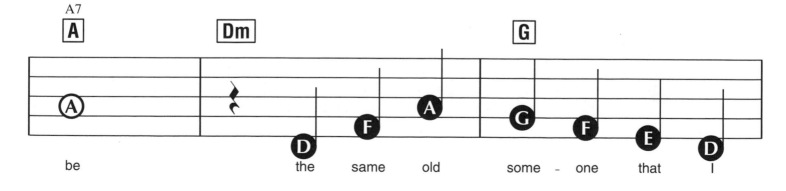

be the same old some - one that I

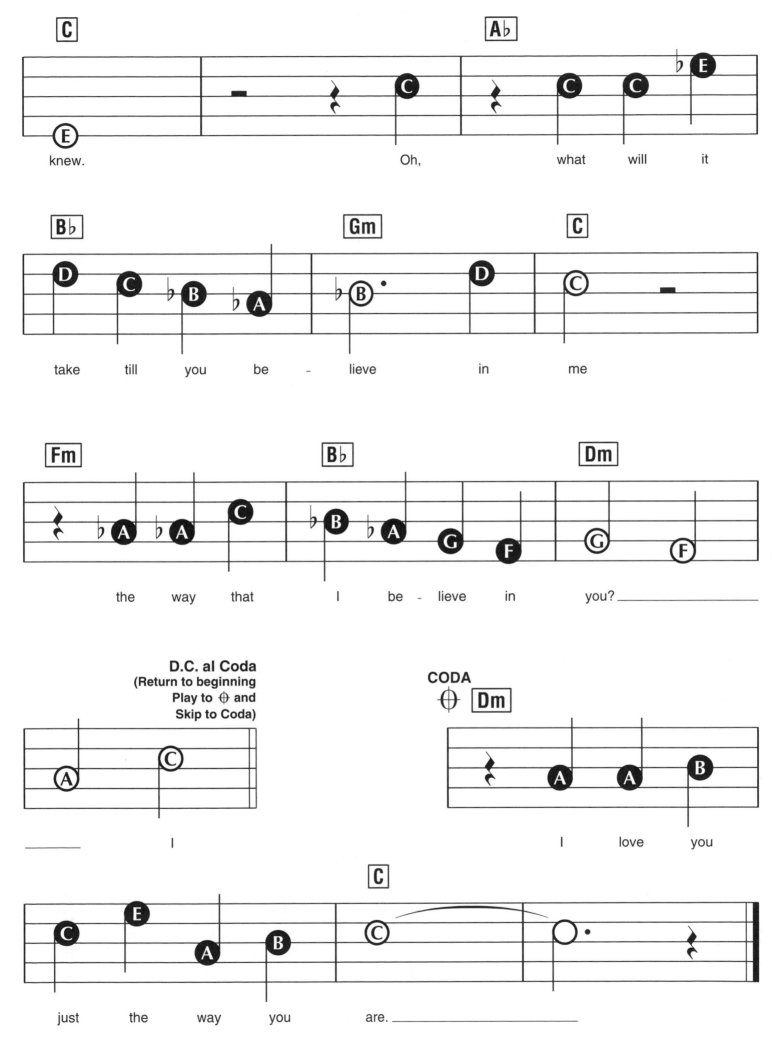

Keep On Loving You

Registration 4
Rhythm: 8-Beat or Rock

Words and Music by
Kevin Cronin

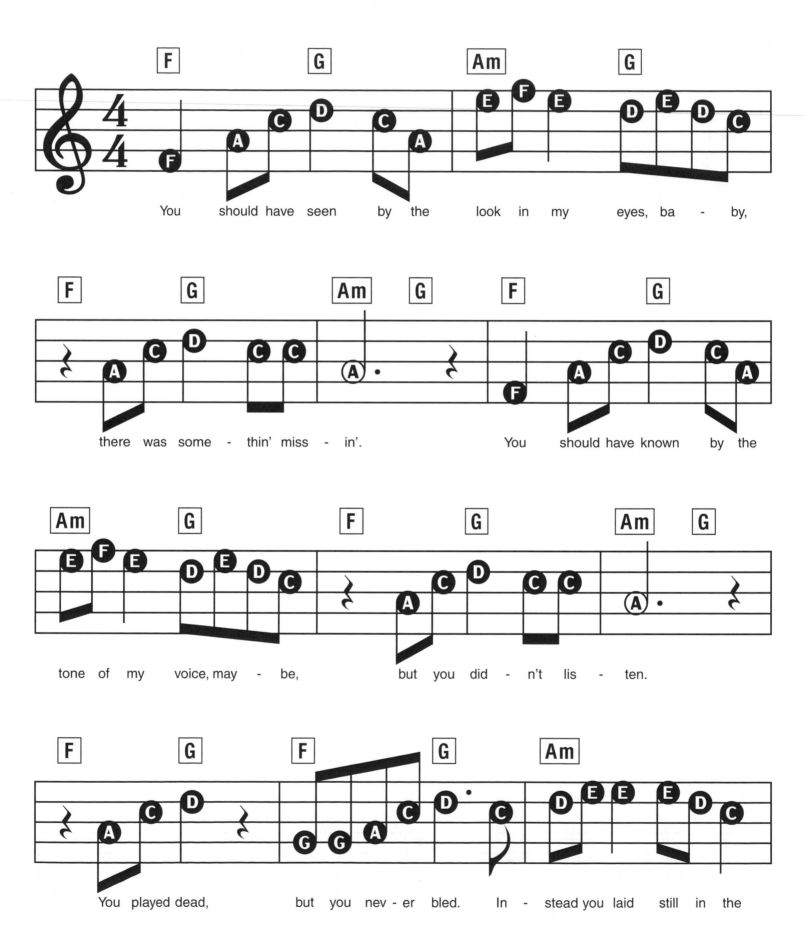

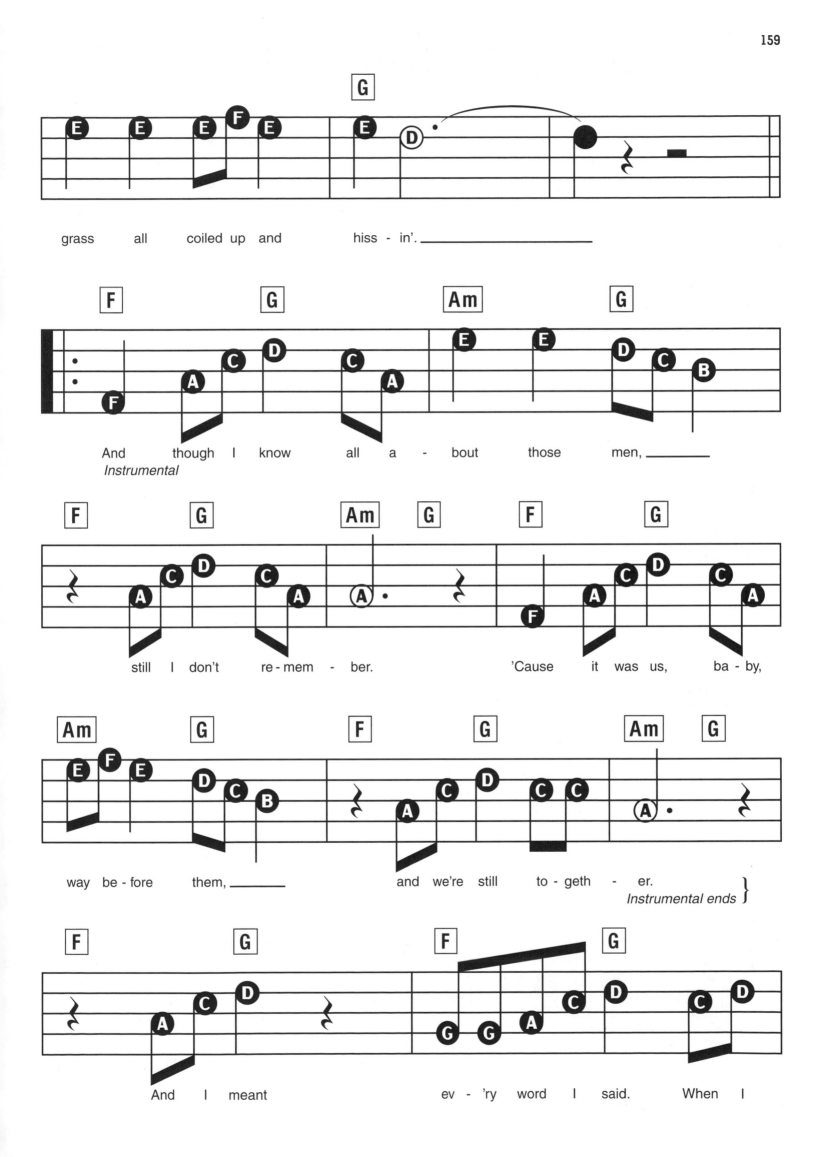

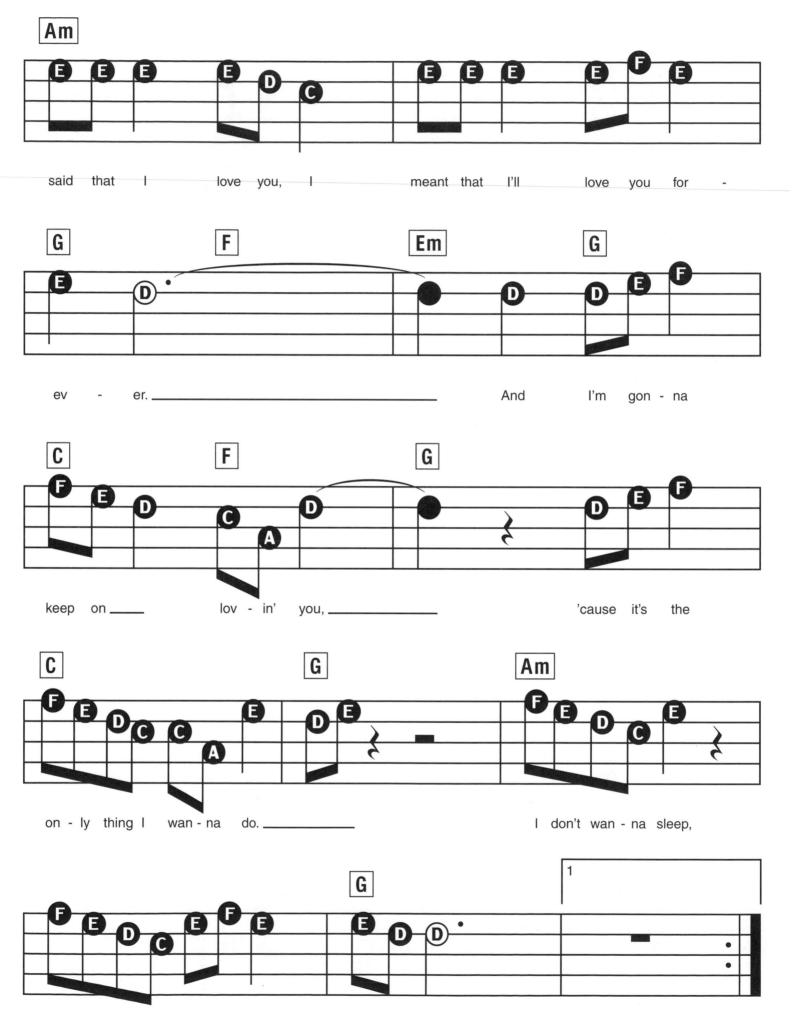

said that I love you, I meant that I'll love you for -

ev - er. And I'm gon - na

keep on lov - in' you, 'cause it's the

on - ly thing I wan - na do. I don't wan - na sleep,

I just wan - na keep on lov - in' you.

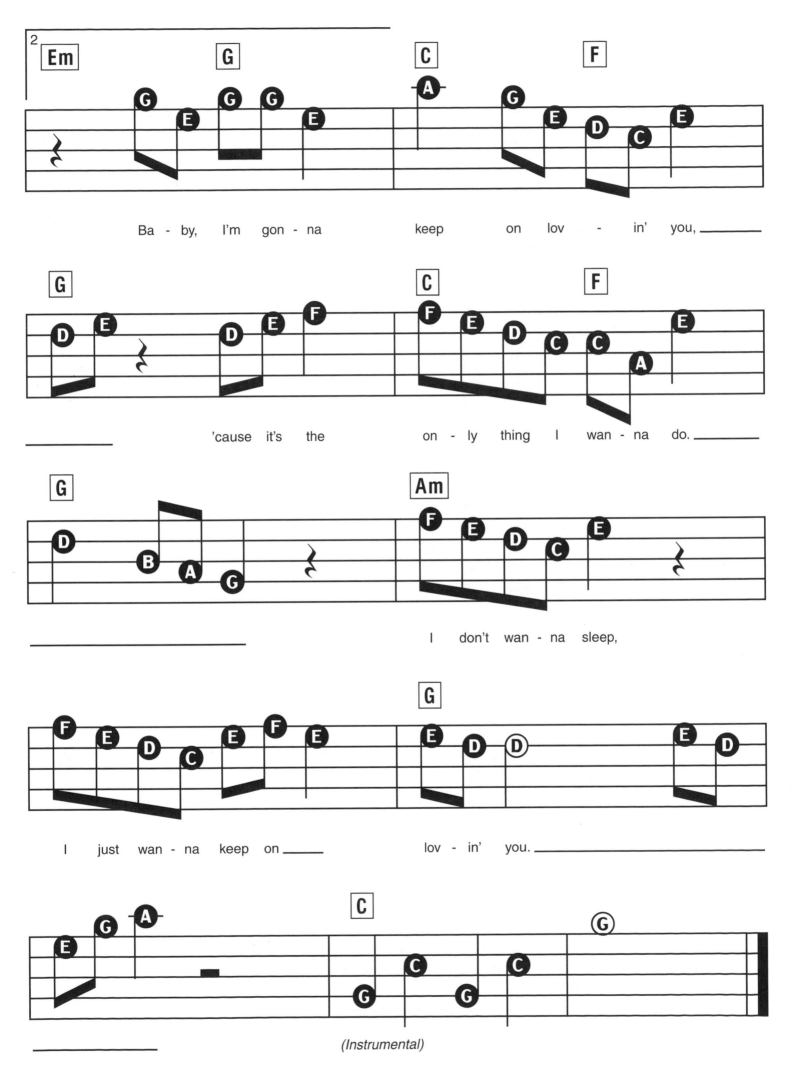

Lady

Registration 3
Rhythm: Ballad

Words and Music by
Lionel Richie

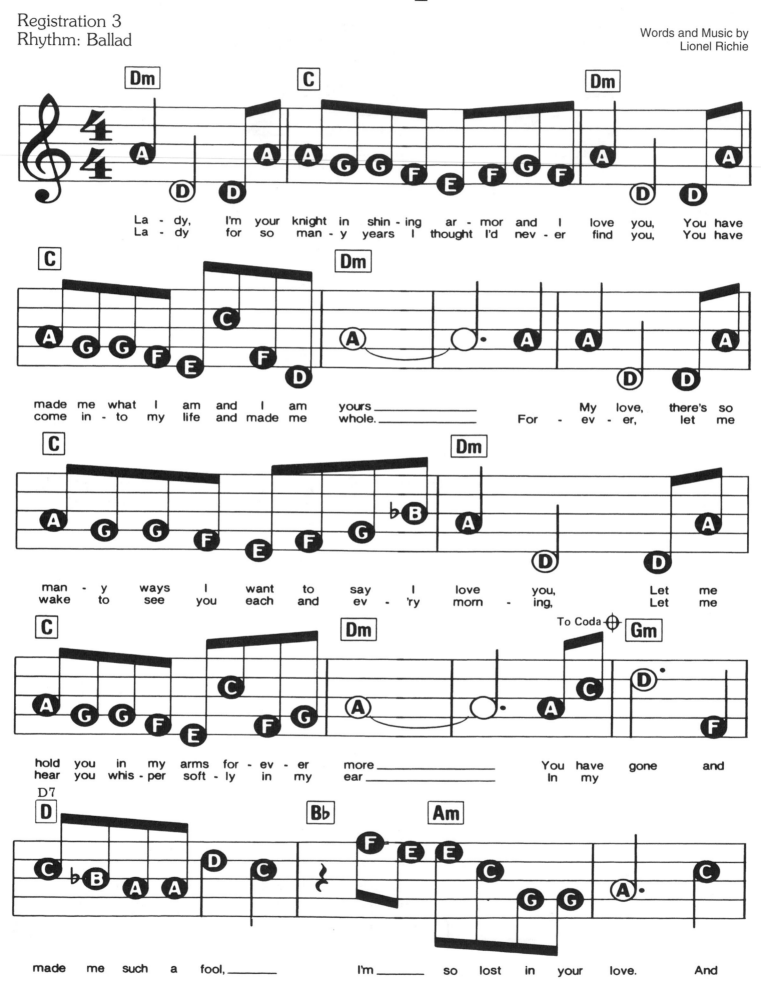

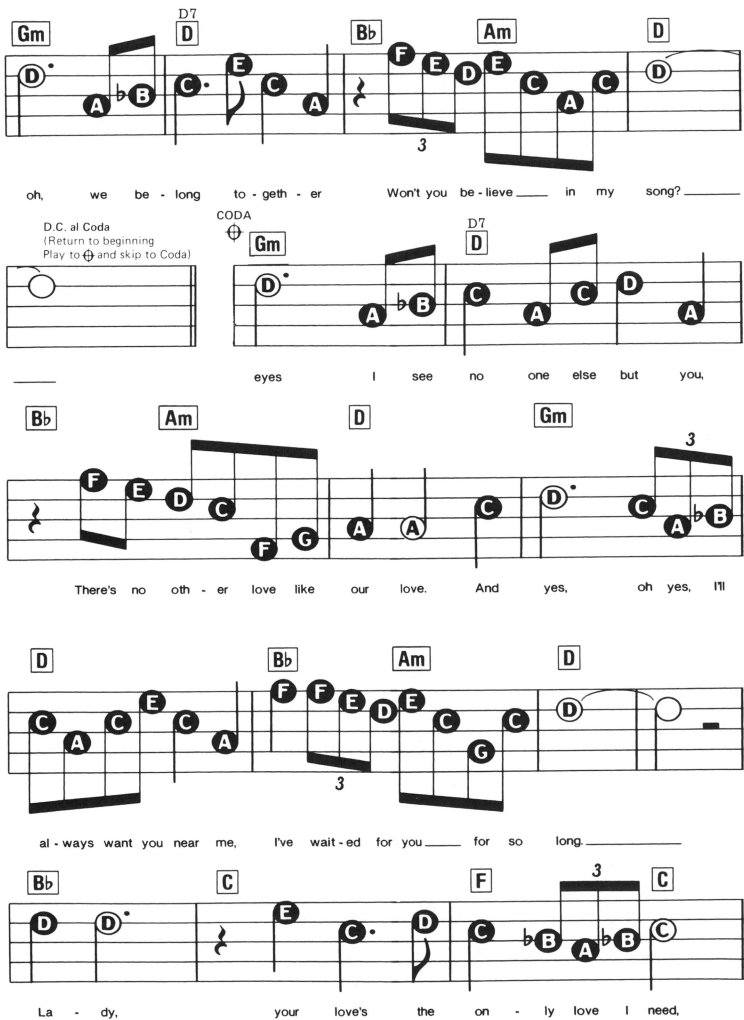

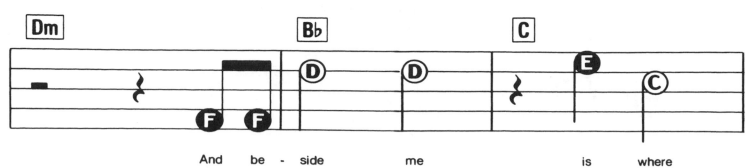

And be - side me is where

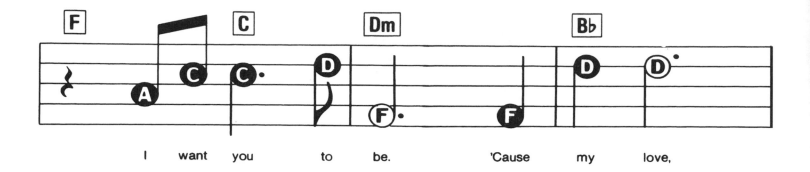

I want you to be. 'Cause my love,

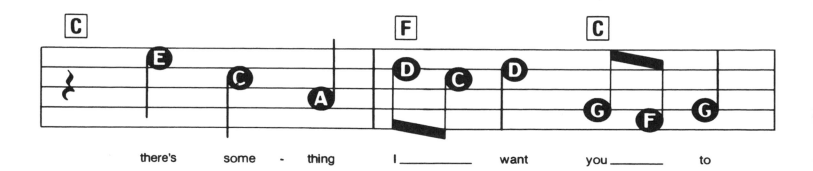

there's some - thing I _____ want you _____ to

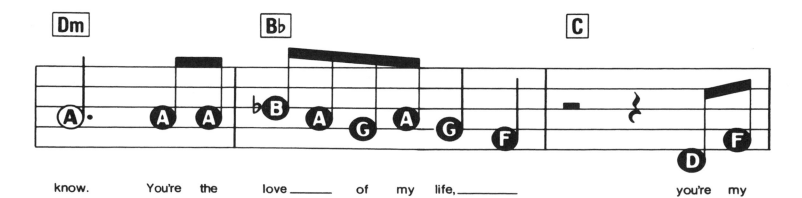

know. You're the love _____ of my life, _____ you're my

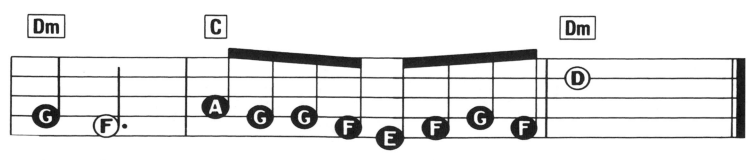

la - dy.

Lady in Red

Registration 1
Rhythm: 8-Beat or Pops

Words and Music by
Chris DeBurgh

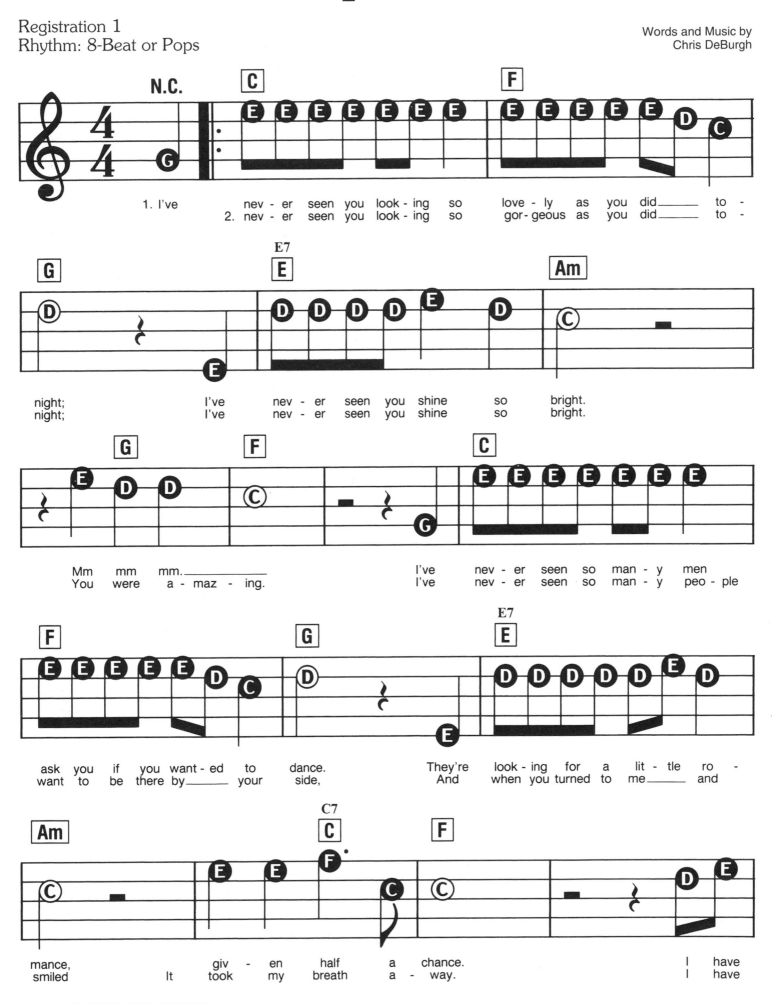

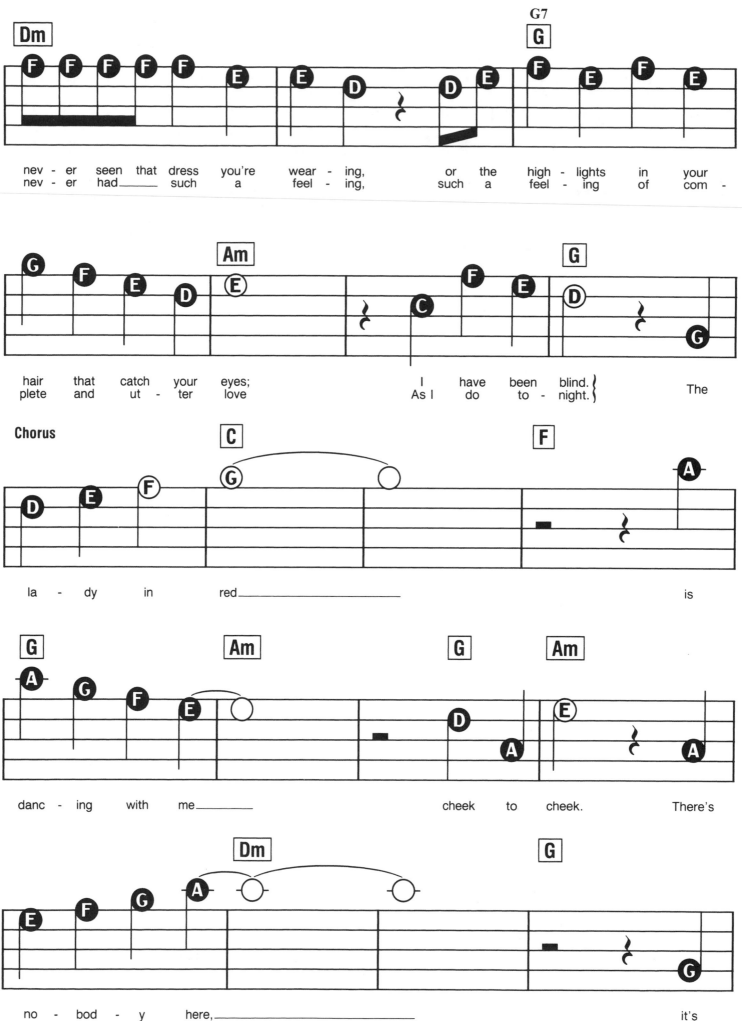

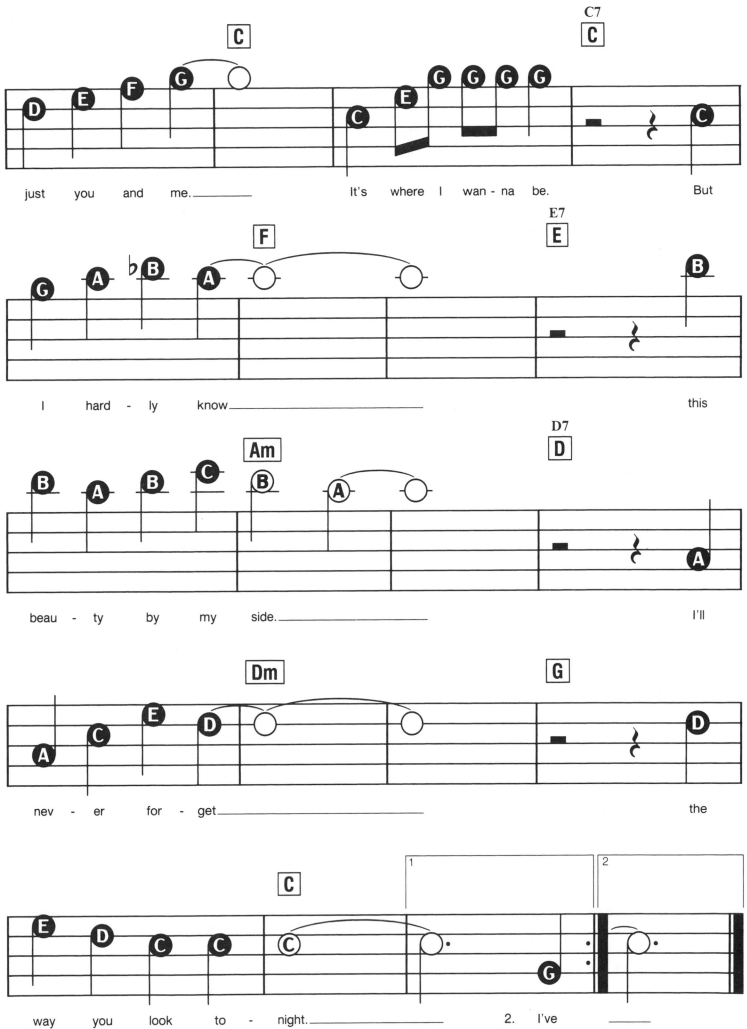

Let It Be Me
(Je t'appartiens)

Registration 8
Rhythm: Rock

English Words by Mann Curtis
French Words by Pierre DeLanoe
Music by Gilbert Becaud

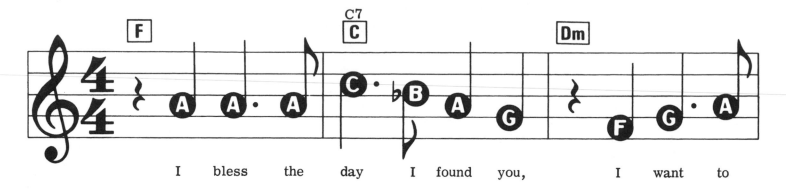

I bless the day I found you, I want to

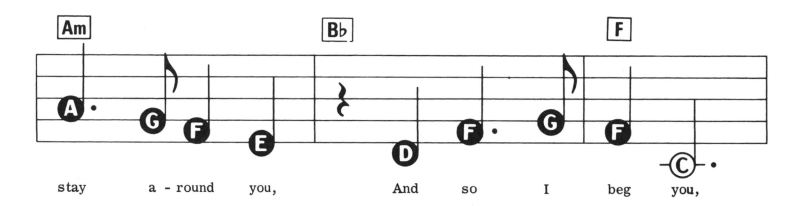

stay a - round you, And so I beg you,

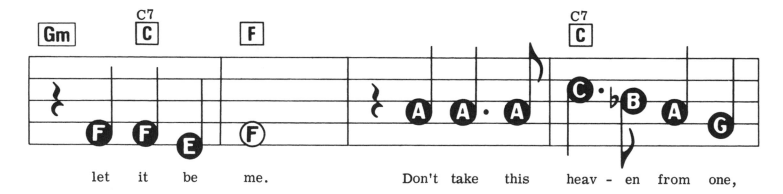

let it be me. Don't take this heav - en from one,

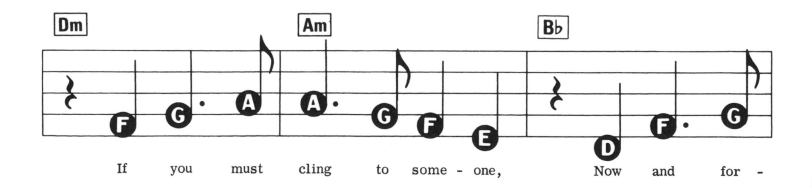

If you must cling to some - one, Now and for -

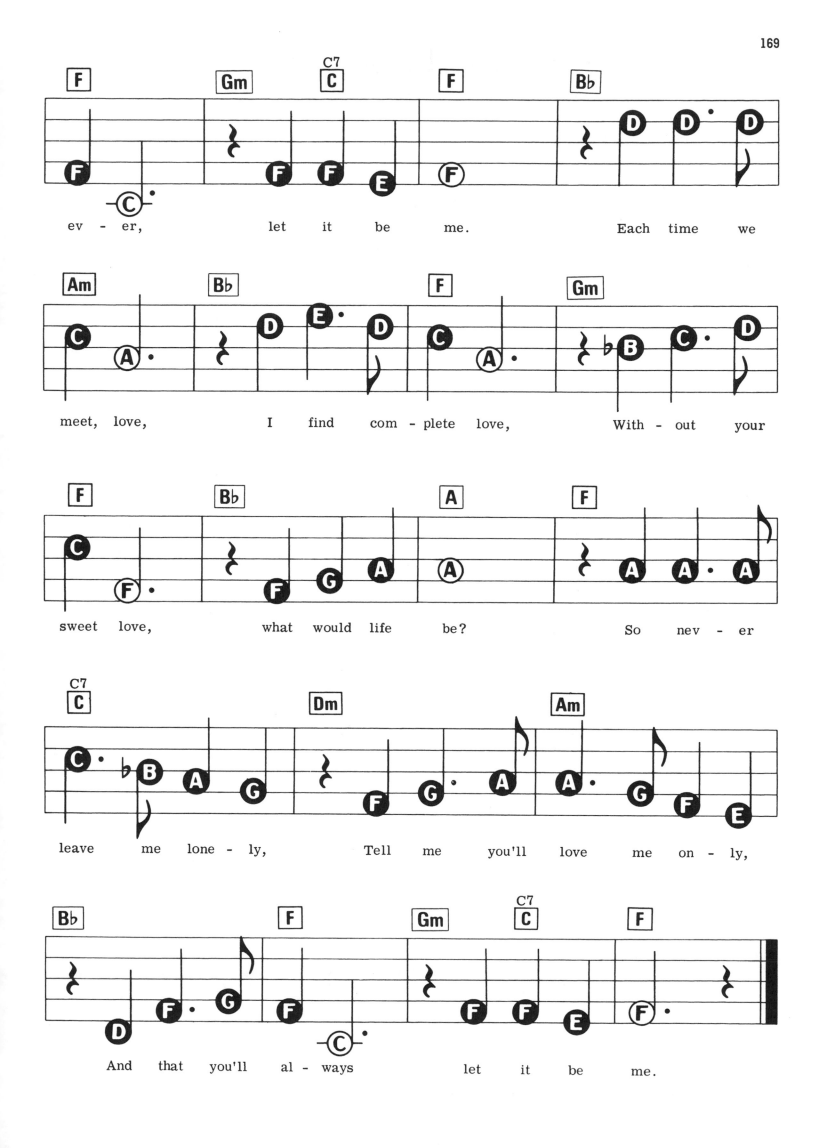

Let the River Run
Theme from the Motion Picture WORKING GIRL

Registration 3
Rhythm: Rock or 8-Beat

Words and Music by
Carly Simon

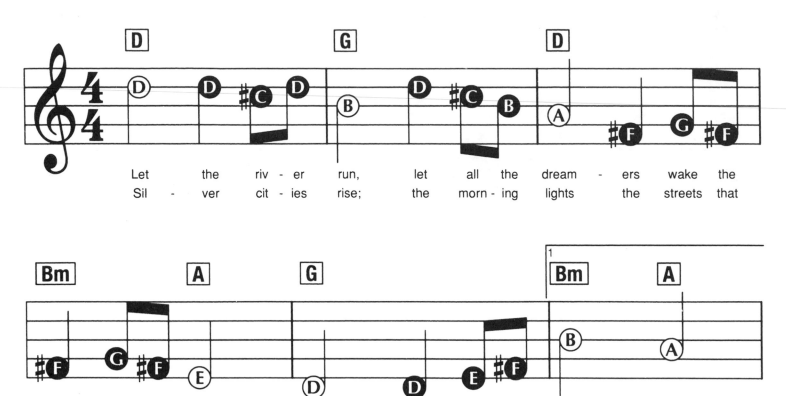

Let   the   riv - er   run,   let   all   the   dream - ers   wake the
Sil -   ver   cit - ies   rise;   the   morn - ing lights   the   streets that

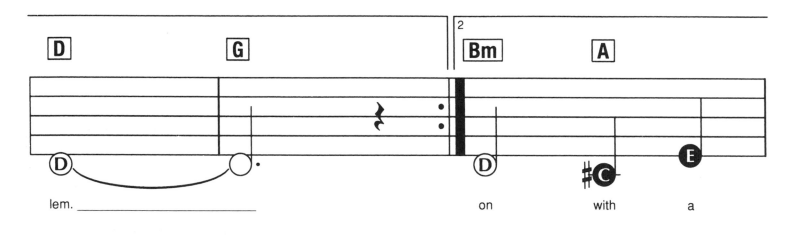

na - tion.   Come,   the   new   Je - ru - sa -
lead   them.   And si - rens   new   call them

lem. _____   on   with   a

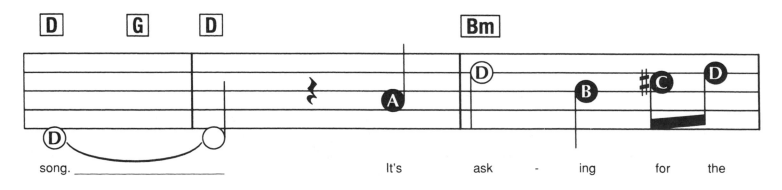

song. _____   It's   ask - ing   for   the

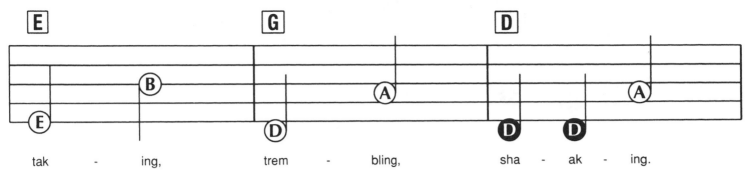

tak - ing, trem - bling, sha - ak - ing.

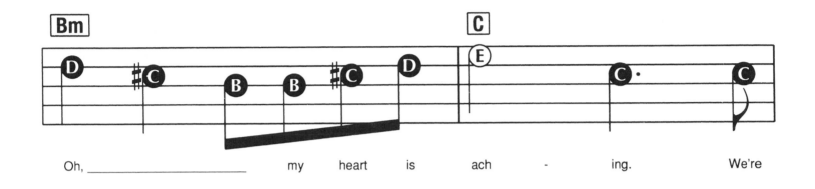

Oh, _____ my heart is ach - ing. We're

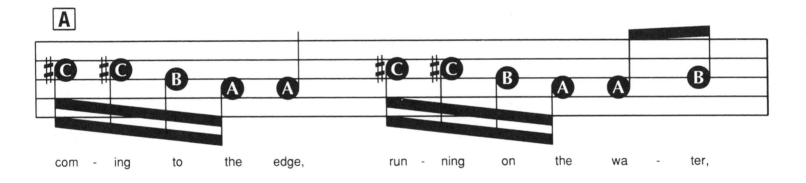

com - ing to the edge, run - ning on the wa - ter,

A7

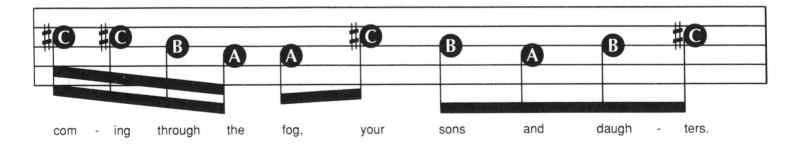

com - ing through the fog, your sons and daugh - ters.

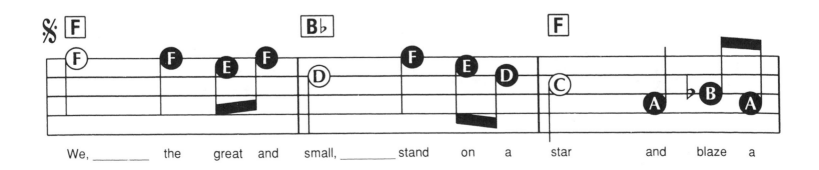

We, _____ the great and small, _____ stand on a star and blaze a

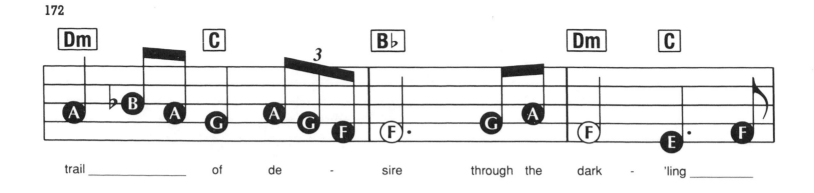

trail _____ of de - sire through the dark - 'ling _____

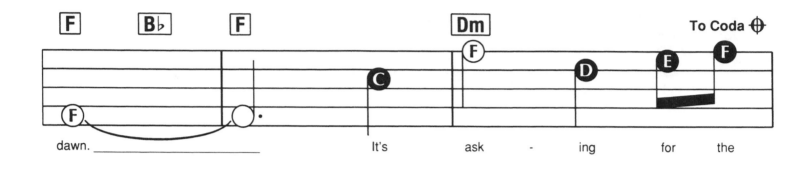

dawn. _____ It's ask - ing for the

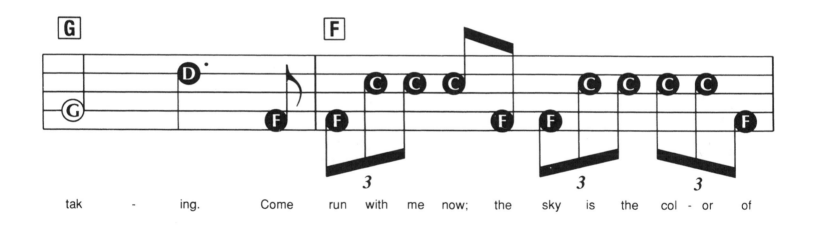

tak - ing. Come run with me now; the sky is the col - or of

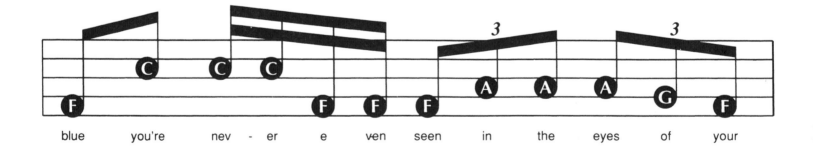

blue you're nev - er e - ven seen in the eyes of your

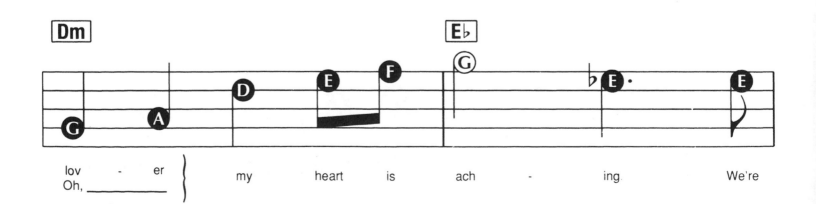

lov - er
Oh, _____ my heart is ach - ing. We're

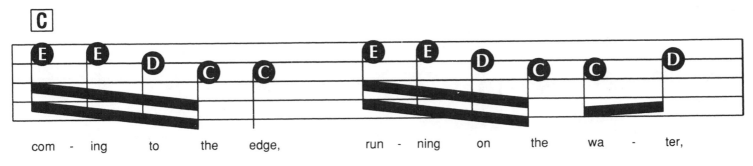

C

coming to the edge, runing on the water,

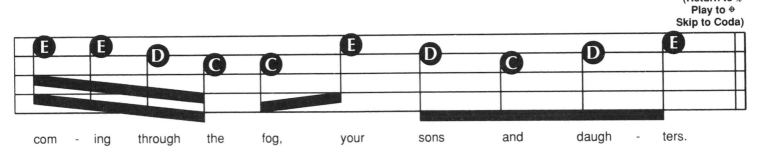

C7

D.S. al Coda
(Return to 𝄋
Play to ⊕
Skip to Coda)

coming through the fog, your sons and daughters.

CODA
⊕

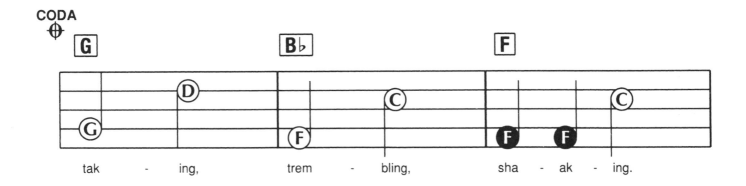

G **B♭** **F**

taking, trembling, shaaking.

Dm **E♭**

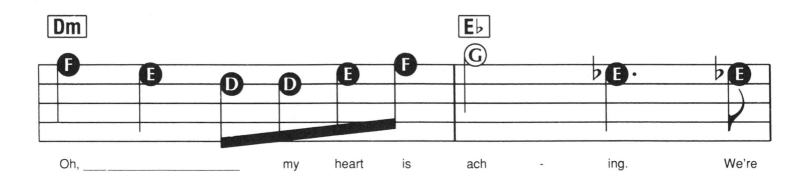

Oh, _____ my heart is aching. We're

C

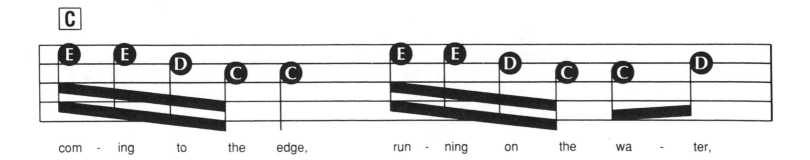

coming to the edge, runing on the water,

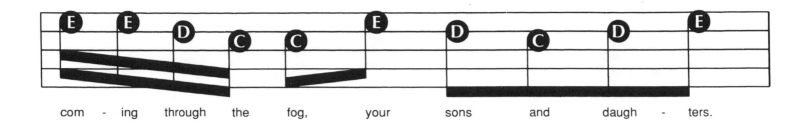

coming through the fog, your sons and daughters.

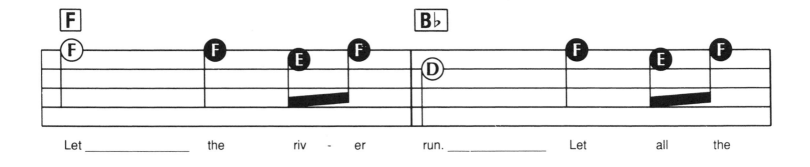

Let _____ the river run. _____ Let all the

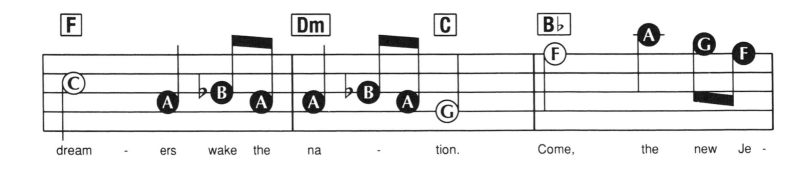

dreamers wake the nation. Come, the new Je-

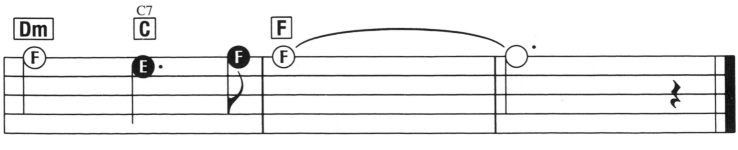

rusalem. _____

Let's Get It On

Registration 7
Rhythm: Rock or 8-Beat

Words and Music by Marvin Gaye
and Ed Townsend

I've been real - ly try - in', ba - by,

try - in' to hold _____ back this feel - in' for so _____ long. _____

And if you feel like I feel, _____ ba - by,

then come on, oh, come _____ on. Ooh, let's get it

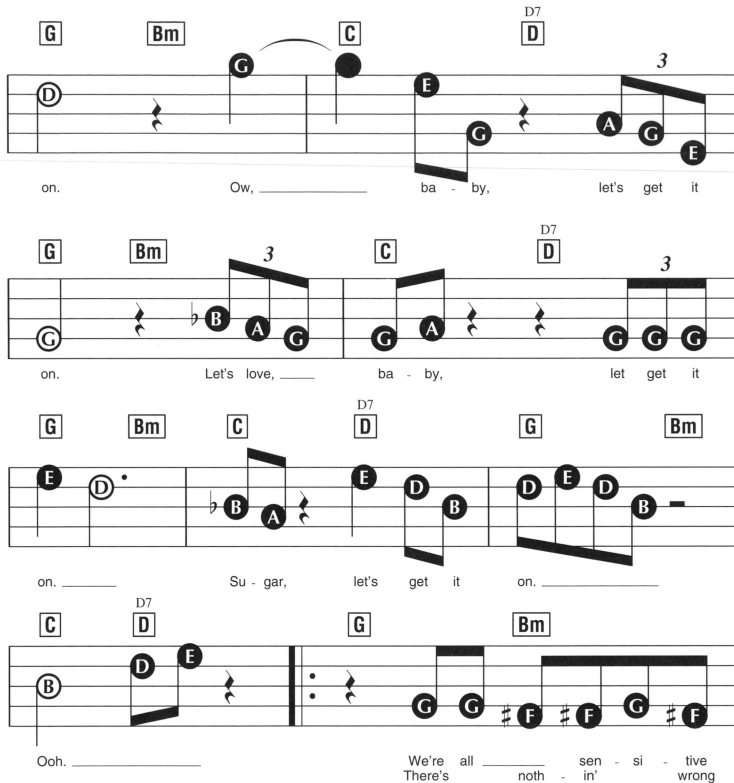

on.   Ow, _____ ba - by,   let's get it

on.   Let's love, ____ ba - by,   let get it

on. _____   Su - gar, let's get it   on. _____

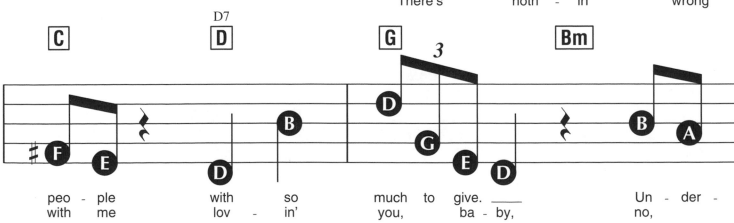

Ooh. _____   We're all _____ sen - si - tive
                          There's ____ noth - in' wrong

peo - ple   with so   much to give. ____   Un - der -
with me   lov - in'   you, ba - by,   no,

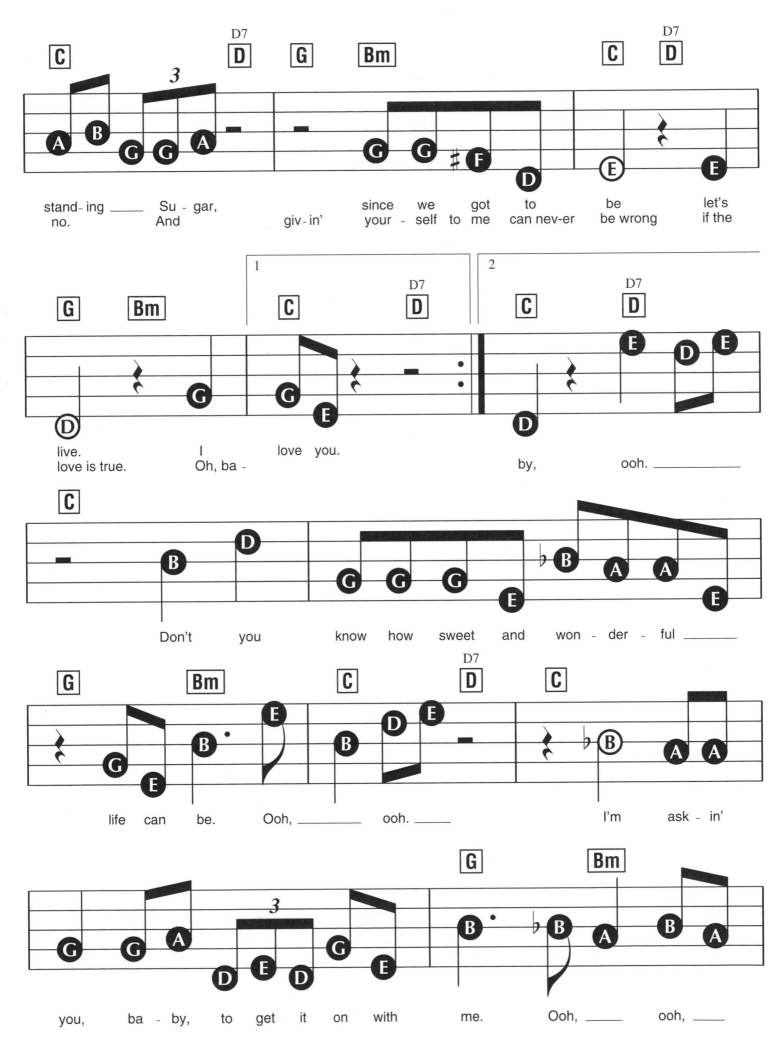

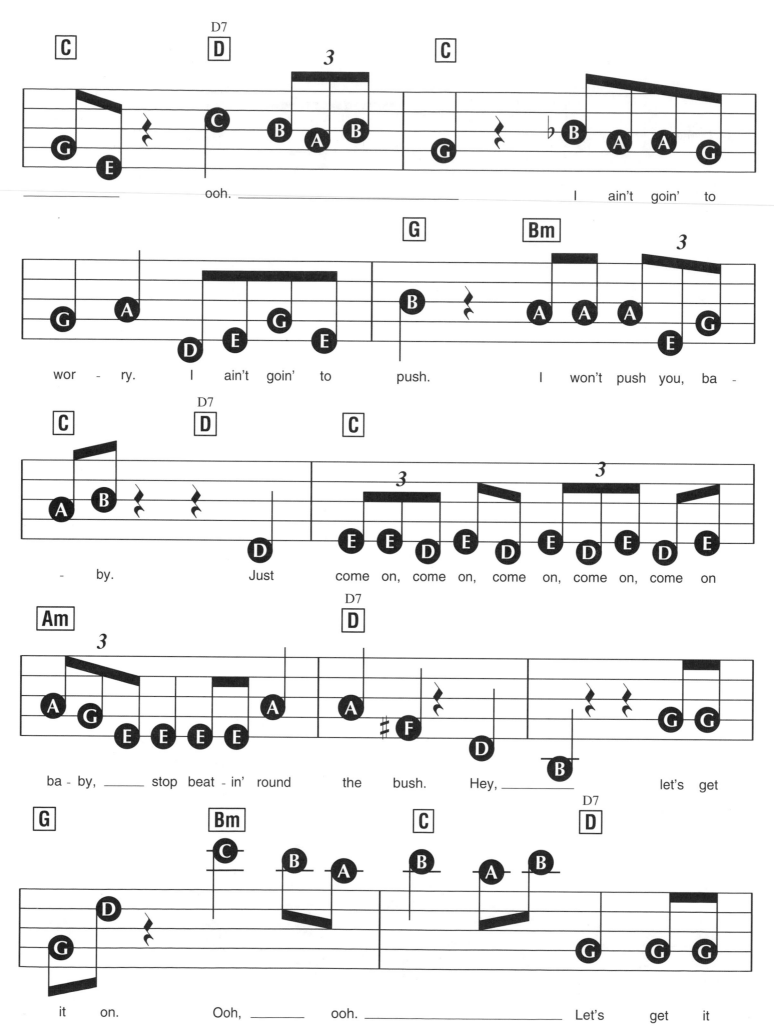

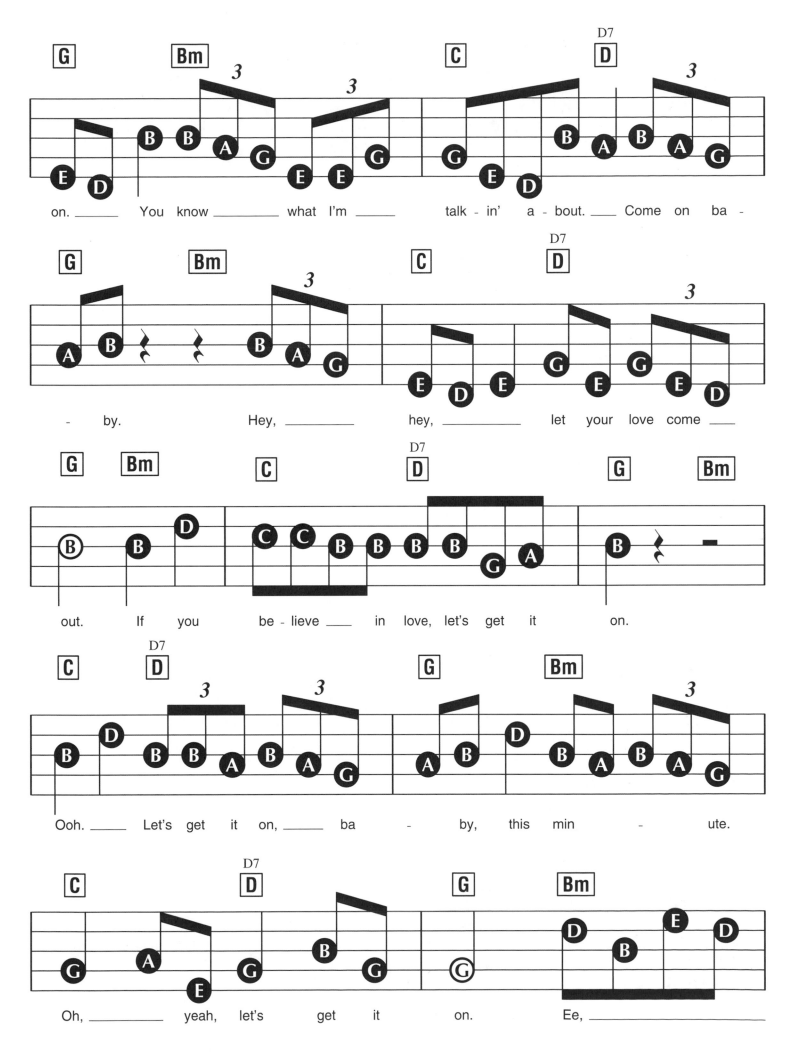

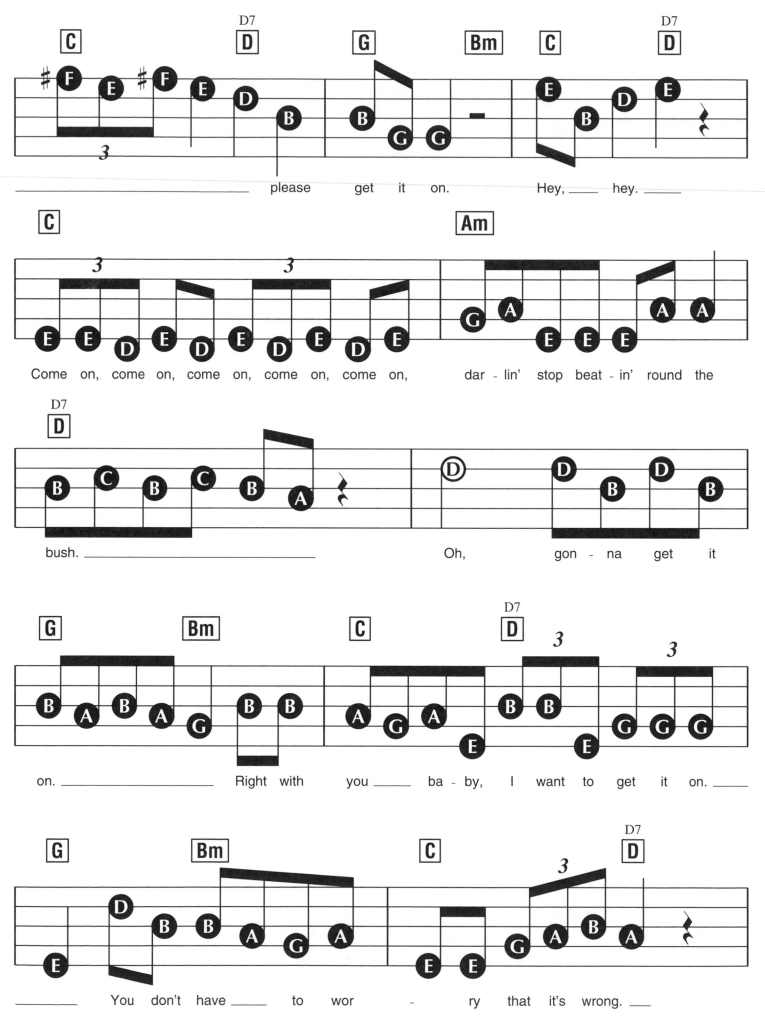

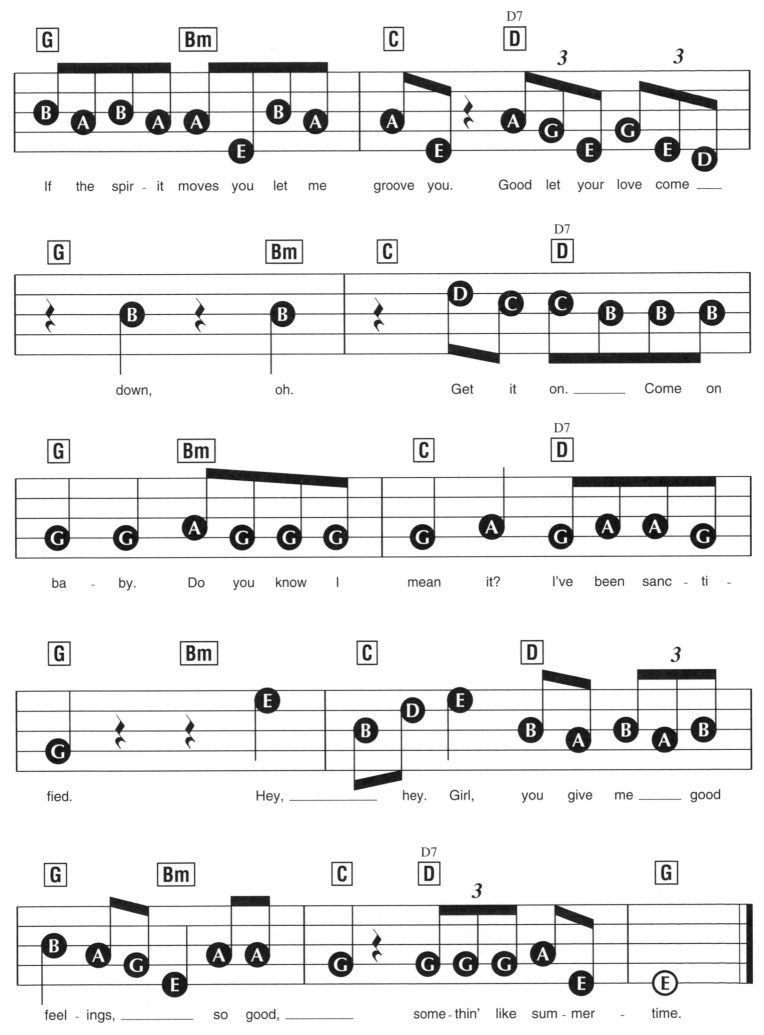

Let's Stay Together

Registration 7
Rhythm: 4/4 Ballad or R&B

Words and Music by Al Green,
Willie Mitchell and Al Jackson, Jr.

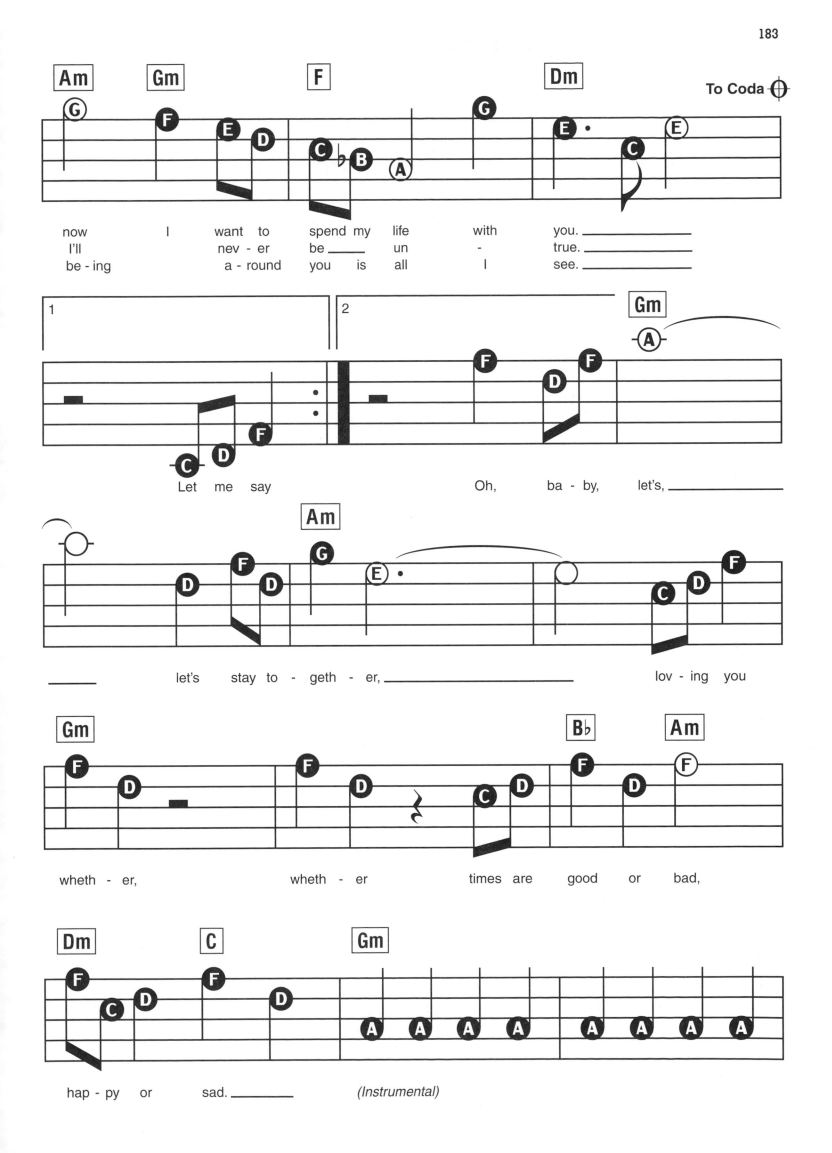

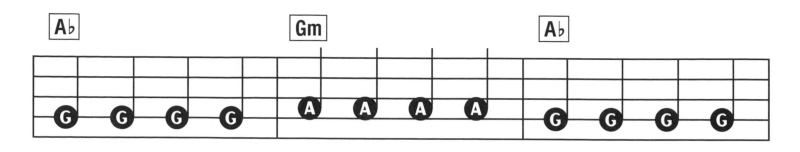

D.C. al Coda
(Return to beginning
Play to ⊕ and
Skip to Coda)

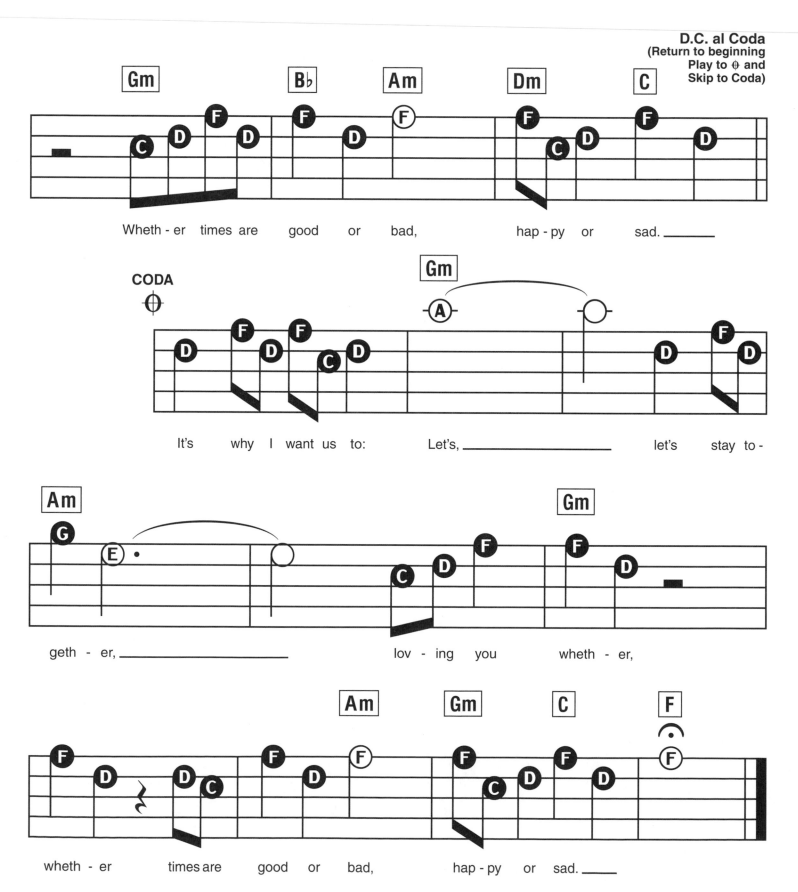

Wheth - er times are good or bad, hap - py or sad. _____

CODA

It's why I want us to: Let's, _____ let's stay to -

geth - er, _____ lov - ing you wheth - er,

wheth - er times are good or bad, hap - py or sad. _____

Love Will Keep Us Together

Registration 8
Rhythm: Rock

Words and Music by Neil Sedaka
and Howard Greenfield

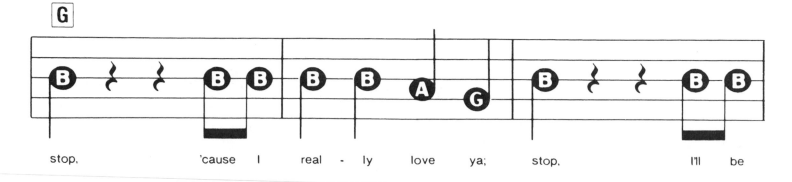

stop,   'cause I   real - ly   love   ya;   stop,   I'll be

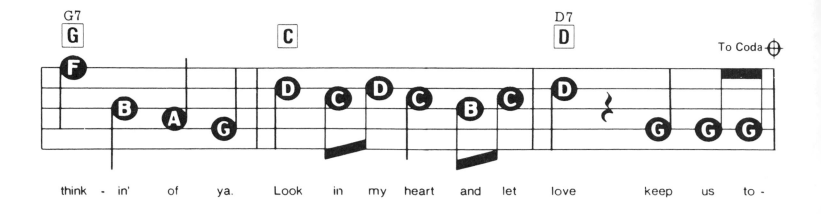

think - in'   of   ya.   Look   in   my   heart   and   let   love   keep   us   to -

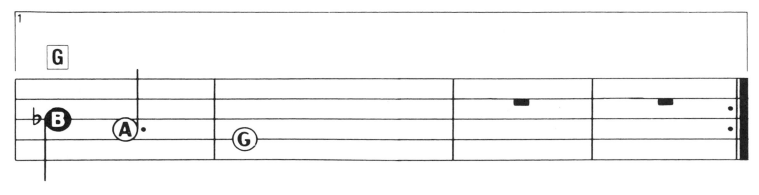

geth -   er.

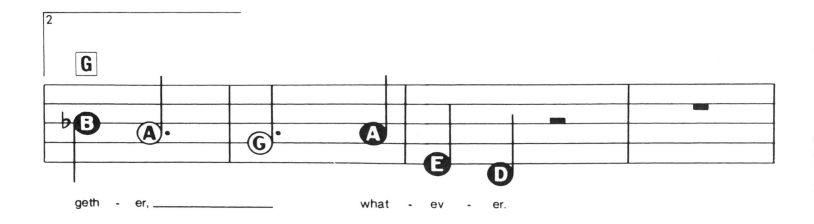

geth - er, _____   what - ev - er.

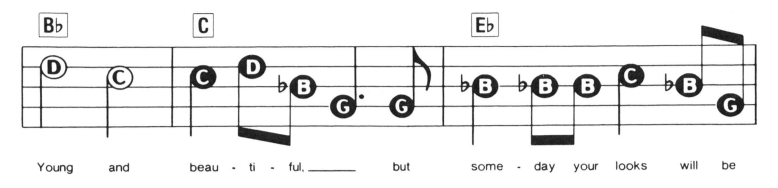

Young and beau - ti - ful, _____ but some - day your looks will be

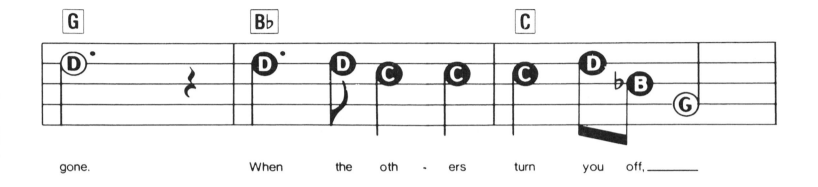

gone. When the oth - ers turn you off, _____

D.C. al Coda
(Return to beginning
Play to ⊕ and skip to Coda)

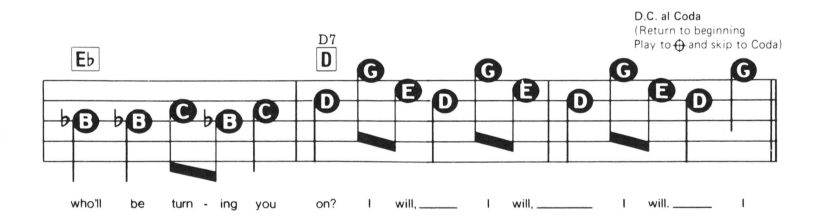

who'll be turn - ing you on? I will, _____ I will, _____ I will. _____ I

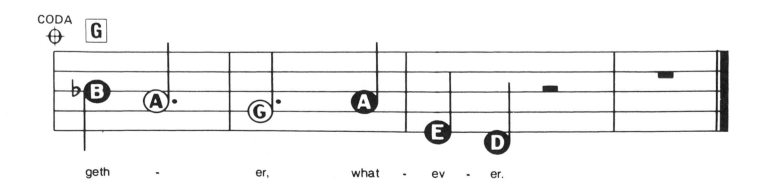

geth - er, what - ev - er.

Longer

Registration 4
Rhythm: Rock or 8-Beat

Words and Music by
Dan Fogelberg

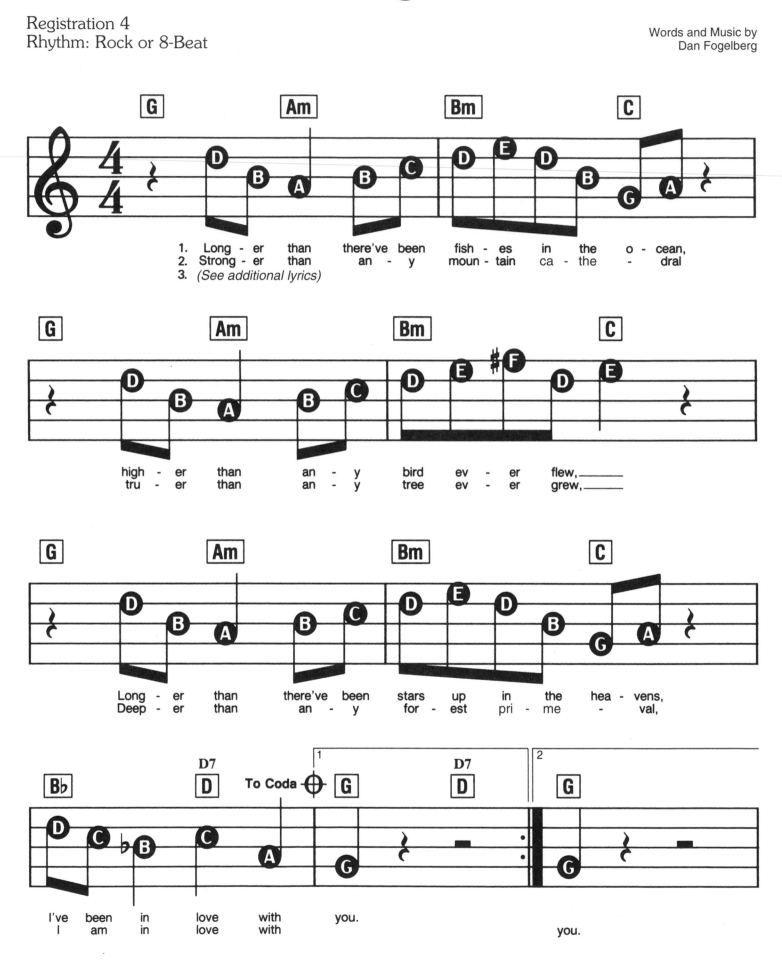

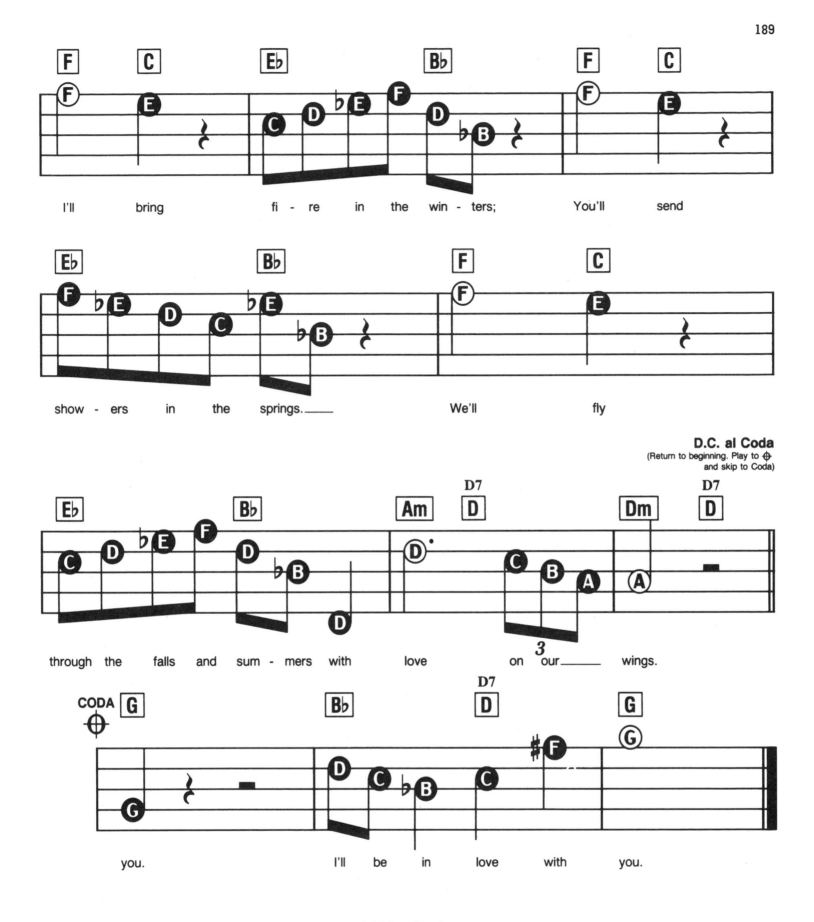

Additional Lyrics

3. Through the years as the fire starts to mellow,
Burning lines in the book of our lives.
Though the binding cracks and the pages start to yellow,
I'll be in love with you.

Love Me Tender

Registration 9
Rhythm: Slow Rock or Rock

Words and Music by Elvis Presley
and Vera Matson

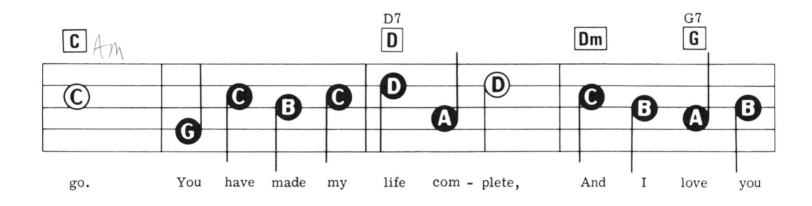

Love me ten - der, love me sweet; Nev - er let me

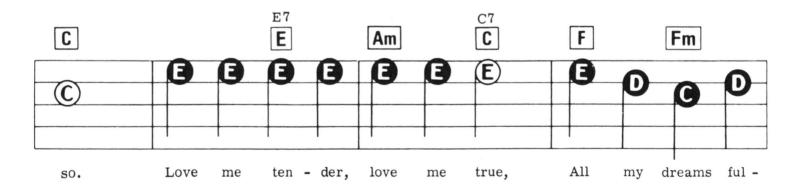

go. You have made my life com - plete, And I love you

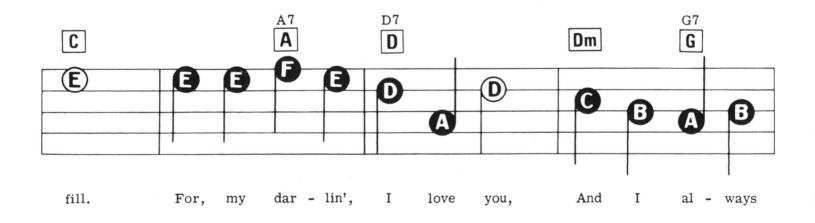

so. Love me ten - der, love me true, All my dreams ful -

fill. For, my dar - lin', I love you, And I al - ways

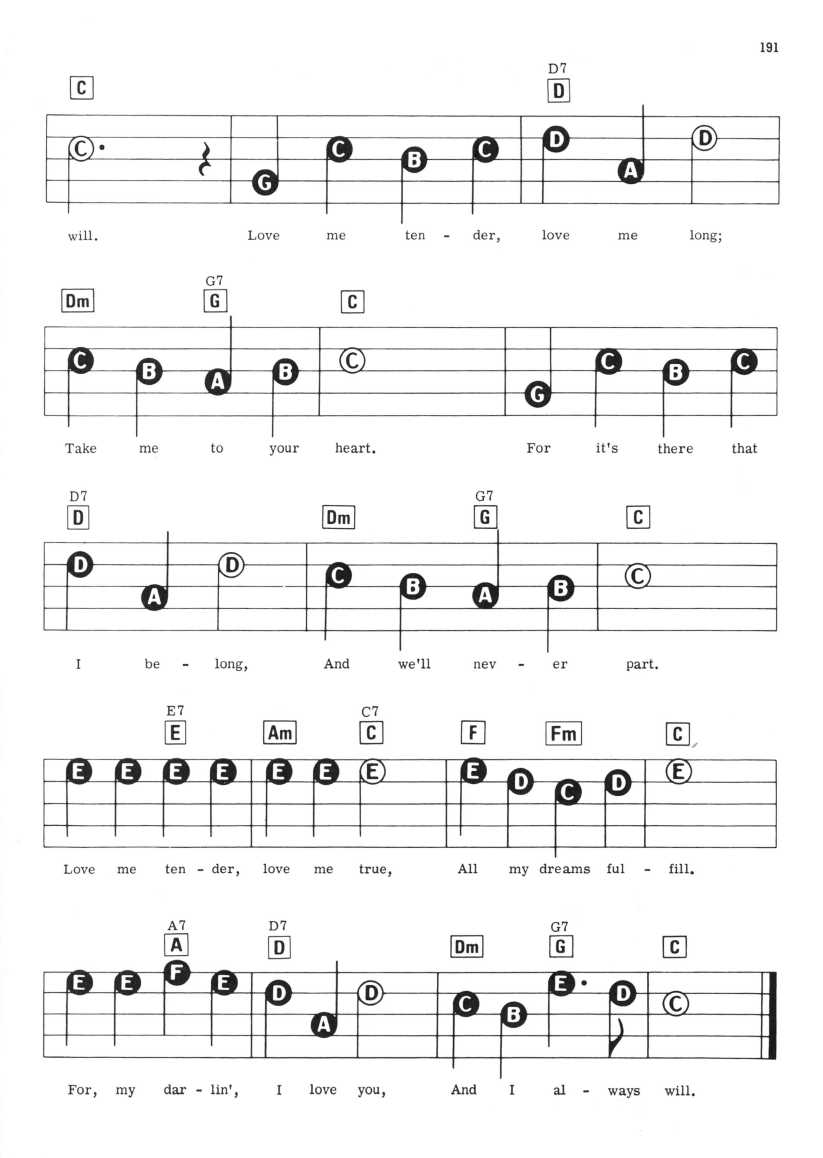

Love Takes Time

Registration 10
Rhythm: 8-Beat or Pops

Words and Music by Mariah Carey
and Ben Margulies

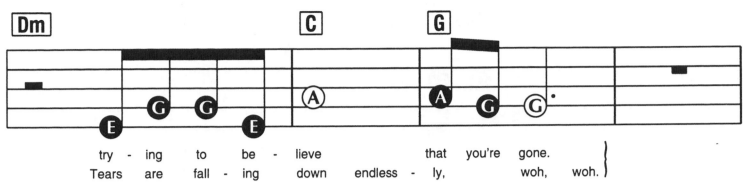

try - ing   to   be - lieve   that   you're   gone.
Tears   are   fall - ing   down   endless - ly,   woh,   woh.

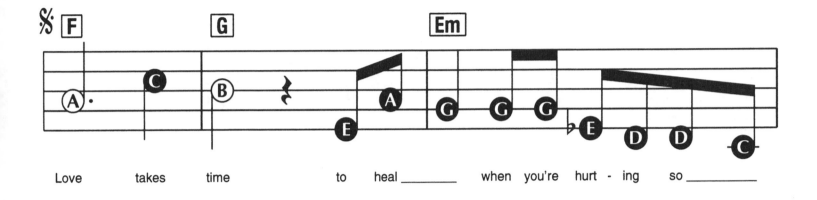

Love   takes   time   to   heal _____   when   you're   hurt - ing   so _____

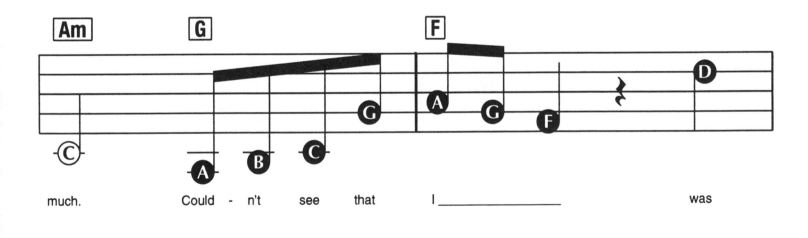

much.   Could - n't   see   that   I _____   was

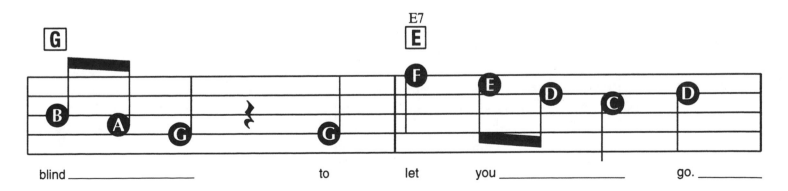

blind _____   to   let   you _____   go. _____

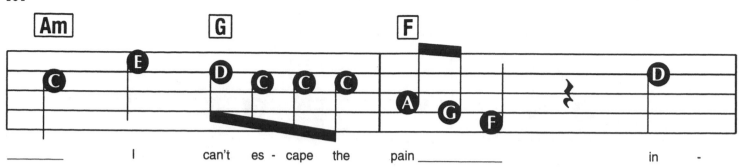

I can't es - cape the pain

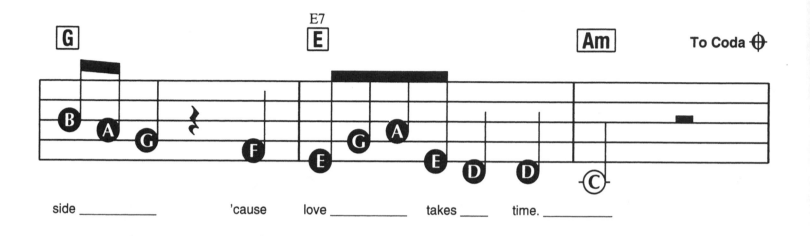

side 'cause love takes time.

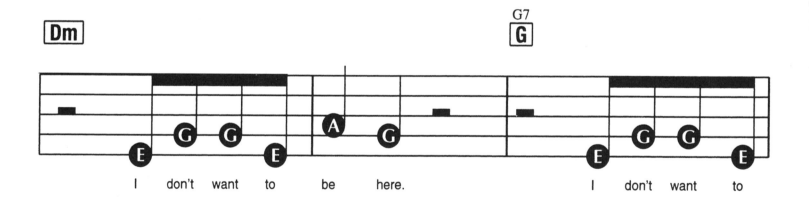

I don't want to be here. I don't want to

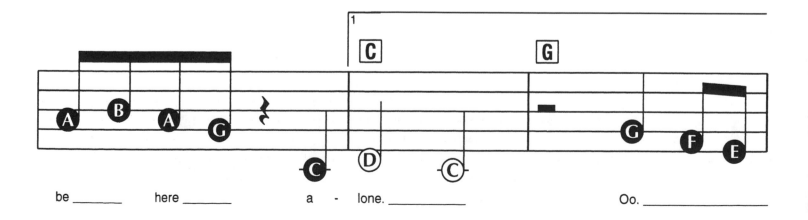

be here a - lone. Oo.

195

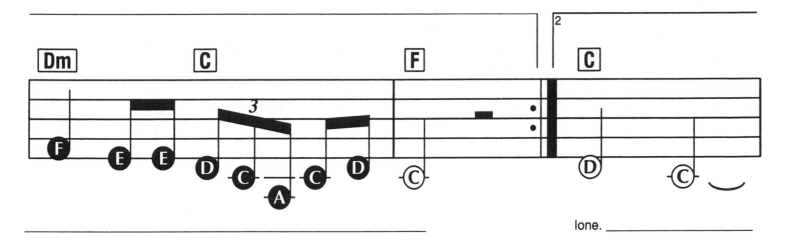

lone.

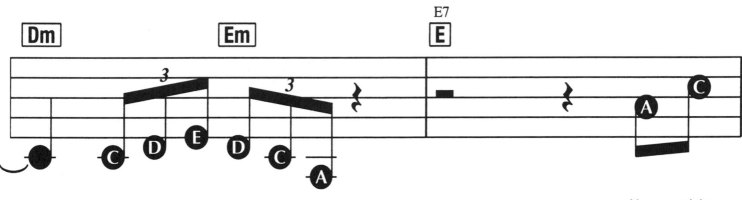

You   might

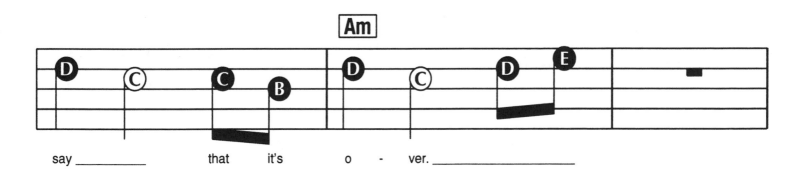

say _____   that   it's   o - ver. _____

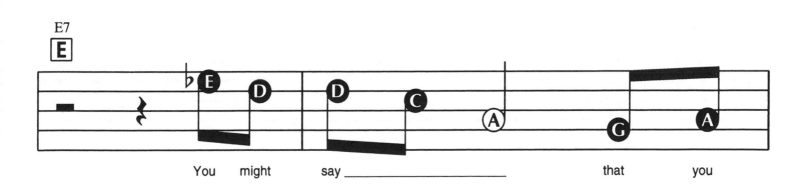

You   might   say _____   that   you

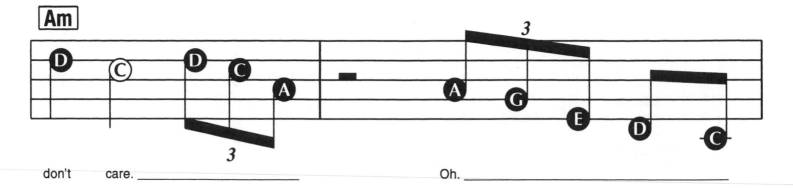

Am

don't   care. _____   Oh. _____

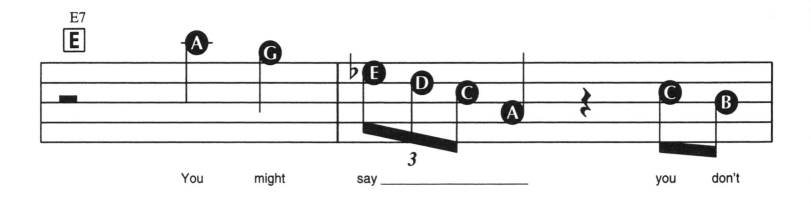

E7

E

You   might   say _____   you   don't

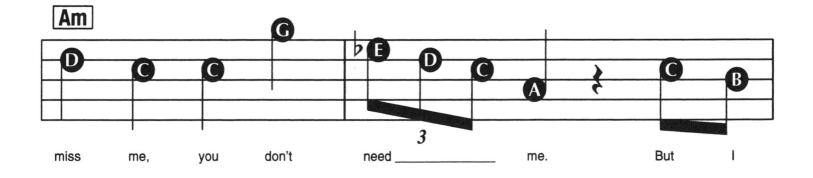

Am

miss   me,   you   don't   need _____   me.   But   I

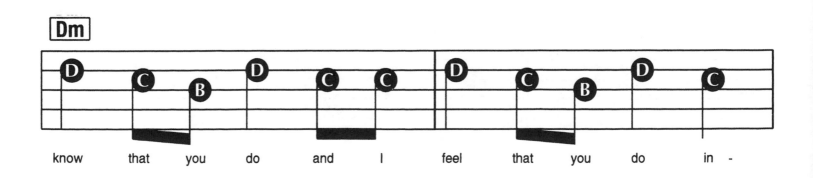

Dm

know   that   you   do   and   I   feel   that   you   do   in -

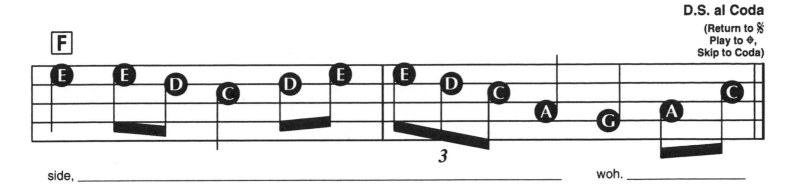

side, _____ woh. _____

CODA
⊕

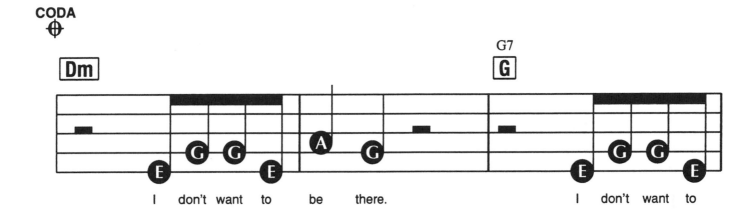

I don't want to be there. I don't want to

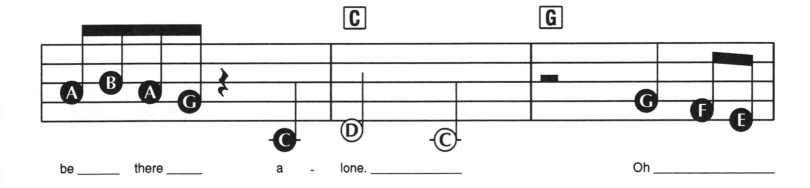

be _____ there _____ a - lone. _____ Oh _____

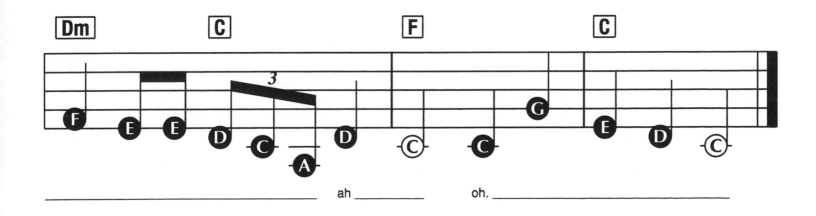

_____ ah _____ oh. _____

Loving You

Registration 4
Rhythm: Ballad or Fox Trot

Words and Music by Jerry Leiber
and Mike Stoller

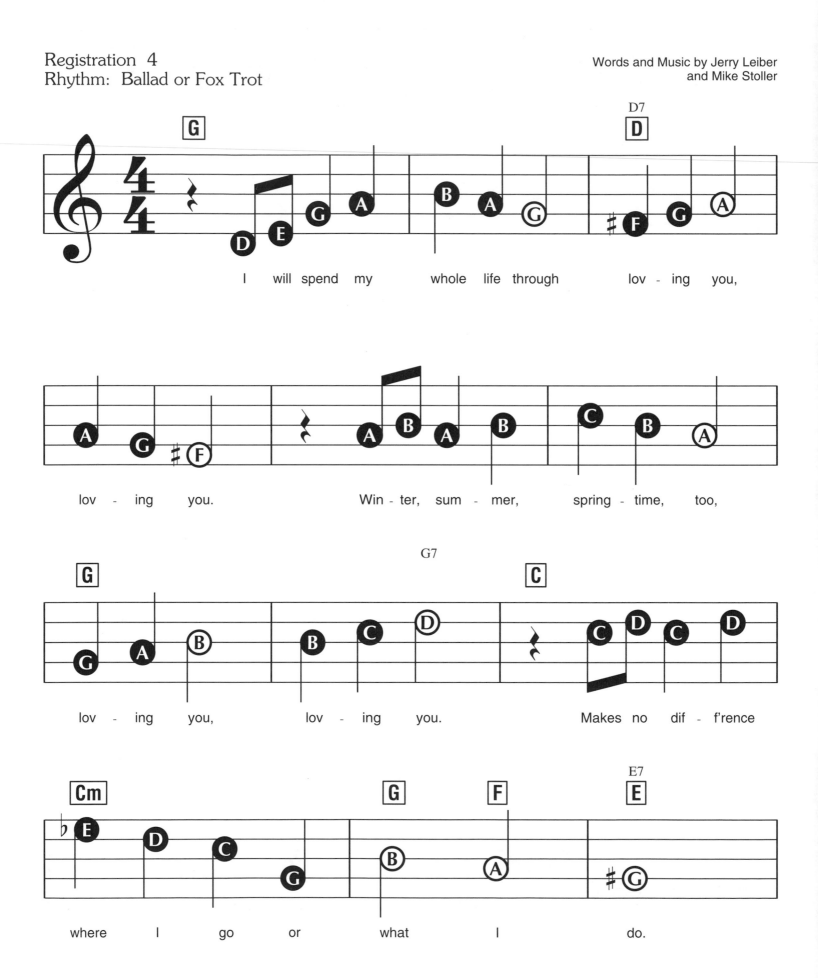

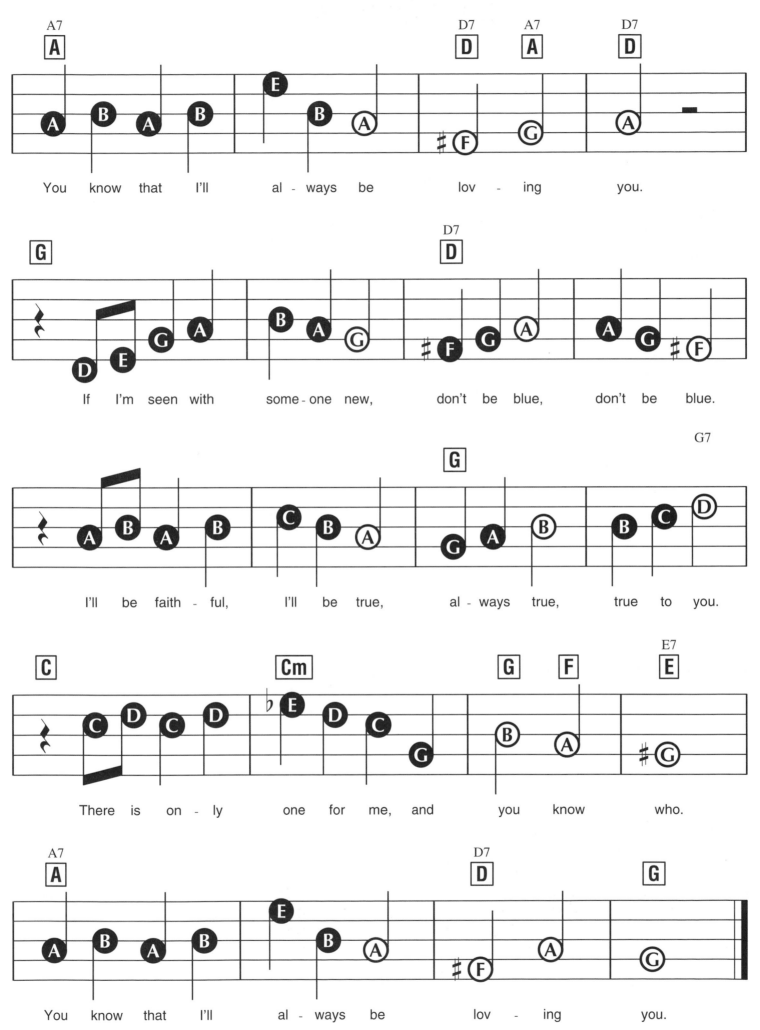

Mandy

Registration 1
Rhythm: Rock

Words and Music by Scott English
and Richard Kerr

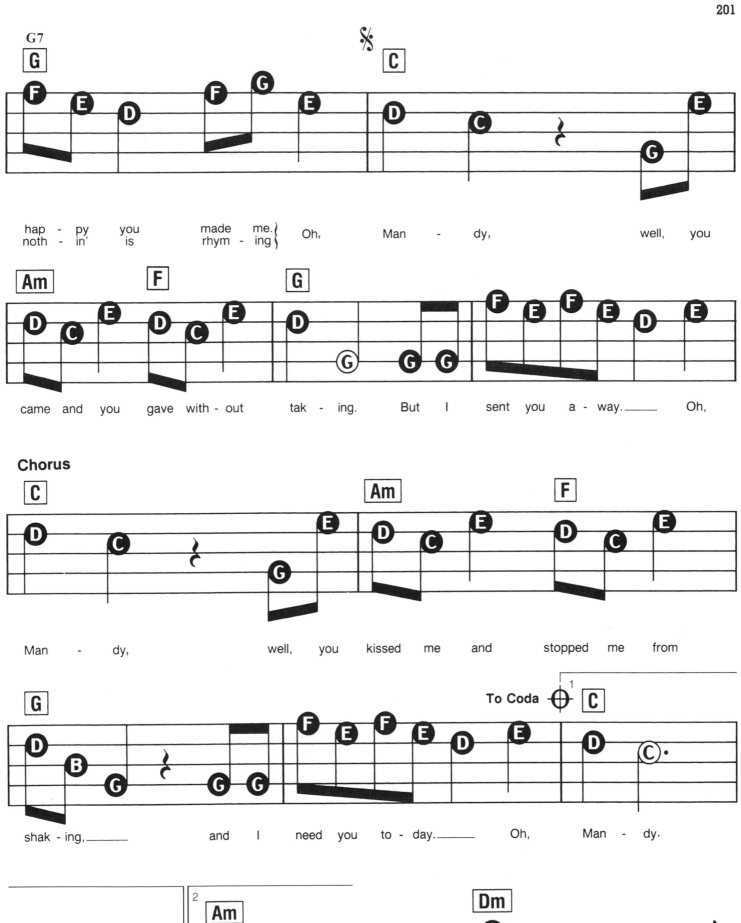

hap - py you made me.
noth - in' is rhym - ing} Oh, Man - dy, well, you

came and you gave with - out tak - ing. But I sent you a - way.___ Oh,

Chorus

Man - dy, well, you kissed me and stopped me from

To Coda

shak - ing,___ and I need you to - day.___ Oh, Man - dy.

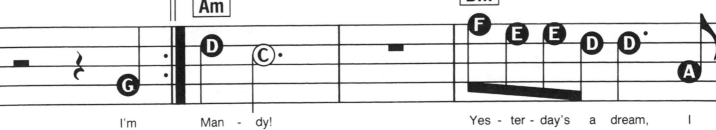

I'm Man - dy!

Yes - ter - day's a dream, I

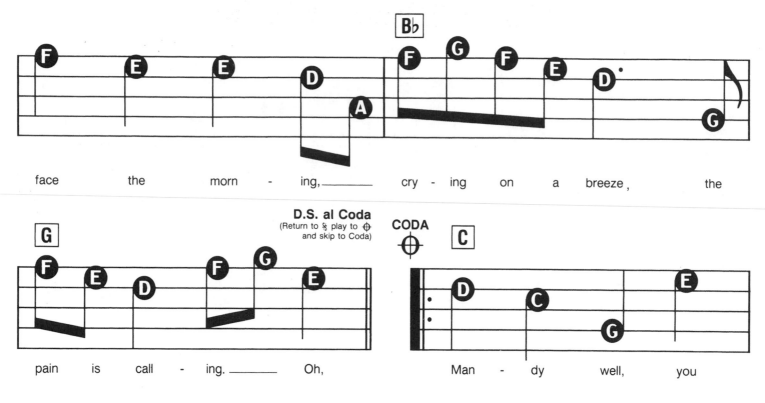

face the morn - ing, _____ cry - ing on a breeze, the

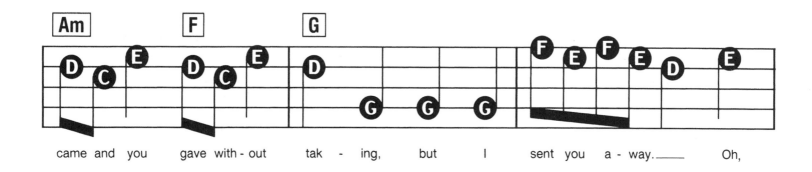

D.S. al Coda
(Return to % and play to ⊕
and skip to Coda)

CODA

pain is call - ing. _____ Oh, Man - dy well, you

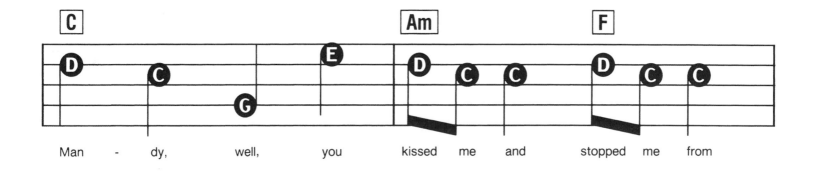

came and you gave with - out tak - ing, but I sent you a - way.___ Oh,

Man - dy, well, you kissed me and stopped me from

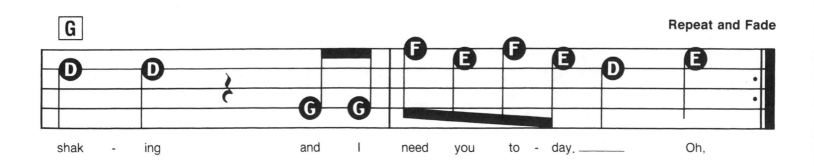

Repeat and Fade

shak - ing and I need you to - day. _____ Oh,

More Than Words

Registration 2
Rhythm: Reggae or Rock

Words and Music by Nuno Bettencourt
and Gary Cherone

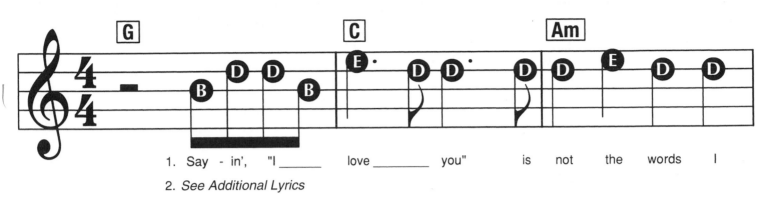

1. Say - in', "I _____ love _____ you" is not the words I
2. *See Additional Lyrics*

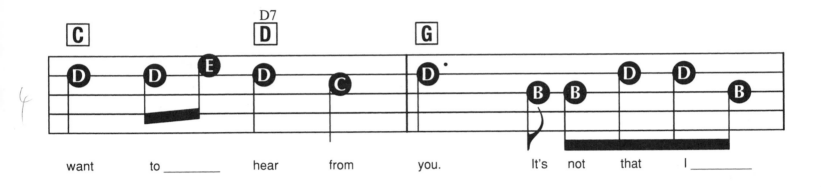

want to _____ hear from you. It's not that I _____

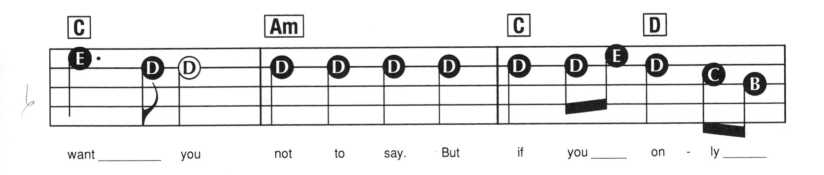

want _____ you not to say. But if you _____ on - ly _____

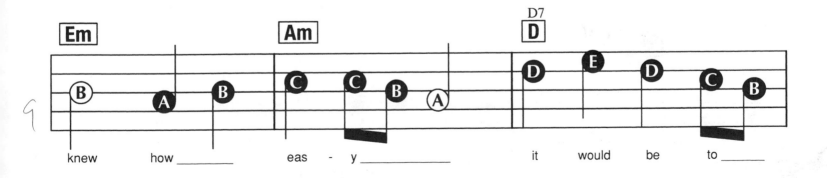

knew how _____ eas - y _____ it would be to _____

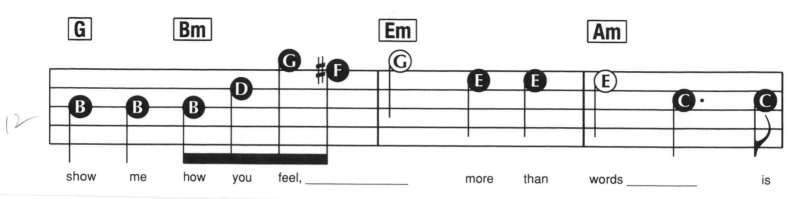

show me how you feel, _____ more than words _____ is

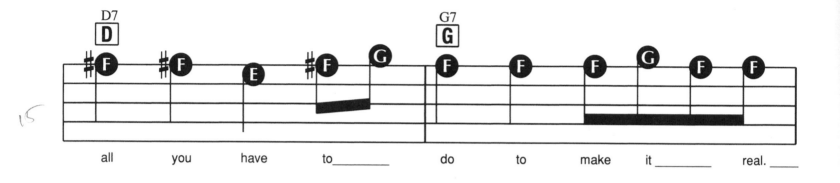

all you have to_____ do to make it _____ real. ____

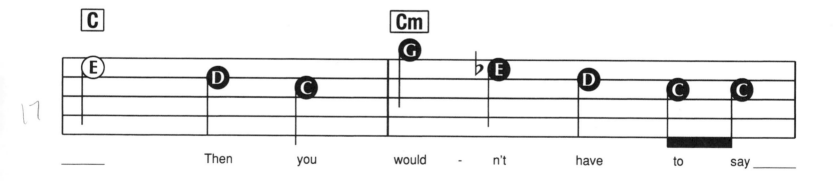

_____ Then you would - n't have to say _____

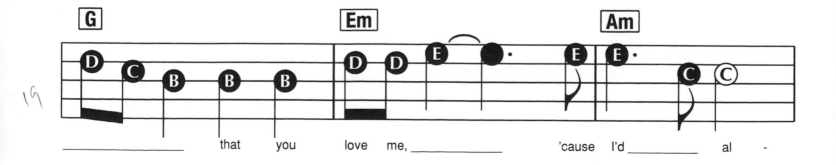

_____ that you love me, _____ 'cause I'd _____ al -

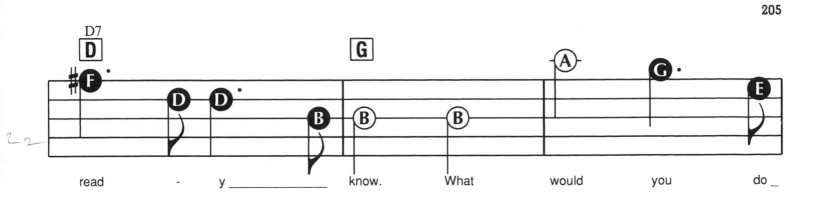

read - y _____ know. What would you do _

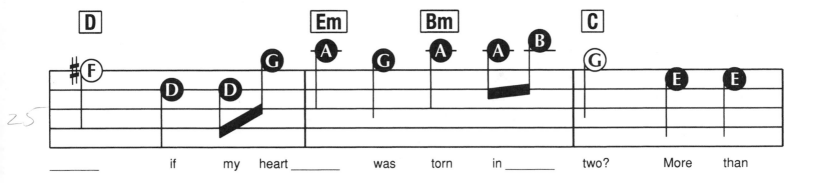

_____ if my heart _____ was torn in _____ two? More than

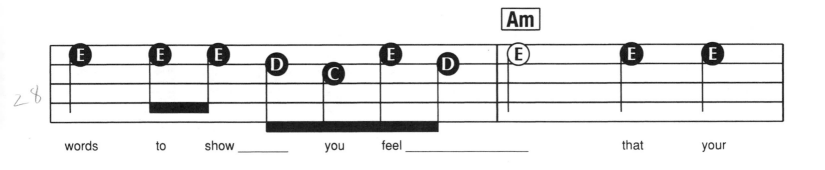

words to show _____ you feel _____ that your

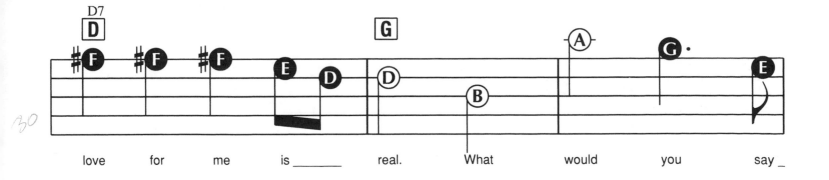

love for me is _____ real. What would you say _

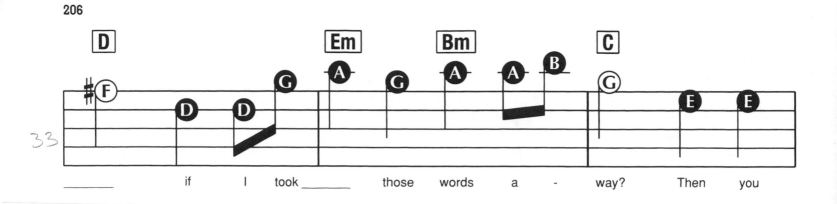

_____ if I took _____ those words a - way? Then you

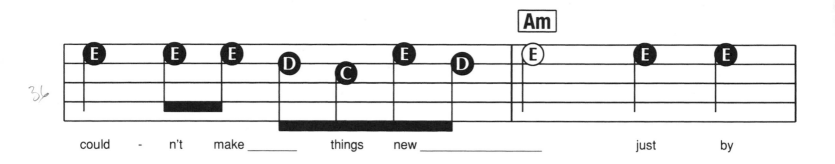

could - n't make _____ things new _____ just by

To Coda ⊕

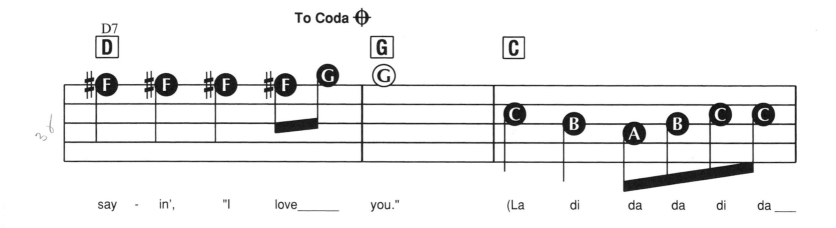

say - in', "I love_____ you." (La di da da di da ___

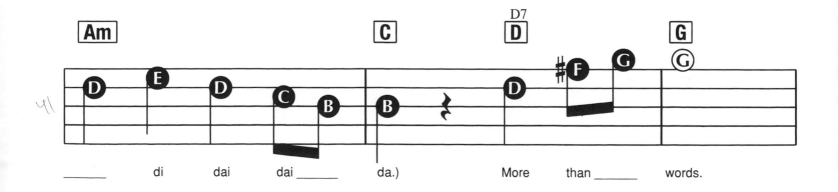

_____ di dai dai _____ da.) More than _____ words.

D.C. al Coda
(Return to beginning
Play to ⊕ and
Skip to Coda)

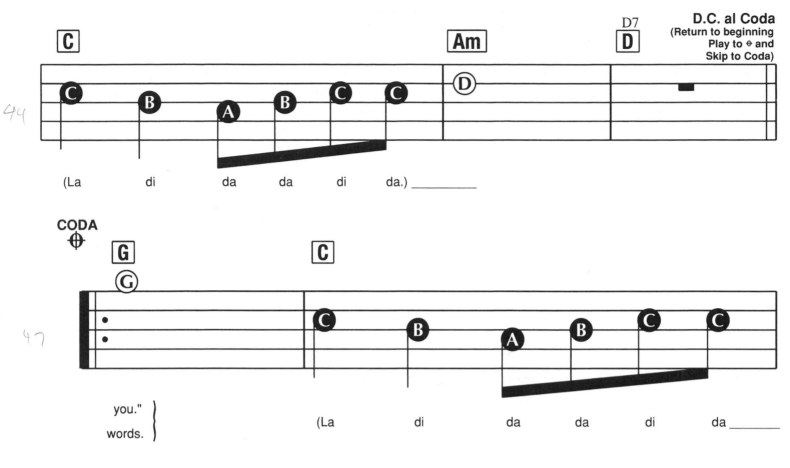

(La   di   da   da   di   da.) _____

CODA
⊕

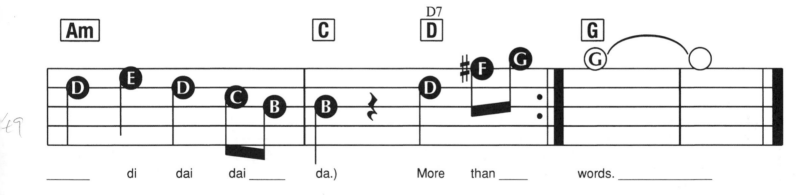

you." ⎫
words. ⎭

(La   di   da   da   di   da _____

_____   di   dai   dai _____   da.)   More   than ____   words. _____

Additional Lyrics

2. Now that I have tried to talk to you
    And make you understand.
    All you have to do is close your eyes
    And just reach out your hands.
    And touch me, hold me close, don't ever let me go.
    More than words is all I ever needed you to show.
    Then you wouldn't have to say
    That you love me 'cause I'd already know.

    Chorus

Maybe I'm Amazed

Registration 1
Rhythm: Rock, Pops or Ballad

Words and Music by
Paul McCartney

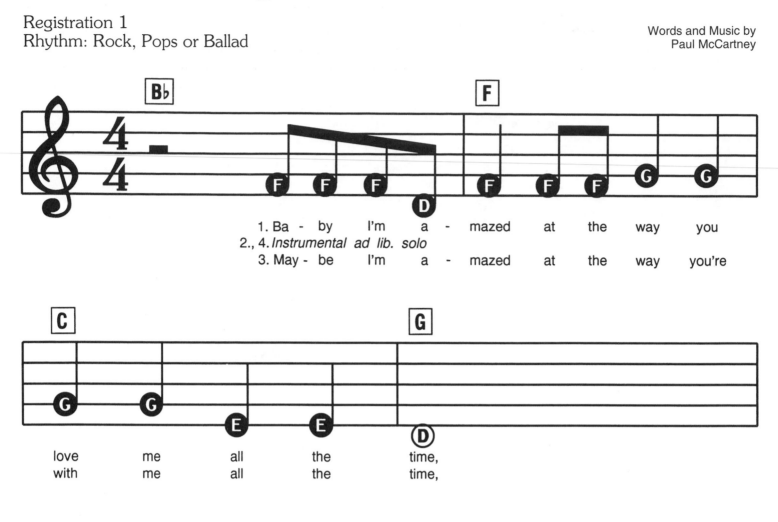

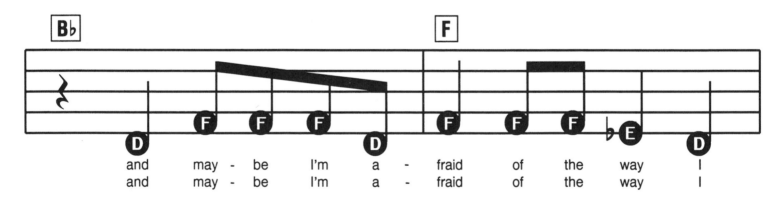

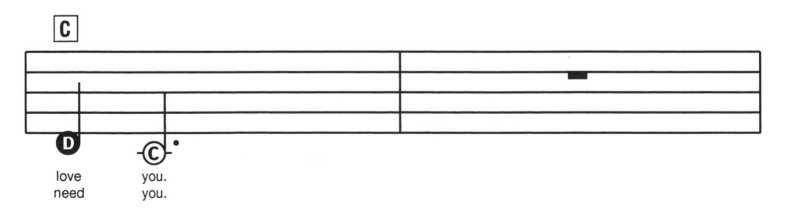

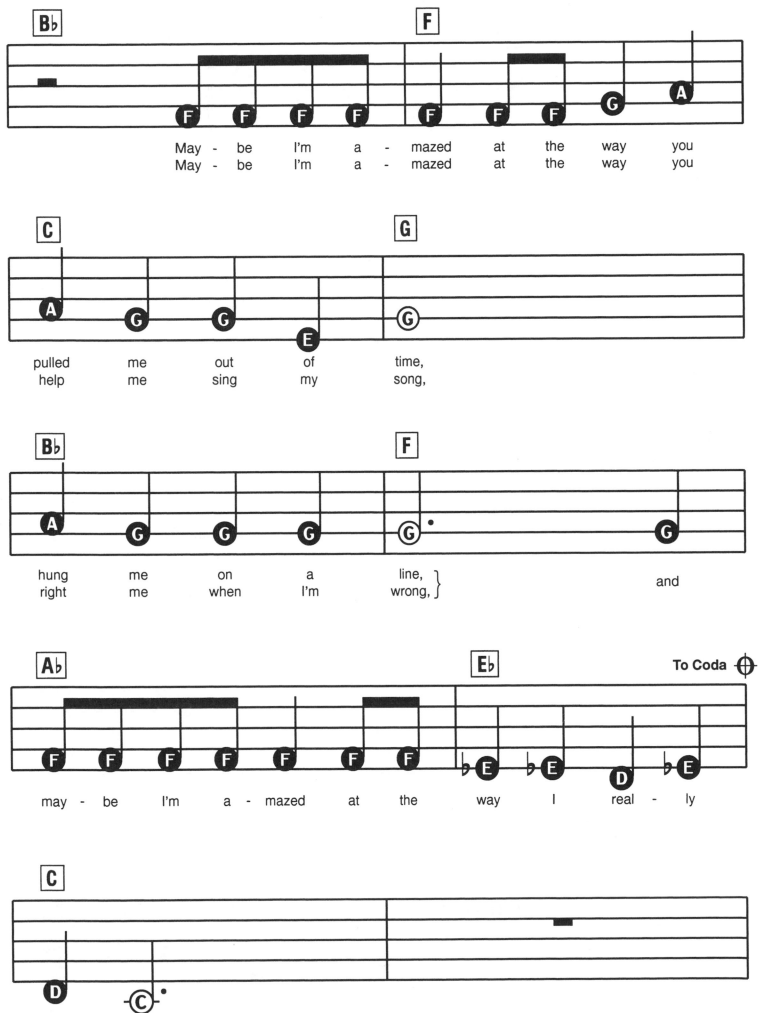

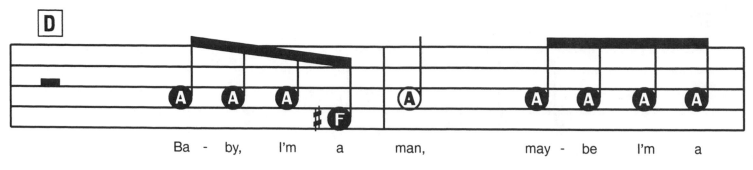

Ba - by, I'm a man, may - be I'm a

D7

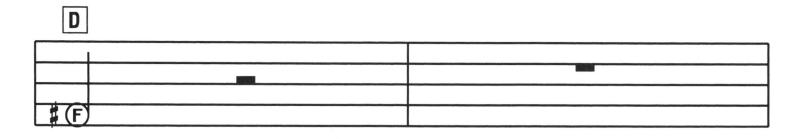

lone - ly man who's in the mid - dle of some - thing____

G

that he does - n't real - ly un - der - stand. ____

D

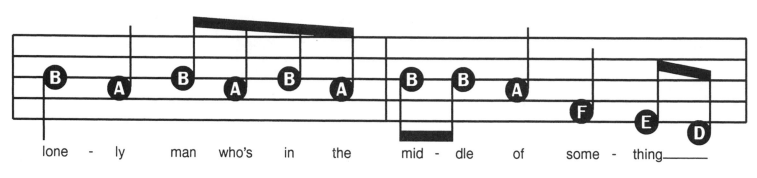

Ba - by I'm a man, and may - be you're the

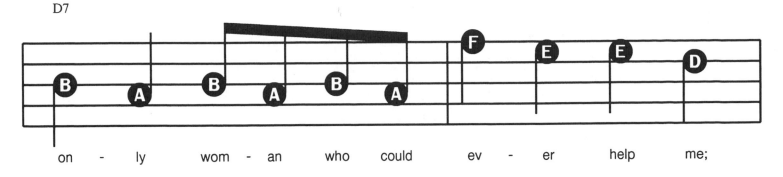

D7

on - ly wom - an who could ev - er help me;

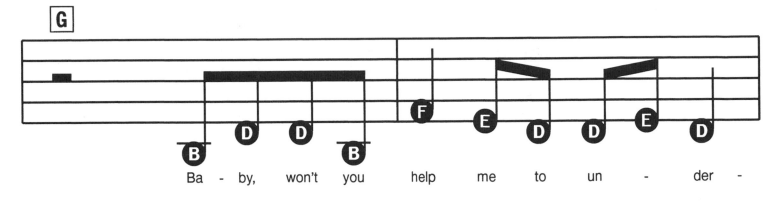

G

Ba - by, won't you help me to un - der -

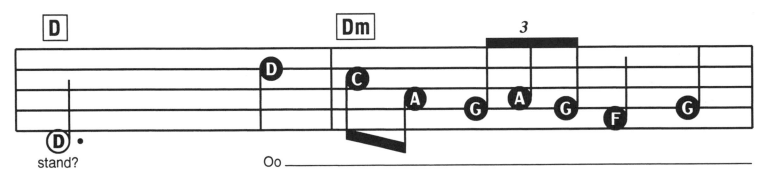

D   Dm   3

stand?   Oo

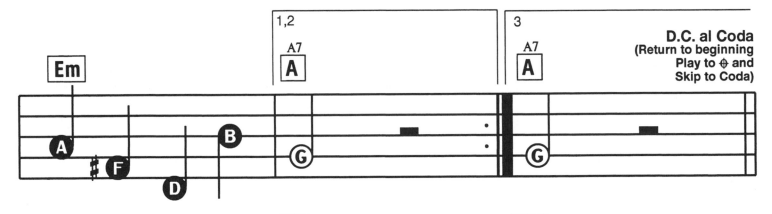

Em   1,2 A7 A   3 A7 A

D.C. al Coda
(Return to beginning
Play to ⊕ and
Skip to Coda)

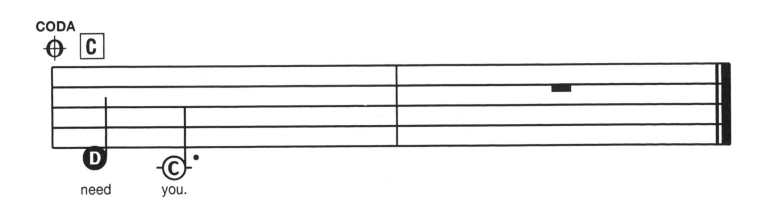

CODA
⊕ C

need you.

My Heart Will Go On
(Love Theme from 'Titanic')
from the Paramount and Twentieth Century Fox Motion Picture TITANIC

Registration 8
Rhythm: Ballad

Music by James Horner
Lyric by Will Jennings

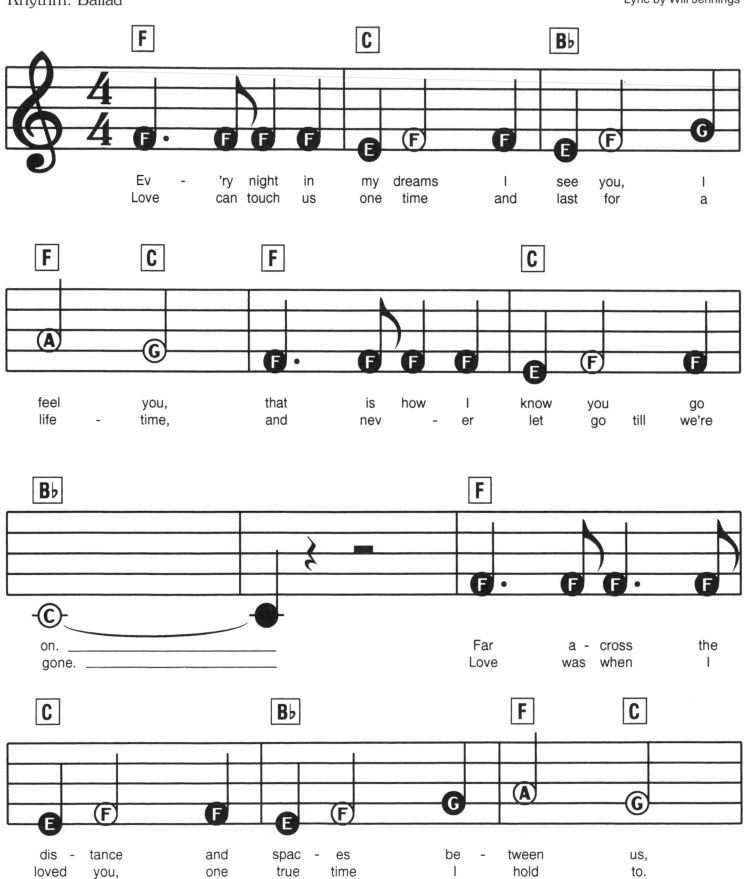

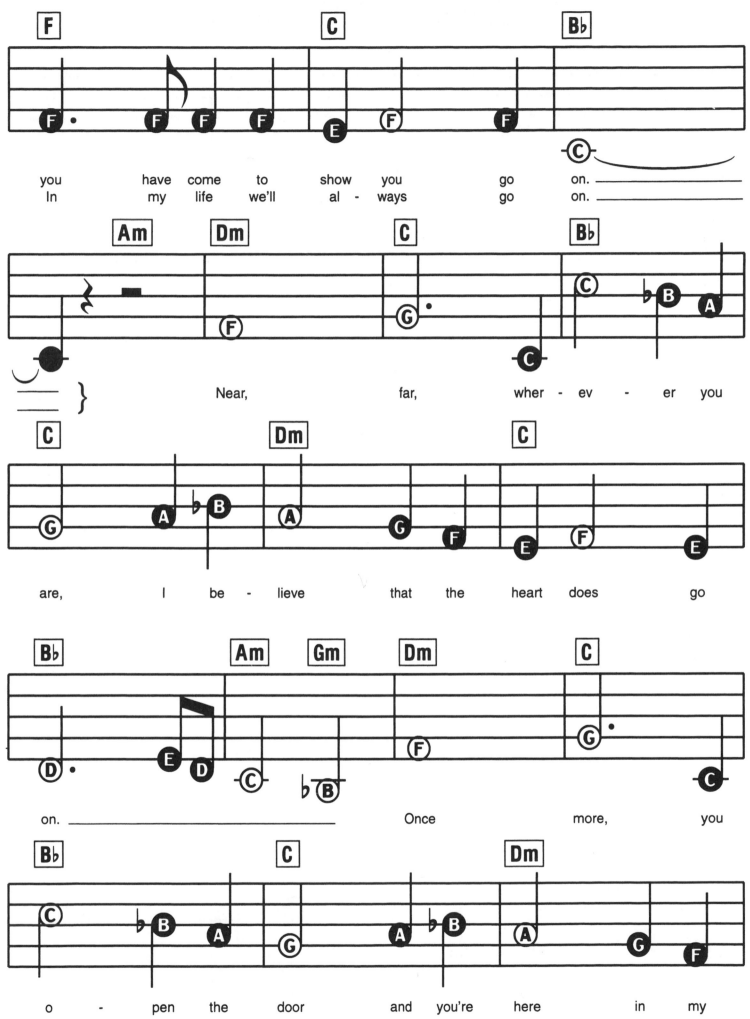

you have come to show you go on. ___
In my life we'll al - ways go on. ___

Near, far, wher - ev - er you

are, I be - lieve that the heart does go

on. ___ Once more, you

o - pen the door and you're here in my

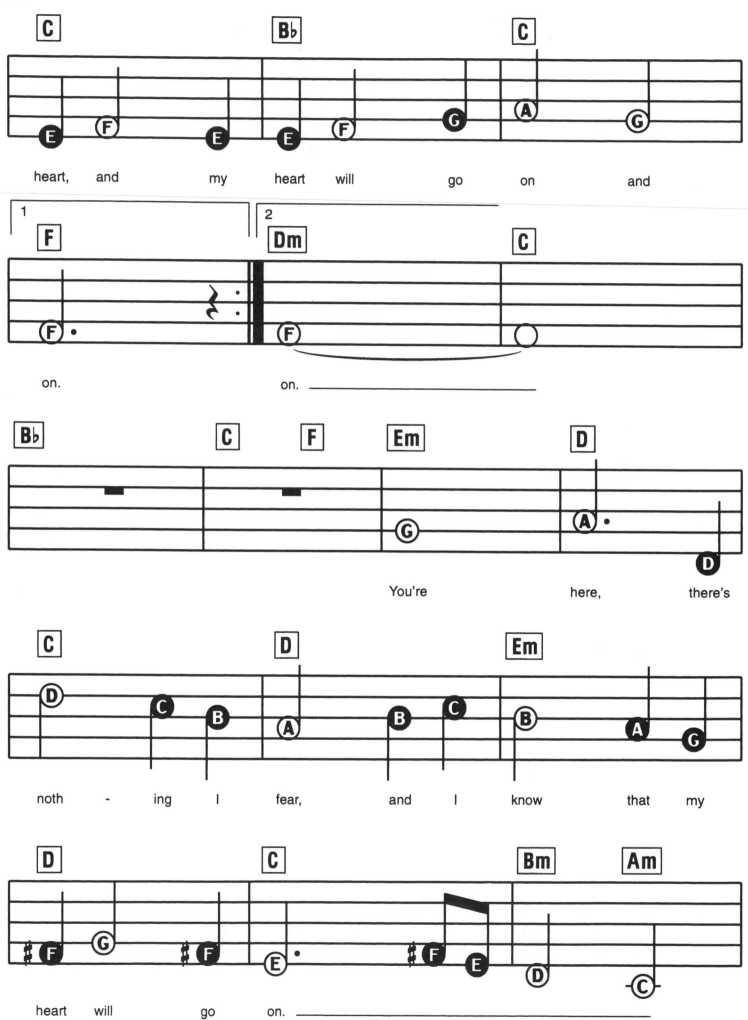

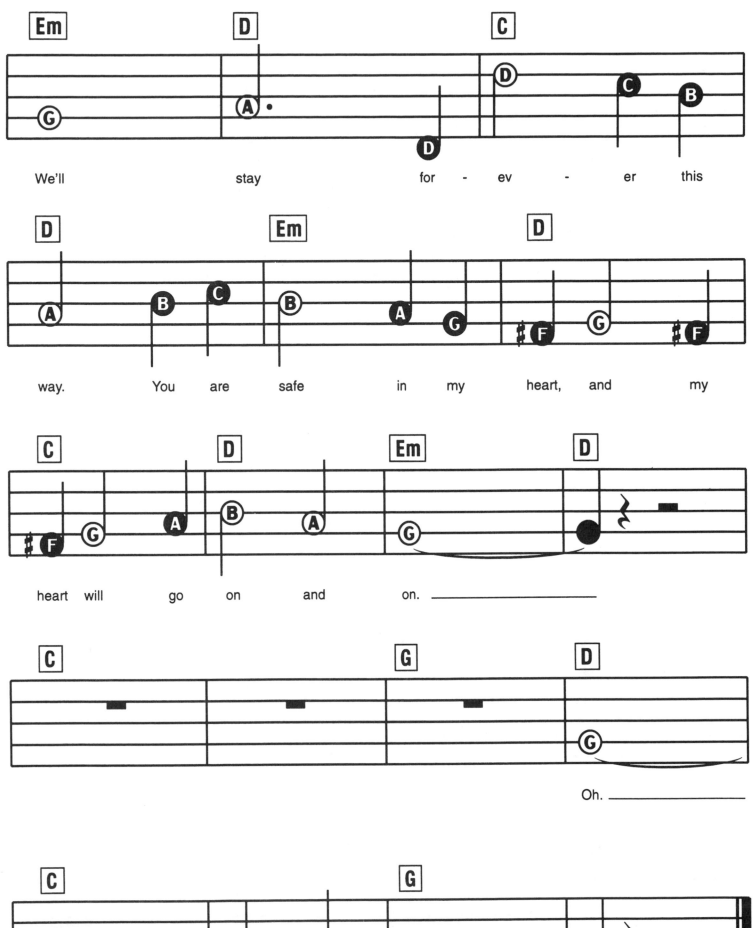

My Love

Registration 10
Rhythm: Ballad

Words and Music by
Paul and Linda McCartney

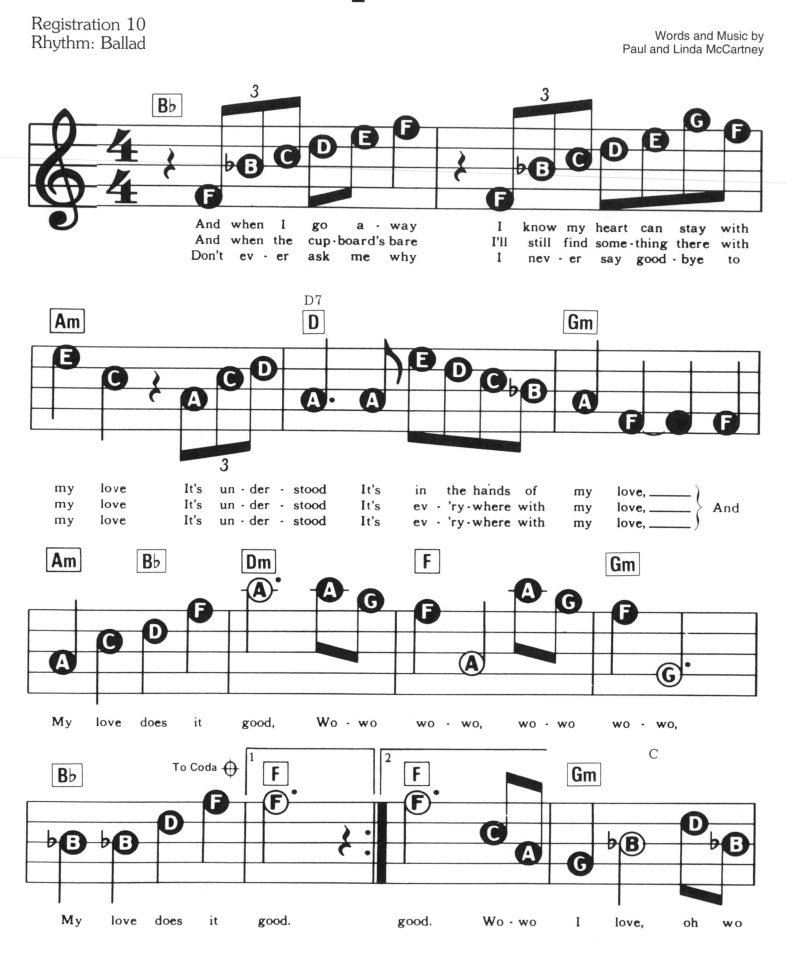

And when I go a - way   I know my heart can stay with
And when the cup-board's bare   I'll still find some-thing there with
Don't ev - er ask me why   I nev - er say good - bye to

my love   It's un - der - stood   It's in the hands of my love, ____
my love   It's un - der - stood   It's ev - 'ry-where with my love, ____ } And
my love   It's un - der - stood   It's ev - 'ry-where with my love, ____

My love does it good,   Wo - wo   wo - wo,   wo - wo   wo - wo,

My love does it good.   good.   Wo - wo   I love,   oh wo

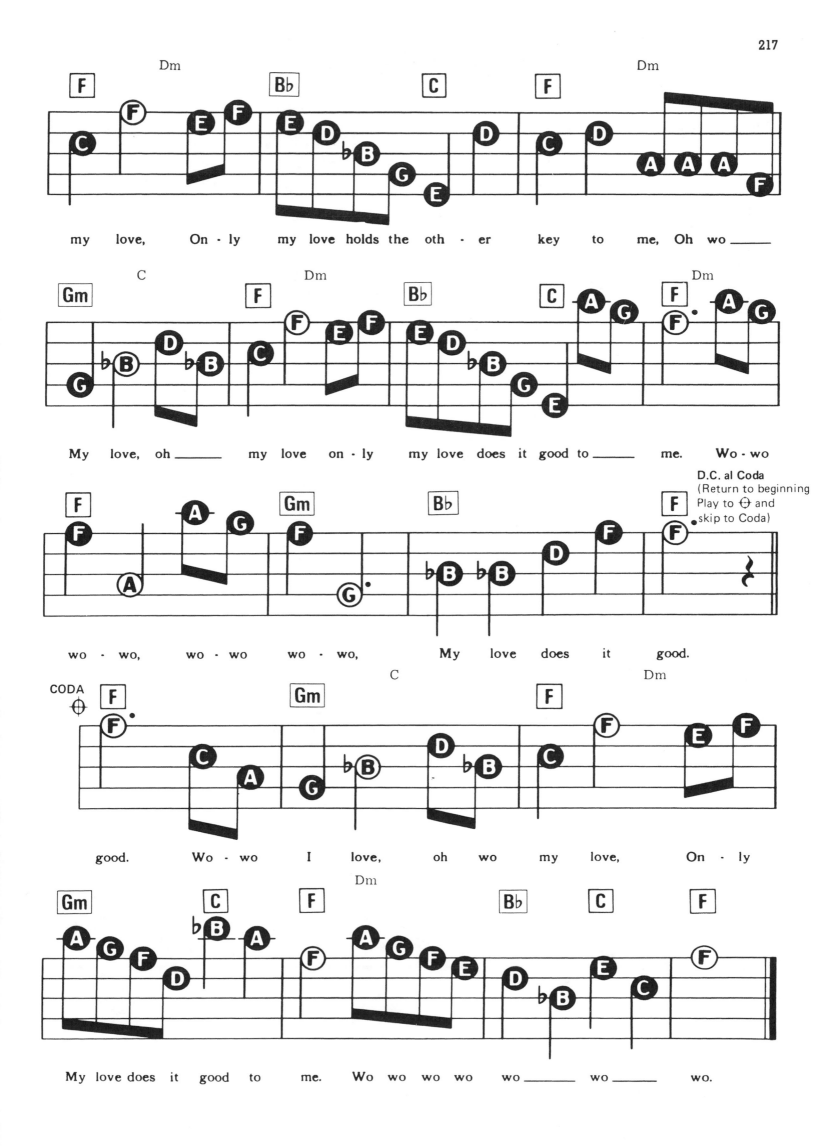

On the Wings of Love

Registration 3
Rhythm: 8-Beat or Pops

Words and Music by Jeffrey Osborne
and Peter Schless

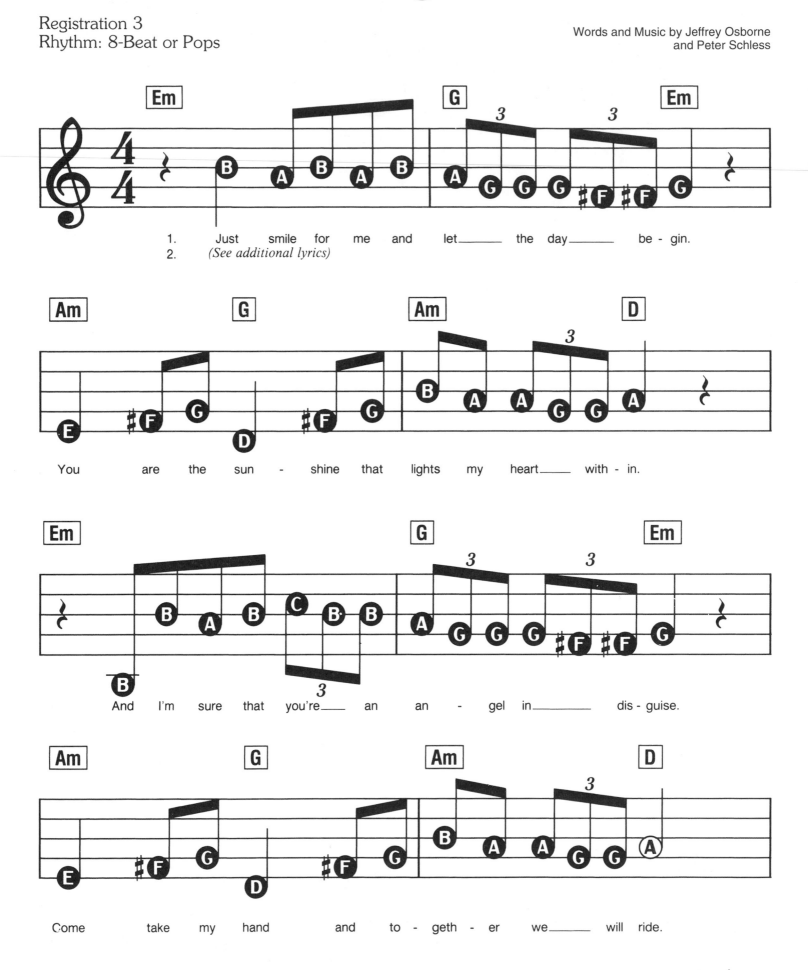

1. Just smile for me and let___ the day___ be - gin.
2. *(See additional lyrics)*

You are the sun - shine that lights my heart___ with - in.

And I'm sure that you're___ an an - gel in___ dis - guise.

Come take my hand and to - geth - er we___ will ride.

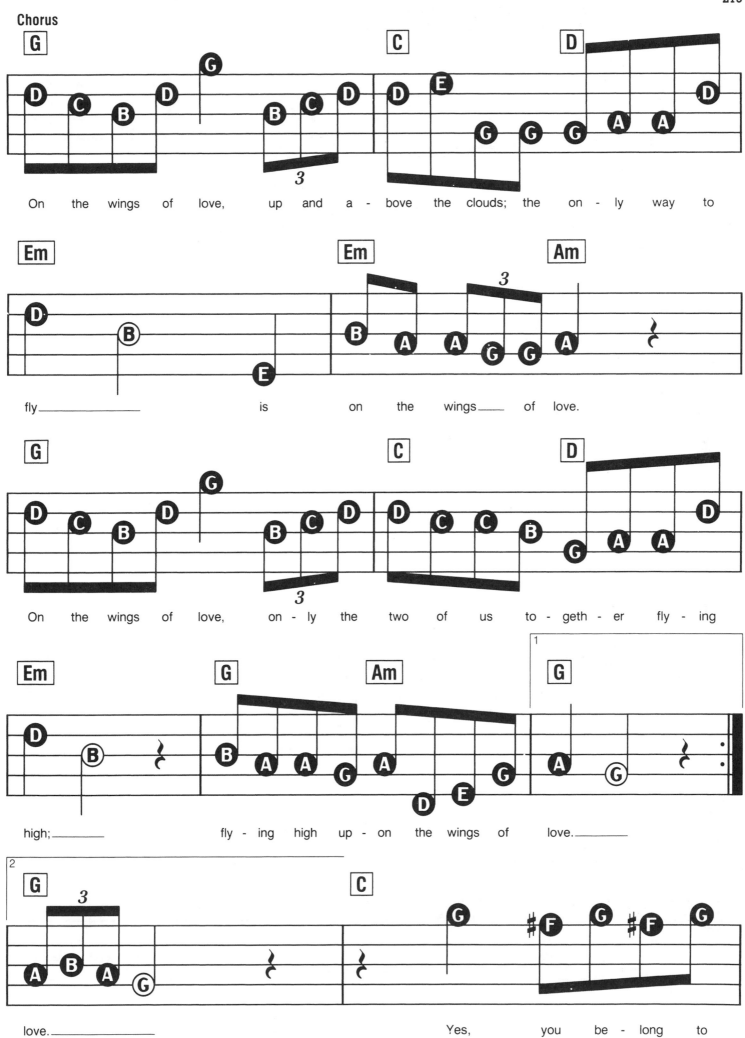

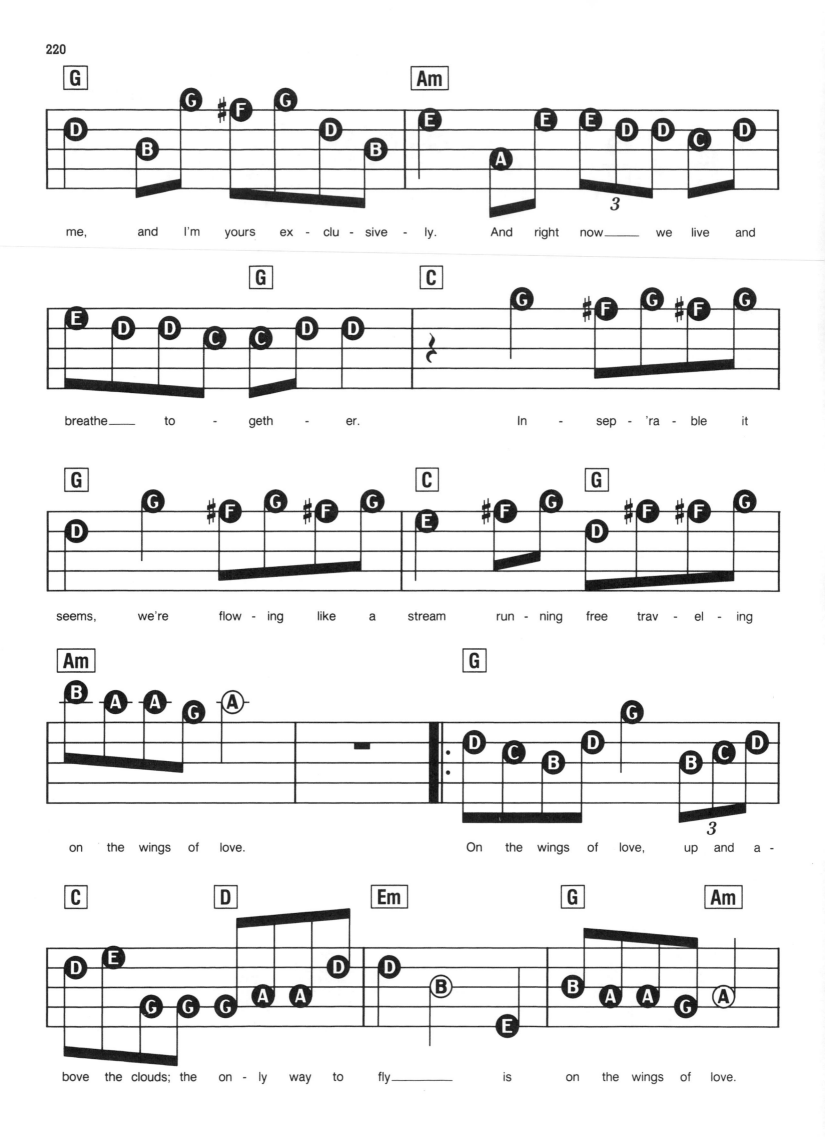

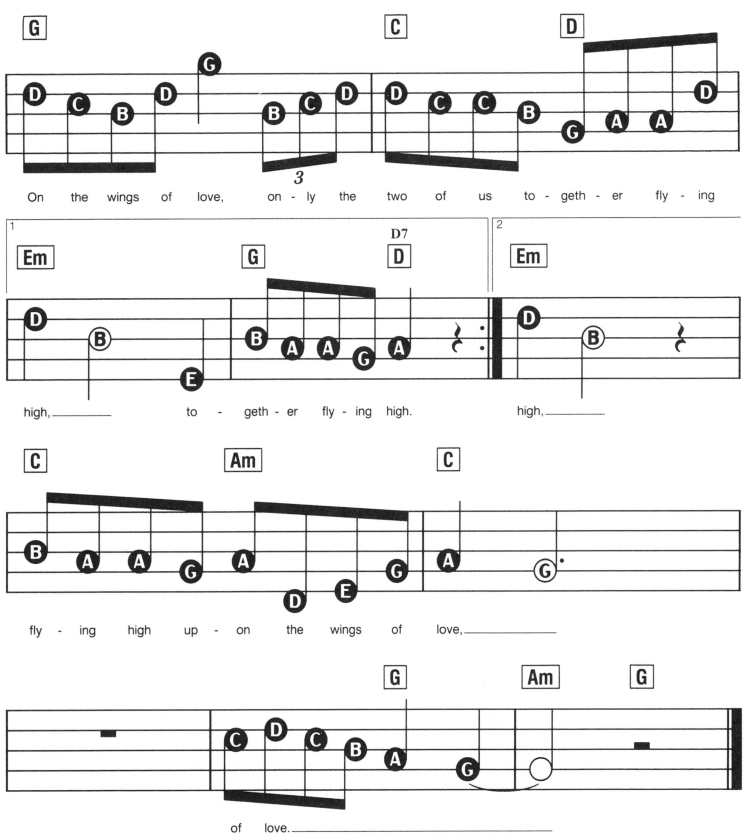

Additional Lyrics

2. You look at me and I begin to melt
   Just like the snow, when a ray of sun is felt.
   And I'm crazy 'bout you, baby, can't you see?
   I'd be so delighted if you would come with me.

   Chorus

Put Your Head on My Shoulder

Registration 2
Rhythm: Slow Rock or Ballad

Words and Music by
Paul Anka

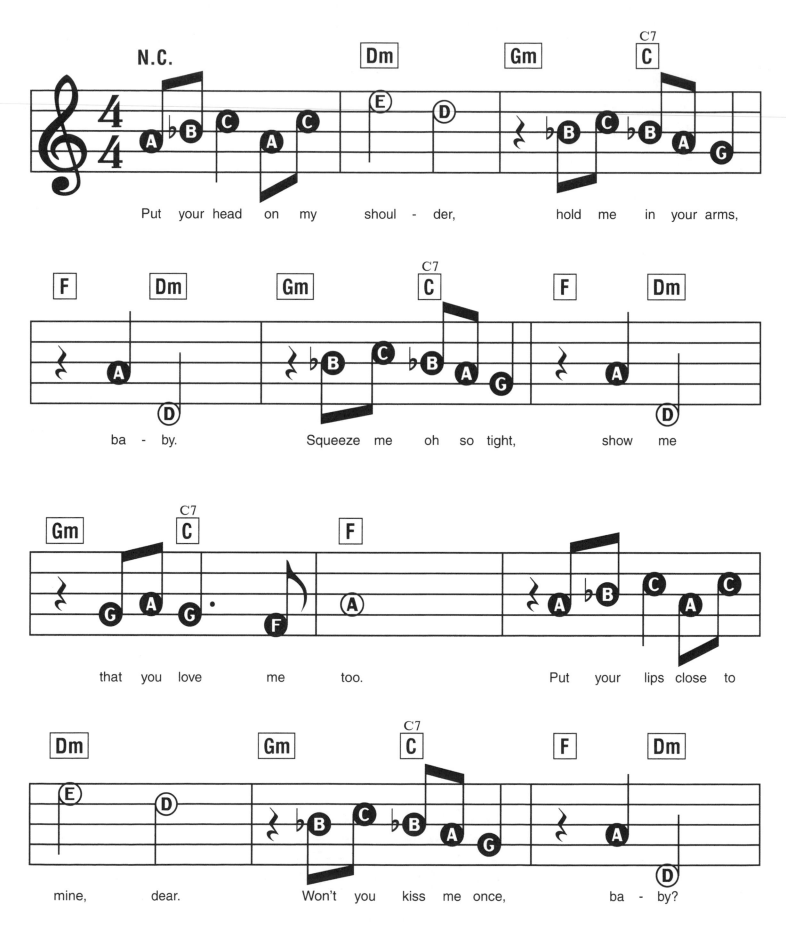

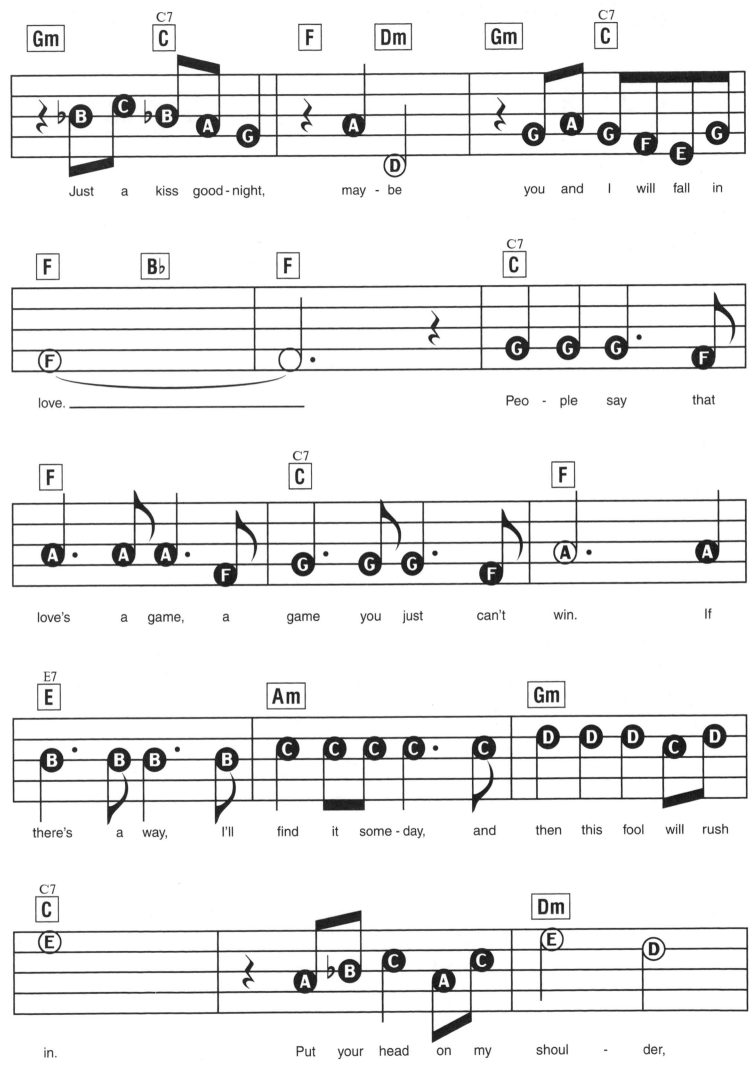

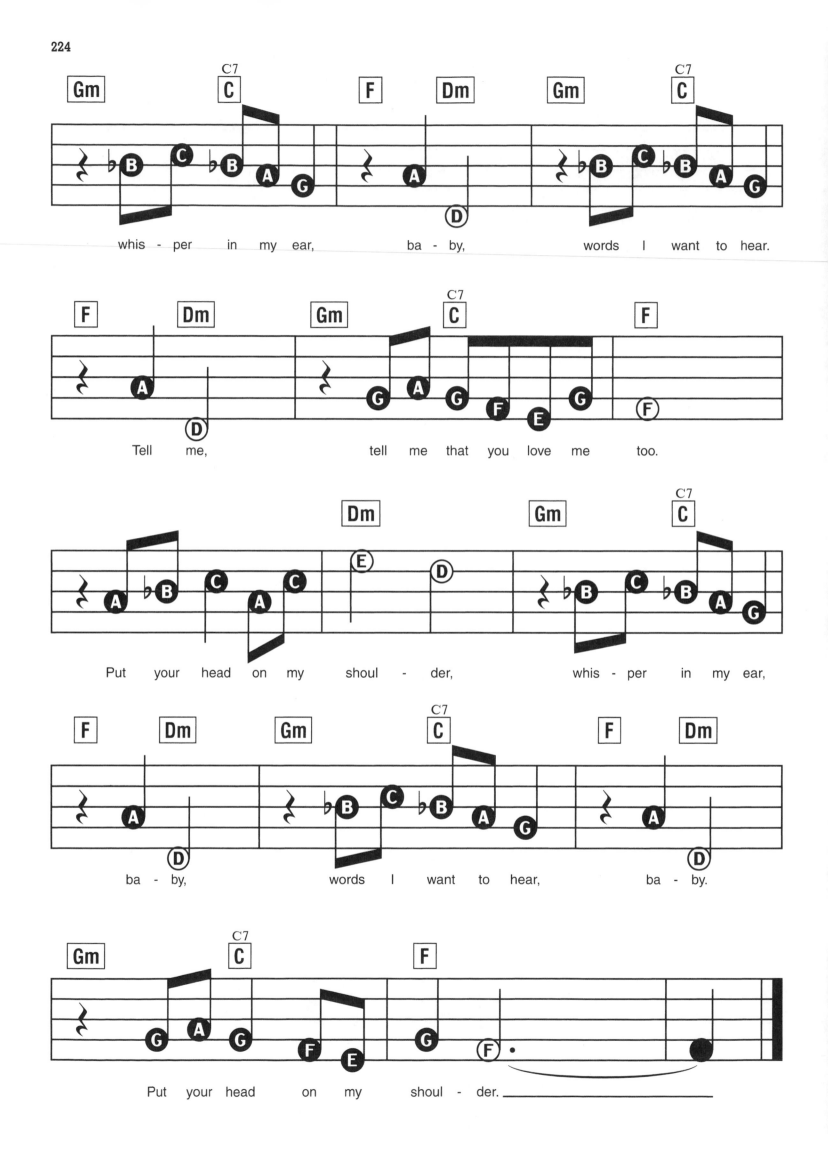

Save the Best for Last

Registration 8
Rhythm: 8-Beat

Words and Music by Wendy Waldman,
Phil Galdston and Jon Lind

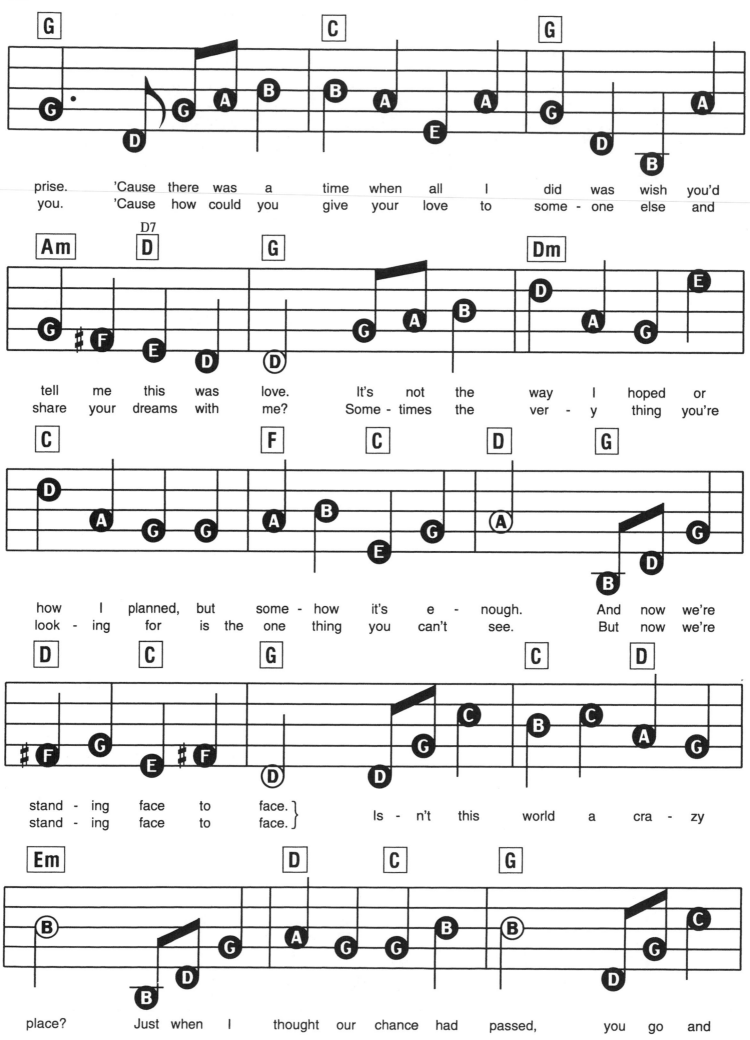

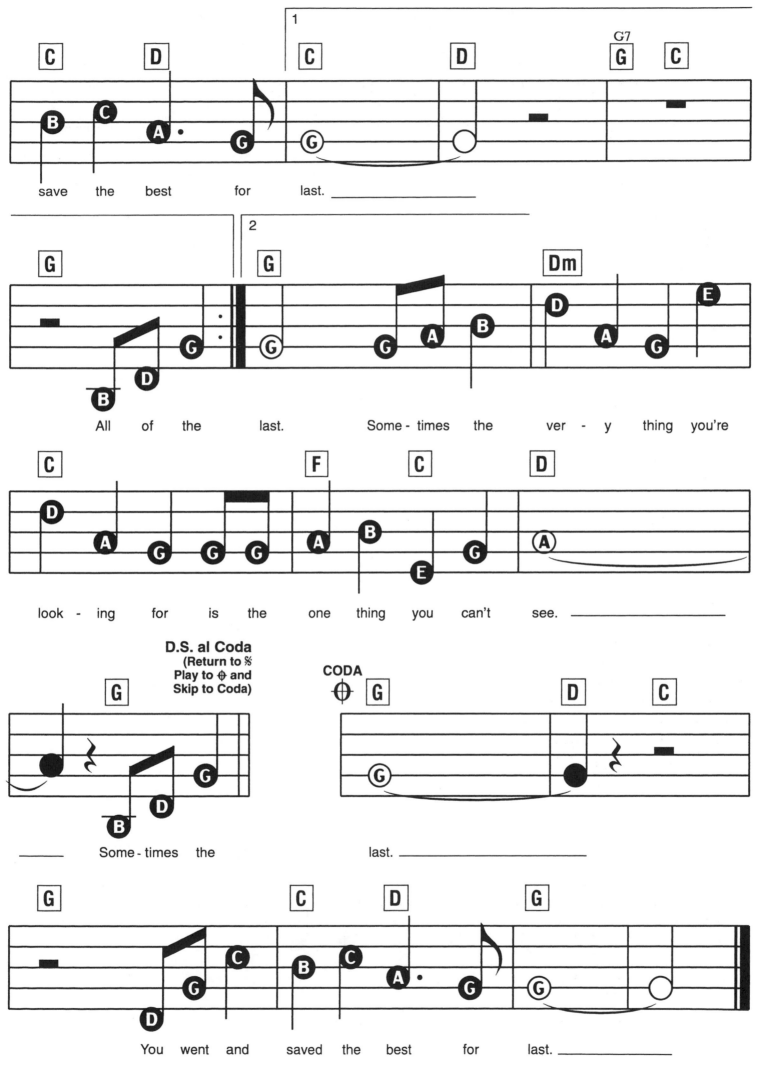

Separate Lives
Love Theme from WHITE NIGHTS

Registration 3
Rhythm: Rock

Words and Music by
Stephen Bishop

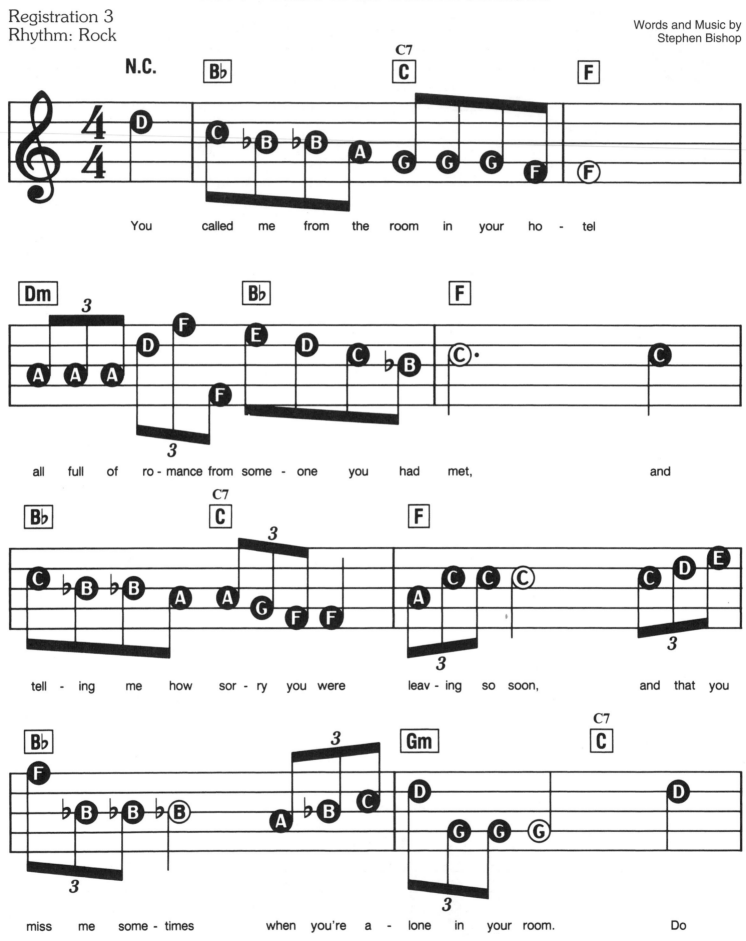

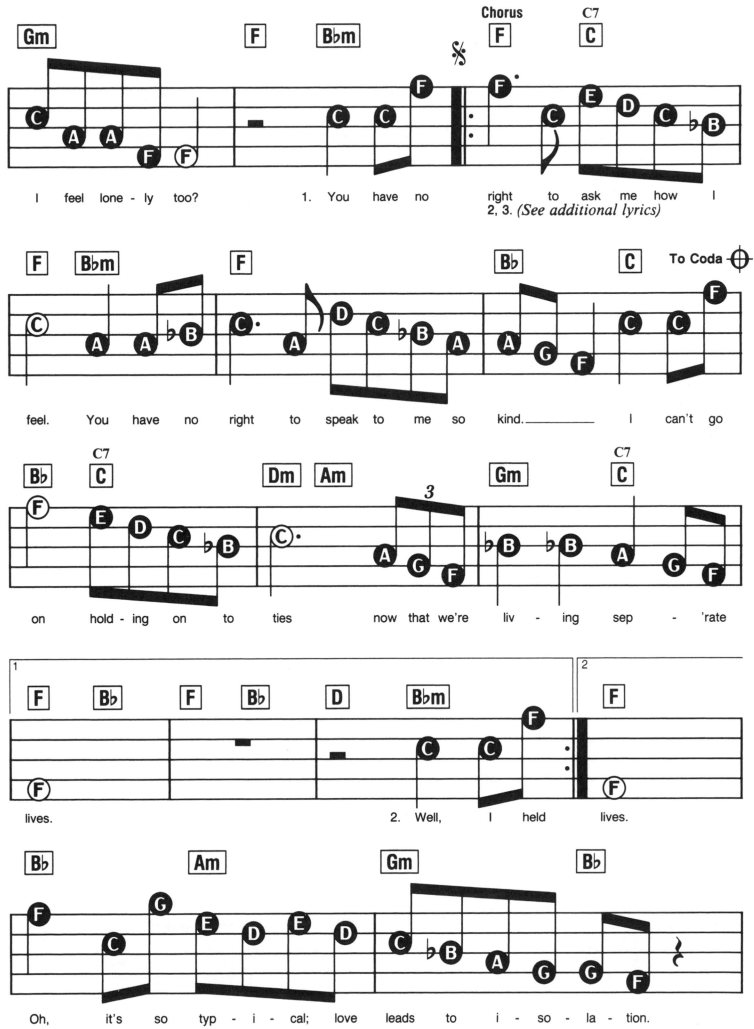

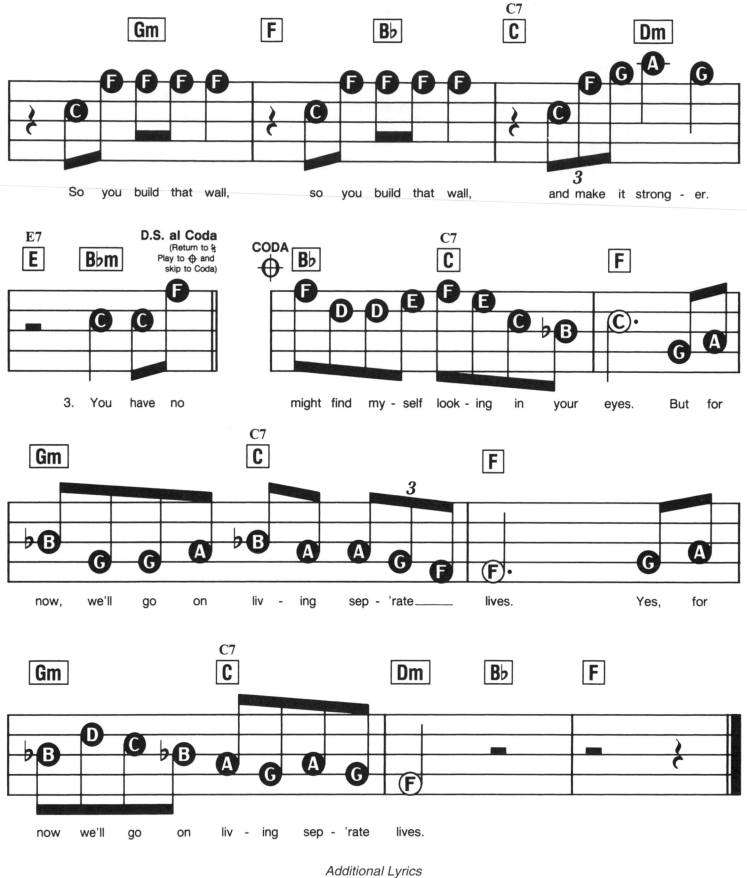

Additional Lyrics

Chorus 2:

Well, I held on to let you go.
And if you lost your love for me,
You never let it show.
There was no way to compormise.
So now we're living separate lives.

Chorus 3:

You have no right to ask me how I feel.
You have no right to speak to me so kind.
Someday I might find myself looking in your eyes.
But for now, we'll go on living separate lives.
Yes, for now we'll go on living separate lives.

September Morn

Registration 2
Rhythm: Ballad or Fox Trot

Words and Music by Neil Diamond
and Gilbert Becaud

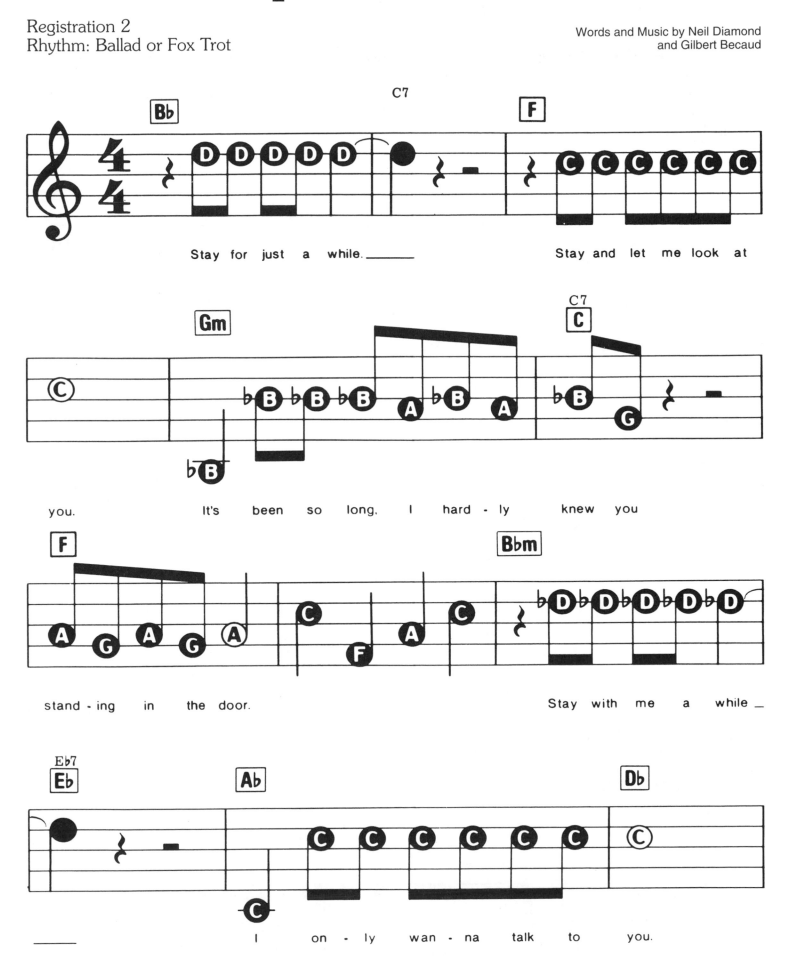

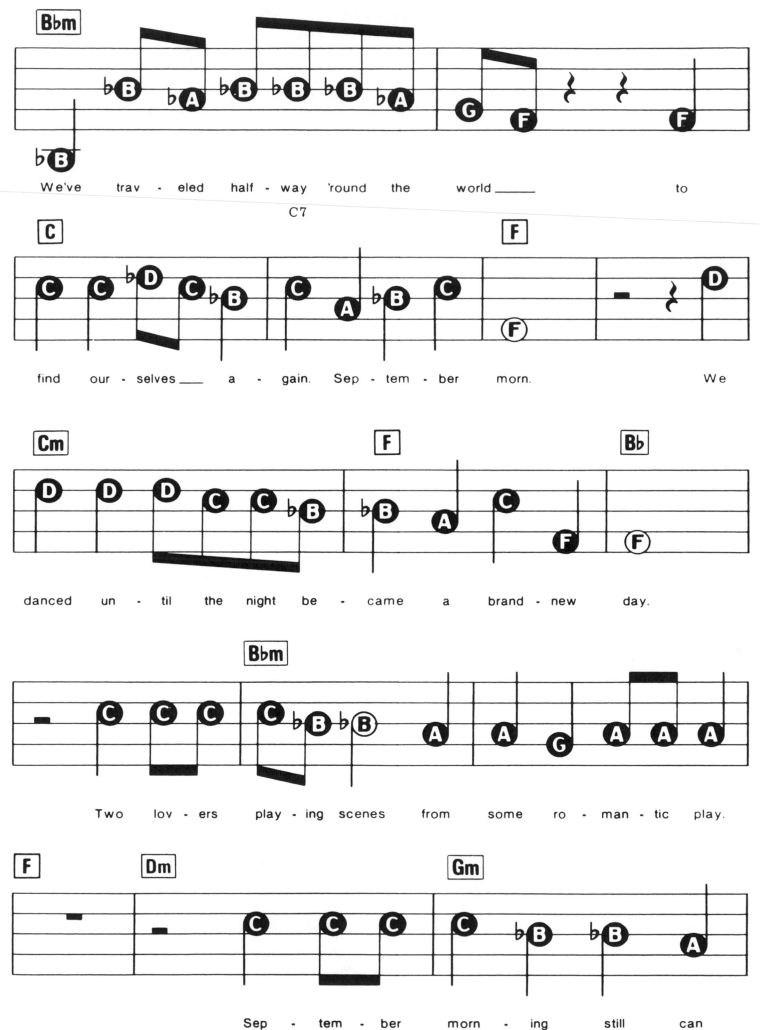

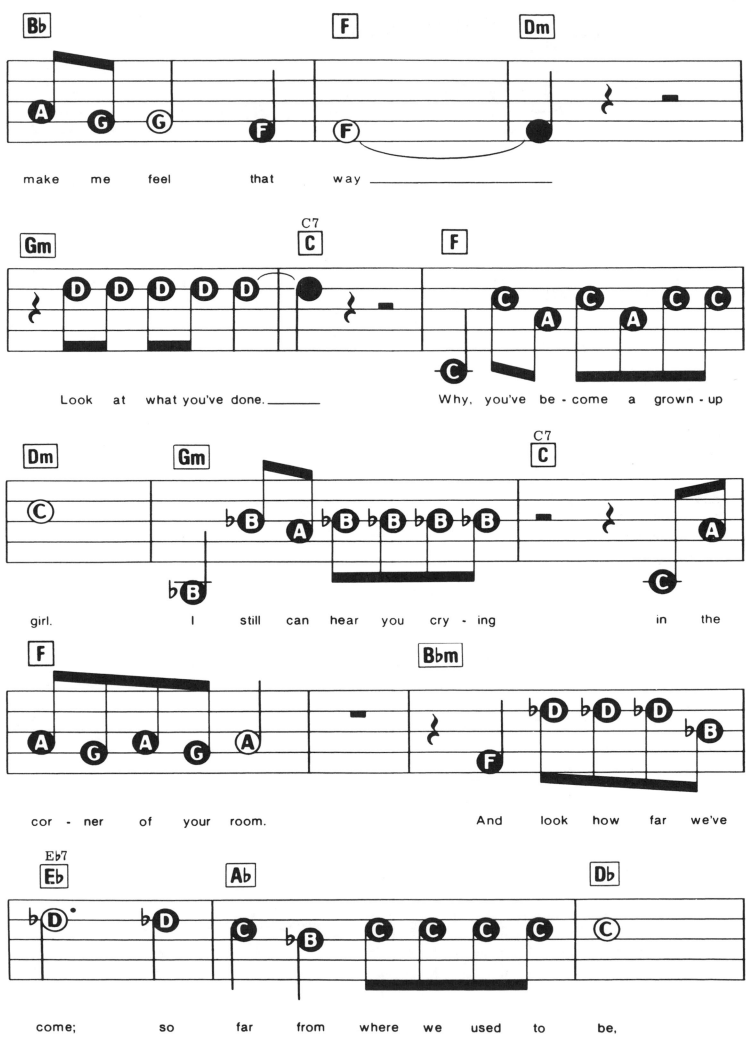

233

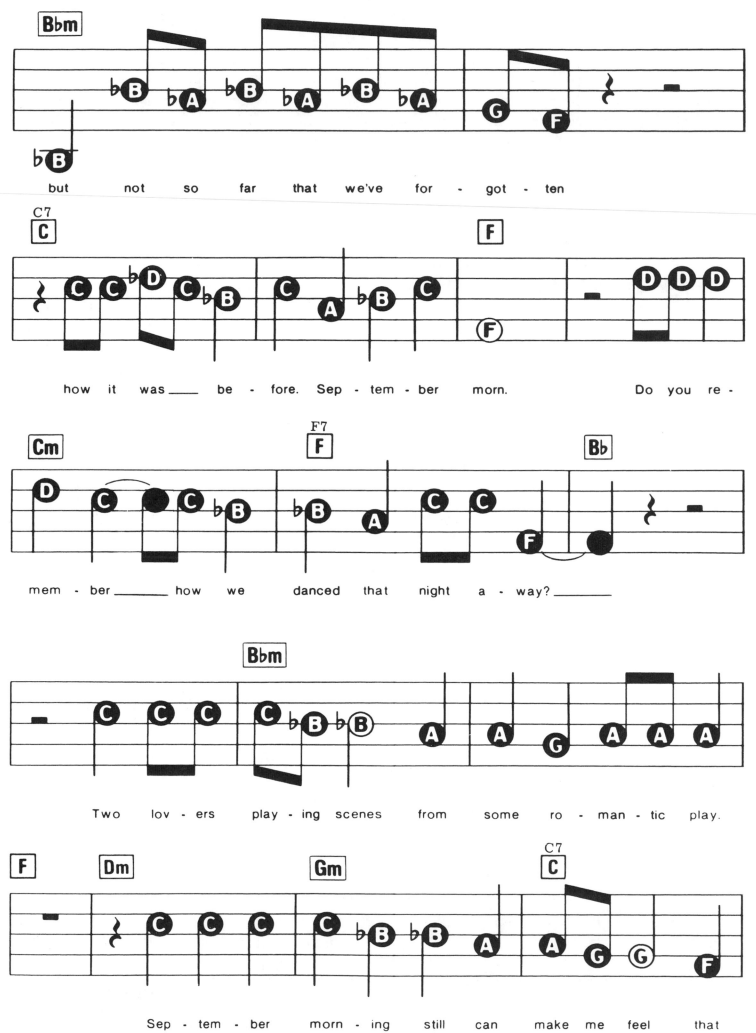

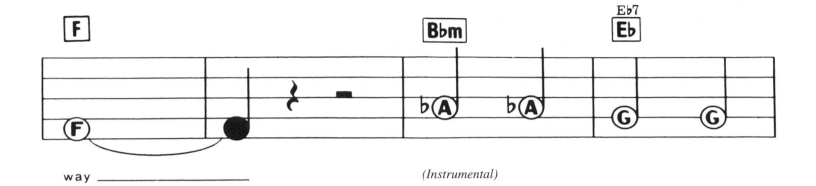

way _____ *(Instrumental)*

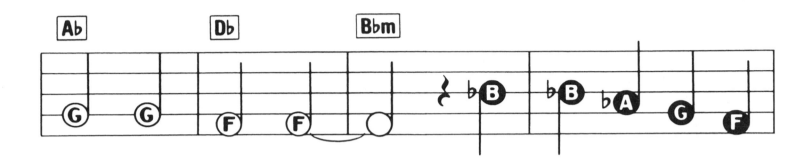

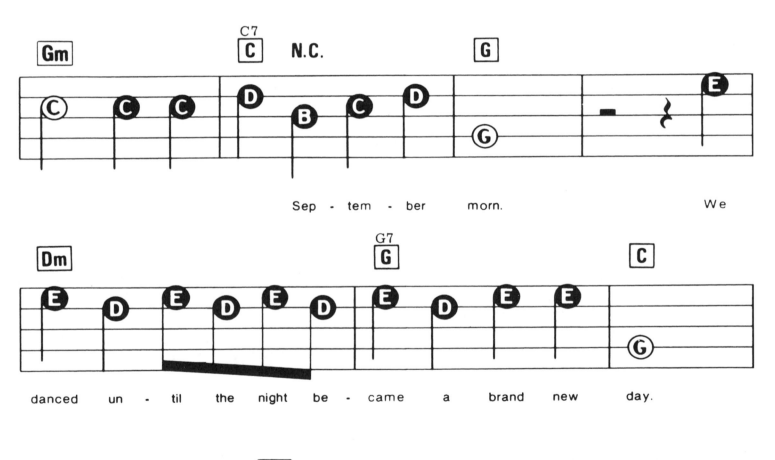

Sep - tem - ber morn. We

danced un - til the night be - came a brand new day.

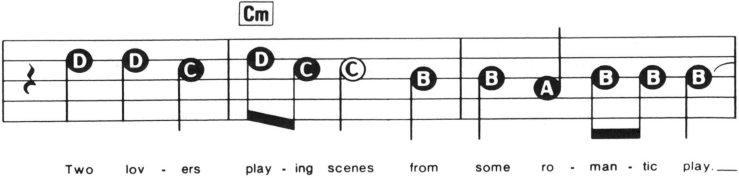

Two lov - ers play - ing scenes from some ro - man - tic play. ___

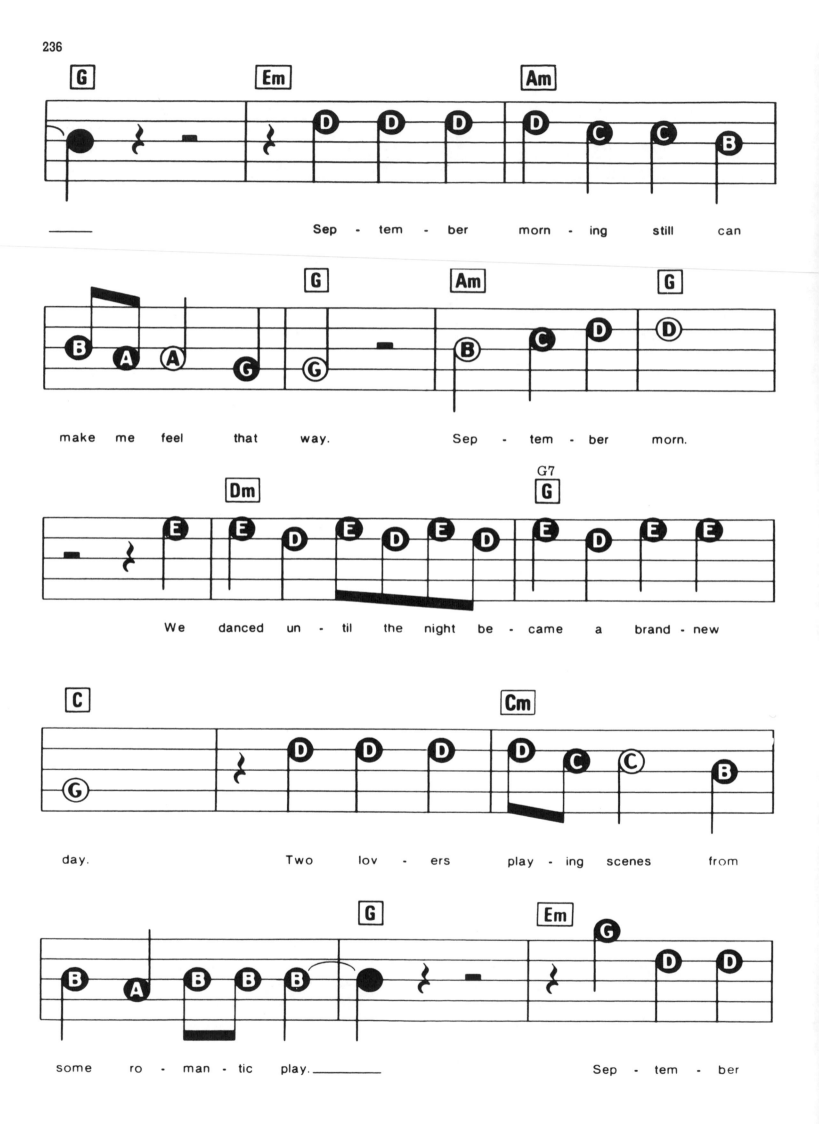

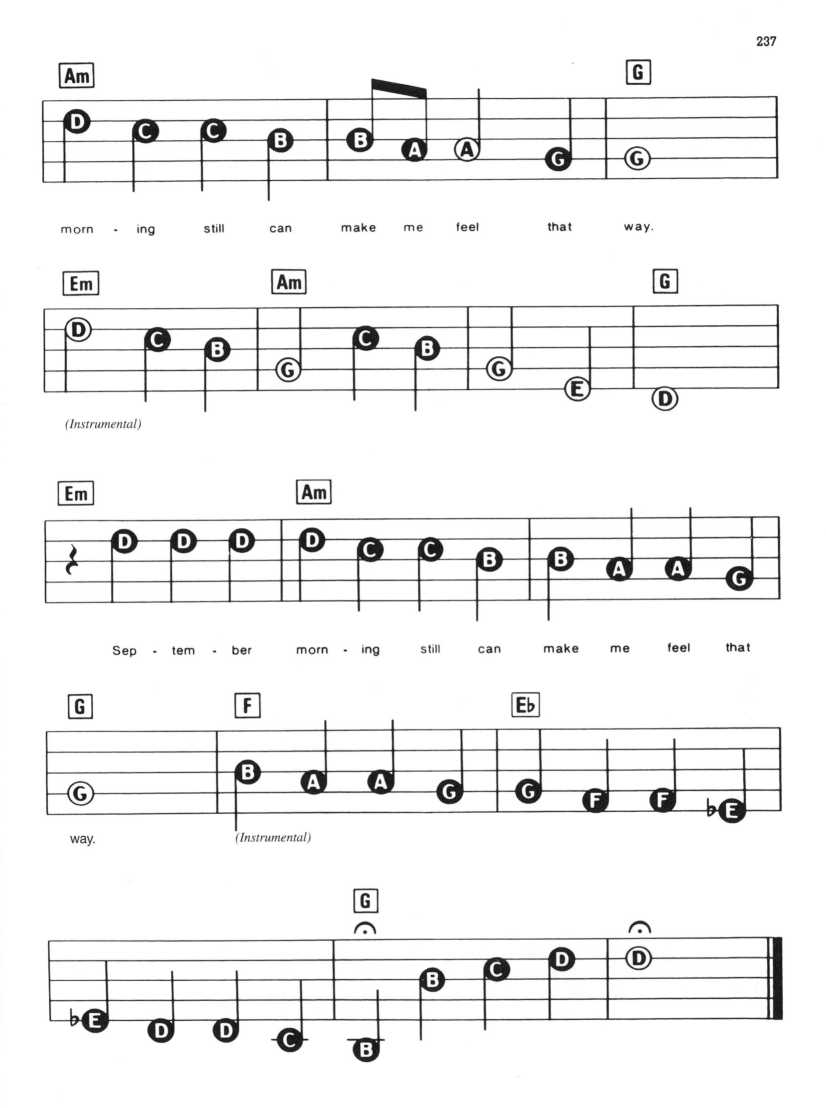

She's Got a Way

Registration 3
Rhythm: Ballad

Words and Music by
Billy Joel

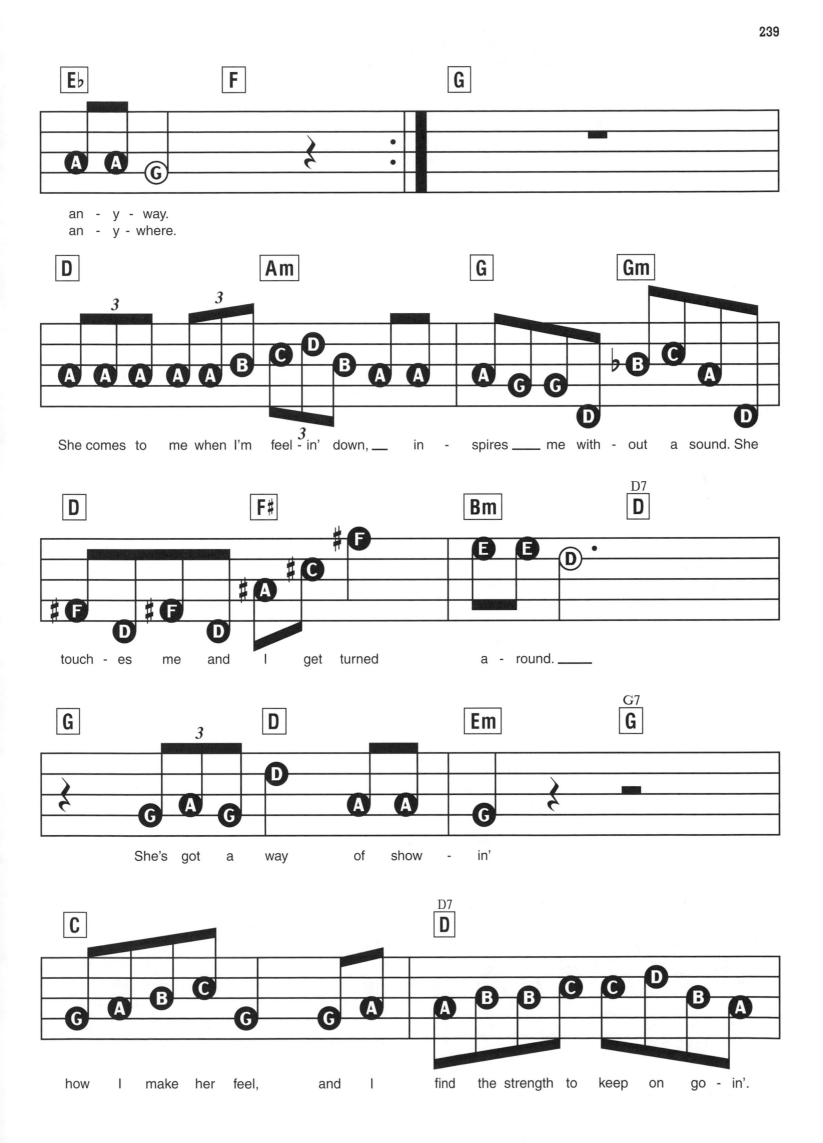

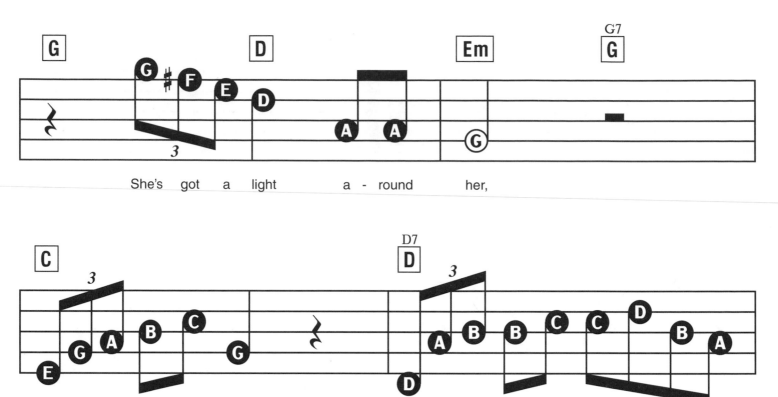

She's got a light a - round her,

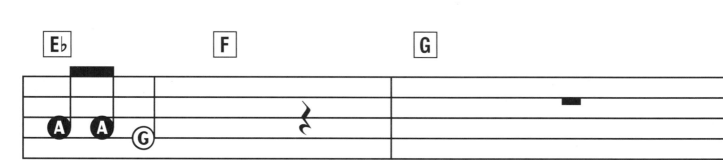

and ev - 'ry - where she goes, a mil - lion dreams of love sur - round her

ev - 'ry - where.

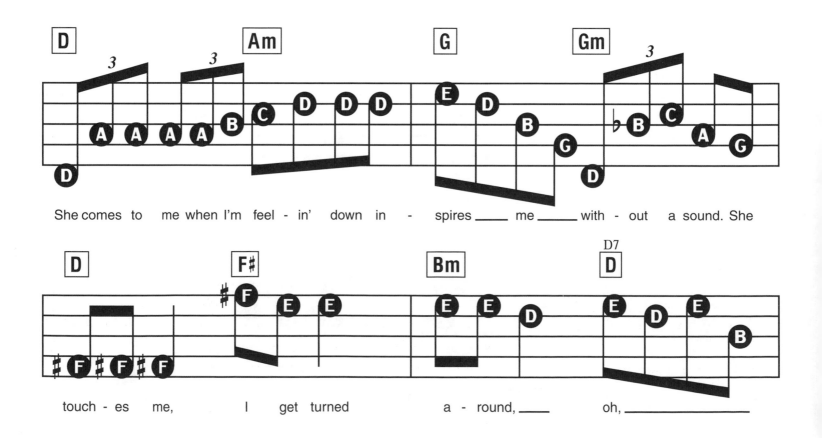

She comes to me when I'm feel - in' down in - spires ____ me ____ with - out a sound. She

touch - es me, I get turned a - round, ____ oh, _____

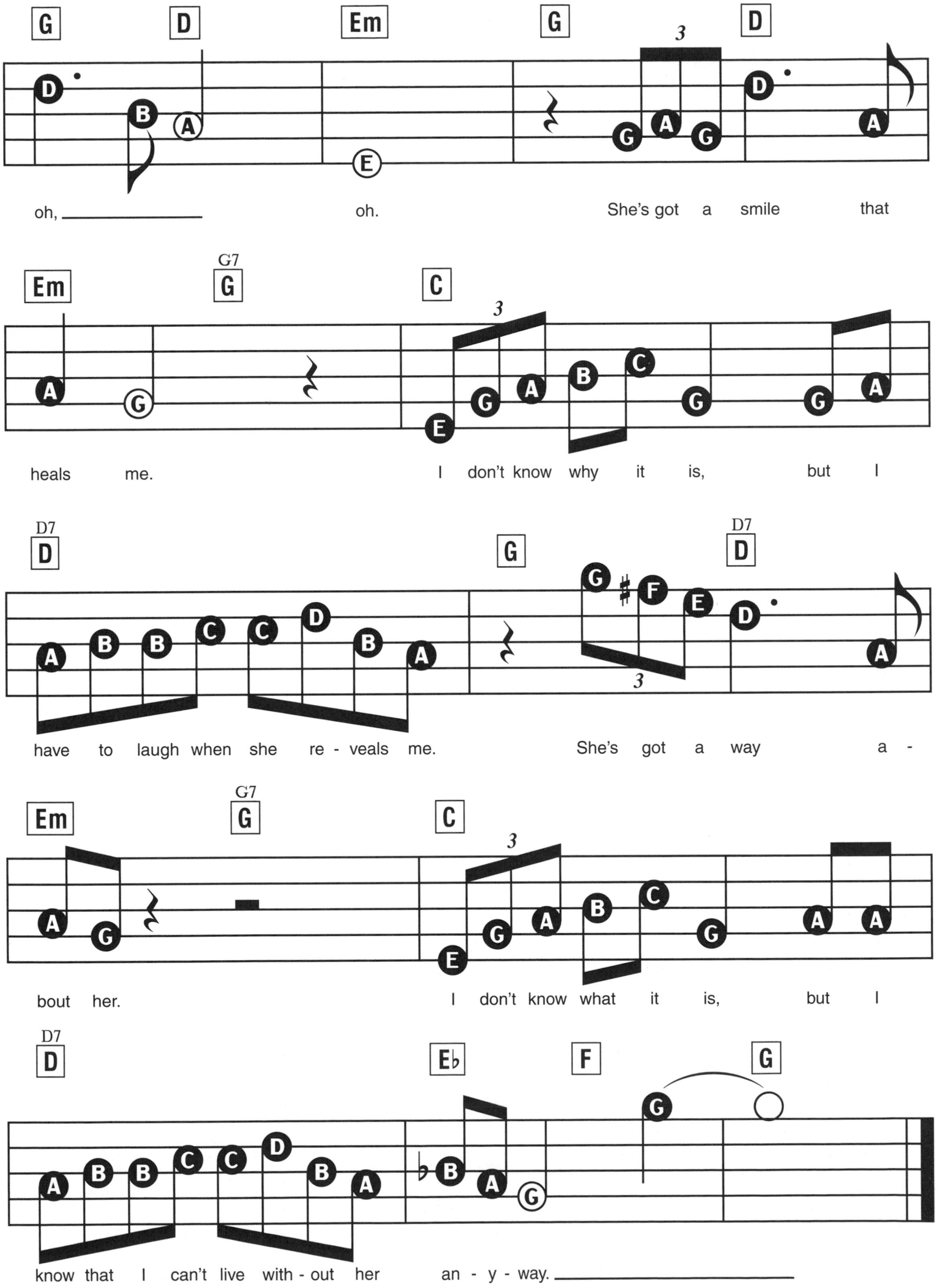

Somewhere Out There
from AN AMERICAN TAIL

Registration 3
Rhythm: Ballad or 8-Beat

Music by Barry Mann and James Horner
Lyric by Cynthia Weil

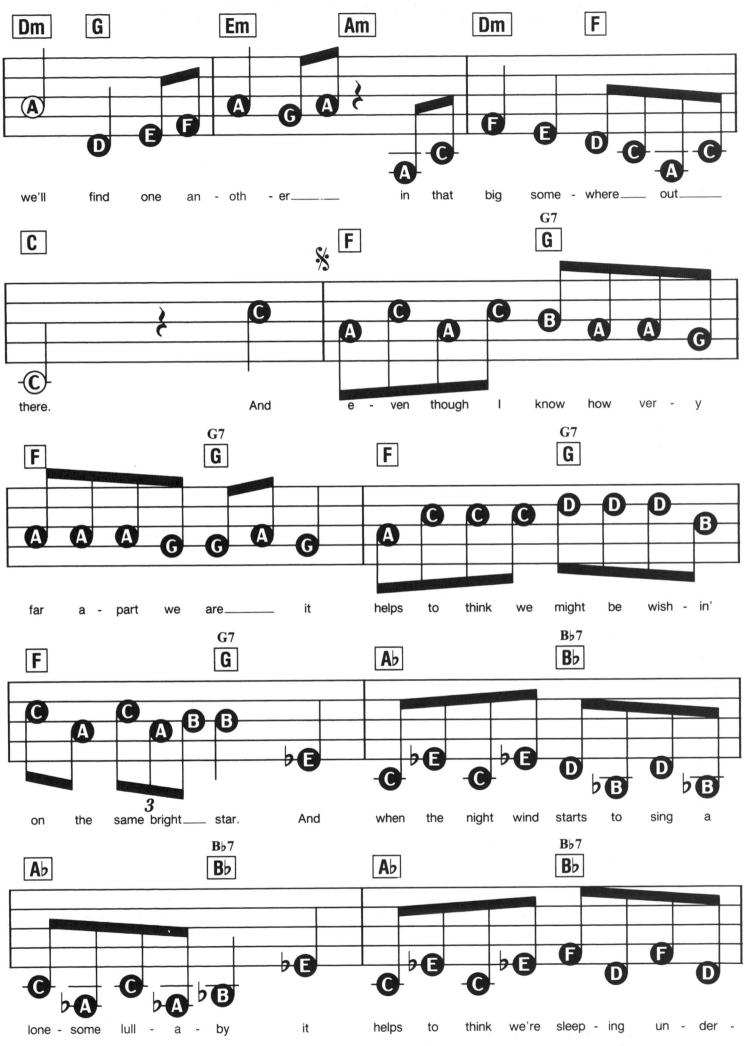

243

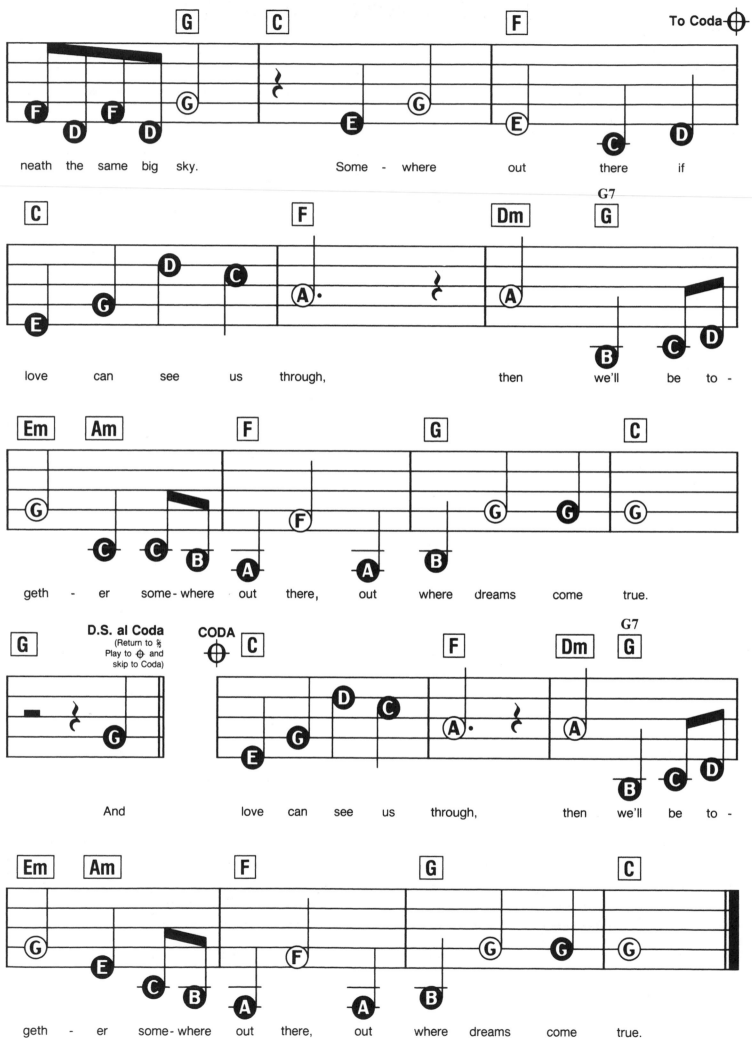

Three Times a Lady

Registration 1
Rhythm: Waltz

Words and Music by
Lionel Richie

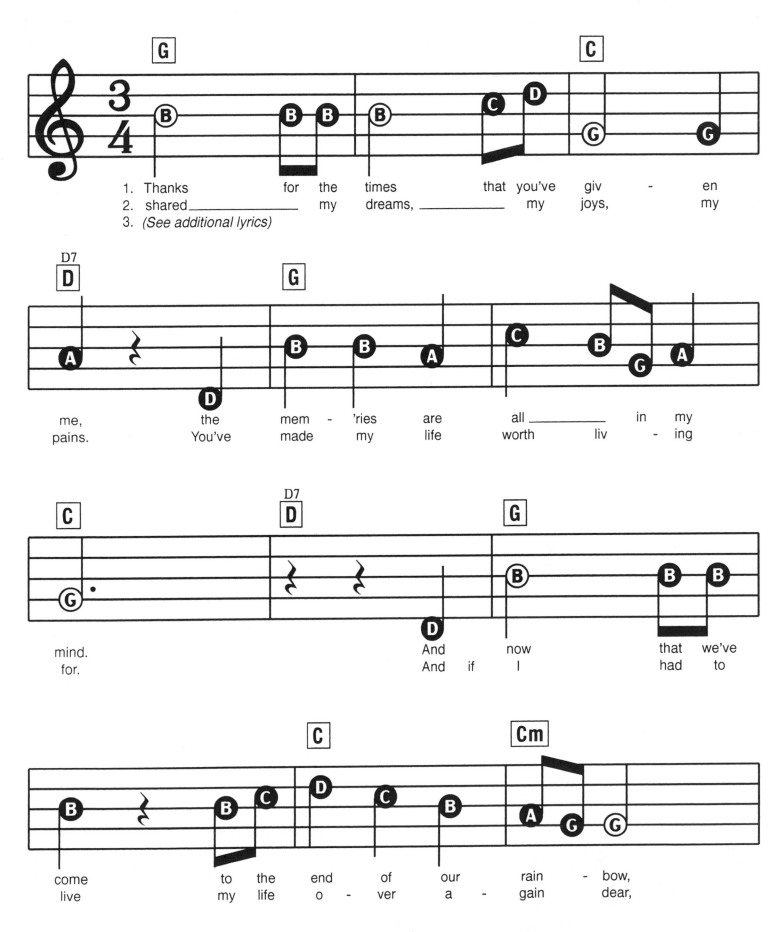

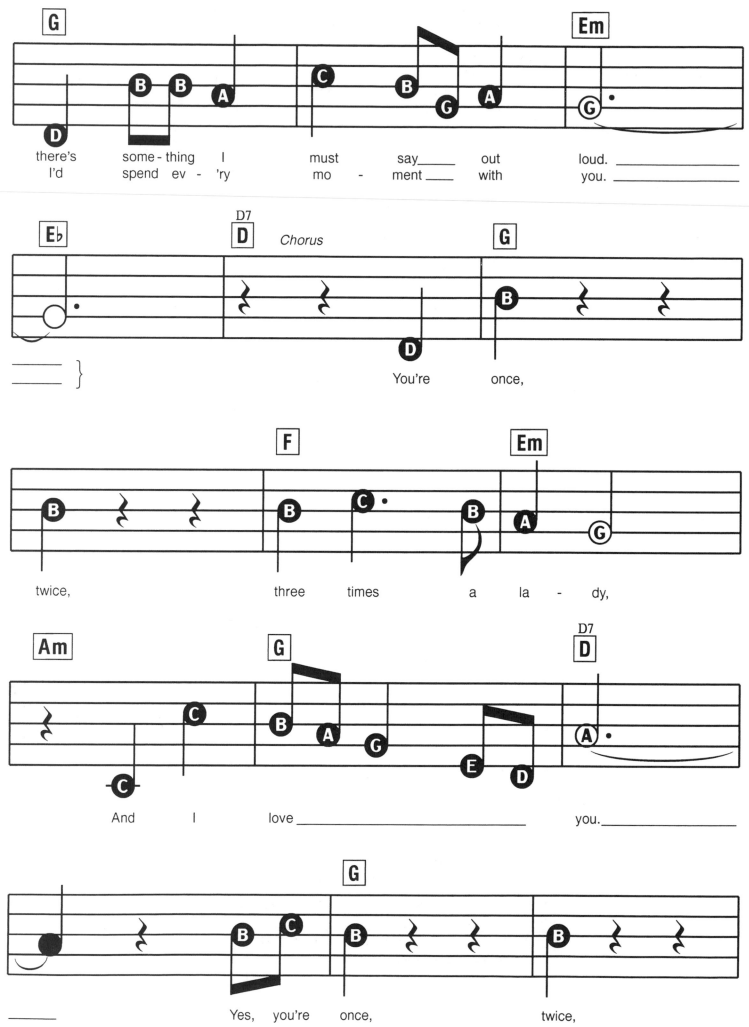

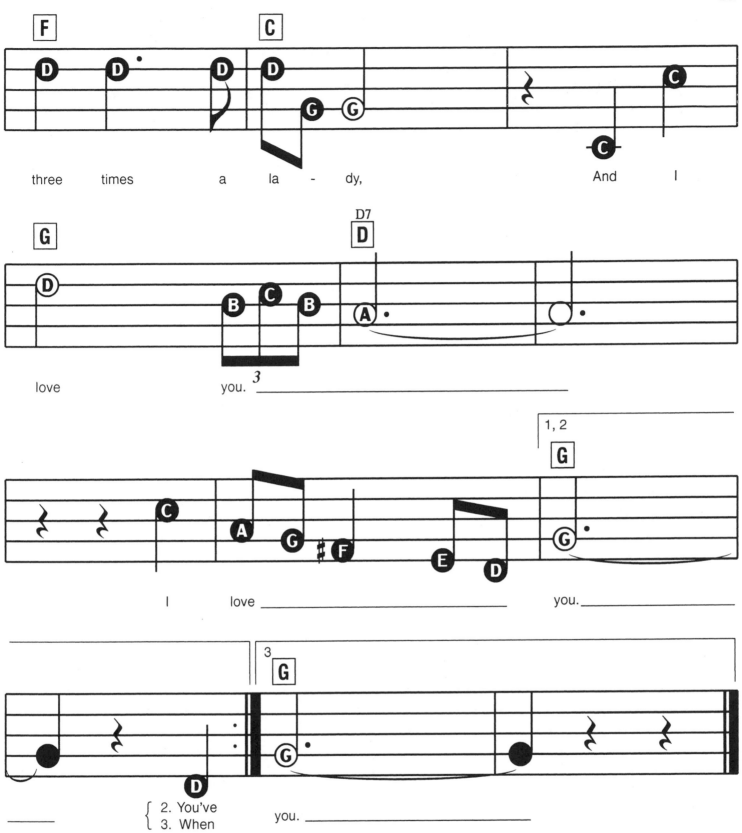

Additional Lyrics

3. When we are together the moments I cherish
   With ev'ry beat of my heart.
   To touch you, to hold you, to feel you, to need you.
   There's nothing to keep us apart.
   Chorus

Strangers in the Night
adapted from A MAN COULD GET KILLED

Registration 5
Rhythm: Ballad or Slow Rock

Words by Charles Singleton and Eddie Snyder
Music by Bert Kaempfert

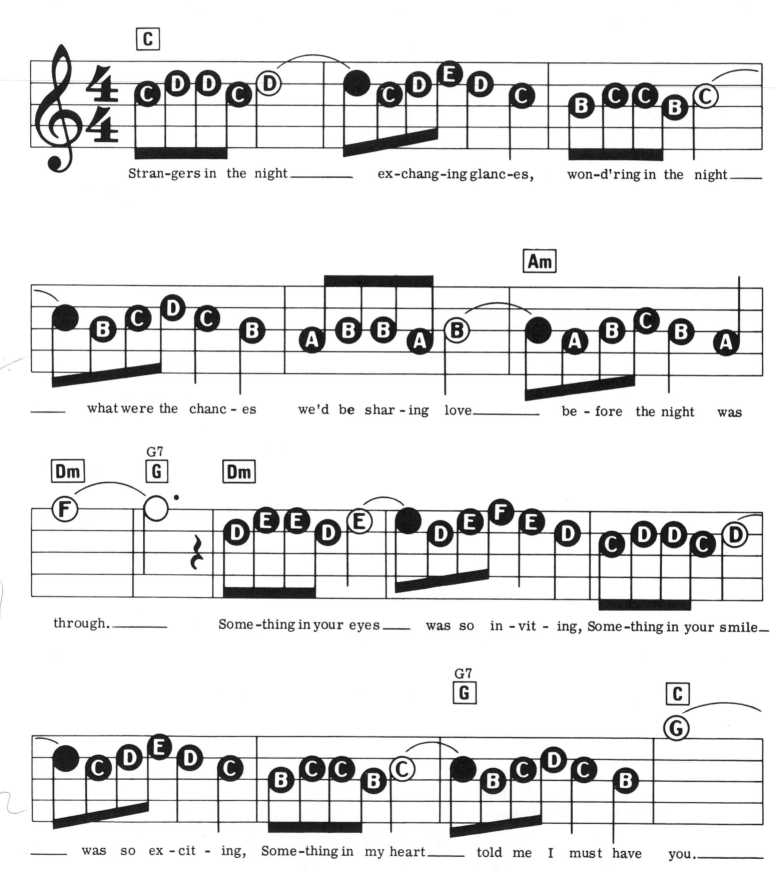

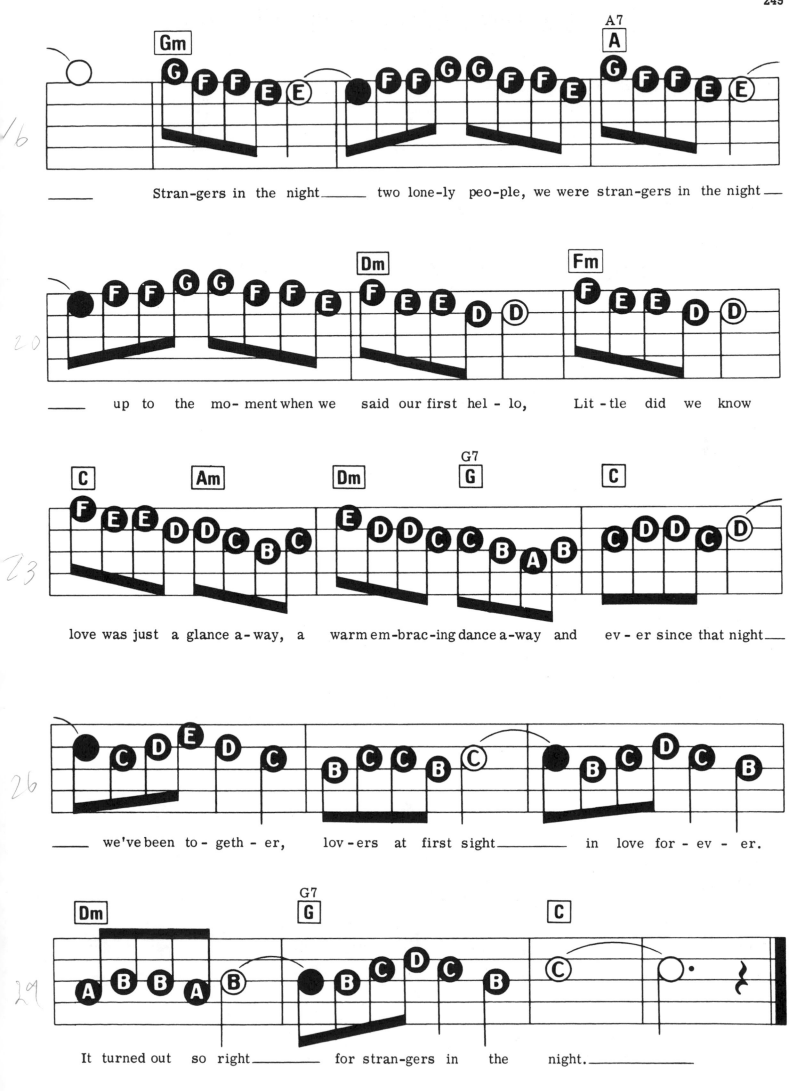

Time After Time

Registration 3
Rhythm: Rock or Jazz Rock

Words and Music by Cyndi Lauper
and Rob Hyman

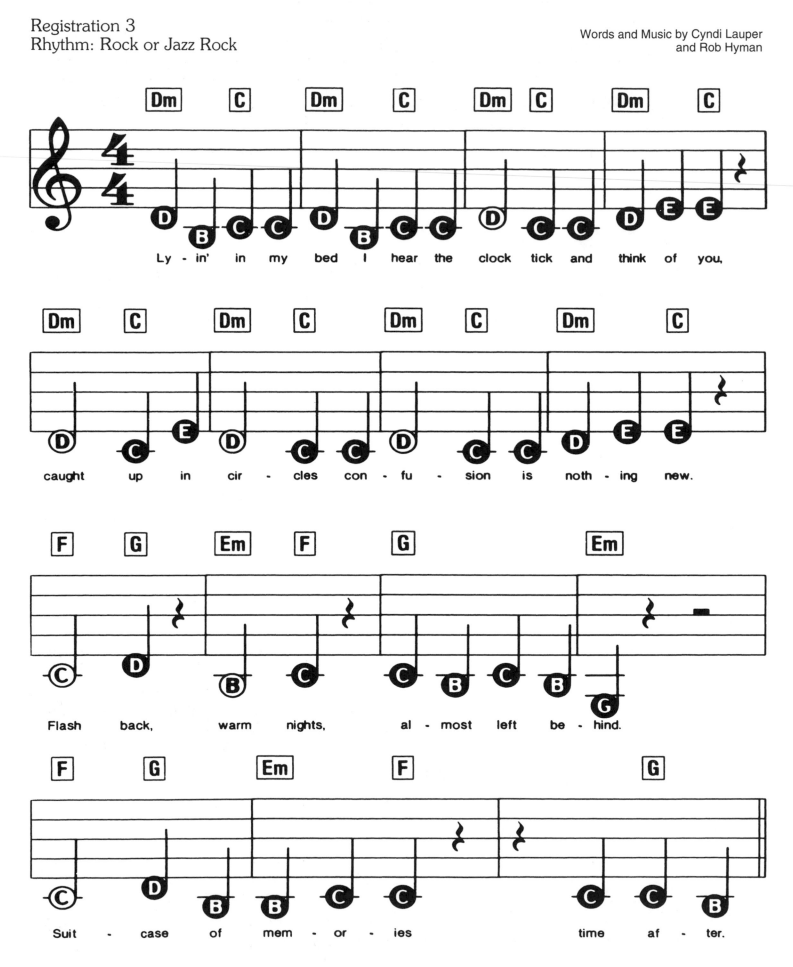

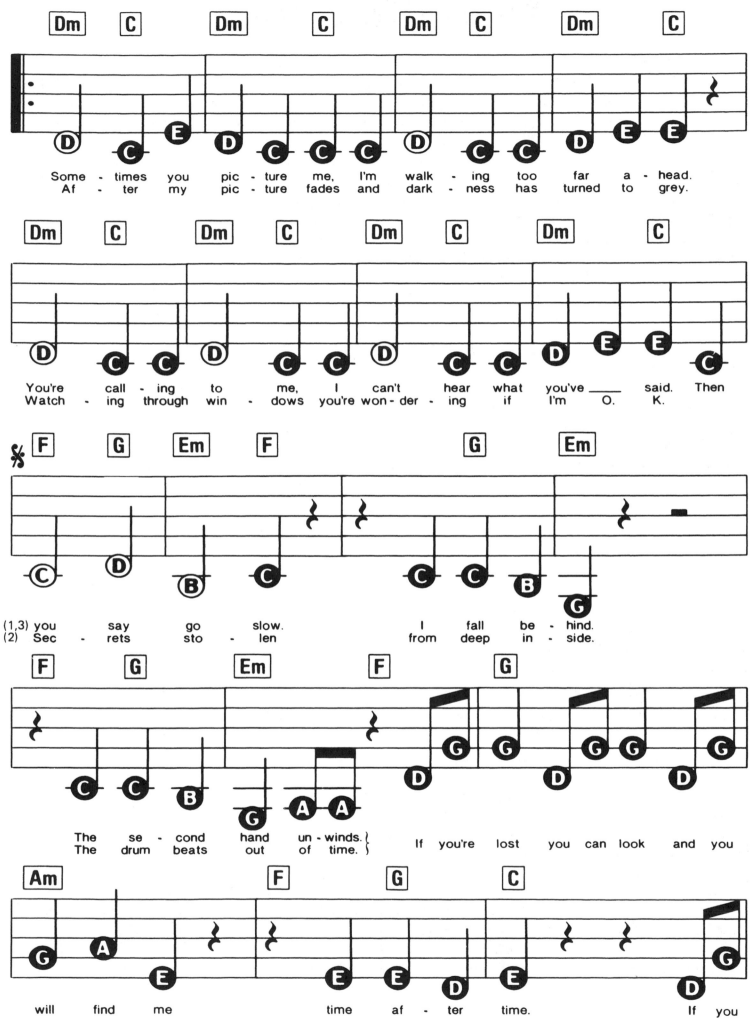

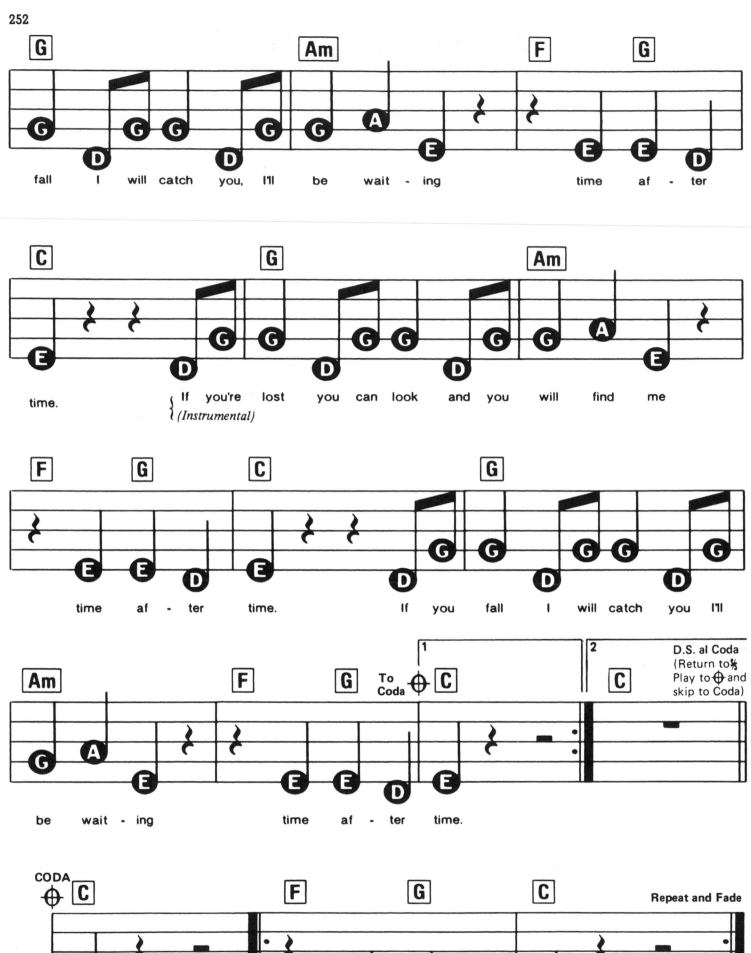

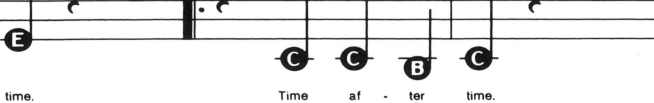

Where Do I Begin
(Love Theme)
from the Paramount Picture LOVE STORY

Registration 8
Rhythm: Ballad or Slow Rock

Words by Carl Sigman
Music by Francis Lai

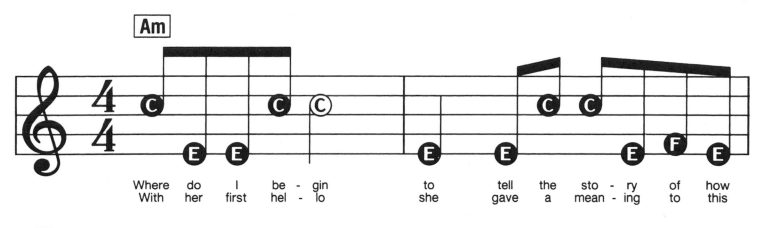

Where do I be - gin to tell the sto - ry of how
With her first hel - lo she gave a mean - ing to this

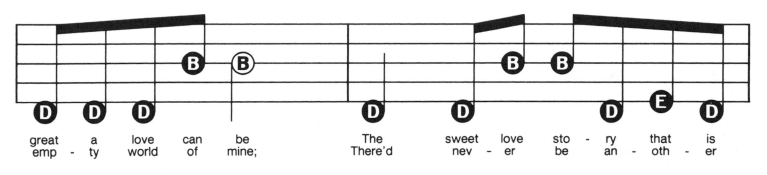

great a love can be The sweet love sto - ry that is
emp - ty world of mine; There'd nev - er be an - oth - er

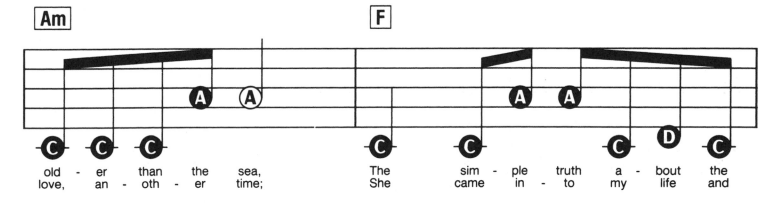

old - er than the sea, The sim - ple truth a - bout the
love, an - oth - er time; She came in - to my life and

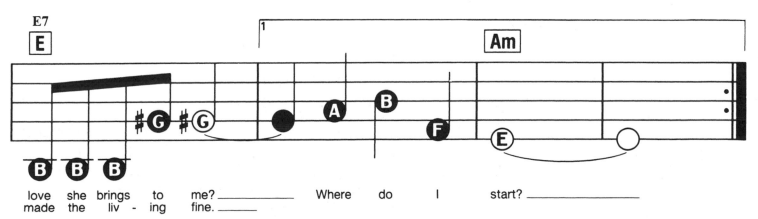

love she brings to me? _____ Where do I start? _____
made the liv - ing fine. _____

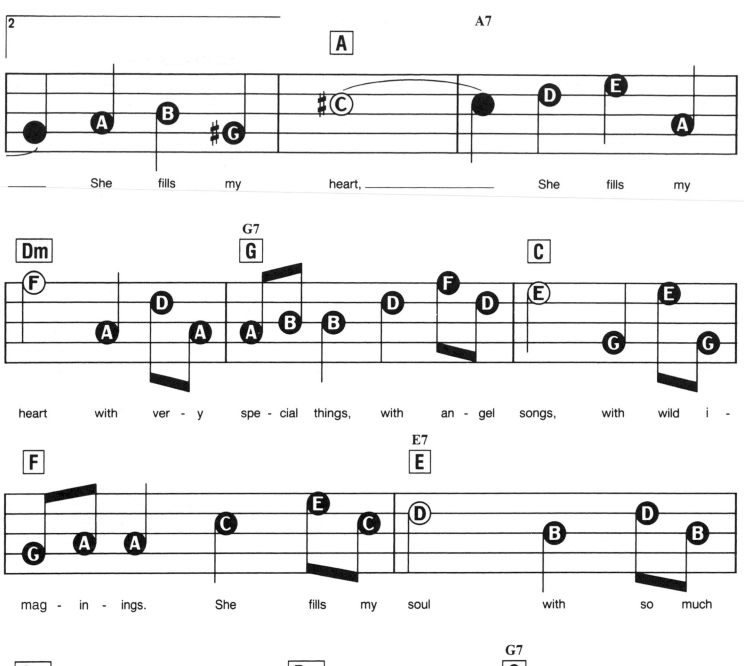

She fills my heart, _____ She fills my

heart with ver - y spe - cial things, with an - gel songs, with wild i -

mag - in - ings. She fills my soul with so much

love that an - y - where I go I'm nev - er lone - ly. With her a -

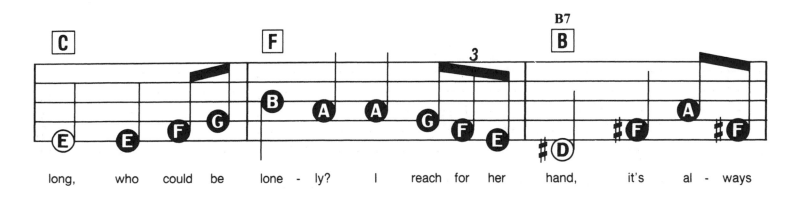

long, who could be lone - ly? I reach for her hand, it's al - ways

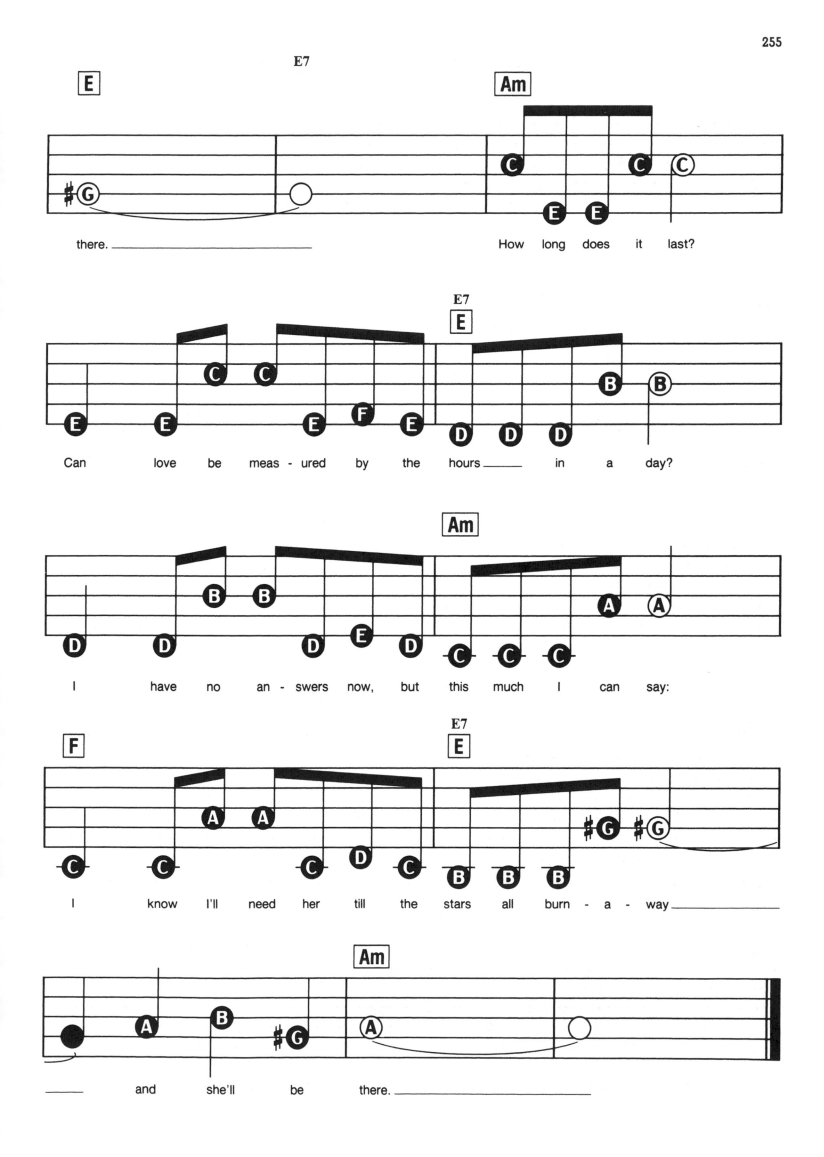

Unchained Melody

Registration 4
Rhythm: Ballad

Lyric by Hy Zaret
Music by Alex North

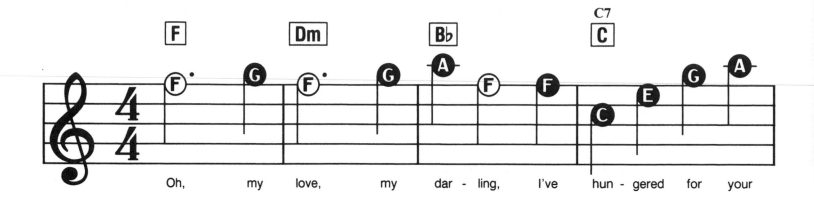

Oh, my love, my dar - ling, I've hun - gered for your

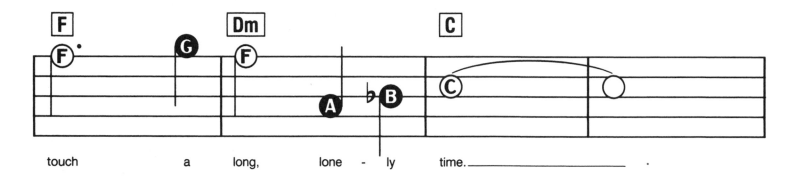

touch a long, lone - ly time. _____

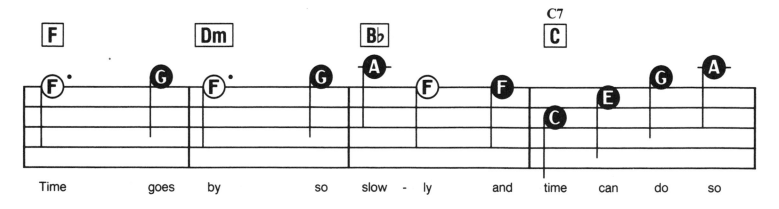

Time goes by so slow - ly and time can do so

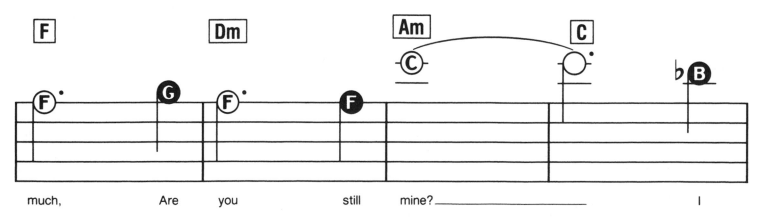

much, Are you still mine? _____ I

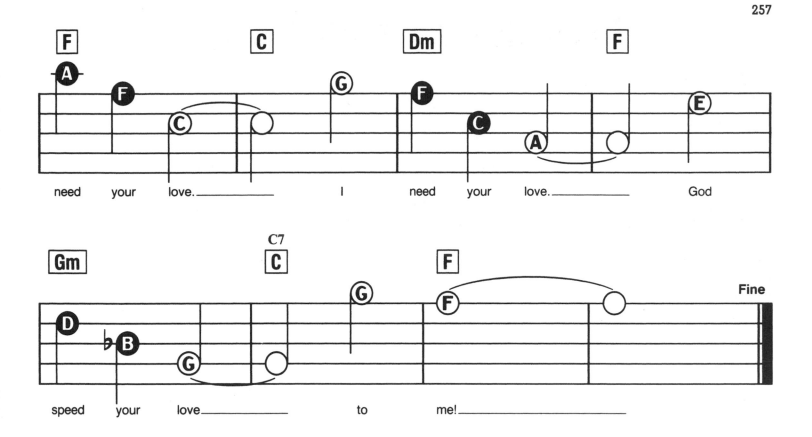

need your love._____ I need your love._____ God

speed your love_____ to me!_____

Fine

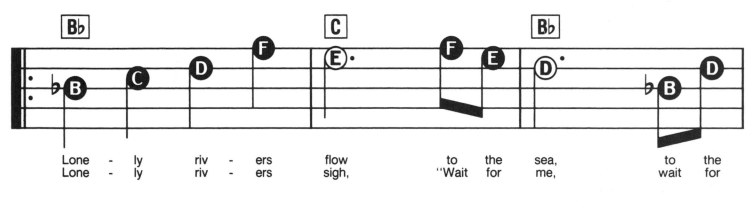

Lone - ly riv - ers flow to the sea, to the
Lone - ly riv - ers sigh, "Wait for me, to wait for

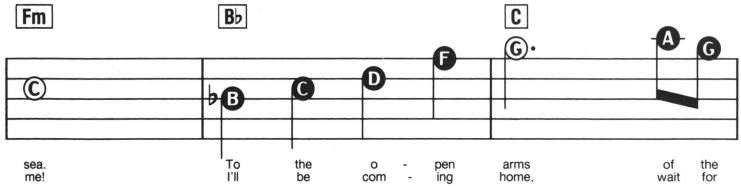

sea. To the o - pen arms of the
me! I'll be com - ing home, wait for

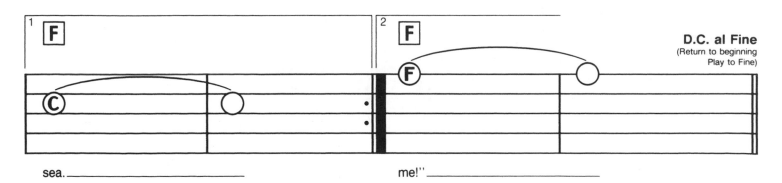

sea._____ me!"_____

D.C. al Fine
(Return to beginning
Play to Fine)

We've Only Just Begun

Registration 1
Rhythm: 8-Beat or Pops

Words and Music by Roger Nichols
and Paul Williams

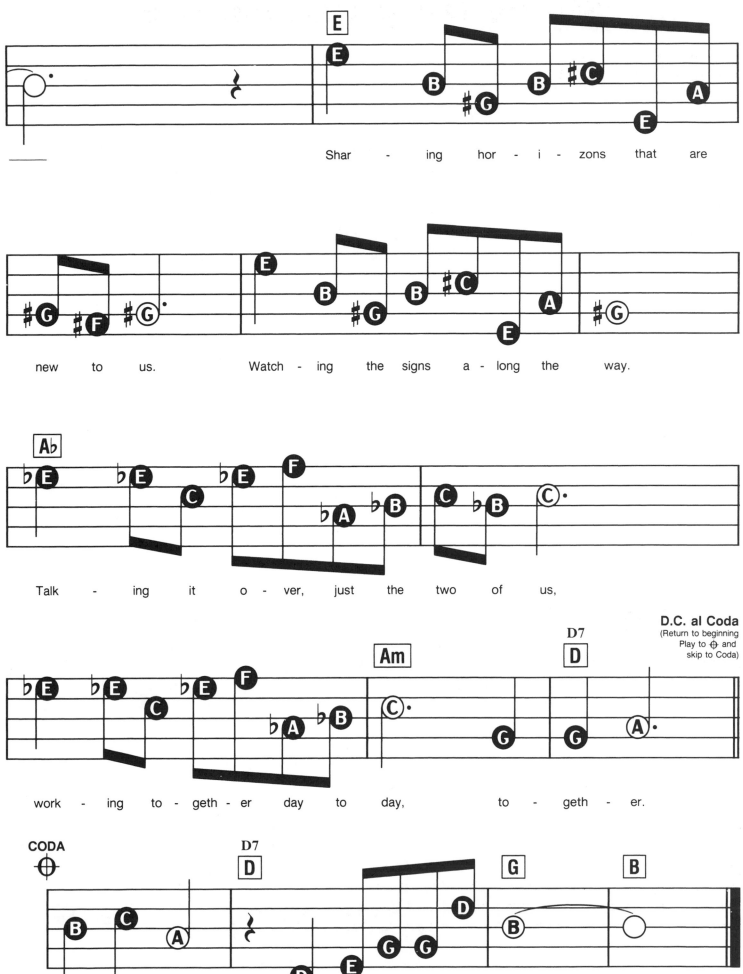

What the World Needs Now Is Love

Registration 2
Rhythm: Jazz Waltz or Waltz

Lyric by Hal David
Music by Burt Bacharach

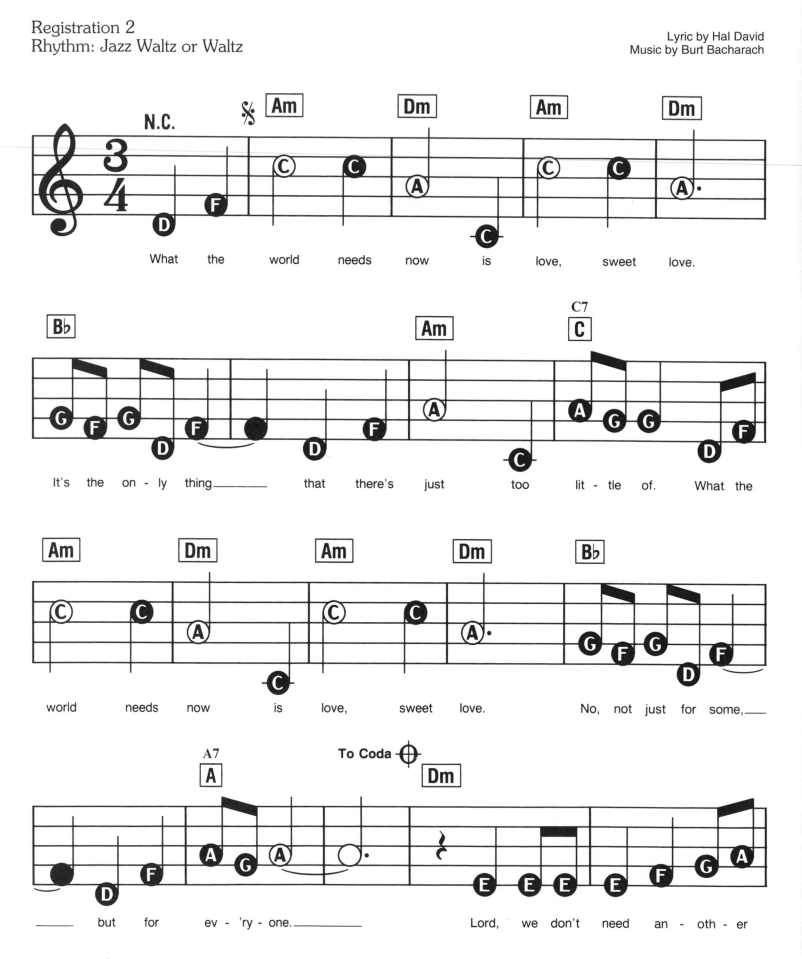

Woman

Registration 3
Rhythm: Rock or Jazz Rock

Words and Music by
John Lennon

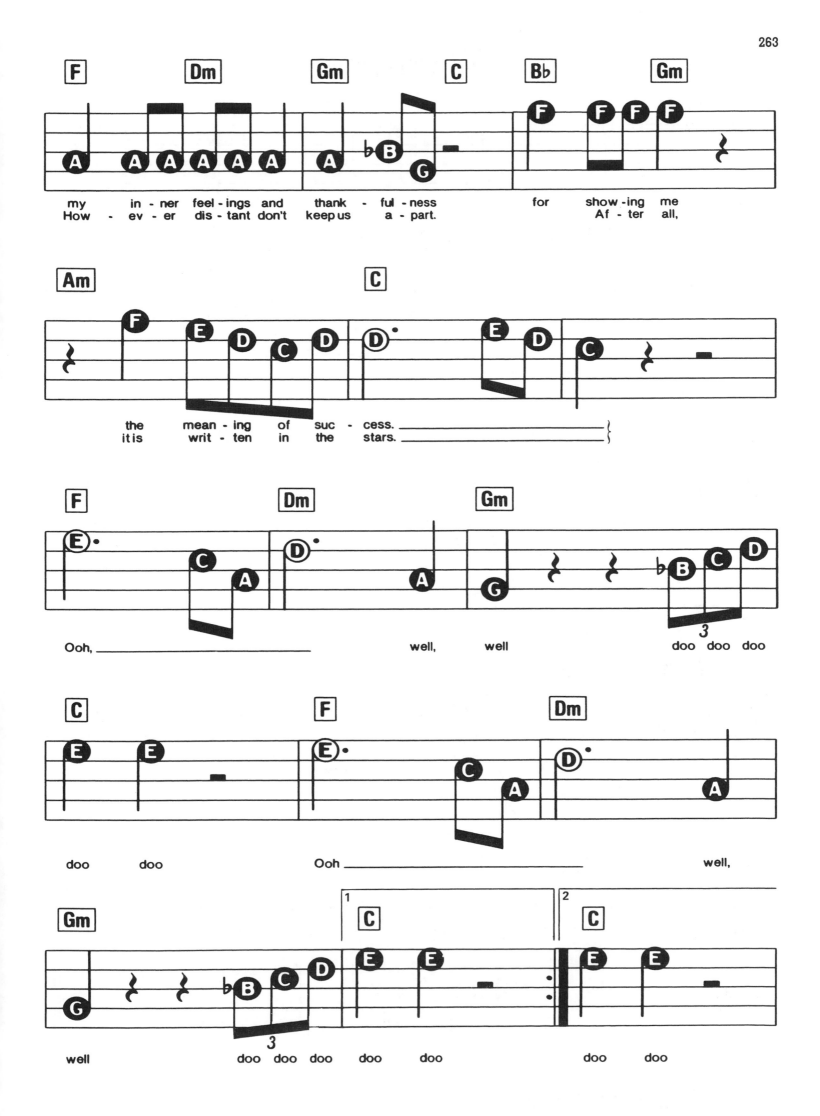

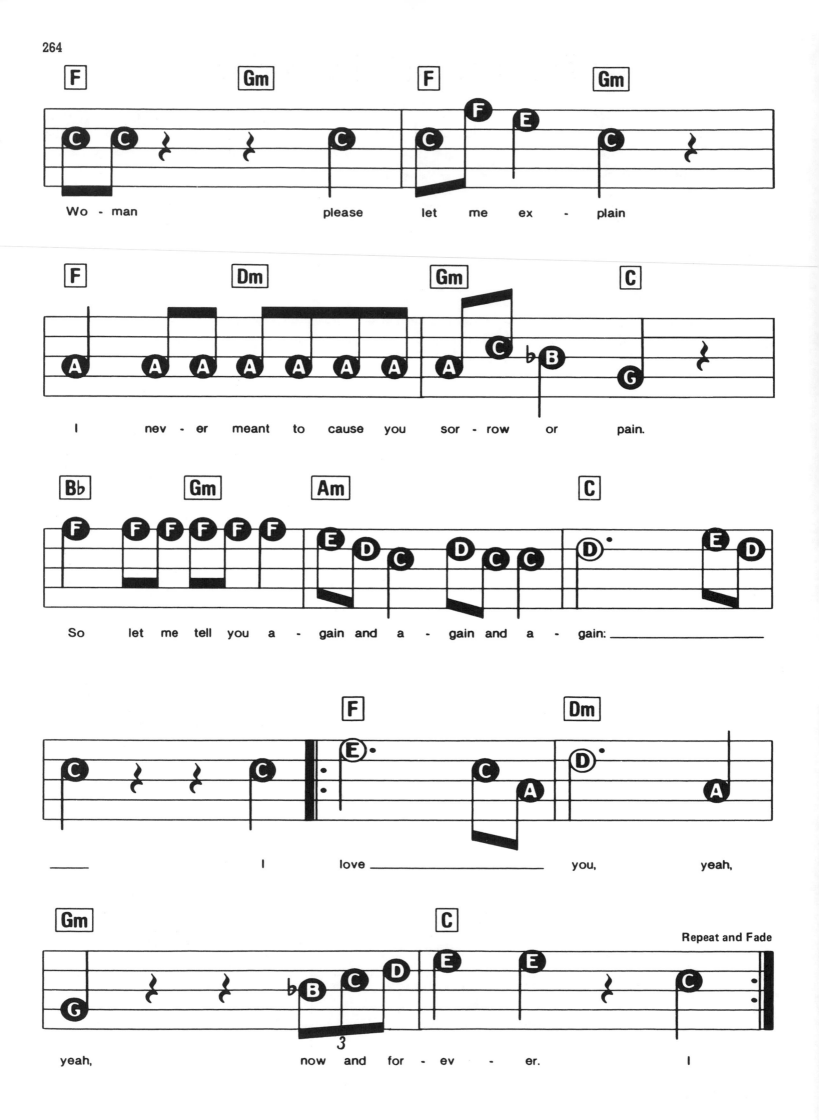

Wonderful Tonight

Registration 4
Rhythm: Pops or Rock

Words and Music by
Eric Clapton

It's late in the eve - ning;
We go to a par - ty,
It's time to go home now,

she's won - d'ring what clothes to wear.
and ev - 'ry - one turns to see
and I've got an ach - ing head.

She puts on her
this beau - ti - ful
So I give her the

make - up
la - dy
car keys

and brush - es her long blonde hair.
is walk - ing a - round with me.
and she helps me to bed. _____

And then she asks me,
And then she asks me,
And then I tell her,

"Do I look all
"Do you feel all
as I turn out the

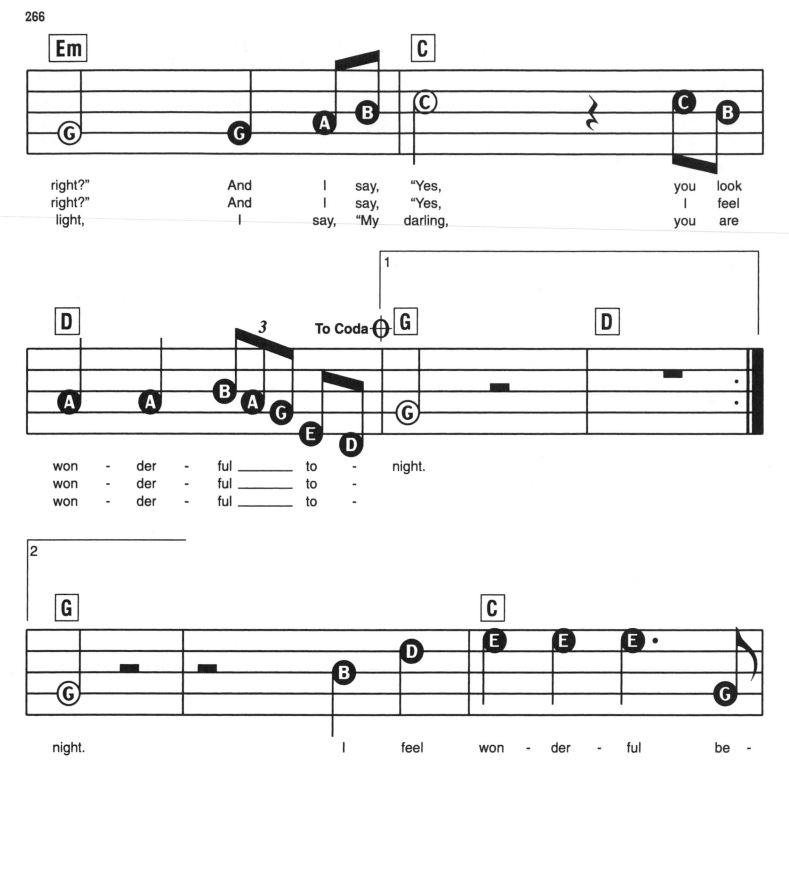

right?"   And   I   say,   "Yes,   you   look
right?"   And   I   say,   "Yes,   I   feel
light,   I   say,   "My   darling,   you   are

won - der - ful _____ to - night.
won - der - ful _____ to -
won - der - ful _____ to -

night.   I   feel   won - der - ful   be -

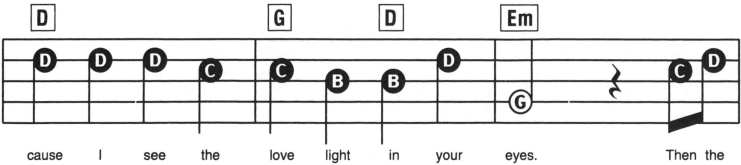

cause   I   see   the   love   light   in   your   eyes.   Then the

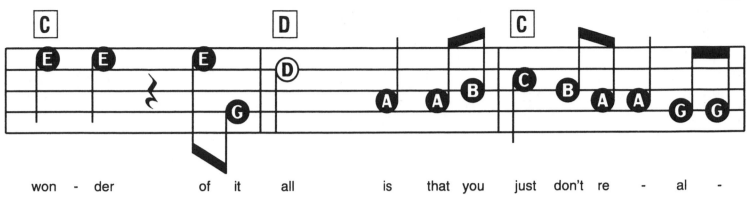

won - der   of it all   is   that you   just don't re - al -

D.C. al Coda
(Return to beginning
Play to ⊕ and
Skip to Coda)

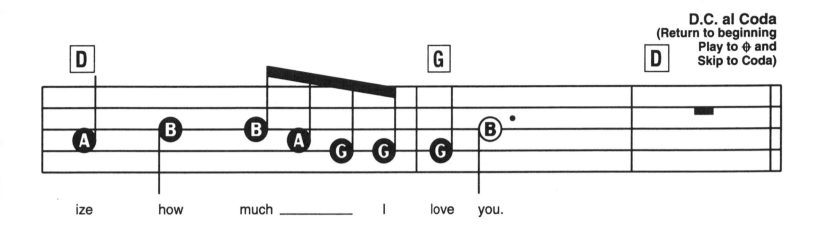

ize   how   much _____   I   love   you.

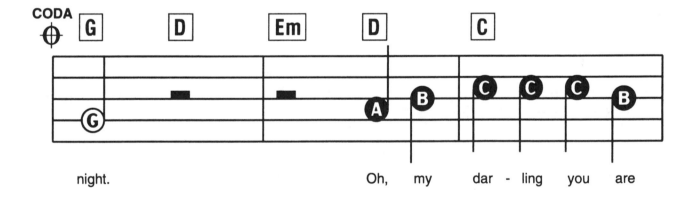

night.   Oh,   my   dar - ling   you   are

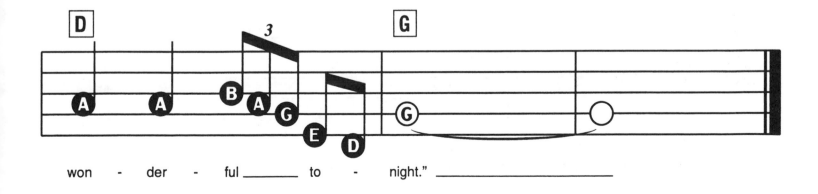

won - der - ful _____ to - night." _____

You Are My Lady

Registration 8
Rhythm: 4/4 Ballad or 8-Beat

Words and Music by
Barry Eastmond

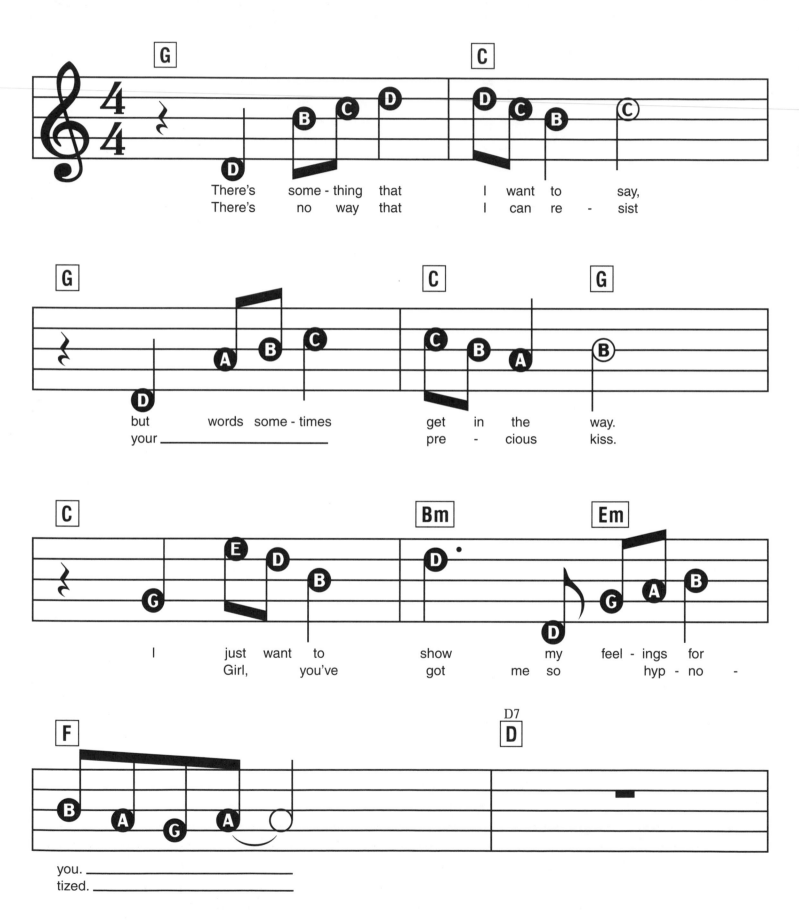

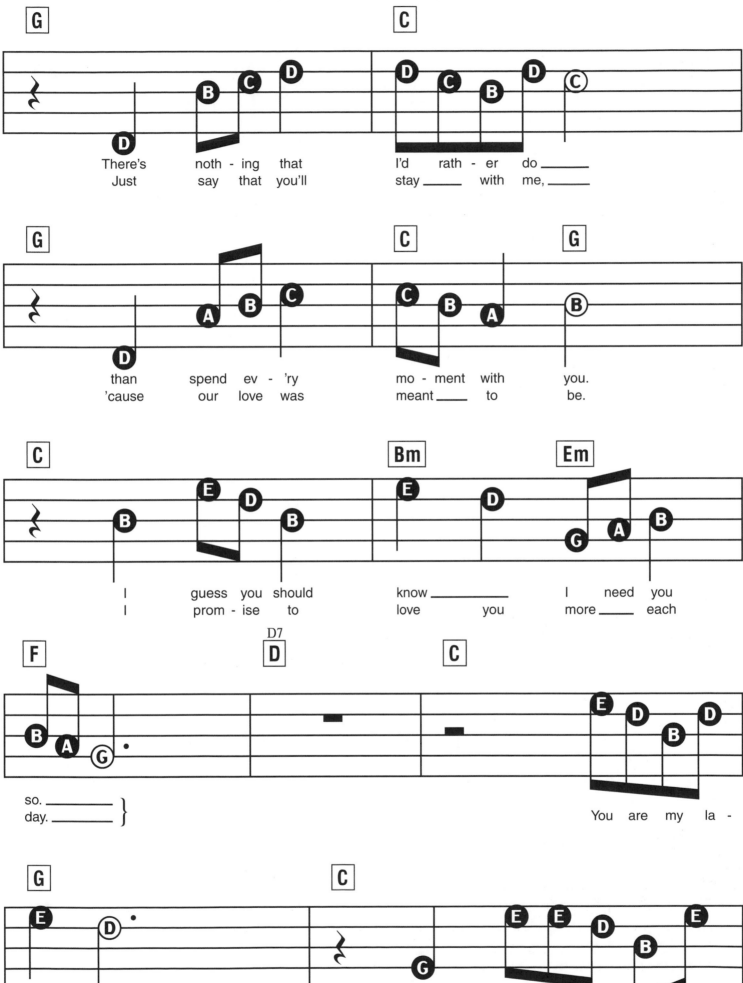

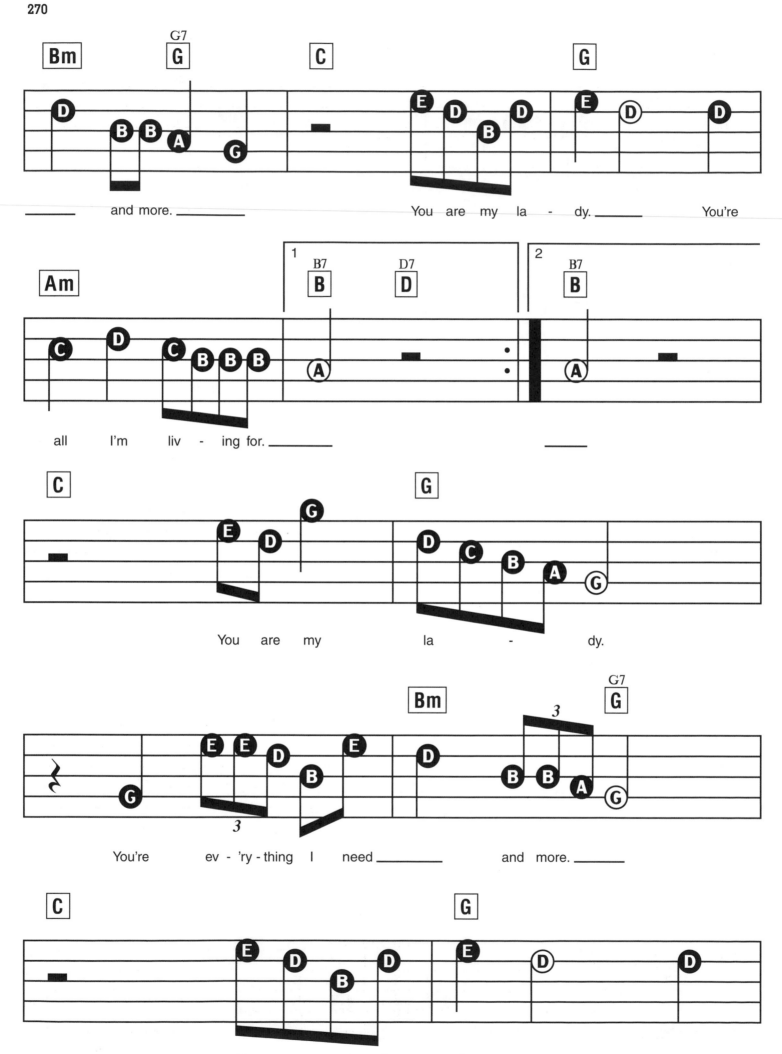

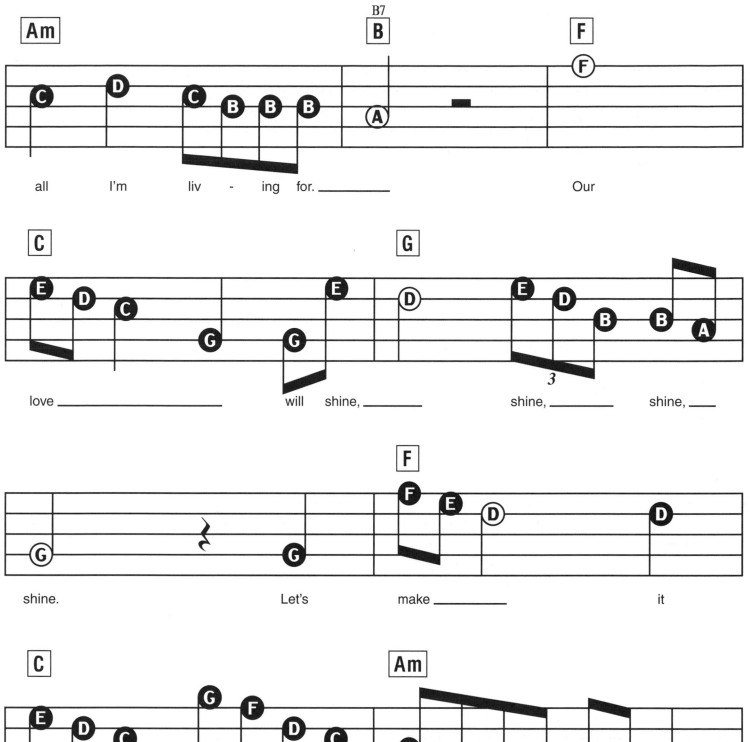

all I'm liv - ing for. _____ Our

love _____ will shine, _____ shine, _____ shine, ___

shine. Let's make _____ it

last, _____ oh, _____ till the end of

time. _____

You Are So Beautiful

Registration 1
Rhythm: Pops or 8-Beat

Words and Music by Billy Preston
and Bruce Fisher

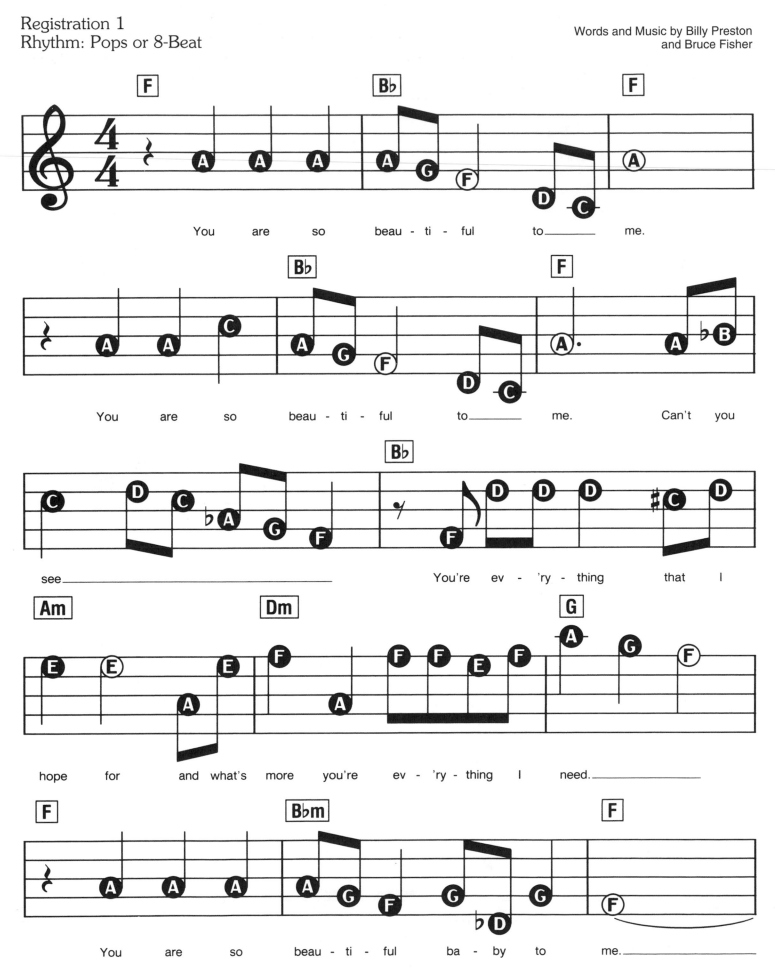

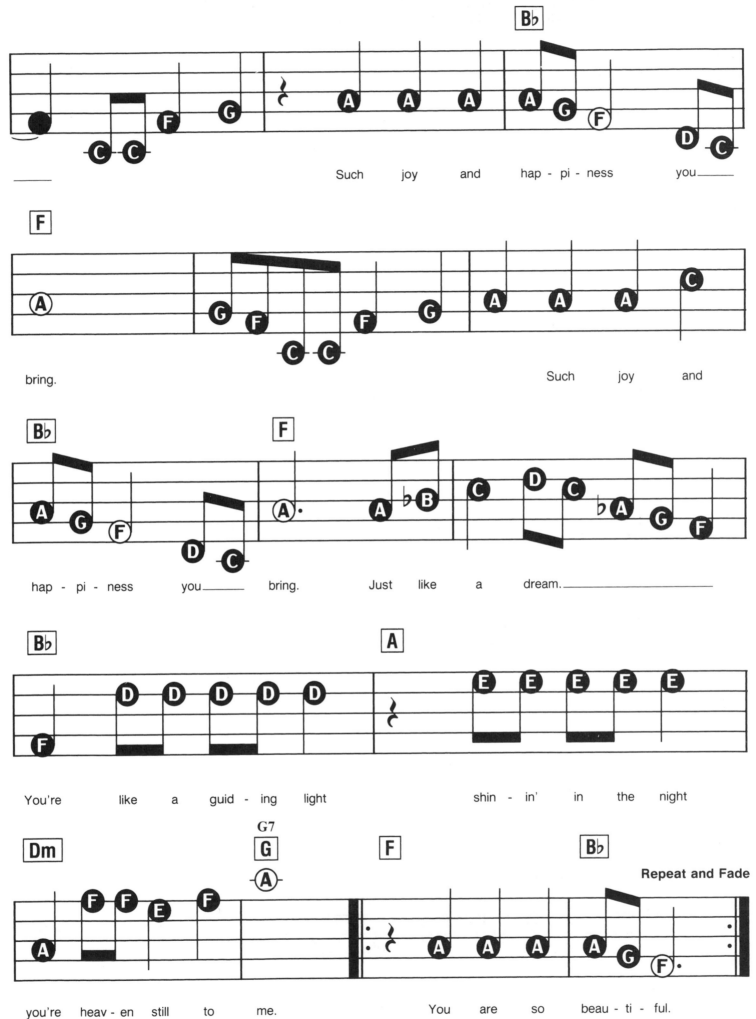

Such joy and hap - pi - ness you____

bring.   Such joy and

hap - pi - ness you____ bring. Just like a dream._____

You're   like   a   guid - ing   light   shin - in'   in   the   night

you're   heav - en   still   to   me.   You   are   so   beau - ti - ful.

Repeat and Fade

You Light Up My Life

Registration 3
Rhythm: Waltz

Words and Music by
Joseph Brooks

Dm / G / C

So man - y nights, I'd sit by my
Roll - in' at sea, a - drift on the

Am / Bm / E7 (E)

win - dow wait - ing for some - one to
wa - ters, could it be fi - n'lly I'm

Am / A7 (A) / Dm

sing me his song.
turn - ing his for home. So man - y
Fi - n'lly a

G / C / Am

dreams I kept deep in - side me, a -
chance to say "Hey!" I love you."

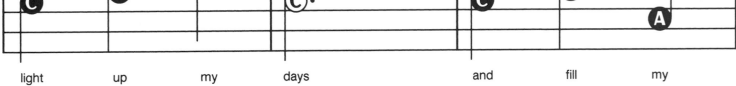

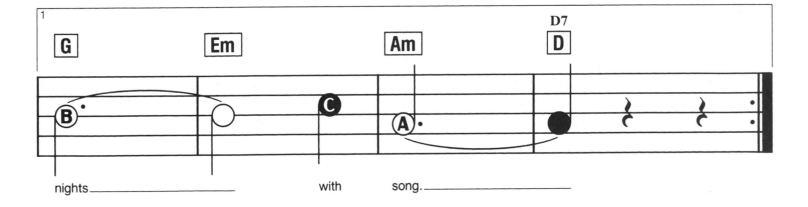

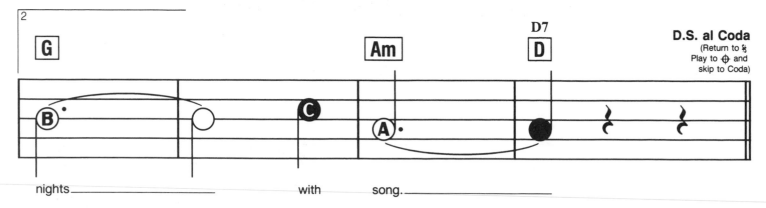

D.S. al Coda
(Return to 𝄋
Play to ⊕ and
skip to Coda)

nights_____ with song._____

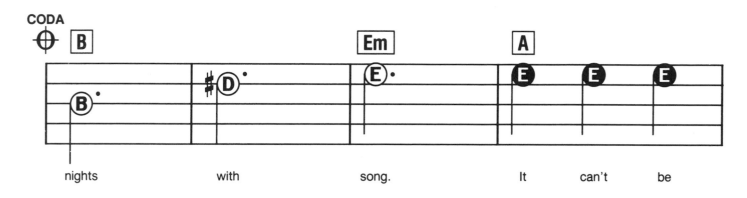

CODA

nights with song. It can't be

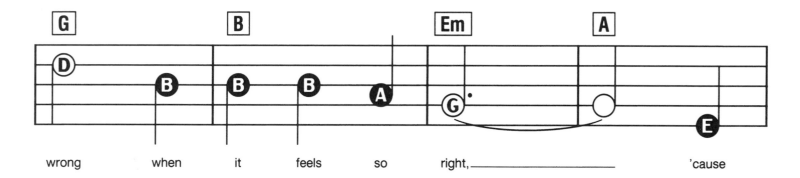

wrong when it feels so right,_____ 'cause

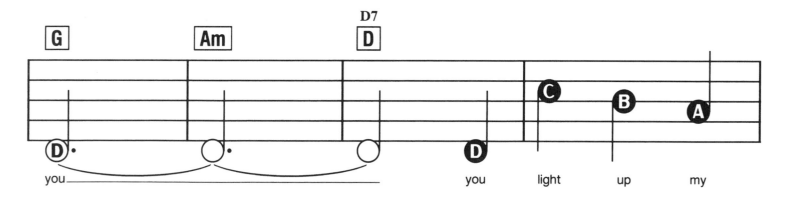

you_____ you light up my

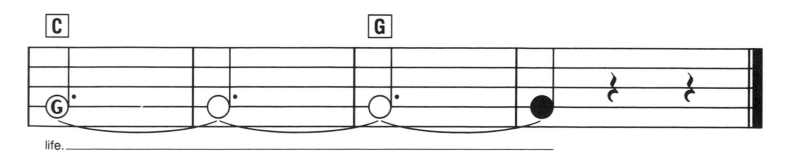

life._____

You're Still the One

Registration 9
Rhythm: Rock or 8-Beat

Words and Music by Shania Twain
and R.J. Lange

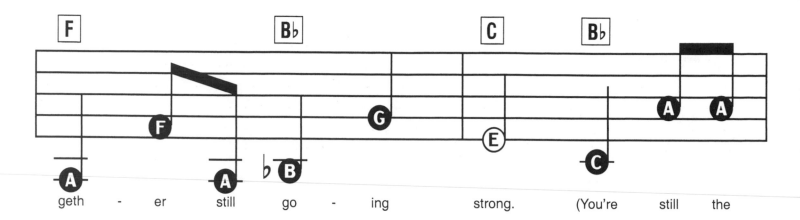

geth - er still go - ing strong. (You're still the

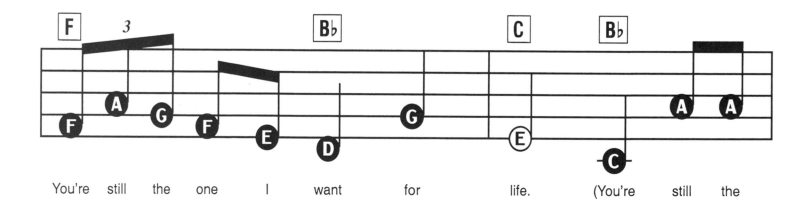

one.) You're still the one I run to, _____ the one that I be - long to. _____

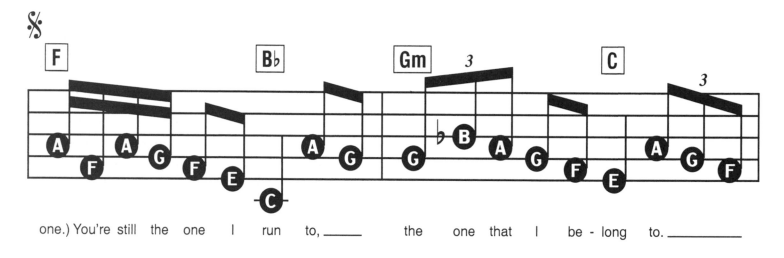

You're still the one I want for life. (You're still the

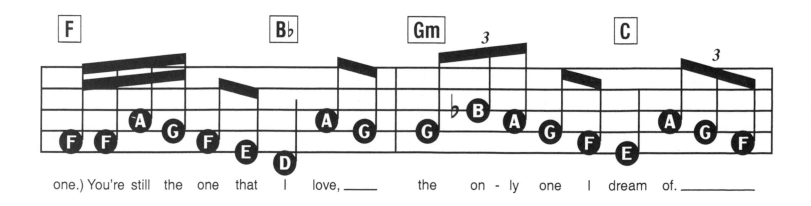

one.) You're still the one that I love, _____ the on - ly one I dream of. _____

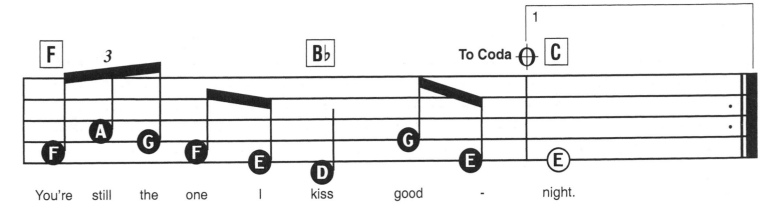

You're still the one I kiss good - night.

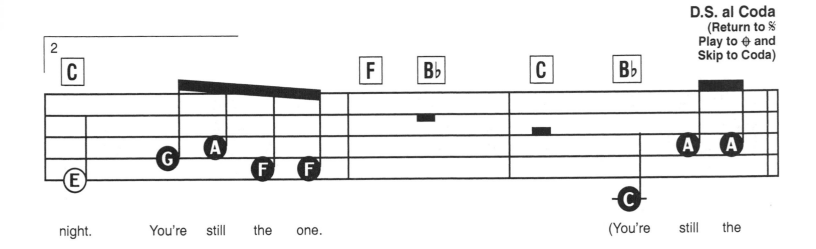

night. You're still the one.

(You're still the

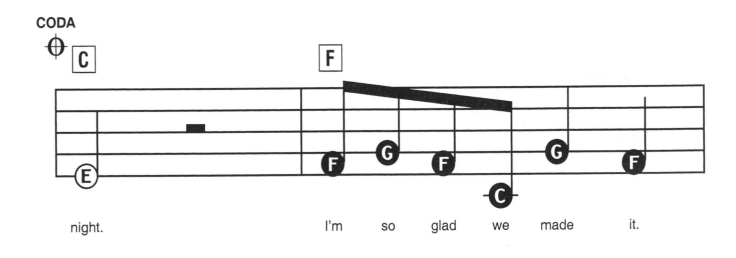

night. I'm so glad we made it.

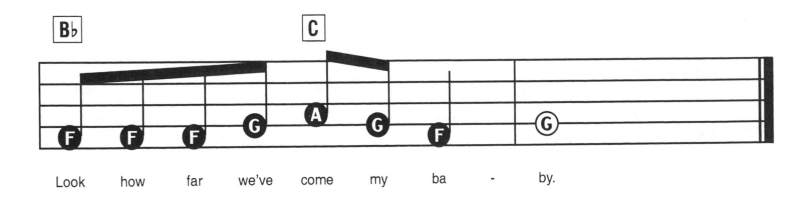

Look how far we've come my ba - by.

You're in My Heart

Registration 1
Rhythm: Shuffle or Swing

Words and Music by
Rod Stewart

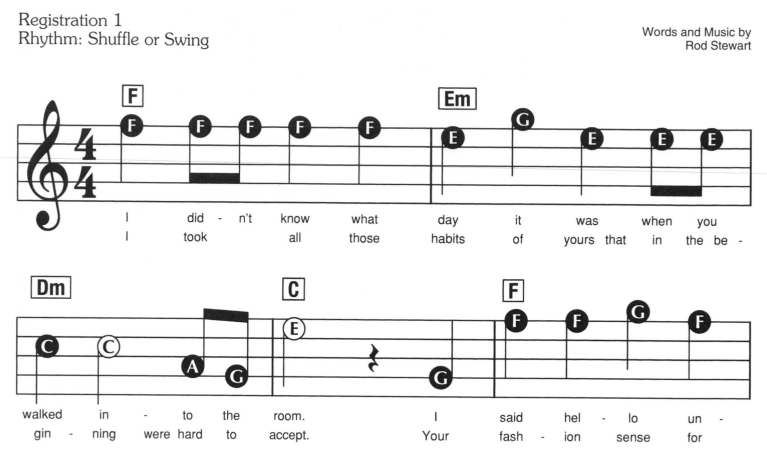

I
I
did - n't
took
know
all
what
those
day
habits
it
of
was
yours
when
that
you
in
the be -

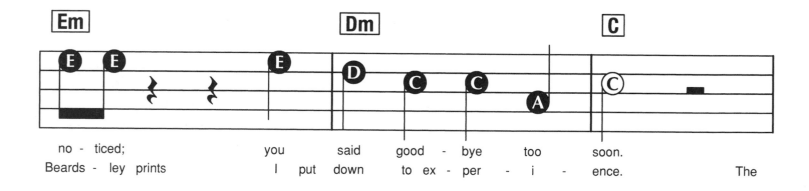

walked
gin - ning
in - to
were hard
the
to
room.
accept.
I
Your
said
fash -
hel -
ion
lo
sense
un -
for

no - ticed;
Beards - ley prints
you
I
said
put
good -
down
bye
to ex -
too
per -
i -
soon.
ence.
The

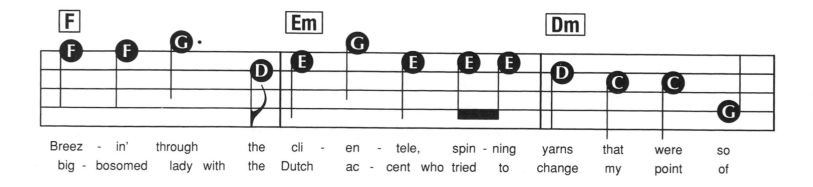

Breez - in' through
big - bosomed lady with
the
the
cli -
Dutch
en - tele,
ac - cent who
spin - ning
tried
yarns
to
that
change
were
my
so
point of

281

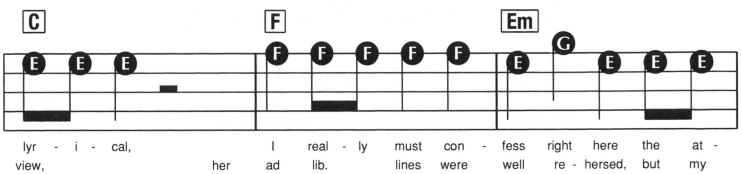

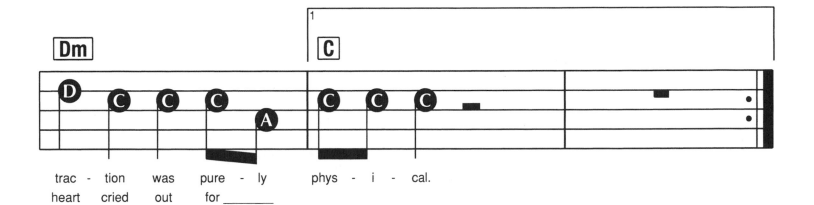

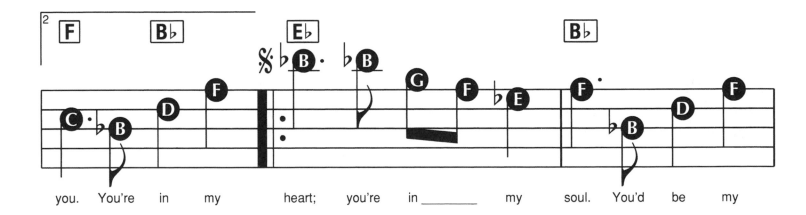

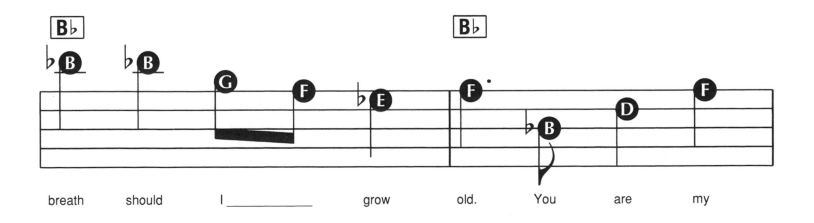

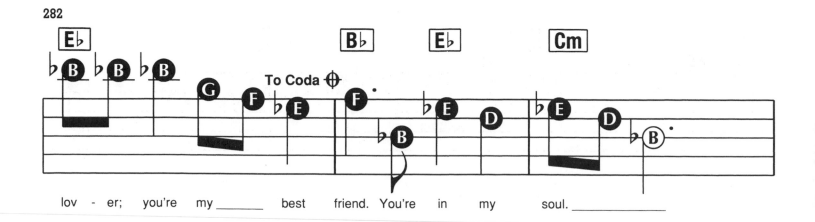

lov - er; you're my _____ best friend. You're in my soul. _____

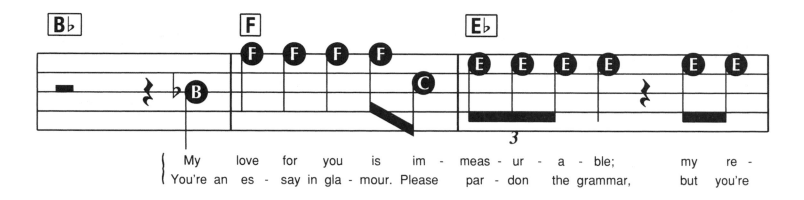

My love for you is im - meas - ur - a - ble; my re -
You're an es - say in gla - mour. Please par - don the grammar, but you're

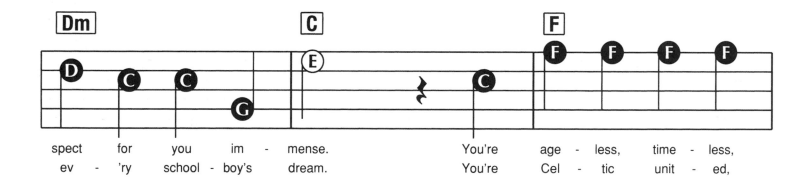

spect for you im - mense. You're age - less, time - less,
ev - 'ry school - boy's dream. You're Cel - tic unit - ed,

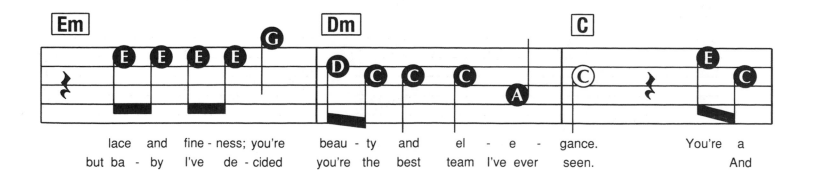

lace and fine - ness; you're beau - ty and el - e - gance. You're a
but ba - by I've de - cided you're the best team I've ever seen. And

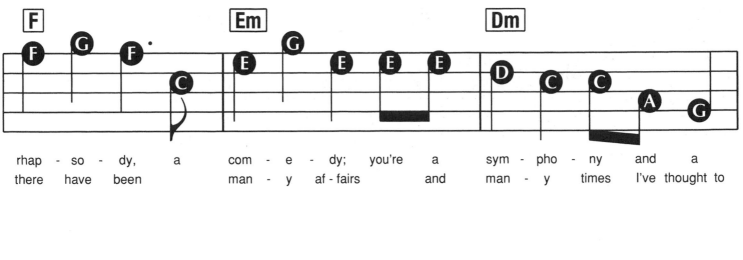

rhap - so - dy, a com - e - dy; you're a sym - pho - ny and a
there have been man - y af - fairs and man - y times I've thought to

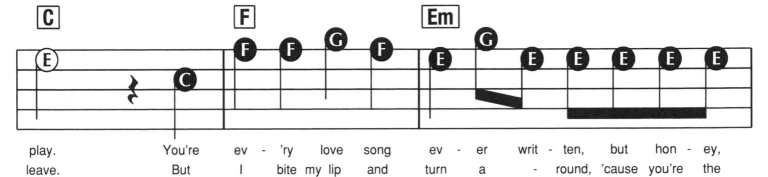

play. You're ev - 'ry love song ev - er writ - ten, but hon - ey,
leave. But I bite my lip and turn a - round, 'cause you're the

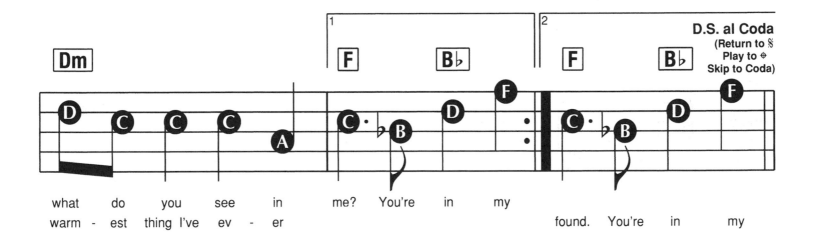

what do you see in me? You're in my
warm - est thing I've ev - er found. You're in my

D.S. al Coda
(Return to %
Play to ⊕
Skip to Coda)

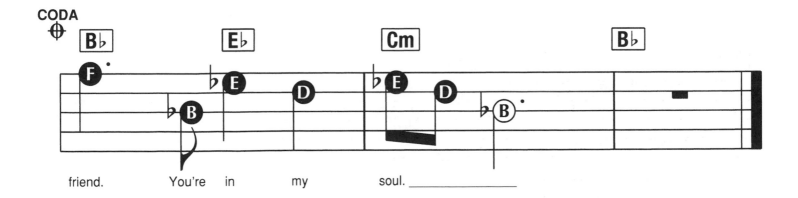

CODA

friend. You're in my soul. _____

Your Song

Registration 3
Rhythm: Swing or Pops

Words and Music by Elton John
and Bernie Taupin

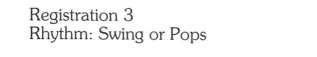

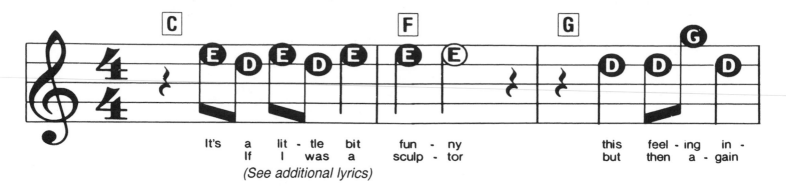

It's a lit - tle bit fun - ny this feel - ing in -
If I was a sculp - tor but then a - gain
(See additional lyrics)

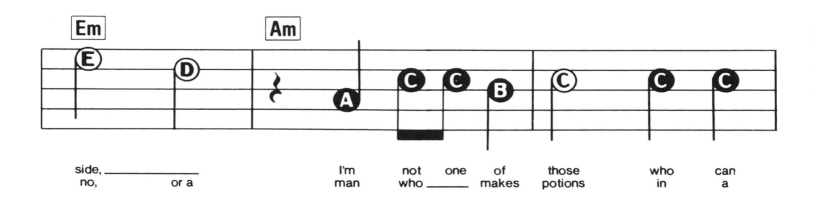

side, _____ or a I'm not one of those who can
no, _____ or a man who _____ makes those potions who in a

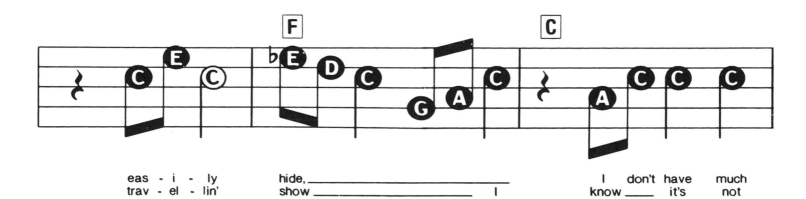

eas - i - ly hide, _____ I don't have much
trav - el - lin' show _____ I know ___ it's not

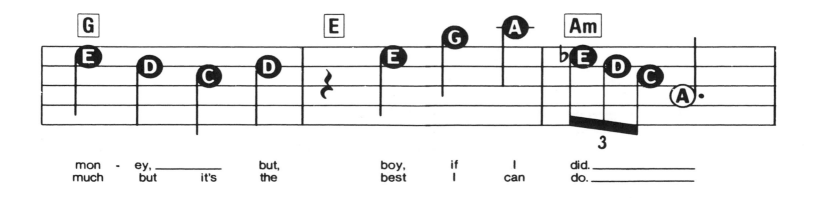

mon - ey, _____ but, boy, if I did. _____
much but it's the best I can do. _____

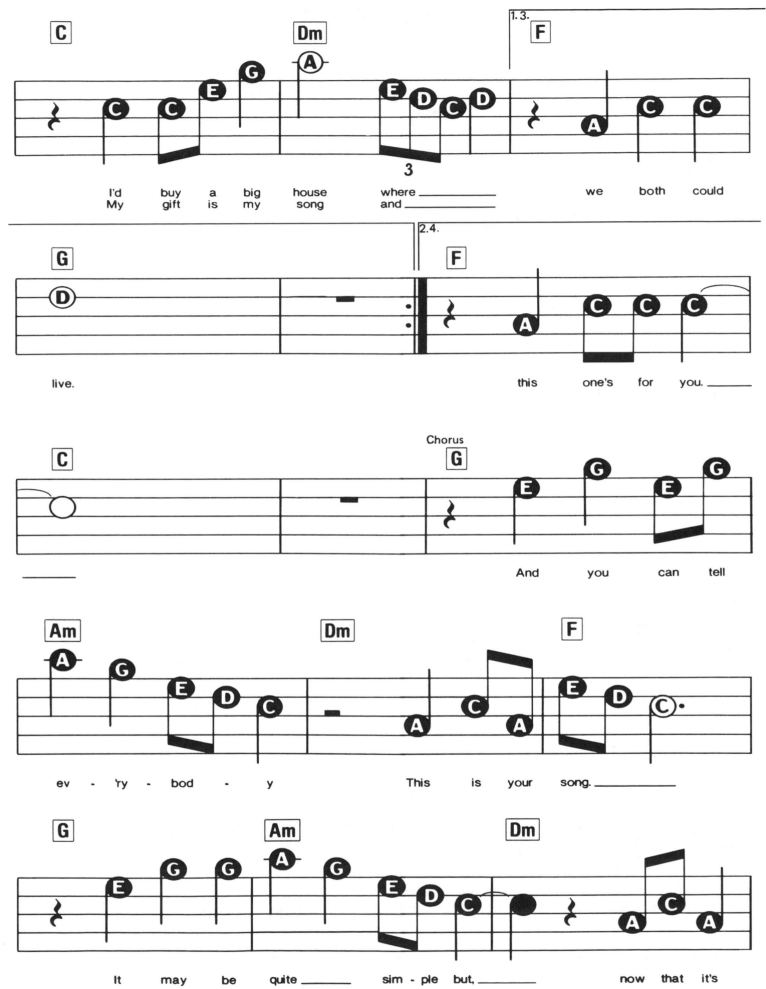

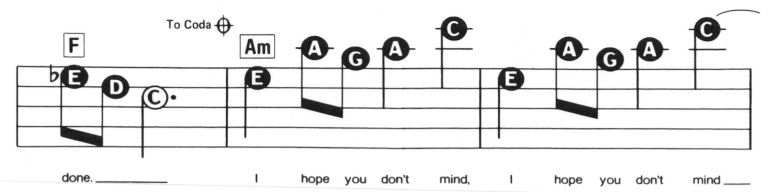

done. _____ I hope you don't mind, I hope you don't mind _____

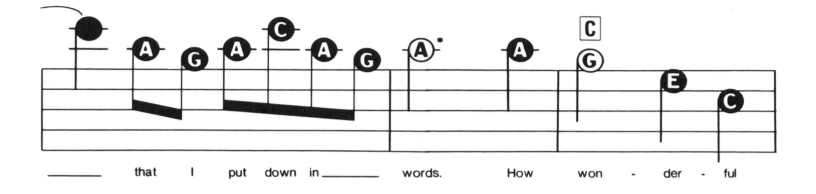

_____ that I put down in _____ words. How won - der - ful

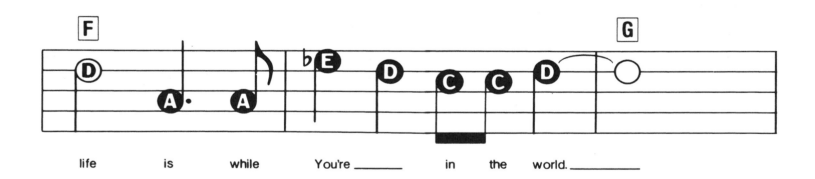

life is while You're _____ in the world. _____

D.C. al Coda
(Return to
beginning,
take 3rd & 4th
endings, Play
till ⊕ and skip
to Coda)

⊕ CODA

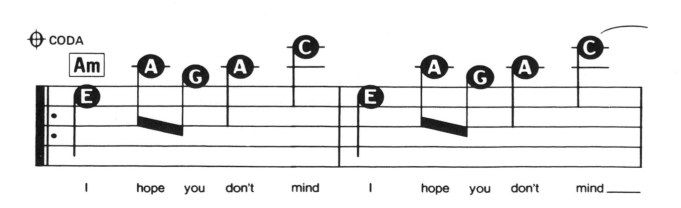

I hope you don't mind I hope you don't mind _____

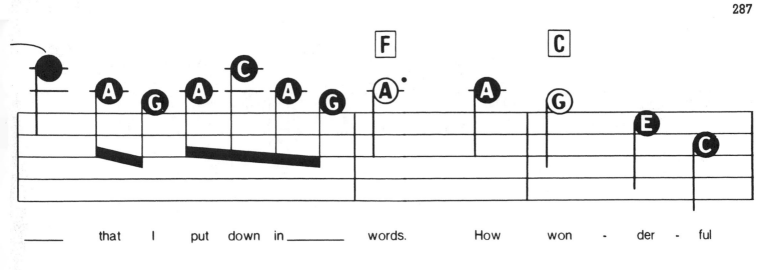

_____ that I put down in _____ words. How won - der - ful

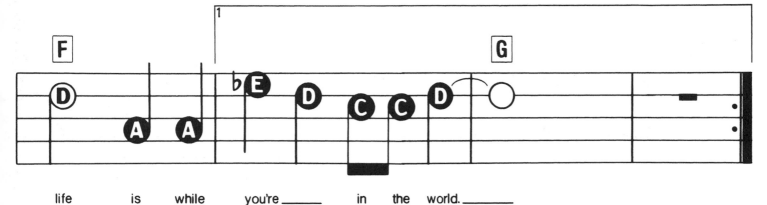

life is while you're _____ in the world. _____

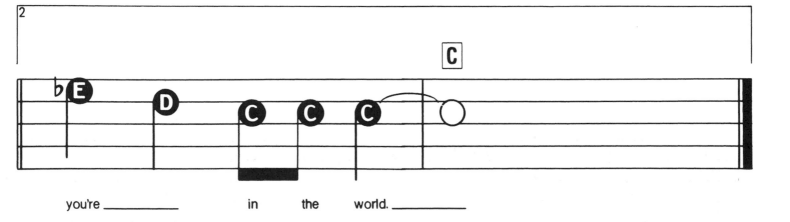

you're _____ in the world. _____

Additional Lyrics

3. I sat on the roof and kicked off the moss.
   well a few of the verses, well they've got me quite cross,
   But the sun's been quite kind while I wrote this song,
   It's for people like you that keep it turned on.
   Chorus

4. So excuse me forgetting but these things I do
   You see I've forgotten if they're green or they're blue,
   Anyway the thing is what I really mean
   Yours are the sweetest eyes I've ever seen.
   Chorus

Registration Guide

- Match the Registration number on the song to the corresponding numbered category below. Select and activate an instrumental sound available on your instrument.

- Choose an automatic rhythm appropriate to the mood and style of the song. (Consult your Owner's Guide for proper operation of automatic rhythm features.)

- Adjust the tempo and volume controls to comfortable settings.

Registration

1	Mellow	Flutes, Clarinet, Oboe, Flugel Horn, Trombone, French Horn, Organ Flutes
2	Ensemble	Brass Section, Sax Section, Wind Ensemble, Full Organ, Theater Organ
3	Strings	Violin, Viola, Cello, Fiddle, String Ensemble, Pizzicato, Organ Strings
4	Guitars	Acoustic/Electric Guitars, Banjo, Mandolin, Dulcimer, Ukulele, Hawaiian Guitar
5	Mallets	Vibraphone, Marimba, Xylophone, Steel Drums, Bells, Celesta, Chimes
6	Liturgical	Pipe Organ, Hand Bells, Vocal Ensemble, Choir, Organ Flutes
7	Bright	Saxophones, Trumpet, Mute Trumpet, Synth Leads, Jazz/Gospel Organs
8	Piano	Piano, Electric Piano, Honky Tonk Piano, Harpsichord, Clavi
9	Novelty	Melodic Percussion, Wah Trumpet, Synth, Whistle, Kazoo, Perc. Organ
10	Bellows	Accordion, French Accordion, Mussette, Harmonica, Pump Organ, Bagpipes